KEY ISSUES IN CORRECTIONS

Jeffrey Ian Ross

Foreword by Richard Tewksbury

First edition published by Prentice Hall in 2007, titled *Special Problems in Corrections*

Second edition published in Great Britain in 2016 by

Policy Press
University of Bristol
1-9 Old Park Hill
Bristol BS2 8BB
UK
t: +44 (0)117 954 5940
e: pp-info@bristol.ac.uk
www.policypress.co.uk

North American office:
Policy Press
c/o The University of Chicago Press
1427 East 60th Street
Chicago, IL 60637, USA
t: +1 773 702 7700
f: +1 773-702-9756
e: sales@press.uchicago.edu
www.press.uchicago.edu

© Policy Press 2016

British Library Cataloguing in Publication Data
A catalogue record for this book is available from the British Library.

Library of Congress Cataloging-in-Publication Data
A catalog record for this book has been requested.

ISBN 978-1-4473-1873-6 paperback
ISBN 978-1-4473-1872-9 hardcover
ISBN 978-1-4473-1875-0 ePub
ISBN 978-1-4473-1876-7 Mobi
ISBN 978-1-4473-1881-1 ePdf

Cover design by Andrew Corbett
Front cover: image kindly supplied by istock

To Mark J. Rochon, Michele A. Roberts,
William P. Barry, and all the other criminal
defense lawyers and public defenders who, on
a daily basis, struggle to protect the rights of
defendants against overzealous prosecutors,
district attorneys, judges, and juries.

Contents

List of exhibit boxes

About the author

Jeffrey Ian Ross, Ph.D., is a Professor in the School of Criminal Justice, College of Public Affairs, and a Research Fellow of the Center for International and Comparative Law and the Schaefer Center for Public Policy at the University of Baltimore, USA.

He has researched, written, and lectured primarily on corrections, policing, political crime, violence, abnormal-extreme criminal behavior, urban subcultures, and crime and justice in American Indian communities for over two decades. Ross's work has appeared in many academic journals and books, as well as popular media. He is the author, co-author, editor, or co-editor of several books including: *Behind Bars: Surviving Prison*; *Convict Criminology*; *Special Problems in Corrections*; *Beyond Bars: Rejoining Society After Prison*; and *The Globalization of Supermax Prisons*.

Ross is a respected subject matter expert for local, regional, national, and international news media. He has made live appearances on CNN, CNBC, Fox News Network, MSNBC, and NBC. Additionally Ross has written op-eds for the *The (Baltimore) Sun*, the *Baltimore Examiner*, *Inside Higher Ed*, *The (Maryland) Daily Record*, *The Gazette* (weekly community newspaper serving Maryland's Montgomery, Frederick, Prince George's, and Carroll counties), *The Hill*, and the *Tampa Tribune*.

Ross has performed consulting services for CSR, Intel Science Talent Search, Maryland Department of Public Safety and Correctional Services, U.S. Department of Defense; Office of Juvenile Justice and Delinquency Prevention, U.S. Department of Justice (USDOJ); The National Institute of Justice, USDOJ; U.S. Department of Homeland Security; and Westat.

From 1995 to 1998, Ross was a Social Science Analyst with the National Institute of Justice, a Division of the USDOJ. In 2003, he was awarded the University of Baltimore's Distinguished Chair in Research Award. From 2005 to 2006, Ross was a member of the Prisoner Advocate Liaison Group for the Institute of Medicine (part of the National Academy of Sciences). Ross worked for approximately four years in a correctional institution. Along with Stephen C. Richards, he is the co-founder of the Convict Criminology school, movement, organization, and network. For more information see www.jeffreyianross.com

Acknowledgements

No major project like this is done alone. To begin with, I want to thank Victoria Pittman, Senior Commissioning Editor, Rebecca Tomlinson, Senior Editorial Assistant, Laura Greaves, Production Editor, Dave Worth, Production Manager, Rebecca Megson, Marketing Coordinator, all at Policy Press, and Dawn Rushen, freelance editor/project manager. They deserve a medal for their encouragement, professionalism, and incredible patience.

I also want to thank Carolyn Fox for copy-editing the book. Additional thanks go out to Rachel Hildebrandt for editing the majority of chapters. My appreciation also extends to the anonymous reviewers of both the first and second editions. They have forced me to re-examine many of my arguments and the evidence upon which they were built.

Since this is a second edition, my gratitude extends back to those who assisted me with the first version of this book, published by Pearson/Prentice Hall. At this publishing house, I would like to thank Mayda Bosco, Frank Mortimer, and Tim Peyton for being part of the cheering section.

I would like to thank my former students, many of whom are former or current correctional, probation, or parole officers and administrators, including Ginger Duke-Miller, Alicia Peak, Abbie Redman, and Dana Valdivia, for enduring many of these chapters as lectures and/or required reading. I have also benefited from a small army of research assistants throughout the years, such as Christine Bevans, Eva Marie Keanely, Chris Brees-Rostveit, and Vickie Sneed who tirelessly tracked down numerous readings for me.

In the first edition, various colleagues, including Bradley Chilton, Francis (Frank) Cullen, David Curry, Ernest J. Eley, Jr., Burk Foster, Richard Hogan, Jay Hurst, Mike (Lee) Johnson, Catherine Leidemer, David Vandivier, Angela West Crews, and Miguel Zaldivar looked at selected chapters and gave me feedback.

I am also beholden to numerous colleagues who have shaped my thinking about crime, criminals, and the practice of criminal justice, not to mention corrections. These include, but are not limited to, Gregg Barak, James Conaboy, Francis T. Cullen, Jeff Ferrell, David O. Friedrichs, Rosemary Gido, Peter Grabosky, Ted Robert Gurr, Mark S. Hamm, Chris Hart, Keith Hayward, Nancy Hogan, Irving Horowitz, Mike (Lee) Johnson, Rick Jones, Victor Kappeler, Eric Lambert, Mike Lenza, Peter Manning, Shadd Maruna, Ray Michalowski, Will H. Moore, Greg Newbold, Stephen C. Richards,

ACKNOWLEDGEMENTS

Dawn L. Rothe, Vincenzo Ruggiero, Marty Schwartz, Michael Stohl, Richard Tewksbury, Ken Tunnell, Austin T. Turk, Loïc Wacquant, Frank (Trey) Williams, Benjamin S. Wright, Aaron Z. Winter, and Barbara Zaitzow.

My fellow Convict Criminologist colleagues, including, but not limited, to Bill Archambeault, Andy Aresti, Bruce Arrigo, James Binnall, Sacha Darke, Rod Earle, Iponwosa (Silver) O. Ekunwe, Preston Elrod, Marianne Fisher-Giorlando, John Irwin, Rick Jones, Mike Lenza, Alan Mobley, Dan Murphy, Greg Newbold, Barbara Owen, Stephen C. Richards, Chuck Terry, Grant Tietjen, Bill Tregea, Denise Woodall and Matt Yeager, should be recognized. And prison activists like Charlie and Pauline Sullivan of National CURE provided a supportive community.

Thanks to Richard Tewksbury, fellow scholar, for writing the Foreword, and for being a great colleague.

Finally, as always Natasha (my wife), and Keanu and Dakota (our children), who tolerated my distraction with this project.

Foreword

The thought of being incarcerated is perhaps the biggest fear for many people in our society. For others, jail or prison is not something to be feared, but rather more of a place or location to wonder about when one will end up there. Institutional corrections in the United States is a massive, exceptionally expensive "system" that reaches into the lives of millions of people. The American correctional system is also fairly complex, often outdated, and for all too many people in our society a common place to spend time. Regardless of whether one believes being incarcerated would be the worst thing that could ever happen to them or that jail, prison, and/or community corrections is just a rite of passage, both views are unfortunate and based on limited, filtered, and most probably biased information. Knowing what incarceration is really like, what jails and prisons are really like and what it is like to live and work in corrections is critical for understanding corrections as an often-overlooked, but critical institution and experience. And, knowing about corrections allows us as a society to know if, when, and where we may need to make changes to this final component of our criminal justice system and what these changes should be. Corrections, rather obviously, serves a very practical purpose for our society. This is the primary way that we have for punishing, as well as (hopefully) changing the behavior of those who cannot, or simply will not, abide by the laws of society. So too do our corrections system and practices exemplify our paradigmatic views of morals, diversities and values of both difference and humanity in general. In short, to know a nation is to know its jails, prisons, and community supervision and vice versa.

Understanding corrections is not a niche issue in the culture of a nation, but it is a major financial investment. If for no other reason, the billions of dollars that are spent on corrections are cause for understanding how this set of places, processes and procedures operates. As one of the only continuously growing industries in our world, many communities rely on jails, prisons and community corrections for jobs and economic stimulation. Billions of dollars of profits are made by corporations that either operate correctional institutions or simply provide goods and services to them. Corrections is one of the largest providers of state jobs in the United States. And, lest we forget, prisons also provide a place for storing our most socially undesirable members and removing them from the communities in which policy makers live, work and play. Examining corrections' role in society allows us to appreciate the nation's fundamental values by looking at the prisons/jails and criminal justice industrial complex. As a long recognized way of assessing a society, if you look at the way that the least desirable, least valued members of society are treated, you can learn about that society's core values. As you move through reading this book – which is an in-depth coverage of most of the many issues that construct what corrections is – think about that. If this is how we treat those "on the bottom" of our social hierarchy, what does this say about us? Do our correctional policies and practices make us look like an advanced, humane, socially just society?

This is not to argue that jails and prisons as a concept is not useful and cannot be a positive aspect of society. But, when corrections becomes a place for social undesirables rather than just the truly dangerous, are we saying something about our values and our views on "difference"? Remember that we tend to incarcerate people for really long periods of time. And, we send people to jails and prison for both big/serious things, and other things that at least some of us may not believe are really worth 20% (10 years for a 50-year-old) of someone's life. For some offenders, yes, corrections is needed, and it should be punitive. But, it should also be humane, based on scientific evidence and in the best interests of all involved, including society as a whole. Do we really benefit from a system that imprisons over 2 million persons at any given point in time? Are there really that many people that just could not be provided less expensive services to facilitate them being members of free society?

Many things may appear to have face validity as support for an approach, practice or structure. But, when we understand such things in context, and in combination, we can see behind the packaging to what is really underneath. At that point we have the necessary resources and understanding to seek to change. But, is change, especially change in the direction of more humane, more socially beneficial outcomes, really what is wanted? For some of us, absolutely. For others, however, it would appear that the answer is no. We know this because, as is stressed throughout this text, illogical, harmful, and sometimes simply inhumane practices are maintained, and even reinforced and strengthened. At these times and in these instances, it is difficult (if not impossible) to believe that policy makers and correctional officials believe we could do better. If they did believe it, wouldn't we make at least some of these positive changes?

Or, for those who arrive at this understanding and do not see a need for change, knowing the information, as well as the ways that corrections is interconnected with other social systems, provides a foundation for building support for the status quo. Knowing what you believe is one thing. Knowing why you believe what you do is probably even more important. This allows for intelligent debate and decisions. Hopefully that debate will consequently produce compromises and consensus based on facts and information rather than emotion, politics and personal investment.

Jeffrey Ian Ross is a scholar who emphasizes the understanding of corrections as a part of the prison industrial complex. The approach he provides in this text is one that recognizes that our correctional systems and practices are heavily influenced by politics, economics and emotion. Knowing that this is how things operate is important. In that vein, books such as this one are critically necessary. Here the reader will see the issues that are of importance in contemporary prison discourse (e.g. the Key Issues!) and be provided with a context in which to see the influences upon, and reciprocal influences from, specific correctional structures, processes, and experiences.

Presenting a clearly critical perspective on corrections, and what it is, how it works and what it produces, *Key Issues in Corrections* shows that it is vital to ask questions and to question what information may be most prominently presented and most loudly argued. This idea introduced in Chapter 2, which highlights the myths about corrections in our society, how and why these myths have come to be "common knowledge," and how widespread acceptance of myths is harmful. Corrections is not an isolated part of our world that is necessarily "out of sight, out of mind." Instead, as readers here will easily see, what happens in corrections is important for society as a whole.

Ross seeks to provide readers with a look at the reality of corrections. Readers need to know, however, that this is a view that is not always pleasant or encouraging. However, if the problems that plague corrections are not identified and discussed, how could we ever expect them to be solved? By honestly and openly looking at the reality of corrections, it becomes possible for corrections to actually be corrected. Providing a foundation upon which to build this correction is what readers will find in *Key Issues in Corrections*.

Richard Tewksbury
University of Louisville, USA

Preface

A brief description

Special Problems In Corrections (hereafter *SPIC*) was published in paperback in 2008 by Pearson/Prentice Hall. In addition to the Foreword by my fellow convict criminologist Stephen C. Richards and the Preface I wrote, the book consists of 16 chapters, each covering a different challenge or controversy in the field of American corrections.

According to the publisher,

> [*SPIC*] identifies the most pressing issues affecting the correctional system today. Maintaining a solutions focus, the book organizes problems into two distinct categories: those impacting the convicts and correctional facilities and those impacting the correctional officers and administrators. It examines long-standing, and emerging issues from a critical perspective, grounding discussion in empirical research and current events. Using the consistent voice of a single author, the book offers a no nonsense approach to explaining the problems of correctional officers, correctional managers, prisoners, and the public.

I explained the rationale behind my organizational concept of a "special problem" in the following manner:

> Given that I do not have the kind of resources to conduct the more comprehensive kinds of studies, almost each semester I survey my students and ask them to rank in order what they think are the most important problems facing the field. Not all the responses fit into distinct categories, but over the years I have discovered a number of consistent themes. Indeed, the problems will not strike the reader as anything new, but the organization and rendering in this book should. (Ross, 2008c: xix)

Although one of the chapters (Chapter 1) discusses the history of corrections, the book primarily focuses on the 1960–2007 period and is geared to an American audience. Not only does *SPIC* review the problems/challenges (including the relevant scholarly research), but it also analyses the solutions proposed and implemented, including their success and failure in solving the relevant problems/challenges. When no discernible solution has been proposed by the field, I suggest one or more potential approaches.

SPIC tackles each problem/challenge in as comprehensive a manner as possible and posits realistic solutions. *SPIC* integrates scholarly analysis with current events by relying on recent news media accounts and information gathered by respected news outlets.

The chapters typically include two boxes (for example, a brief review of an important historical event, a well-known, respected, and/or relevant book, a summary of a film that is pertinent to the chapter, and so on). These are items that students and/or instructors may wish to explore in greater detail. There are also a handful of figures (i.e., lists and tables) throughout the book. The "exhibit boxes" provide background details on items that may be of interest to students and instructors, and help break up the flow of the text.

The book is primarily written for undergraduate students who have already had an introduction to corrections class. It attempts to avoid the nuts-and-bolts approach that is typical to an introduction to corrections text. Thus, the book is targeted toward upper-level university students (typically referred to as juniors and seniors at American universities) and entering graduate students. It may also be used as a supplement in an undergraduate introduction to corrections class, or a class with a title such as "Special Issues in Corrections."

SPIC is easy to read and designed to answer common questions asked by undergraduate and graduate students taking a class in corrections. This book is also accessible to practitioners (including individuals aspiring to work in the fields of criminal justice and corrections in particular) and policymakers in the corrections field, as well as members of the news media covering stories on corrections.

Background to both first and second editions

SPIC was based not only on my practitioner experience (working close to four years in a correctional facility), but also on my over two decades of scholarly research, publishing, and teaching in this field. Over time, the focus of my research and writing on corrections has changed, as has my pedagogy in this subject area. I can say in general and with confidence that my undergraduate corrections class, where I use this text, is one of the most popular courses I teach. A large part of the reason why it is so successful is because of this text.

The need for a second edition of *SPIC*

Needless to say, a number of significant events in the field of corrections have occurred and a respectable amount of academic literature has been published since *SPIC* was originally released, thus making certain sections of the first edition obsolete. Additionally, since the publication of *SPIC*, no other publisher has released a single-author text concentrating on special issues in corrections. The other books that have been produced are all edited compilations. I believe there is still room in the market for a reasonably priced, single-author "Key/Special Issues in Corrections" book tailored for juniors, seniors, and graduate students, which is user friendly and has classroom adoption potential.

New title

Although there are logical arguments for and against using the original title *Special Problems in Corrections* (2nd Ed.) or developing a new one, because of the move to a different press, I believe the *SPIC* title should be avoided. Given the significant changes in terms of content, length, and updates that this second edition has involved, a new title, *Key Issues in Corrections*, was chosen.

Content of *Key Issues in Corrections*

Under the assumption that instructors who previously assigned the first edition of the book might want to use the second edition and may prefer not to substantially redesign their courses, the book largely retains the original table of contents, which captures, in logical sequence, the most important problems/challenges facing the correctional system in the United States.

Additionally, one topic that has risen to prominence since the first edition was published is the challenge of privatization. A chapter titled "Privatization of corrections," placed in the second half of the book, is included. This new chapter includes not only the building and managing of private jails and prisons, but also the contracting out of medical care, mental health care, and education services, all of which have been expanded over the past decade. Likewise a chapter on the death penalty is included. This chapter reviews the history of the death penalty in the United States, including arguments for and against its use. On the other hand, although the subject of juvenile corrections is relevant to the book, neither an extended discussion nor a chapter specifically devoted to this challenge has been included in this text.

Most introductory corrections texts are pretty basic and simplistic in character. They are designed for practitioners or students who are considering or want to enter the profession. These books typically present the facts and then instructors require their students to whom they assign these to memorize and hopefully understand this information. These are important building blocks for understanding the scope of the field of corrections. They provide a considerable amount of content. This material, often technical and vocational in nature, may be irrelevant to the central point of the discussion, and end up distracting and overwhelming students. Unfortunately, these introductory texts rarely encourage students' critical thinking.

In order to minimize these shortcomings, *Key Issues in Corrections* frequently rank orders both problems/challenges and solutions from least to most important. This is done because of the realization that not all problems and solutions are of equal magnitude. The reader may disagree with my ordering, but it serves as a point of departure in argumentation.

In *Key Issues in Corrections*, each chapter is organized in the same manner: history of the problem/challenge, delineation of the components of the problem/challenge (especially the scholarly research that has been produced on the subject or the popular conceptions of the problem/challenge), and a systematic presentation of solutions and why they may or may not work. I believe this manner of organization instills an analytical and critical thinking framework.

The ideas presented in *Key Issues in Corrections* are succinct, and the key points are highlighted in each single chapter. As such the book is written in a manner that sparks discussion on these topics.

In general, the revision involves an updating of the original text, an inclusion of literature that was not reviewed in the preparation of the first edition, a review of additional scholarly literature that has been published since the original version, and a discussion of other noteworthy and newsworthy incidents and episodes from current affairs. The text also includes additional case studies, either within the actual text or in the form of exhibit boxes, as well as updated statistics. The updated text is written in a way that makes it more appropriate for classroom adoption, and possibly the general public.

Below is a list of the features of the new book:

- integration of eight years' worth of new scholarship in this field;
- addition of new lawsuits that have had an impact on corrections in the United States;
- review of the increased use of technology in the field of institutional and community corrections;
- significant expansion of the chapter on "Management and administration";
- inclusion of additional information in the chapter on "Misuse of jails";
- addition of two completely new chapters: "The death penalty," and "The privatization of prisons";

- Foreword by Richard Tewksbury, a prominent scholar in today's field of corrections;
- additional exhibit boxes;
- key terms, listed at the end of chapters;
- increase of word length by approximately 25% in comparison to the first edition.

The book will be as up to date as possible (up to 2016).

Ancillary pedagogy

An ancillary website with multiple choice, short answer, and essay questions will help students gauge whether they have understood the content of the chapter. PowerPoints will be supplied to instructors on demand.

Market

Most university departments of criminology/criminal justice offer at least one corrections class. They are pitched at a very general and descriptive level. *Key Issues in Corrections* not only covers the basics, but also applies an analytical and critical thinking framework that is rarely present in corrections texts.

This book has the most amount of utility for upper level criminology/ criminal justice classes that have titles like "Special Issues in Corrections" or "Special Topics in Corrections." These kinds of classes will be found in larger departments of criminology/criminal justice that are typically located at larger state universities (e.g., University of Maryland, University of Illinois at Chicago, etc.). Rarely will they be found in departments of sociology, which may have only a few criminologists on faculty. Depending on the instructor's orientation, *Key Issues in Corrections* may also be used as a supplement for an "Introduction to Corrections" class.

Introduction

How to determine the most important challenges facing corrections in the United States

The average person is not likely to be too concerned about corrections, incarceration, or inmates/prisoners.[1] But I am. The problem of jails and prisons has intrigued me since the early 1980s, when I took my first and only job in a correctional facility. My interest in this topic has since ebbed and flowed due to a variety of life and career circumstances. Nevertheless, over the two-and-a-half decades that I have been teaching about and conducting research in the field of corrections, I have become interested in identifying the most important challenges within this field as well as their solutions.

I am under the belief, misguided as it may seem, that this information will help us focus our efforts at meaningful reform. I am not alone. At any given time, correctional consultants, alone or part of a team, are crisscrossing the country providing all sorts of evaluations of correctional policies and practices. This work is typically underwritten by state departments of corrections, the federal government, and sometimes by philanthropic foundations. I am also aware of the politically charged atmosphere in which prison reform exists and which can significantly affect meaningful efforts for change. Suggestions may be ignored because they run counter to the views of politicians, practitioners, and the public; and poorly researched programs, and those which were never subject to evaluation, may be funded simply because they have temporary political cache.

Reflexive statement

I wrote this book because of the limitations I found with standard nuts-and-bolts texts on corrections. Although most corrections books used for introductory college and university courses provide an overview of the history and practices, and mention some of the problems of jails, prisons, and community corrections in the United States, too often this field of study and practice is approached in an uncritical (i.e., politically conservative) fashion. This is understandable.

Most prison research and writing tends to reflect the language and special interests of the correctional bureaucracy. After all, the government typically funds the studies and therefore, because of its agenda-setting function, limits the parameters, and often decides if the final report will be distributed widely and used to understand existing problems and suggest new policies and procedures (Ross and Richards, 2003).

Regardless of whether the research is state sponsored, foundation sponsored, or self-funded, the methodology that many researchers use can also be faulted because it often consists disproportionately of complicated statistical analyses. This typically means that investigators do not have to "get their hands dirty" by interacting with convicts, ex-cons, or correctional professionals in order to gain a better contextual understanding of their subject matter and findings.[2]

It must be noted that this book is not an anti-corrections text per se. Many correctional officers and administrators will find various things I say in this book disturbing. My approach might seem overly confrontational, opinionated, provocative, ideological, and "political." Or perhaps I may be accused of editorializing too much. I attribute these impressions to a number of factors. These include a poor understanding of what constitutes an opinion in academic discourse, what ideology and politics mean exactly, and their relationship to policy and practice. I also blame the socialization process that most correctional professionals are subjected to, which I believe fosters a kind of tunnel vision, an us-versus-them mentality, and a perception that anyone critical of the practice of corrections must have an axe to grind. Indeed, there are often large perceptual gaps among inmates, correctional professionals, and scholars, and as a result, it frequently seems like these groups are operating in separate worlds. In short, this book challenges traditional dogma in the field of corrections.

On the other hand, many of my critical criminology colleagues may fault me for not taking a more radical stance that deals with the root causes of crime, criminality, and the perils of capitalism. For example, this book does not advocate the abolishment of jails and prisons, although I am personally familiar with this position (for example, Mathiesen, 1974), having covered the very first prison abolition conference as a reporter for *Now Magazine* in Toronto (Ross, 1983) and having worked for almost four years in a correctional facility.

How to identify the problems

In any given field, there are several different ways and perspectives from which to identify and judge the severity of a problem. Difficulties can be determined and examined at the micro or macro level, or at one of several levels of analysis in between. Caution, however, must be exerted in this task. The method investigators use to identify problems will naturally impact the findings. One must also be sensitive about who is going to use this information.

Looking at root causes versus outcomes to determine problems is also an issue of concern. Investigators need to acknowledge who is doing the evaluation, as well as any biases they may bring to the research. For example, is the person or entity an insider or an outsider? Insiders may have considerable practical experience, but they may suffer from undue bias. Outsiders may not be sensitive to the internal dynamics of organizations and end up missing important cues. The goal here is to determine who has the appropriate knowledge and skills, and who is the most objective. Another matter to consider is the principal of least eligibility. In short, it is the notion that conditions inside correctional facilities must be worse than the inmates experienced on the outside for the sanction to have a deterrent effect (Sieh, 1989).

In order to minimize these problems during the course of my research, in addition to a traditional literature review, I spoke to a wide variety of individuals. I interviewed, observed, and/or corresponded with numerous convicts, ex-cons, correctional, probation and parole officers, and administrators, in addition to visiting several correctional facilities, both private and public, not only in the United States but elsewhere. I also relied on and integrated the relevant literature, contextualized the numerous problems (citing statistics where appropriate), and proposed what I believe are realistic solutions. Some of the problems – like too much red tape, which is an all too familiar complaint of all bureaucracies – were too ambiguous and not given much attention.

Micro level

At the institutional level (individual jails and prisons), for example, one way to identify and judge the severity of a problem is to thoroughly review performance indicators (for example, Logan, 1993). One such example is the *Key Facility Report*. This document lists the various incidents that have happened in a correctional facility over a certain period, and provides a statistical summary of how many verbal and physical altercations have occurred among concerned parties (for example, staff and inmates). These numbers can be compared with those from previous days, weeks, months, or years to determine if things are improving, remaining the same, or, in fact, worsening. Alternatively, human resource statistics may reveal other subtle dynamics. Key variables to understand the health of an institution may include the number of job vacancies over a relevant period of time. Employee turnover rates can be an indicator of job dissatisfaction, since some employees may believe that they are not being paid enough or that there is too much job-related stress. Alternatively, the number of employees out sick per week, month, or year might be an indication of the prevalence of disease/illness, or even dissatisfaction with work. Other variables might be the presence of unrest in a facility, the number of inmate lawsuits, the number of employee grievances, and the number of private facilities in a jurisdiction.

Another way to get a handle on the problems is to review the number and kinds of *Administrative Remedy Reports* that have been turned in to a coordinator. Typically, these documents, much like a complaint form, are submitted by inmates in a secured ballot-type box. The coordinator is usually a high-ranking correctional officer, and the investigation is conducted by another officer. Some of the complaints are legitimate, while others are of questionable merit; they cover the gambit from poor medical treatment to the bad selection of entertainment options.

Prisoners can and do complain. However, if this is perceived to be a nuisance or if a convict is deemed a "troublemaker," inmates may incur retribution from correctional officers and management. This can involve bringing an inmate up on disciplinary charges (often referred to as receiving a *shot*) for even a small infraction, sending a convict to solitary confinement, special management, administrative segregation (or in prison argot, the *hole*), or repeatedly transferring an inmate to another facility (known as *riding the bus* or *diesel therapy*). There are countless ways that correctional officers and managers can retaliate against convicts who are perceived to complain excessively or unnecessarily.

That is why many inmates are reluctant to complain through official channels. Likewise, this state of affairs may contribute to learned helplessness or surplus powerlessness in which, after numerous rejections, a person simply does not try to address his or her grievances (Lerner, 1991). Additionally, the performance of correctional officers can be determined through activity reports or periodic personnel evaluations (Freeman, 1999: 329–32). In most organizations, this process is done on an annual basis, but it may produce very superficial and sanitized results, which generally do not go into enough detail for scholars to draw meaningful conclusions.

Finally, gathering anecdotal or confirming evidence by interviewing sources, experts, or "key informants," such as convicts, correctional officers, administrators, and prison scholars, is often done. Correctional officers and prisoners are probably the best sources to provide this kind of information because they are on the front lines every day (Conover, 2001; Ross and Richards, 2002; 2003). Preferred by journalists and ethnographic researchers, this method produces information that is typically current and rich in detail, but it is also potentially biased because it is difficult to judge the veracity of the information.

Sources may lie, embellish, or forget critical material. Thus, it is essential that several individuals from the same institution be consulted and ideally watched over a sufficient period of time, because often workers under observation are on their best behavior, but they have difficulty sustaining this demeanor over time (for example, the Hawthrorne Effect, i.e., when those observed − typically by researchers − change their behavior to what they believe is the investigator's expectations). Alternatively, key personnel may be absent from the facility (e.g., on vaction or out sick). Finally, one of the biggest challenges to studying corrections is gaining access, which for some facilities, especially high security and Supermax prisons, is next to impossible.

Macro level

There are approximately six methods by which researchers, practitioners, and policymakers can obtain a larger picture of the problems within the corrections field (Welsh and Harris, 2004). They are listed from least to most useful.

First, *thoroughly assess peer-reviewed scholarly journal articles* in the field of corrections. This method provides researchers with an idea of academics' perceptions of the most dominant problems, and also editors' and reviewers' judgments of which papers are the most worthy of journal publication. However, just because journal editors decide to publish an article on a specific topic does not mean that this issue is the most important for practitioners or convicts; it could simply be a reflection of the kinds of manuscripts that have been submitted, the availability of space, or the current editor's (or editorial board's) predilections.[3]

Second, *review practitioner-relevant publications.* In the field of corrections, the American Correctional Association publishes a handful of newsletters and *Corrections Today.* These periodicals are practitioner friendly, and the decisions about what to include in the magazine are based on the editor's or editorial team's perceptions of what would appeal to the readership/membership and not necessarily the rigorousness of the research.

Third, *perform a content analysis of news media,* such as television and/or radio news broadcasts as well as newspaper and magazine reports, to see which corrections-related issues are cited most frequently (for example, Krippendorf, 1981). The drawback to this is that these reports may simply be snapshots in time, and they suffer from the same constraints as scholarly journals.

Fourth, *collect and/or analyze so-called social indicators* (i.e., data on such factors as crime rates, victimization patterns, and incarceration rates) located in diverse sources like the Uniform Crime Reports, or the National Crime Victimization Survey. Similarly, the Bureau of Justice Statistics (BJS), a division of the Department of Justice, systematically collects data on jails and prisons in the United States, from the number of inmates to the type of correctional officers employed.

Fifth, *hold a community forum.* Often when a department of corrections (DOC) is about to choose a new site for a jail, prison, or halfway house a community forum is held. This is similar to the method of the 2005–6 National Commission on Safety and Abuse in Prison (www.prisoncommission.org)

(hereafter Commission on Safety and Abuse) (Gibbons and de Katzenbach, 2006), which on June 8, 2006, released its final report on conditions in correctional facilities throughout the United States. The downside here is that community forums often tend to be opportunities for people to vent, and they are geographically constrained to the regions in which they are held. One way around these drawbacks is to hold multiple well-organized public forums in different parts of the country and to systematically integrate an on-line component.

Finally, *systematically administer a survey to a broad constituency of individuals who have a strong interest and/or expertise in the field of incarceration* (for example, officers, administrators, and convicts).[4] One popular method involving experts in the field is commonly referred to as a Delphi study and has been perfected in several branches of the criminal justice system (for example, Tafoya, 1986). Unfortunately, this method is like a snapshot in time and may not be useful for long-term planning.

In the end, although each method of data collection has advantages, almost all have drawbacks. Thus, how should one proceed? Combining all these methods, and triangulating among the results, may be the most useful course of action, since it would come closest to achieving a balanced approach. To do this properly, however, researchers need adequate resources.

Solutions to problems

Few of the solutions proposed for the field of corrections are easy to implement, and all may lead to unintended consequences (for example, Merton, 1936; Clear, 2001; Preston and Roots, 2004). It might be easiest to achieve success at the institutional level rather than at the state or federal level of corrections. There is also a realization that many problems seem to simply snowball. Problems can be linked together and can affect each other, and the population interviewed or surveyed may not be able to disentangle them. It is also recognized that the history of prison reform is fraught with intractable challenges (Sullivan, 1990). Moreover, solutions to correctional problems may be initiated or may originate from several sources, including the state or government, the private sector, religious bodies, self-help organizations for convicts, or inmates themselves. Finally, some of the more extreme suggestions, like prison abolition (Mathiesen, 1974), are not widely held and perhaps impractical at this point in history.

Unintended consequences. It must also be understood that corrections is ultimately a system in which each component typically performs a function,[5] and as systems theory suggests (Parsons, 1951), if you tinker with one aspect of the organization, it will have an effect somewhere else. It is like a ripple effect, and the ripples are felt in many places that are often not immediately apparent or easy to distinguish. What do I mean by this statement? In simple terms, some of the solutions implemented by practitioners can and do have negative and unintended consequences that correctional planners fail to account for or intentionally minimize in terms of the impact they may have. Nothing in life is perfect, but some of the negative effects might be controlled. The trick in proper criminal justice planning is to adequately predict and prepare for this possibility with contingency plans (Welsh and Harris, 2004).

Survey end users. Given that I do not have the kind of resources to conduct the more comprehensive kinds of studies previously reviewed, almost each semester that I teach the class in which this book is used, I survey my students and ask them to rank in order what they think are the most important problems facing the field. Not all the responses fit into distinct categories, but over the years, I have discovered a number of consistent themes. Indeed, the challenges will not strike the reader as anything new, but the organization and rendering in this book should. Additionally, to the extent possible, the problems identified in each chapter are presented from least to most important in terms of how they affect corrections.

Certainly, there will be disagreements among correctional officers, administrators, inmates, and other corrections experts with respect to what they think are most important. But I believe that an expert's most important job is to contextualize information and issues for the audience. Some readers may also question the utility of students' perceptions as an organizing tool. Indeed most students have not yet been exposed to the realities of the criminal justice system; however, the reader should understand that my approach serves as a benchmark or pedagogical starting point for communicating the problems with corrections to them and not an end in itself.

Problems for convicts and correctional officers. One set of difficulties I have identified focuses on the problems for convicts and correctional facilities, and the other difficulties encountered by correctional officers and administrators. It is with this knowledge that I organize my courses, lectures, and this book. As I have argued in my other books (Ross, 1995/2000a; 2000b), although it is important to discuss problems (and, in general, most people are reasonably good at doing this), it is more important to propose and implement realistic solutions to address or solve these difficulties. The reader should also realize that some of the solutions proposed in one part of the book reappear frequently because they are capable of solving more than one difficulty.

Relevance of social justice. Mention should also be made of the social justice (Arrigo, 1998) or restorative justice approach (e.g., Braithwaite, 1989). Many observers of corrections, including myself, recognize the limitations with the current criminal justice system, particularly its emphasis on retributive justice, and its inability to address the higher order societal goals of human respect and dignity. That is why the criminal justice system and corrections, in particular, should be working in this direction. To the extent possible, this book emphasizes these themes.

Best practices. Another issue that should be addressed is the best practices approach (Bogan and English, 1994). Over the past two decades, there has been a tendency in policy circles to admire what works best in institutional settings. What the supporters of this perspective often fail to recognize is the diversity of agencies or the difficulty in transferring methods from one setting/jurisdiction to another. An inability or unwillingness to consider the contextual differences between the private sector and the public sector and an assumption that framework-specific solutions do not have to be tinkered with can precipitate unintended problems.

Missing subject matter. Additionally, the reader will notice that some problems are not discussed in any great detail. These are juvenile corrections, racism in prison, and reentry. This is not to suggest that these issues are not important or problematic, but their exclusion reflects the consensus of those to whom I have administered my survey.[6]

Terminology. Finally, a note on terminology is in order. To the extent possible, and apologies if I sound too politically correct, this book avoids using the term *offender.* In normal usage, most people do not think twice about uttering this word as a synonym for "convict," "inmate," or 'prisoner." But, on closer examination, "offender" is derived from the same set of words that includes the term *offensive.* Granted, many of the things convicts have done or do are or appear offensive. Yet, because of the fallibility of our criminal justice system, it should come as no surprise that some people are wrongfully committed (Christianson, 2004).

In addition, some things that individuals have done which land them in jail or prison are so minor (for example, possession of small amounts of recreational drugs) that we might question why they are incarcerated in the first place. Thus, to call all convicts offenders is probably unnecessarily derogatory. Likewise, to the extent possible, the labels *boss, bull, cap, guard, hack,* or *screw* are avoided as these synonyms for correctional officers are also perceived to be pejorative, ignoring the professional nature of this occupation. True, many correctional officers act in a deviant manner (Ross, 2013; Ross, Tewksbury and Rolfe, 2016), but in a scholarly text such as this, nuance should be observed. That is why I will strive to use the term *correctional officer.* Finally, there are few synonyms for jails, prisons, and correctional facilities outside of institutions and facilities. In the same manner as above, I have refrained from using the colloquial words *can, hoosegow, joint,* and *pokey.*

Corrections as a global problem. Finally, corrections is not only an American problem but also a global one (Ross, 2013a). Keep in mind that when other countries are considering how to improve their corrections system, they typically look toward the United States to see what has been done here. Thus, for the sake of focus, the majority of examples within this book are rooted in the United States. In sum, *Key Issues in Corrections* reviews and examines the critical, longstanding, and emerging issues that affect the way correctional facilities are operated, and how convicts, correctional officers, and administrators experience this unique setting.

Notes

[1] Despite subtle differences in usage, I use the terms "convicts," "inmates," and "prisoners" interchangeably throughout this book.

[2] See, for example, critiques by Liebling (1999) and Wacquant (2002).

[3] In general, this discussion deals with the impact of findings.

[4] This is selectively done with different constituencies (for example, Gibbs, 1993).

[5] See, for example, the theoretical literature on structural functionalism and systems theory.

[6] For research connected to race in prison, see for example, Carroll (1988). For the graying prison population, see for example, Aday (1994). For American Indians behind bars, see for example, Archambault (2003; 2006; 2014).

PART I

Laying the groundwork

ONE

What is corrections, and what are its problems?[1]

Introduction

It bears mentioning that criminology is primarily the study of the causes and effects of crime, and that criminal justice consists of the analysis of the organizations responsible for monitoring, investigating, and responding to crime, in addition to those processing the individuals who have been charged or convicted of a crime and those who have been victimized by crime. The criminal justice system, in particular, is composed of four interconnected branches: law enforcement, the courts, corrections, and juvenile justice. Corrections encompasses jails, prisons, and a variety of community-based programs and sanctions (for example, probation, parole, and the like).

The term "corrections" usually means "the institutions, policies, procedures and other nuts and bolts of the system" (Welch, 1996: 3). It also subsumes "the great number of programs, services, facilities and organizations responsible for the management of people who have been accused or convicted of criminal offenses" (Cole, 1994: 544). Corrections are typically divided into two parts: institutional corrections, which is the bricks-and-mortar side of jails and prisons, and community corrections, which encompasses such programs and practices as probation, parole, and intermediate sanctions.

Additionally, it must be understood that the practice of corrections is generally intended to have three objectives: punishment, community safety, and rehabilitation. One side benefit of jails and prisons is that they are supposed to deter individuals from committing crime. Sometimes the system achieves these goals, while at other times it does not.

Another important distinction should be made between the state and federal correctional systems. Those who are sentenced to state prisons have violated a state criminal code. People who have committed a relatively minor crime are often given some form of community corrections. If, on the other

3

hand, they are sent to jail, depending on the sentencing structures of the state in which they were convicted, they may be incarcerated for up to one year.[2] Individuals sent to federal prisons, run by the Federal Bureau of Prisons (FBOP), have engaged in at least one of a select number of crimes, such as income tax evasion, counterfeiting, trafficking across state lines, kidnapping, bank robbery, political crimes, and crimes on a federal property.

Relevant statistics

Over the past four decades, the United States has experienced one of the largest expansions in its jail, prison, and community corrections populations. This phenomenon has alternatively been called "the imprisonment binge" (Austin and Irwin, 2001) or the "race to incarcerate" (Maur, 2006). In the United States (for the year 2013), 6,899,000 people were under the control of adult correctional systems. Approximately 2.3 million were behind bars in jails or prisons and 4,751,000 on probation or parole (Glaze and Kaeble, 2014). State and federal correctional systems (not to mention private prisons) employ roughly 650,000 people, who work as administrators, correctional officers (COs), case managers, classification officers, probation and parole officers, counselors, and social workers.

Although it is difficult to determine the total costs of operating correctional facilities in the United States, it is not impossible. It currently costs taxpayers approximately $39 billion a year to fund state correctional systems (Henrichson and Delaney, 2012: 69),[3] both federal and state systems combined have been estimated to cost about $112 billion (Austin and Irwin, 2001: 13).

Why has this occurred?

Approximately four general reasons account for the increase in the number of people being sentenced to jails and prisons:

1. the construction of new facilities;
2. sentencing guidelines (particularly "truth in sentencing" legislation, mandatory minimums, and determinant sentencing);
3. new laws (for example, "three strikes, you're out" legislation);[4] and, most importantly,
4. the war on drugs.[5]

These factors include several ironies. Why? The bulk of individuals who are sentenced to jail or prison are there because they were convicted of nonviolent, drug-related crimes. On the other hand, violent criminals are frequently released back into the community to make way for first-time nonviolent criminals. Many of those who are let out are angry, have not received any special vocational training, and thus leave with few marketable skills. The majority who are released come out worse than when they entered (Clear, 1994). This is why the process of incarceration is sometimes called a revolving door and/or turnstile justice (Gido and Alleman, 2002).

Those entering the system are also disproportionately ethnic or racial minorities (for example, African Americans, Hispanics, and Native Americans), and poor whites from rural and remote areas. They are usually drawn from lower socioeconomic segments of society and are either unemployed or underemployed (Miller, 1996; Welch, 1996; Austin and Irwin, 2001: 3).

One might assume that an increased rate of incarceration might result in a lower rate of crime, and many individuals take comfort in this assumption. However, there is no proven relationship between the crime rate and the number of people who are locked up (Lynch, 2007). Thus, our crime rate increases and decreases in a cyclical fashion, and rarely is this connected to the number of people that are incarcerated (Blumstein et al., 1977; Blumstein et al., 1981).

Finally, although the United States champions itself as a democratic country, putting a disproportionate number of people behind bars restricts the civil liberties of an unnecessarily large number of its citizens. This approach to dealing with individuals who commit crimes seems unnecessarily harsh and counterproductive when the United States is compared with Scandinavian countries (that is, Denmark, Finland, the Netherlands, Norway and Sweden), where the crime rates per capita basically match those of the United States, although they have lower incarceration rates (Christie, 1993/1994). Moreover, the United States' policy and practice of hyperincarceration appears to be hypocritical when you consider that, even though the nation claims to be a protector of human rights, it actually incarcerates more people than the former authoritarian regimes of the Soviet Union and apartheid South Africa (Welch, 1996: 4).

What has been the response?

Unsurprisingly, the prevailing impression among many correctional administrators, officers, experts, and activists is that the jail and prison system is failing. One of the classic statements echoing this idea is Reiman's study, *The Rich Get Richer and the Poor Get Prison* (1979/2003). This book argues that the criminal justice system encourages the existence of a criminal class and promotes the notion that the poor are disproportionately responsible for the majority of crimes. That is why Reiman and others "focus on the class bias inherent in the criminal justice system" (Welch, 1996: 5). This approach is shaped by a critical perspective that involves

> questioning, challenging and examining all sides of various problems and issues. Instead of uncritically accepting punishment and corrections as natural extensions of society, the critical approach delves under the surface of punishment to explore corrections at greater depths ... it dispels many myths and misconceptions surrounding corrections ... it demystifies the objectives, processes and outcomes of correctional intervention and offers alternative interpretations and solutions. (Welch, 1996: 6)

This combination of ideology and methodology typically looks for the hidden meanings behind myths, and explores their utility, purpose, and function in an effort to better inform the subject matter under investigation (for example, Taylor et al., 1973; Lynch and Groves, 1986/1989; Ross, 1998/2009). I do not suggest that one needs to adopt a critical perspective to examine issues at a deeper level, but this is a central feature of such an approach.

Crime and corrections as social problems

Not only do special problems exist in relation to selected aspects of jails, prisons, and community corrections, but there are also a number of difficulties intrinsic to the American correctional system as a whole. Over the past few decades, because of our inability to solve many of the problems with corrections, some analysts believe that the field in and of itself is a problem (Welch, 1996: 8). It has been called a social problem (Welch, 1996) or a "national tragedy and disgrace" (Austin and Irwin, 2001), while others have suggested that not only our overreliance on jails and prisons, but the way we incarcerate people is part of a correctional industrial complex, an informal network of correctional workers, professional organizations, and corporations that maintain and expand the jail and prison systems (Christie, 1993/1994; Hallinan, 2003).

In the state of California, for example, jails and prisons are the largest state employer. Moreover, the California Correctional Peace Officers Association is one of the most powerful unions in the state, and the California Public Employees' Retirement System (CalPERS), the benefit coordinator for the state's jail and correctional workers, is a multi-billion dollar entity. Therefore, those seeking changes to these systems are always up against powerful lobbying interests.

Some correctional observers and critical criminologists have said that although conditions are problematic, they will not be solved until the underlying causes of crime are addressed. They argue that until we eradicate the conditions and processes that lead to and reinforce inequality, poverty, and racism, and guarantee universal access to housing, health care, and education, we will not be able to solve the prison crisis (Richards, 1998). Thus, it could be argued that requiring COs to have more training or improving classification, for example, are simply inefficient means of tinkering with the symptoms, rather than an actual holistic attempt to deal with the root causes. Undoubtedly, jails and prisons are the consequence of enduring and underlying systemic problems in society.

Although addressing, minimizing, and even solving the underlying issues that cause crime are extremely important, this book is primarily intended to sort out the present-day problems affecting corrections.[6] This study recognizes that many of these difficulties have endured for a long time, and their relative importance is subject to change over time. In order to bring us up to date and to contextualize matters, however, a brief history of corrections is provided.[7]

A short history of corrections in the United States

The origins of corrections in the United States can be traced back to colonial times. In general, during this period, deviance and law breaking were primarily handled through the process of shaming. The Puritans in New England used correctional punishment as a means to enforce their strict moral codes. They viewed the deviant as willful, a sinner, and a captive of the devil. Informal community pressures, such as gossip, ridicule, and ostracism, were found to be effective in keeping most citizens in line. "Fines, confinement in the stocks and the public cage, and whippings were other frequently used methods of control" (Bartollas, 2002: 46). Mutilations, burnings, and brandings were used as punishments for serious crimes. "Most punishments were public and involved either quick, corporal tortures or more prolonged humiliation. Among the punishments designed to deter crime by inflicting pain, the colonials often used the whipping post, branding, and maiming, gags, and ... the ducking stool" (Meskell, 1999: 841). The sanctions that were more directed towards humiliating the offender included "public penance, the stocks, the pillory, and the scarlet letter" (842). With respect to capital punishment, "the colonial criminal system liberally used capital punishment. Colonials punished offenders increasingly harshly for repeat crimes" (842). Those who were repeat offenders and could not be banished were typically given the death penalty by hanging.

Execution (especially by hangings) and banishment were rare occurrences. Why? Especially if a community was small, why would the populace want to get rid of a valuable helping hand? It would not have made economic sense, as this would result in them metaphorically shooting themselves in the foot. In terms of detention, "The jail, which was brought to the colonies soon after the settlers arrived from England, was used to detain individuals awaiting trial and those awaiting punishment" (Bartollas, 2002: 46).

One of the earliest correctional facilities, the Walnut Street Jail, was built in 1790 in Philadelphia by the Quakers (that is, a Christian religious order also known as the Religious Society of Friends). They believed that deviants and lawbreakers should be left in isolation, preferably with a copy of the King James version of the Bible by their sides, to reflect on the sins they committed. This approach was called the Pennsylvania, or *silent but separate, system*. No sooner had the first prison been built than efforts to change correctional facilities started appearing – ranging from architecture to the programs they provided. After several reforms were proposed, larger and more comprehensive structures were built as part of the Pennsylvania correctional system, including Eastern State Penitentiary (built in 1821) and Western Penitentiary (built in 1826). Later, as the country grew in population, a competing corrections philosophy and practice developed at the prison in Auburn, New York (built in 1816). The administration of this prison believed that a military regime, in which convicts lived and worked together but remained silent, would have a rehabilitative effect on them. This alternative was called the Auburn, New York, or *silent but congregate system*.

Exhibit 1.1

Classics in corrections

Michel Foucault's *Discipline and Punish* (1975)

French historian and philosopher Michel Foucault's (1926–84) seminal book focuses on how powerful entities, initially the Church, later the state, punished heretics and individuals who violated the law. This study also discusses how punishment has shifted from a focus on the body of a person to the mind and/or soul. In so doing, Foucault looks at the power relationships among those in control and those who have to submit to the control. He begins his famous book with a description of an execution that took place in the mid-seventeenth century. Foucault points out that after the French Revolution (1789–99), punishment changed from torture and death to the imprisonment of people. Central to the culture of prisons and penitentiaries is the process of surveillance embodied in Jeremy Bentham's notion of the Panopticon. Increasingly powerful entities controlled people through surveillance, and Foucault notes that this kind of sanctioned watching has spread beyond the prison and into society.

By the late 1800s, most states completed building their first "big house" prisons (for example, Sing Sing, San Quentin, Joliet, and so on), also known as penitentiaries. These large structures, typically constructed out of local stone, built by convicts, and echoing the architectural style of castles, were usually located in rural or remote parts of their respective states.[8] Why? The farther the facility was located from the major urban locales, the cheaper was the land. Also if there was an escape, it would take the convicts a long time to reach "civilization." Thus the location would increase the possibility that escapees would be caught on their way home. Siting these facilities in rural or remote locations also appeared to minimize urbanites' levels of fear. One final reason for these locations is that, to some extent, the construction of correctional facilities in rural and remote areas can maintain or spur economic growth.

Physically, penitentiaries are characterized by high walls, large tiers, a yard, shops, and industries.

> The prisoners, averaging about 2,500, came from both urban and rural areas, were poor, and outside the South, were predominantly white. The prison society was essentially isolated; access to visitors, mail, and other kinds of communication was restricted. Prisoners' days were strictly enforced by guards. ... In the big house there was little in the way of treatment programs; custody was the primary goal. (Cole, 1994: 579)

This was generally known as the custodial model.

In 1876, in a sharp departure from the Auburn and Pennsylvania correctional systems, the State of New York opened the country's first "reformatory" in Elmira. The reformatory architecturally resembled a military barracks or a summer camp, with inmates living communally in dormitories. Under its new warden, Zebulon Brockway, the facility, geared to younger inmates (ages 16–30), emphasized rehabilitation and indeterminate sentencing tailored to each individual inmate. This regimen included courses taught by "inmates, college professors, public school teachers, and lawyers teaching a wide range of general subjects, as well as sports, religion, and military drills" (Stone, 2005: 287). Over the next 35 years, the Elmira Reformatory served as a model for the construction of similar correctional facilities in different states in the United States and elsewhere.

During the 1940s and 1950s, more jails and prisons were built, and corrections became recognized as a profession. Big houses were becoming obsolete, and the architecture of prisons started changing, as did their locations. This was also the beginning of a number of experiments in the field. One noticeable change was the introduction of a classification system that placed prisoners into different levels of security (that is, minimum, medium, and maximum). Another experiment involved rehabilitative programs that were couched in the medical model (for example, Rothman, 1980). Crime was perceived as a disease, and convicts afflicted with this malady were to be cured. In this context, a variety of psychological, and drug and alcohol treatment programs were introduced. This was also the beginning of the professionalization of corrections. COs were now required to take tests in order to qualify for jobs in jails and prisons, and this increasingly became the norm for the more senior positions in the facilities and within the state departments of corrections (DOC).

In the 1960s, correctional experts and practitioners experimented with various community corrections programs. These initiatives went beyond simply probation and parole, and included innovations such as diversion, work and educational release, and house arrest (McCarthy and McCarthy, 1997). These were attempts to decrease the number of people in the jails and prisons, especially for those who could be optimally treated, rehabilitated, or monitored within their communities.

During the 1980s, however, as a response to the public's fear of crime combined with simplistic interpretations and stereotypes connected to previous crime-reducing experiments (Austin and Irwin, 2001: xiii–xiv; Austin, 2003), a progressively conservative agenda took hold of criminal justice research, policy, and practice. Many of the gains that were part of the so-called community corrections era were scaled back. Congress and state legislatures passed draconian criminal laws that reversed such time-honored practices as indeterminate sentencing and ushered in a whole host of laws that made prisoners spend more time in custodial facilities. Politicians also enacted legislation that enabled states to build more correctional facilities. In short, prisons and jails were now to be more harsh and punitive than before. Many people with progressive agendas, on the other hand, advocated social and restorative justice as higher-order alternatives to the current criminal justice system, which focused disproportionately on retributive justice (for example, "an eye for an eye").

In the meantime, the jail and prison-building boom increased, as towns and cities lobbied their state legislators and federal representatives for the construction of new correctional facilities to make up for the job loss that happened as a result of manufacturing businesses closing and, in some cases, moving away (Welch, 1998; Hallinan, 2003). This trend was facilitated by the passage of the Violent Crime Control and Law Enforcement Act of 1994. According to Hallinan, "[t]hese communities profit most from the prison boom: from the construction jobs and the prison jobs and all the spin-off business that prisons create. Yet it is hard to ignore that those getting rich are usually white and those in prison are usually not" (xii).

In the 1990s, one the most significant changes in the growth of prisons came with the building and use of Supermax facilities (see Chapter 5). These controversial structures are used to house the most violent and escape-prone inmates. At the federal level, this group includes political prisoners, and organized crime and gang leaders. Prisoners are locked up 23 out of 24 hours a day, and over time they often suffer problems associated with sensory deprivation (Ross, 2007; Ross, 2013a, b). A brief chronology of these events is contained in Exhibit 1.2.

Exhibit 1.2

Major developments in the chronology of corrections in the United States

1796	Newgate Prison is built in New York City, New York
1790	Quakers build Walnut Street Jail in Philadelphia, Pennsylvania (initiates silent and separate system)
1816	State of New York builds Auburn Prison (institutes silent and congregate system)
1821	State of Pennsylvania builds Eastern State Penitentiary in Philadelphia
1826	State of Pennsylvania builds Western Penitentiary in Pittsburgh
1876	Zebulon Brockway leads first juvenile reformatory in Elmira, New York
1890	Federal Prison System established, later evolving into the Federal Bureau of Prisons (FBOP)
1934	Federal government designates Alcatraz Prison, located in San Francisco harbor, to hold the most dangerous prisoners in the United States
1974	National Institute of Corrections formed
1983	FBOP converts United States Penitentiary Marion (Illinois) into a Control Unit, where inmates are locked down 23 out of 24 hours a day, closely resembling a Supermax prison
1994	Violent Crime Control and Law Enforcement Act of 1994 (aka Crime Bill) passed. Places caps on the number of times inmates sentenced to the death penalty can appeal their conviction at the federal level. Also provides funding for the construction of new jails
1994	FBOP builds first Supermax prison in Florence, Colorado

Current goals of incarceration

As the number of people being sent to jail and prison has doubled and the system has become more punitive, additional challenges face the American correctional system. For example, the events of 9/11 have had an effect on both the state and federal prison systems (Ross, 2014).

In the field of criminal justice, money has been disproportionately spent on law enforcement. In times of budgetary crunches, the justice system has cut back in several areas, and jails and prisons feel the brunt of these changes. Correctional workers (a term used to describe all personnel who work in a jail or prison) are increasingly leaving the profession because many do not believe the risks are worth the rate of pay. In some jurisdictions, COs are being furloughed and laid off. They are not allowed to work overtime, and they may regularly come to work overtired or exhausted because they are having to hold down other jobs to make ends meet. To make up for the loss of personnel, some state DOCs are hiring younger COs. We have seen the age slip from 21, to 19, and when this proved unworkable, back up to 20. Whereas jails and prisons are supposed to punish convicts, keep the community safe, and rehabilitate inmates, rehabilitation is rarely attempted when money is scarce.

These and other challenges face the correctional system of today. Before exploring them in greater detail, the next chapter reviews some of the myths of jails, prisons, and convicts, and the history of their creation. These misperceptions frustrate rational debate, analysis, and policy creation.

Key terms

Big house: Prisons/penitentiaries. Typically large structures, constructed out of local stone, built by convicts, and sometimes resembling castles. Usually located in a rural or remote part of the state.

Conservative: Political ideology that stresses individual rights, small government, and minimal government intervention into the daily lives of its citizens.

Correctional officer (CO): Individual who is responsible for maintaining custody of inmates and order in the cellblocks, tiers, and wings of a correctional facility.

Corrections: Broad encompassing term for the institutions/facilities, policies, procedures, programs, and services that we associate with jails, prisons, inmates, correctional officers (COs) and administrators, and other correctional workers.

Critical criminology: A branch of criminological theory that stresses the importance of class bias and the influence of power relations as the determining factor in crime causation and response. Questions, challenges, and tries to demystify crime and criminal justice.

Custodial model: Sees security, order, and discipline as the primary goal of corrections. Prisoners are isolated from the rest of society and their daily activities are closely monitored by COs.

Department of Corrections (DOC): The typical name given to the bureaucracy in each state in the United States that runs the state correctional facilities.

Determinate sentencing: Specific penalty (that is, length of time incarcerated) that an individual convicted of a crime must complete. Does not allow any discretion on the part of the judge.

Federal Bureau of Prisons (FBOP): Runs the federal prison system. Incarcerated inmates convicted of a federal criminal offence.

Indeterminate sentencing: Penalty that specifies a range that an individual convicted of a crime must complete while incarcerated. Allows discretion on the part of the judge.

Jail: State run correctional facilities where inmates are sentenced for up to one year. (Maryland, unlike other states, has jail sentences up to 18 months.)

Liberal: Political ideology that advances greater redistribution of wealth and government intervention into the lives of its citizens. Advocates government-funded social programs like education, health, and welfare.

Mandatory minimum sentences: If convicted of particular crimes, offenders must spend a specific period of time incarcerated, no matter the extenuating circumstances.

Parole: When an inmate is released from a correctional facility back into the community in advance of the expiration of their term. They are subjected to numerous sanctions that they must abide to.

Prison: A physical institution where individuals who are convicted of a crime are incarcerated. Typically the individual has committed a felony and the duration of the sentence is more than a year.

Reformatory: Correctional facility, originated with Zebulon Brockway during 1876. Housed younger inmates. Emphasized rehabilitation. Used dormitory settings.

Reiman's hypothesis: The criminal justice system is designed to fail.

Sentence: Legal penalty/sanction handed down/imposed by the judge to a person convicted/found guilty of a crime.

Sentencing guidelines: Provide a proscriptive plan that judges use to determine the appropriate sentence for an individual convicted of a crime. Takes into account the offense the individual was convicted for, and their criminal history.

Silent but congregate system: Type of prison regime originally implemented in the New York State prison system at Auburn. Prisoners were required to be silent but ate, worked, and slept together. Rigid military like discipline was enforced.

Silent but separate system: Type of prison regime originally designed by Quakers implemented in Walnut State Jail and then carried on in Pennsylvania prisons. Prisoners were required to be silent and were kept in separate cells 23 hours a day. Usually given a bible and encouraged to reflect upon their deeds.

Supermax Prison: Highest level security prison in the United States. Inmates are in their cells 23 out of 24 hours a day.

Three Strikes: In some states where this law exists, individuals who have committed a third serious crime (typically a felony) are automatically sentenced to an extended period of incarceration.

Truth in Sentencing: Policies enacted in different states that have essentially abolished indeterminate sentencing and in some cases parole.

Notes

[1] An earlier version of this chapter benefited from comments by Richard G. Hogan.

[2] Some states like Maryland incarcerate individuals in jail for up to 18 months.

[3] These numbers do not include what is normally considered to be the collateral consequences (both social and economic) of incarceration felt by families and other loved ones of inmates and the communities in which they live.

[4] In 1984, Congress passed the Violent Crime and Control Law Act, which enabled tougher sanctions for those accused of particular kinds of crimes. Shortly after the federal system implemented its changes, most of the states followed suit. In 1986, Congress passed mandatory minimum sentencing laws, which instructed judges to sanction those convicted of a crime to fixed lengths of time behind bars.

[5] In addition to these factors, there are numerous micro and macro level processes which have led to the current incarceration rate (Pfaff, 2012).

[6] Those interested in attempts to solve the underlying causes of crime might wish to turn to a number of introductory textbooks on the more general field of criminology.

[7] Several capable histories of corrections in America have been written. Readers could benefit from these works if they want a more in-depth historical treatment (for example, Rothman, 1971/2002).

[8] Obviously there are exceptions. The Maryland Penitentiary, the second oldest facility of its kind in the United States, was built in 1804 and is located in downtown Baltimore. Additionally, other variations exist, like the industrial prisons and the plantation model in the South. In August 2015 the facility that formerly housed the Maryland Penitentiary was finally closed.

TWO

Misrepresenting corrections

Introduction

T he correctional systems in the United States and elsewhere suffer from numerous problems (Austin and Irwin, 2001). One issue is the difficulty in obtaining accurate information about jails, prisons, incarceration, correctional officers (COs), and prisoners. More importantly, many individuals, organizations, and institutions tend to develop misconceptions and stereotypes about correctional systems and convicts.[1]

This chapter identifies the dominant common falsehoods about corrections; reviews the leading cultural industries responsible for developing these misconceptions; and provides examples that demonstrate how these myths are created, perpetrated, and perpetuated.[2]

More specifically, in this chapter I examine the importance of mythmaking about crime, criminal justice, and corrections; look at why myths are often believed and taken as fact; and review the important role of the cultural industries. I conclude with some suggestions on how to remedy the problems intrinsic to these myths.

The importance of mythmaking about crime, criminal justice, and corrections

Most people have never been inside a holding cell, jail, or prison as an arrestee, inmate, CO, support staff, administrator, teacher, or visitor. Thus, the general public depends on secondary sources of information and their own (often inadequate) inferences about correctional facilities and the individuals who live and work within (for example, Freeman, 2000: 3; Ross, 2015). Too often, the information on which the general public relies is a myth (Pepinsky and Jesilow, 1985; Kappeler et al., 1996).

A myth is not necessarily arbitrary, false, or the result of poor research or differences of opinion. Rather it is "a traditional story of unknown authorship, with a historical basis [that] ... explain[s] some event" (Kappeler et al., 1996: 2). Myths are "nonscientific, spoken or written fiction used as if it were a true account of some event" (2). Kappeler et al. add, "These crime fictions often take on new meanings as they are told and retold – and at some point ... [are accepted as] truth for many people" (2). Myths are powerful windows into the beliefs of a society. In short, they exaggerate reality.

The average person is exposed to numerous myths on a regular basis. We have myths about certain individuals, professions, places, and experiences. Most of us do not stop to question the veracity of these stories. Why? We do not have the resources (that is, time, money, expertise, and so on) to evaluate every single piece of information we receive. We also have limited attention spans, we lack a compelling interest, and we have competing pressures. We accept myths for a variety of reasons. Myths make our lives easier, which is why we do not question the truth behind many things in our lives. We manage to function reasonably well with most myths.

Even though they are faulty, myths are also presented as if they are true, told by someone who typically has some expert status, and repeated on a frequent basis. Frequently, each time myths are told, these stories are slightly changed, incorporating new information with each new teller. They take on new meanings and are believed by an increasing number of people.

The notion that the criminal justice system (for example, Reiman, 1979/2003; Pepinsky and Jesilow, 1985; Kappeler et al., 1996; Anonymous, 1997), corrections in general (for example, Freeman, 2000), and various dimensions of corrections (for example, Klofas and Toch, 1982; Schicher, 1992; McAuley, 1994; Saum et al., 1995; Peterson and Palumbo, 1997) have their fair share of myths is not new. Needless to say, what we know about the criminal justice system has some basis in fact and reality. Indeed, "[m]any of our contemporary issues of crime and justice are the product of some real event or social concern. Whether or not these events are based on 'truth' is largely irrelevant" because they gain a "larger than life" reality (Kappeler et al., 1996: 2).

Perhaps nowhere is mythmaking more prominent than in the field of corrections. According to Roberts (1994: 1), "Prisons, as debated in political campaigns, dissected in university classrooms, and portrayed in newspapers and motion pictures, are often a caricature. The truth about prisons is at once less dramatic, less fixed, less utopian, less dystopian, and less frightening than stereotypes would suggest." To expand upon these ideas, I examine the interrelated topics of the existing myths within the crime and corrections arenas, as well as their creation, effects, and perpetrators.

What are the myths?

There are at least 16 interrelated myths about prisons, convicts, and COs, including but not limited to those surrounding living conditions, prisoners, and COs.[3] In general, they are:

A. Quality of living conditions
- cleanliness of correctional institutions
- food quality
- appropriateness of health care
- presence and cost of certain amenities
- access to educational programs and recreational opportunities
- frequency of sex and/or male rape

B. Convicts
- convicts' physical appearance
- prisoners' violent tendencies
- inmates' guilt

C. Correctional officers
- correctional officers' lack of concern for inmates

D. The effectiveness of the correctional sanction
- the effectiveness of community corrections
- the relationship between incarceration and crime rates
- the cost of jails and prisons
- the types and lengths of punishment for convicted criminals
- prisoners' inability to be rehabilitated
- the utility of jails and prisons as a deterrent to crime.

In short, these issues are related to facilities, processes, prisoners, correctional personnel, and sentences. Although each of the myths themselves deserves special attention, the focus of this chapter is on their creation and on the means through which this is accomplished.

How are the myths created?

Myths have deep roots in our beliefs about people, society, and institutions, including folklore and cultural expectations; they are often timeless. Stories are passed on from one person to another, from one community to another, from one generation to another, and they are often accepted without much regard to (or knowledge about) the evidence that challenges them.

Several factors enable the development of myths, particularly those about crime and criminals. These include effective presentation and dissemination; adherence to certain well-known themes; involvement of one or more credible sources, particularly an individual or an organization that is respected; targeting unpopular groups in society as perpetrators; projecting victims as helpless and innocent; and, most importantly, using a variety of dissemination vehicles (for example, the mass or social media).

All this is facilitated through a process usually referred to as the importation/exportation hypothesis (Irwin and Cressey, 1962). Within this framework, attitudes, behaviors, fashions, ideas, and styles (that is, elements of a particular lifestyle) that originate in prison make their way into the streets, ghettos, and barrios, and trends from the outside enter into correctional facilities. We do not know exactly where this transmission belt starts, but origination is not an important issue in this discussion. This interrelationship, however, suggests that a complex and important dynamic exists between attitudes and behaviors that come into the jails and prisons, and those that go out of it.

In sum, ideas and beliefs are socially (Berger and Luckmann, 1966) or culturally (Heiner, 2001) constructed.[4] Orientations do not exist in a vacuum but are shaped by a variety of individuals and organizations. By the end, the final message often bears little relation to the original communication. With reference to information about corrections, in general, our lack of firsthand knowledge makes it understandable that our opinions are based upon mediated truths (Jones and Schmid, 2000).

What are the effects of crime myths concerning corrections?

Crime myths "have numerous effects on our perceptions; we may not even be conscious that they are at work" (Kappler et al., 1996: 3). There are six main purposes of crime myths, and these are also applicable to corrections. First, myths "organize our views of crime, criminals, and the proper operation of the criminal justice system" (3).

Second, they "support and maintain prevailing views of crime, criminals, and the criminal justice system" (Kappeler et al., 1996: 3).

Third, these misrepresentations "reinforce the current designation of conduct as criminal, support existing practices of crime control, and provide the background assumptions for future designation of conduct as criminal" (Kappeler et al., 1996: 3–4).

Fourth, the myths are "convenient[ly] used to fill gaps in knowledge and to provide answers to questions social science either cannot answer or has failed to address" (Kappeler et al., 1996: 5).

Fifth, the stereotypes "provide for an outlet for emotionalism and channel emotion into action" (Kappeler et al., 1996: 5). In general, they "seem[] to follow a series of recurrent patterns. These patterns allow a disproportionate amount of ... attention to be focused on a few isolated criminal events or issues" (5).

Finally, with respect to corrections, myths prevent rational discussion about related issues and usually contribute to the perpetuation of the same failures and mistakes in this policy arena.

Who perpetrates the myths?

By all means, criminals, convicts, ex-cons, and COs often embellish their personal lives and experiences behind bars. Likewise, powerful groups with vested interests, craft, develop, disseminate, perpetrate, and shape the majority of myths about corrections. Many of the misrepresentations originate or are reinforced in the news media, government (through various politicians and bureaucracies), correctional institutions, interest groups, universities, and consulting companies by reporters, broadcasters, editors, elected and appointed officials, bureaucrats, public relations specialists, information officers/specialists, prisoners and COs alike, wardens, experts, academics, and consultants. These interests can have either competing or complementary agendas. These actors disseminate myths about jails, prisons, correctional officers, and convicts, while promoting policies and practices that are favorable to their own objectives and constituencies.

Their efforts are typically concentrated on minimizing external involvement in their programs or in the operation of correctional facilities, and they may also be motivated by a desire sell products or services to increase their organizations' revenues. If successful, these endeavors provide a greater degree of autonomy for the relevant organizations.

Why are myths about corrections successful?

There are roughly four interconnected reasons why myths about crime and corrections are so effective. They include, but are not limited to, the power of those creating the myths, the costs involved in obtaining accurate information about jails and prisons, the apathy of the public, and the convincing nature of the myths.

Many who promote myths about corrections possess a considerable amount of resources (that is, money, personnel, expertise, and access). Membership organizations, like the American Correctional Association (ACA) and the American Jails Association (AJA) (the largest professional associations for correctional practitioners in the United States), can and do perpetrate myths about corrections. The ACA, for example, is a large dues-paying organization with many influential members. Although the goal of the

ACA is to "improve the image of those who work in corrections ... [through] ... improving the conditions of corrections professionals and those who are incarcerated through the development of standards" (Gondles, 1999: v), the group also shapes the dialogue on prisons. The AJA at the local government, state, and federal levels, to whom jails and prisons are accountable, and many media outlets are also well funded through tax revenues and the sales of their products (that is, advertising) respectively.

One way to gather important information about corrections is through qualitative research, especially ethnographic studies (Wacquant, 2002). This typically means face-to-face interviews and/or observation of subjects under investigation. Conducting research inside prisons, regardless of the research method, is extremely difficult, and one of the biggest problems is access. Complex and protracted negotiations with prison officials often needs to occur before researchers can interview convicts, correctional workers, and/or administrators. Even if this opportunity is granted, gaining the trust and cooperation of the subject participants is still a challenge.

Because many correctional facilities are usually located in relatively remote areas, researchers, policymakers, and the news media rarely conduct independent research and learn firsthand about prison conditions. Unless you have the cooperation of the correctional facility administration inside, usually the visit you are allowed is very short, and if it is a particular inmate you want to talk to it is usually in the visiting room. Most correctional professionals have too many resource constraints to make this work; thus, outsiders typically have to rely on less than ideal information. Meanwhile, the lion's share of the public is simply overburdened with the everyday challenges of making a living, taking care of children, and so on; thus, an objective and detailed analysis of correctional practices becomes a luxury, especially when this involves a time-consuming information search (119–20). Furthermore, most COs and administrators do not want to talk to outsiders (that is, researchers or journalists) because they are worried that they will uncover some sort of problem and reveal this to the public, unnecessarily embarrassing them or their correctional facility and resulting in sanctions (that is, suspension, demotion, firing, and so on) by their organization (Ross, 2011b). Additionally, some convicts are also moved around quite frequently. If a person is convicted of a federal offense, they might be originally incarcerated in New York City but eventually be moved to Alabama or Oklahoma or Alaska, if the FBOP (Federal Bureau of Prisons) so desires it. Finally, myths appear to be convincing. Mythmakers are very skilled at communicating their messages and tapping into issues that the public feel are important (Beckett and Sasson, 2003).

The public forms its knowledge of corrections through a complex interaction of mythmakers (that is, initiators, sources, propagandists, and gatekeepers), mediums, and recipients. This knowledge is predicated on shared or misinterpreted meanings among convicts, reporters, researchers, prison information officers, and the public, and these messages are spread through a vast array of cultural industries.

The contribution of cultural industries

Some businesses exploit the styles and images of deviant subcultures or make references to these groups to generate income (Lopiano-Misdom and De Luca, 1997; Klein, 2000: chapter 3). This process, referred to as the commodification of culture, may use images and symbols about jails, prisons, COs, and incarceration to convey a particular lifestyle, to sell products and services, and – consciously or unconsciously – to perpetrate and perpetuate the myths about corrections. Cultural industries do not simply exist in a vacuum; they function within a social context and have ideological implications. Schiller (1989) identifies cultural industries that "provide symbolic goods and services" (30) and divides them into two tiers. The first one he categorizes as "publishing, the press, film, radio, television, photography, recording, advertising, sports, and ... the information industry" (30). The second category, on the other hand, consists of "services ... displayed in relatively permanent installations," like "museums, art galleries, amusement parks ..., shopping malls, and corporate 'public spaces'" (30–1). The former is more transitory, and the latter is more permanent. Schiller notes that "all economic activity produces symbolic as well as material goods. In fact, the two are generally inseparable" (31).

Cultural industries reflect and shape public opinion. They can influence policymakers and legislators, ultimately impacting the policies, practices, and laws that are, introduced, debated, accepted, passed, and implemented. In some cases, cultural industries glamorize or romanticize jail and prison life. The settings, individuals, and issues are typically dramatized for entertainment value. For instance, the camaraderie with or conflict between COs/administrators and prisoners is often romanticized or exaggerated, giving the public a false impression of the range of relationships that exist inside correctional facilities.

Cultural industries are important in constructing the popular culture of corrections, a culture that is "the product of a complicated, ongoing evolutionary process organized around the creation and consistent reinforcement of a core set of negative stereotypes and their associated imagery. This core of negative stereotypes imagery defines the constructed image template of corrections" (Freeman, 2000: 10).

There are eight primary cultural industries that perpetuate myths about incarceration.[5] Organized from least to most important, they are fashion, advertising, music, fiction, documentaries, television, motion pictures, and the news media. Needless to say, these cultural industries are typically interwoven.[6] Understanding that the styles of deviant or criminal subcultures are often glorified may increase the appeal of jail or prison to those who have never served time.

Fashion

It has long been recognized that clothing, jewelry, and accessories – and, by extension, the fashions and styles we wear or adopt – consciously or unconsciously reflect our values, moods, personality, or self-image, and provide us with a sense of belonging or identity. Clothing can also be used to separate people and categorize them into groups, thereby providing a type of psychological and, later, physical distance between real, imagined, or potential antagonists. It should be noted that fashions are not simply embedded in dress but can extend to speech, hair, and body customization (Goffman, 1959; Miller, 1996). Scholars have long recognized that particular subcultures wear unique styles of clothing (for example, Tunnell, 2000: 48–51). Over the past four decades, prisoners' clothing styles have been copied by some mainstream clothing manufacturers.[7] Because certain articles of clothing are seen as hip, they are adopted into mainstream culture, often through middle-class voyeurism or fascination. In turn, this connection can make prison seem acceptable and those who wear the articles somewhat radical or rebellious.

Advertising

Prisoners, COs, jails, and prisons are occasionally used in advertising campaigns for shock and/or entertainment value. By grabbing the public's attention, commercials enable corporations and political organizations to gain attention, sell products and services, and promote and gather support for certain points of view. Although convict and correctional themes are traditionally used in the sales of security-related products through mediums that sell products to the Correctional Industrial Complex (for example, Christie, 1993/1994), a handful of recent marketing efforts include television advertisements.

The potential to incorporate jails, prisons and corrections into advertising campaigns and branding is limitless. This process largely depends on the creativity and ability of commercial artists and copywriters to link the symbols and images of this environment with the products and services to be sold.

Music

The connection between music and prisons is hardly new (Fisher-Giorlando, 1987). Several famous musicians have done time, and many individuals formerly incarcerated have gone on to successful musical careers after being released. Moreover, a handful of musicians have been granted access to correctional facilities to play concerts, and a number of well-known musicians have written popular protest songs focusing on the plight of the incarcerated. Some of these musicians draw upon their own jail or prison experiences as they write and record songs. Naturally, this prompts the questions of why these individuals become successful musicians, and what kind of role prison played in their career? In short, did this time help or hinder their success? These musicians might have turned their prison experiences into something positive, but this does not necessarily imply causality.

The music-prison phenomenon is prevalent across a number of different music genres, including country and western, rock and roll, blues, bluegrass, rap, and hip-hop (Tunnell, 1992; 1995; Hamm and Ferrell, 1994). Additionally, there have been successful record labels such as Death Row Records, founded by the late and controversial Suge Knight, that draw on the convict theme.

Fictional treatments

Each year, an increasing number of fictional treatments – including poems, short stories, and novels that are set in correctional facilities – are written and published (Franklin, 1982; 1998; Massey, 1989). Perhaps the most important fictional medium is the novel because of its potential use as the basis for films or television series. In general, "the prison novel balances attention on the bureaucratic or institutional setting or atmosphere with a focus on the character caught up in it" (Massey, 1989: 3). "Some, like *Cool Hand Luke* by Donn Pearce or Edward Bunker's *No Beast So Fierce*, received recognition when movies based on the novels became popular. The vast majority of these novels appear briefly, often only in paperback, and then ... [go] out of print" (2).

Fictional books based on prison settings can be divided into two camps: those written by "professional writers who have not served extensive time behind bars" and those produced by convicts or ex-convicts (Massey, 1989: 2). The first category includes Stanley Elkin's *A Bad Man*; John Cheever's *Falconer*; Stephen King's *The Green Mile* series, which includes *The Two Dead Girls*, *The Mouse on the Mile*, *Night Journey*, *Coffey's Hands*, *The Bad Death of Eduard Delacroix*, and *Coffey on the Mile*; and Tim Willocks' *Green River Rising*.[8]

There is also a growing number of well-known books written by American convicts or ex-cons about prison life, including Jack London, Malcolm Braly, and Edward Bunker. Massey (1989), who performed an in-depth study of these books, said that there is "a progression of experiences found in virtually all prison novels: entry, the world of prisons, and crisis" (5–6). Additional themes are repeated in each novel: "the alien world of the cell block, the animosity between the convict and his keepers, the macho inmate in a violent social environment, and the criticism of a country that treats humans this way" (6).

The setting in fictional prison stories "is often pictured as a refuge from the trivial or prosaic" (Duncan, 1996: 13). As a refuge, its importance lies in the "prison as the quintessential academy and prison as a catalyst of intense friendship" (13). Given that the reading public for these novels is much smaller than the readership of mass media outlets, it is difficult to measure the importance of this influence.

Documentaries

A growing number of documentaries and docudramas have attempted to present the reality of prisons. Some of these have been made for television news shows, such as *48 Hours* and *Primetime*, or cable TV stations such as Court TV now called truTV. To accomplish their goals, these productions often trace the history of different correctional institutions, cite statistics (including the number of cells and the cost of housing prisoners), and use archival photographs, newsreel footage, reenactments, and interviews with current or ex-prisoners, COs, chaplains, and others. They often also incorporate copious footage of the prison (including its graveyard and cellblocks), dramatic language to describe individuals and incidents, and haunting music as a backdrop. News personalities like Ted Koppel, Bill Kurtis, Hedrick Smith, Mike Wallace, and Tom Wicker or actors like Andre Braugher, Tim Robbins, or Paul Servino narrate some of these productions. Other documentaries mainly consist of a series of "talking heads," including convicts, COs, prison wardens, reformers, and judges.

Regardless of who produces and distributes these documentaries, they routinely feature stereotypical images of prisoners who are tattoo laden, muscle bound, and intimidating. Although viewers may enjoy these videos, these films often serve to reinforce the myth of convicts as violent predators.

Television

For the average viewer, television is easily accessible and relatively pervasive (for example, airports, bars, and doctors' offices). Anyone who has access receives its message. Many people watch hours of television each day, and viewers do not have to be literate or even speak English to understand the content of a program. Television is also a powerful disseminator of style, which has a predominant visual component.

Two basic types of programs relevant to corrections have been produced for television broadcast: "reality TV" shows and the series.

First, since 2000, MSNBC, the cable news station, has aired the *Lockup* series (Cecil and Leitner, 2009). The weekly show goes inside an extensive number of well-known maximum security prisons and interviews inmates, correctional workers, and administrators. The series is "careful not to be overly sympathetic to the inmates, yet want to hold up a mirror to them in a way to show the viewers what happens. Most inmates do their time and get out" (Tucker, nd). The *Lockup* "franchise" has spawned five related shows under its domain: *Raw, Extended Stay, World Tour, Special Investigation*, and *Life After Lockup*. The series will be coming to an end June 29, 2016.

Likewise, the National Geographic Channel aired two corrections relevant series: one called *Lockdown*, and the other Locked Up Abroad. The first, aired between 2008-2010, "takes viewers inside the closed world of three maximum-security U.S. prisons to observe violent clashes, covert rules, and secret codes of justice."[9] The second, which started broadcasting in 2006 and ended in 2013, "takes viewers inside accounts of capture, incarceration, and terror far away fro home with intimate personal interviews and dramatic reenactments."[10]

Finally, in 2011, A&E introduced *Beyond Scared Straight*. The series builds upon the controversial program and documentary introduced in the late 1970s, that would temporarily introduce juveniles who have engaged in crimes to prison. Each episode introduces a handful of teenage youths to different programs run in correctional facilities in the United States. The series ran for a total of nine seasons, with the series finale airing on September 3, 2015. All series have encountered criticisms and sparked different ethical controversies.

Second, few prison series have been produced for the American TV market. Yet, there are a few exceptions: In 1997, the Home Box Office (HBO) cable station introduced *Oz*, which lasted six seasons. Created by Tom Fontana and produced by both Fontana and Barry Levinson (known for his critically acclaimed police series *Homicide: Life on the Streets*), the program, acknowledged as being HBO's first and longest series, the program looked at the lives of convicts and correctional workers in an urban correctional facility. This series somewhat resembled a soap opera with secretive relationships among the staff and inmates, and it frequently portrayed prisoners as predatory homosexuals or psychopathic killers who suffered from severe psychological problems. Only six to eight shows were aired each season.

Seemingly, both the viewing public and many criminal justice practitioners – particularly COs – thought the show was an accurate reflection of reality. On the other hand, many convicts found the series to be a gross distortion of prison reality. They did not accept this program as an honest representation of prison life. In fact, in the spring of 2000, the popular television comedy series *Saturday Night Live* aired an episode poking fun at and parodying *Oz* (see Exhibit 2.1).

In the fall of 2005, the Fox Broadcasting Company debuted a new series called *Prison Break*. Directed by Paul Scheuring, the show focuses on the exploits of the character Michael Scofield, played by actor Wentworth Miller. The protagonist's brother has been sentenced to death (naturally, for a crime he did not commit) and is awaiting his execution at the fictitious Fox River State Penitentiary. Scofield, who just happens to be a structural engineer with plans of the prison, commits a crime and is fortuitously sentenced to the same prison as his brother. Scofield's objective is to help his brother escape and, until this is accomplished, to survive the prison experience.

In 2014, streaming service Netflix started airing the comedy–drama series, *Orange is the New Black*. This effort was initially based on the memoir of the same title, written by Piper Herman documenting her 16 months incarceration at the all women's' Federal Correctional Institution Danbury. The fictionalized Netflix series is set in Litchfield Correctional Institution, which encounters considerable challenges in its day-to-day running. The series brings in and deals with themes of bisexualism and lesbianism, correctional officer deviance, addiction, racism, and administrative incompetence. Almost each episode features a back-story regarding one or more inmates or correctional officers. Unlike other series, inmates are portrayed as human beings struggling with addiction, lack of friendship and parenting.

Exhibit 2.1

Television series

Oz (1997–2003)

Between 1997 and 2003, HBO, a cable television station, aired *Oz*, a one-hour drama that was set at a fictional maximum-security prison called Oswald State Correctional Facility. Developed by Tom Fontana and Barry Levinson, this series captured the lives and struggles of inmates, correctional workers, and administrators in an experimental part of the prison called the Emerald City. Here the emphasis was on rehabilitation and learning responsibility while inmates were behind bars. The characters appeared to be made up of the "requisite" number of races and ethnic groups.

Many people who work or have worked in the field of corrections saw a considerable amount of reality in the series, especially with respect to the relationships that developed. Others found the setting quite claustrophobic. Unlike the characters in *Law and Order* or the now-defunct *NYPD Blue*, who could and did get out of the station house, those in *Oz* were always confined.

Motion pictures

Our attitudes and beliefs about jails and prisons are also shaped by movies (Crowther, 1989; Parish, 1991; Rafter, 2000: chapter 5). Many of the images we have about correctional facilities come from movies (Jones and Schmid,

2000). Whether these Hollywood films are screened in movie theaters, or available on or through other screening methods (e.g., DVDs, television, or streaming via Netflix, Amazon, etc.),[11] they present us with numerous images of prison life. Indeed, movies that deal at some level with corrections could probably be placed on a continuum that ranks each film according to the amount of time it devotes to a correctional theme. For example, the Hollywood movie *Shawshank Redemption* (with actors Tim Robbins and Morgan Freeman) contrasts with *The Rock* (with actors Sean Connery and Nicholas Cage). "The prison film, a claustrophobic offshoot of the gangster film, was by 1933 a thriving sub-genre in its own right" (Shadoian, 1979: 169). "Public attitudes toward criminals in general, the types of people who are or should be incarcerated, and prison conditions that should be tolerated become evident through the treatment of criminal characters in film" (Munro-Bjorklund, 1991: 56–7).

Since the 1930s, there have been more than 100 movies made about adult male prisons alone (Cheatwood, 1998). Like television, this form of communication is accessible to most people. One need not have skills, like literacy, in order to understand the motion picture industry's basic message.

Few people have systematically investigated films about prisons. Although Munro-Bjorklund (1991: 56–61) examines the motion pictures made in the aftermath of the Attica riot (1971), it was not until Cheatwood that we had a more comprehensive treatment of Hollywood movies on incarceration. As Cheatwood notes, "[M]uch of the research that does exist is highly impressionistic or treats only one film, one national event, or one limited time period" (1998). According to Travisino, "Hollywood and the television writers continue to portray the vilest aspects of prison life, and the public is led to believe that nothing can be accomplished because that's 'the way it is' with the system" (1980: 1, as quoted by Cheatwood: 21).

A handful of scholars have written about motion pictures that depict prisons. Rafter (2000), for example, suggests that prison movies serve four purposes: "to identify with the perfect man; ... to participate in perfect friendships; ... to fantasize about sex and rebellion; and ... to acquire insider information about the apparent realities of prison life" (123). According to her, "[t]raditional prison films invite us to identify with heroes, even superheroes" (123). Prison films contain an abundant supply of "ideal companions, buddies more loyal and true than any on the outside" (124). She adds, "[P]rison films with male inmates often have a homosexual subtext in which the buddy gets both a perfect friend and a lover" (125). Finally, prison movies "offer the inside scoop, a window onto the inaccessible but riveting world of the prison" (127).

Cheatwood (1998) analyzes fictional movies about adult male civilian prisons produced between 1929 and 1995, classifying the films into four categories based on different eras: Depression, 1929–42; Rehabilitation, 1943–62; Confinement, 1963–80; and Administrative, 1981–95. He claims that movies about prisons "revolve around the themes of confinement, justice, authority and release. These components ... enable us to see how our theories and public positions are translated and presented to the public" (210).

Cheatwood believes that Hollywood movies on prison have a "subtle" rather than an "immediate" impact on the viewing public (1998: 211). He states, "[p]eople see pictures that support their established and currently held views of the world, and films can only gradually reshape or crystallize amorphous visions, perceptions, or ideas that the viewing public holds" (211).

In covering films about prisons, Cheatwood mentions, "[t]hese have varied from military prison escape films to musicals about maximum security institutions" (1998: 211). He limits his sample to

> films whose predominant subject was incarceration in a male, adult, civilian correctional facility. There are several pragmatic reasons for this limitation. In the public, the "prison problem" tends to be identified with adult, male, civilian facilities. So few "probation and parole" films exist that they do not constitute a genre at all. Although there are quite a few films about women's prisons, many are sexploitation films. (211)

Cheatwood further argues, "[w]ithin each of these eras, the treatment of distinct elements and the manner of their combination have been relatively consistent through the films produced. Further, the nature of these films displays a relationship both to the academic theories of corrections predominant in the era and to changes and events in the pragmatic operations of corrections in the nation" (1998: 215).

Many of these movies have become very predictable. Rafter (2000: 117–23) suggests that stock characters, plots, and themes are prevalent in all prison movies. With respect to characters, we typically have "convict buddies, a paternalistic warden, a cruel guard, a craven snitch, a bloodthirsty convict and the young hero" (118). In terms of repeated plotlines, we see riots, escapes, or the planning that goes into these events (120). A particularly redundant theme is "rebellion against injustice. Innocents, ... are being punished by diabolical officers and nasty fellow convicts. ... To restore justice, the prisoners sometimes take matters into their own hands. ... At others, someone comes to their rescue" (121–2).[12]

Finally, one of the biggest misrepresentations embedded in motion pictures is that of female prisoners (Morey, 1995; Faith, 1997). Few Hollywood films give accurate accounts of incarcerated women. Those that are available are generally pornographic in nature (often referred to as *B movies*) and include buxom blondes and "butch" guards. These films emphasize themes of domination, lesbianism, lust, and voyeurism.

Exhibit 2.2

Selected commercial and fictional movies with settings that take place in jails, prisons, or include correctional themes

American Me
Bad Boys
Birdman of Alcatraz
Brubaker
CB4
Con Air
Dead Man Walking
Felon
The Hurricane
The Green Mile
Iceman
Law Abiding Citizen
The Longest Yard (1974 and 2005 versions)
One Flew over the Cuckoo's Nest
Prison Song
The Rock
Shawshank Redemption
Sleepers
Stir Crazy

News media

Americans receive their news from a variety of sources: television, radio, magazines, newspapers, and the internet. In fact, according to Cheatwood, "[m]ost people in the general public have formed their images of what prison life is 'actually' like from the mass media" (1998: 210).

As a result of advances in communications technology, the mass media has gained enormous influence over the kinds of messages communicated, heard, and seen, as well as the interpretation of important events. The mass media is probably the most important vehicle for conveying and shaping the cultural construction of crime and criminals. The media operates under the myth of objectivity – that reporting is balanced and fair. However, on closer examination, we find that most outlets have ideological and political agendas. News media outlets, in particular, are in a perfect position to communicate these misrepresentations.

By the same token, members of the news media serve a variety of functions including, but not limited to, and in increasing order of importance: providing information, educating the public, sharing opinions, stimulating debate, reinforcing dominant stereotypes, and most of all, making a profit for their owners (Lichteret al., 1986; Barak, 1995; Brownstein, 1995; Parenti, 1995).

In most news organizations, the staff consists of a variety of reporters. The variability is largely a function of the organization's resources, and this, in turn, is fuelled by revenues and perceptions of audience demands (Ross, 1998; 2000c: chapter 2). Larger newspapers typically employ a crime or police reporter. Some, like *The New York Times*, can have upward of ten police or crime reporters. Unfortunately, few journalists are assigned to cover the prisons or jails on a full- or part-time basis (Ross, 2011b). According to Chermack, "News media do not have a corrections beat that fulfills the same function as a police or court beat" (1998: 97).

One must also recognize that, in most news organizations, crime reporting is often an entry-level position. As part of a natural career path, many reporters may begin with this beat and then graduate to covering city hall, state politics, and eventually – if they are lucky or so inclined – federal politics.

> Prompted by the nature of the media industry, television and newspaper reporters focus on "hot topics" of entertainment value. In the early stages of myth development, media frenzy develops, which allows for expanded coverage of isolated and unique events. Typically, the appearance of an uncritical newspaper or magazine article exploring a unique social problem starts the chain of events. (Kappeler et al., 1996: 6)

The journalist has "uncovered a 'new' social evil. Other journalists, not wanting to be left out, jump on the band wagon" (Kappeler et al., 1996: 6).

Few content analyses of newspaper coverage of corrections have been performed (Jacobs and Brooks, 1983; Freeman, 1998; Ross, 1999). First, Jacobs and Brooks (1983) examined newspapers, periodicals, and television news broadcasts about prison, which appeared in 1976. Second, Freeman (1998) explored "the content of 1,546 newspaper articles concerning corrections that appeared through the United States between September 8, 1994 and November 24, 1995" (1998: 203).[13]

Finally, Ross (1999), in an attempt to understand the issues focused on in corrections reporting, the prominence of the stories, the reporters who were covering this topic, and the sources of the stories, performed a content analysis of a year's worth (that is, 1999) of criminal justice reporting appearing in *The Baltimore Sun*. Unfortunately, these studies are mere snapshots in the overall picture of corrections reporting. Moreover, the last two studies might depict regional patterns of corrections reporting more than they do national content.

Members of the news media have been accused of a whole host of failings including, but not limited to, sensationalism, bias (selectivity), censorship, lack of interest in "serious and complicated questions," and superficiality. Needless to say, reporters encounter various obstacles when trying to research articles or stories on correctional facilities.

According to Davis (1998), "Much has been written about the emergence of the correctional 'boom' in America, yet for all the media attention, prisons remain a largely unchecked arm of American governance. In many states, corrections is among the largest budget items, yet coverage of correctional facilities and the convicts incarcerated in them is scarce" (1998). Despite the United States having the highest incarceration rate and a so-called prison crisis, corrections is typically not a hot topic in the news. Why are criminal justice agencies avoided by the news media? There are probably two major reasons: lack of access by reporters and lack of interest by the public.

The amount of access reporters have to jails and prisons varies according to the type of facility and jurisdiction (Talbott, 1988; 1989; Anonymous, 1989; 1998a; 1998b; Hincle, 1996; Kindel, 1998). Most correctional facilities rarely allow prisoners to be interviewed by reporters. Much of what *is* reported often comes from limited or biased sources, such as prison public information officers. In most cases, members of the media are not allowed access to correctional facilities or to the convicts housed within. For example, jails and prisons generally do not share with the media news concerning the murders or assaults of prisoners. Each correctional facility has its own policies and procedures, and some are stricter than others. The Supreme Court has derived "three major principles concerning prison access": The First Amendment "does not guarantee the public or the press a right to obtain information from prisons." Second, "[j]ournalists have no greater rights of access than [does] the general public." Third, "[t]he public's need for access to information will be balanced against other societal needs, such as law enforcement interests and personal privacy" (*Pell v. Procunier*, 1974; *Saxbe v. Washington Post*, 1974).

Another reason for the lack of coverage may have to do with a "self-fulfilling prophecy" of sorts. In other words, it could be that the news media rarely reports on corrections; thus, the public is not interested. Since a wider audience is not interested, neither is the news media. This is somewhat ironic given the "if it bleeds, it leads" mentality of the media. How can they focus so much time, especially on TV, to murders, shootings, and criminal trials, but not turn to the inevitable result – prisons and corrections?

Solutions

How can we change this state of affairs? The following seven solutions, listed from least to most important, could possibly minimize or counterbalance the production and dissemination of myths produced by the cultural industries.

First, building on Sir John Fielding's (a British magistrate, 1721–1780) original desire that prisons need to be more open to inspection and investigation, correctional facilities must do more to allow the prisoners in their custody to be interviewed by the media, policymakers, and academic researchers. Hopefully, these reports will document how problems with jails and prisons and with COs are commonplace.

Second, correctional facilities need to submit to periodic open houses that permit the public a relatively comprehensive look at what happens within jail and prison walls. Admittedly, not all parts of correctional institutions will or should be open to the public. And these visits must be conducted in such a fashion as to not encourage a zoo-like atmosphere. Facilitating the public to see as much as possible about what goes on behind the razor wire will help them get a better picture of the concerns of convicts and COs.

Third, the mass media and especially Hollywood need to make a better effort to produce films with more accurate and less sensational portrayals of convicts, COs, and the criminal justice system. Criminology and criminal justice instructors should endeavor to use realistic accounts of life in prisons in their classroom instructional material (for example, documentaries, autobiographies, and the like).

Fourth, we also should help journalists gain access to prisons. The reporters need to be better educated about the conditions of prisoners and the powers of COs and administrators. Journalism schools could be advantageous in this respect; perhaps some sort of partnership with journalism schools and academics might be beneficial.

Fifth, guest lecturers who have done time or who work in correctional facilities should be used more often and more effectively to talk about the reality of prisons. Ex-cons, correctional employees, and administrators should be invited to speak to news organizations and to groups of students. They can offer a needed dose of realism to the classroom, more so than can many of the academic texts we currently use. We should caution our speakers against the overuse of sensationalism and counsel them to avoid conveying a succession of "war stories."

Sixth, we might also depend more heavily on autobiographical materials, such as books written by convicts and ex-cons (for example, Jackson, 1970; Abbott, 1981; Abu-Jamal, 1996; Baca, 2001; Ross and Richards, 2003), COs (for example, Conover, 2001; Wilkinson, 2005), and administrators (for example, Bruton, 2004; Willett, 2004). Other experts, although often biased or sensationalized for effect, can sometimes bring to light issues that are overlooked in other texts.

Seventh, a public relations or awareness campaign could bring to people's attention the powerful effects of our cultural institutions in shaping what we know about jails and prisons. Building on the success of the Adbusters efforts, documented in books like *No Logo* (Klein, 2000), such a campaign should hold these entities more accountable.[14]

We live in a time when more is demanded of the public, because the issues are so numerous, complex, and interrelated. Some people "tune out," but a modern representative democracy demands a public that is alert, well informed, and engaged (Ross, 2000a: chapter 7). The ability to critically analyze controversial evidence is so badly needed in the complex world in which we live.

Finally, the misrepresentation of corrections, the misinformation, and the outright lies propagated by the government and media need to be regularly challenged (Herman and Chomsky, 1988). Unfortunately, there is a tendency among the general public to believe popular conceptions and myths about correctional facilities and convicts, especially their entitlements in the jail and prison system, and to adopt popular misconceptions. Most are, in fact, sweeping generalizations that contradict empirical reality.

Key terms

American Correctional Association (ACA): Member based organization for correctional officers (COs) in the United States with large dues paid.

Commodification of culture: Process whereby images and styles of deviant and criminal groups are used to sell products and services.

Content analysis: A scientific research method that counts the number of times a word or phrase is mentioned in one or more types of mass media, and its relation to other themes.

Cultural industry: Businesses that reflect and shape public opinion and are important in constructing the popular culture of prisons.

Documentary: A nonfictional film about a subject.

Importation/exportation hypothesis: Process whereby sources of fashion language, and subcultures that exist in correctional facilities, are taken to the street and then back into jails/prisons as each new generation enters prison.

Mass media: News media, Hollywood films, television, fictional books, etc.

Myth: Nonscientific, spoken, or written fictional story presented to an audience as if it were a true account of some sort of event, person, or place.

News media: Radio, television, newspapers, internet news source.

Style: A type of fashion (includes clothing, jewelry, body modification, haircuts), or the way a person carries themself.

Notes

1 This chapter uses the words myths, misconceptions, misrepresentations, and stereotypes interchangeably.

2 This chapter's interpretation is mainly confined to the United States; however, the findings can be generalized to many of the advanced industrialized democracies.

3 For a detailed examination of these myths see, for example, Ross (2012a). A detailed description and analysis of these myths was not included in this text because of space limitations.

4 Although Surette (1998: xvii) suggests that there are actually three "dominant social construction of reality engines," a discussion of this issue is beyond the scope of this chapter.

5 Cultural industries are often analyzed through the academic prism of cultural studies or research on popular culture. Radio and sports are not covered in this chapter.

6 For example, it is difficult to separate the origins of the messages conveyed in a movie set in prison and, say, the book upon which the film was based (for example, *Dead Man Walking*).

7 This has probably evolved from or is interwoven with what might be referred to as gang style (for example, Miller, 1995).

8 Some outsiders have criticized these professional writers "as writing primarily for profit, ... Needless to say, those profits, even for the most famous novelists ... have been meager" (Massey, 1989: 2).

9 See http://channel.nationalgeographic.com/series/lockdown

10 See http://channel.nationalgeographic.com/series/locked-up-abroad

11 The DVD and online (for example, Netflix, Amazon Prime, and so on) markets, an offshoot of the Hollywood movie industry, help to shape teenagers' thinking. They are impressionable and may desire, but lack, many of the entertainment venues available to adults. Bored by family TV shows, they look elsewhere. Numerous outlets are available for prison movies that are X- or R-rated.

12 Not only academics, but also members of the correctional industry have commented on the stereotypical images presented by Hollywood films (for example, Zaner, 1989).

13 A more complete review of these is available in Ross (2003).

14 Many of these solutions may amount to prison voyeurism (Ross, 2015). A detailed discussion of this phenomenon, however, is not covered in this text.

PART II

Challenges for convicts and correctional facilities

THREE

Misuse of jails

Introduction

Almost every town, city, municipality, and county has a jail. These can be very small facilities or large institutions, like Rikers Island in New York City or Los Angeles County Jail, which resemble mini-cities in their own right (Irwin, 1985; Thompson and Mays, 1991).

Most of the public fail to distinguish between jails and prisons. People who are sent to jail are typically either pre-trial detainees or individuals convicted of relatively minor crimes (known as misdemeanors). Pre-trial detainees are those individuals who have been determined by a judge, magistrate, or commissioner as being unable to make bail; they cannot be released on their own recognizance; or they have been accused of committing a serious felony and are perceived to be a flight risk (that is, they will not voluntarily return to court). These detainees are kept in jails, awaiting further processing by the criminal justice system.

Individuals who cannot make bail are typically poor and powerless, and come from the lower socioeconomic classes in society. Thus, it should come as no surprise that jails and correctional facilities in the United States predominantly house African Americans, Hispanics, Native Americans, and poor whites.

They are often young, uneducated or poorly educated, and unemployed. This phenomenon has been pejoratively called warehousing (Miller, 1996; Welch, 1996: 172; Irwin, 2005). Very few of these pre-trial detainees will have the nerve and financial resources to fight their cases. Instead they often plead guilty and then are released to the street for "time served." Regardless, they are saddled with criminal records that haunt them for the rest of their lives (Miller, 1996). Despite their legitimate uses, holding cells and jails are routinely used as makeshift "drunk tanks, truant halls, and shelters for the homeless and mentally ill" (Welch, 1996: 167).

Who runs the jail? In most jurisdictions the municipality operates the jail. In many places in the United States, however, especially where a county form of government exists, the sheriff (an elected position) runs the jails.

Exhibit 3.1

Classics in corrections

Jerome G. Miller's *Search and Destroy* (1996)

Longtime social worker, prison activist, and researcher Jerome Miller (1931–2015) reviewed his experience and the research conducted by his organization, the National Center on Institutions and Alternatives, in an attempt to explain what happens to the average inmate in an American big-city jail. He discovered that a disproportionate number of individuals (mainly poor African-American and Hispanic youths) who are confined in jails cannot be released on bail or their own recognizance and are thus forced to remain locked up for long periods of times before their release can be secured by a public defender. They often plead guilty to lesser charges and are released on time served. The second part of Miller's book consists of his interpretation of criminological theory's racist aspects. He blames police and probation officers, social workers, courts and academics, for unnecessary bias in their work which results in the over incarceration of African Americans.

Functions of jails

Jails have approximately ten interrelated functions:

1. "receive individuals pending arraignment and hold them awaiting trial, conviction, or sentencing";
2. "re-admit probation, parole, and bail-bond violators and absconders";
3. "temporarily detain juveniles pending transfer to juvenile authorities";
4. "hold mentally-ill persons pending their movement to appropriate health facilities";
5. "hold individuals for the military, for protective custody, for contempt, and for the courts as witnesses";
6. "release convicted inmates to the community upon completion of their sentence";
7. "transfer inmates to Federal, State, or other authorities";
8. "house inmates for Federal, State, or other authorities because of crowding of their facilities";

9. "relinquish custody of temporary detainees to juvenile and medical authorities"; and
10. "hold inmates sentenced to short terms (generally under 1 year)" (Gilliard, 1999: 5).

Experiencing jail

Shortly after being arrested, individuals soon learn if they are charged with a misdemeanor or a felony. The first typically carries a maximum sentence of less than a year in jail,[1] and is considered by the criminal justice system to be a relatively minor crime. If the person is charged with a felony that carries a sentence of one year to life or death, then, in the eyes of the law, the individual has committed a serious offense.

After being handcuffed, patted down (searched for weapons and contraband), and forced into a police car or van, arrestees will arrive at the local lockup. Depending upon which law enforcement agency made the arrest, arrestees may be transported to the nearby district or division police station, "central booking" located in or near the municipal courthouse, the federal courthouse, or directly to the county jail. Alternatively, individuals may spend a couple of hours at the local police station in a holding cell and then be transported to central booking, where they will wait an hour or two before being booked.

The facilities vary in physical appearance (for example, layout, state of disrepair, and so on) and comfort (for example, amenities, air quality, and so on) usually with no bed and only a bench to sit on. The newly arrested are held in their own cell, either alone or with another person, or they are placed in a "bullpen" or "drunk tank" with 50–100 other inmates. These spaces might be dark or bright, have graffiti on their walls, and can smell of urine, excrement, sweat, and vomit.

No matter where the police take the accused, the routine is basically the same. Arrestees are booked, which means being fingerprinted and photographed (also known as having one's mug shot taken). Any shoelaces, belts, and neckties will be confiscated because the jailers do not want the person to use them to attempt suicide or to hurt other detainees. Valuables and identification are placed in an envelope for safekeeping, then arrestees are taken to a holding cell. Those staying longer will be strip-searched and typically given an orange jumpsuit.

All trips to prison begin with some jail time. If computed properly, this time is typically deducted from a person's sentence as "credit for time served." Most prisoners (and COs (correctional officers)) consider city and county jails to be worse than prison, especially the facilities in large cities and in the Deep South (Ross and Richards, 2002). Regardless of their location, jails have few, if any, medical, recreational, or educational services.

Jails have five primary drawbacks. In general, they are, from least to most important:

- lack of privacy;
- poorly trained and paid personnel;
- overcrowded and unsanitary conditions;
- bad food and living conditions; and
- substandard or nonexistent medical treatment (Zupan, 2002).[2]

Lack of privacy

There is little privacy in jail. Although it might seem like an invasion of privacy, in the case of high-profile defendants, every incriminating word said, phone call made, or letter written will be used in court to make a case against an arrestee or to drum up additional indictments against them or others. Jailhouse holding tanks are usually "bugged" with hidden microphones and video cameras.

This technology is rarely used for the convicts' protection. Instead, it provides the judicial system another opportunity to gather incriminating evidence. The jailers tape everything, yet the facility does not need to rely on sophisticated electronic surveillance, as cellmates may be more than happy to inform law enforcement of anything their cellmates say. These "jailhouse snitches" will convey details of conversations entered into or overheard to law enforcement as a means (or so they hope) to extract special benefits and/ or reduce their own sentences or jail time. And, if it is an important case, like homicide, rape, or large-scale drug conspiracy, sometimes an undercover police officer will be placed in the suspect's cell to pose as his new best friend. Access to phones is limited. Those who are in custody may have to wait a day or two to place calls.[3] Toilets are usually made out of stainless steel and do not have lids, door stalls – if they ever existed – are removed, and rarely is toilet paper found on the rollers.

Poorly trained and paid personnel

Many lockup and jail facilities are staffed by "turnkey" officers, who are paid close to minimum wage, and who appear nearly as economically desperate as the prisoners. They are also typically less educated and have less on-the-job training than their CO counterparts who work in state and federal prisons. There are constant staff shortages at jails, largely due to the turnover of employees. Few chances for higher advancement exist, and the personnel often form low opinions of the work they do (Welch, 1996: 184; Kiekbusch et al., 2003).

Overcrowded, unsafe, and unsanitary conditions

Generally, jails consist solely of holding cells, cellblocks with dayrooms, dormitory-style rooms, and solitary confinement. Cells are usually crowded with bunk beds stacked two or three high, with a dozen or more men in each cage. These facilities are also jammed with men sleeping in the dayrooms, gymnasiums, and on mattresses along the hallway floors. Some institutions do not have smoke and CO_2 detectors, fire alarms, fire extinguishers, or sprinkler systems. Or if they do, they are faulty or inoperable. Heating systems are typically poor, and little or no air conditioning or proper ventilation may be available, or may be broken or missing. Medical equipment may be nonexistent, expired, or unsanitary. Likewise, basic electrical and plumbing systems may be inadequate, broken, unsafe, and unsanitary. The facilities are frequently filthy and infested with different types of vermin (that is, bedbugs, cockroaches, fleas, lice, mice, rats, and so on), with toilets that do not function properly, walls and ceilings that are dirty, plaster that is cracked and falling, paint that is peeling off the walls, and broken windows.

Inedible food

Jails have a reputation for serving horrible food. If prisoners have money, they may have the option to buy food through a commissary or canteen.[4] In some facilities, COs who feel sorry for the prisoners because of the horrible food – but more likely because they can make some money on the side – make their rounds late at night with a cart to sell snack food. In other lockup facilities, particularly when an individual is being transported or arraigned, they are given bologna or cheese sandwiches and orange Kool-Aid, which has a diuretic effect.[5] It must be understood that not all inmates can afford the commissary nor the benefits derived from being able to pay for their own food.

Poor medical care

Medical care is almost nonexistent in jail. Drug addicts, prisoners in methadone programs, and alcoholics frequently enter jail. They will suffer withdrawal symptoms and rarely is something given to the detainee to ease the transition. In the process, these individuals may have seizures or delirium tremors. If health care is given, it is typically slow and inadequate, and medical equipment is often primitive and unsanitary.

In some cases, the care is dangerous, inhumane, and unconstitutional. Part of the reason is that the medical and psychiatric care may be administered by private health companies, like Prison Health Services, which predictably and continuously focus on the bottom line (Von Zielbauer, 2005a; 2005b).

Summary

Jails often fall short of the provisions of the Eighth Amendment, which reads "Excessive bail shall not be required nor excessive fines imposed, nor cruel and unusual punishments inflicted." Additionally, "prison authorities may not ignore a condition of confinement that is sure or very likely to cause serious illness and needless suffering the next week or month or year merely because no harm has yet occurred" (*Rhodes v. Chapman*, 1981) (see Exhibit 3.2).

Exhibit 3.2

Documentary

The Second City: Inside the World's Largest Jail (1999)

This documentary, originally produced for Bill Kurtis's *Investigative Reports* (1999), takes the viewer on a tour of the Los Angeles County Jail, the largest facility of its kind in the world. People are admitted 24 hours a day and are charged with all kinds of criminal offenses. The jail is administered by the Los Angeles County Sheriff's Department. The documentary focuses on the challenges and fears of convicts, COs, and correctional administrators. It reveals jail conditions, such as overcrowding, seemingly inedible food, weapons, and the violence and frustration of inmates. The documentary depicts how rival gangs, such as the Crips and the Bloods, are kept in separate holding cells, how they earn points for good behavior, and how they may eventually return to the general population. The film also shows an inmate demonstrating to correctional officers how to make a shank or knife from a tooth brush. To add an individual face to the jail, the film tracks the trials and tribulations of a young African American male who was sent to the jail for allegedly failing to pay several traffic and speeding tickets.

Solving the problem

Four primary approaches have been used to reduce the misuse of jails:

- improve the physical structure or layout;
- seek accreditation;
- file legal suits against jail or prison systems; and
- prevent those charged or convicted of a relatively minor criminal offense from either stepping foot inside the jail or expediting their removal from this kind of correctional institution.

The following section explores these options in some detail.

Improving the physical structure

There is considerable variability in the design of jails. In some settings large rooms are set up dormitory style with countless rows of cots and bunk beds, while others reflect a traditional design with separate cells that contain one to six bunk beds. As part of the desire to improve the physical structure of jails, *new-generation* (also known as *direct supervision*) jails (and prisons) have been designed and constructed. "These buildings are intended to maximize security and efficiency by means of easy observation and electronic surveillance of inmates. Such patterns utilize advancements in electronic communications and shatterproof glass materials to replace steel bars and stone blocks, creating a lighter, more comfortable environment that is also very secure" (Roots, 2005: 628).

In the 1970s a new design and accompanying management philosophy was introduced in many jails across the country. Through podular/unit architecture and direct supervision, podular/direct supervision (PDS) jails have been created. Often built in a system of "pods," or modular self-contained housing areas linked to one another, direct supervision jails have helped eliminate the old physical barriers that separated staff and inmates. There are typically two tiers stacked on top of each other. Access to the second floor is by stairs on each side of the first tier. The main activity of the unit is concentrated on the first floor, where one or more correctional officers sit at a desk near the entrance.

It is hoped that these new designs will prevent many of the blind corners where prisoner and staff assaults occur, and that a more "participative" and "proactive management philosophy" will increase communication at all levels. In this design, traditional aspects of secure facilities have been eliminated, including "bars and the isolated, secure observation areas for officers" (Bayens et al., 1997). Instead, there is a more

> open environment in which inmates and correctional personnel could mingle with relative freedom. In a number of such "new-generation" jails, large reinforced Plexiglas panels supplanted walls and served to separate activity areas, such as classrooms and dining halls, from one another. Soft furniture is the rule throughout such correctional facilities, and individual rooms take the place of cells, allowing inmates a modicum of personal privacy. (Schmalleger, 2006: 376)

Direct supervision jails have been praised for reducing the number of escapes, suicides, sexual assaults, rapes, and incidences of violence among inmates and for reducing violence toward correctional officers. These types of facilities have also been known to lead to higher staff morale (Schmalleger, 2006: 377).

Direct supervision facilities are not without their critics. First, changing the architecture is not enough. "[N]ew generation jails are too frequently run by 'old-style' managers and correctional personnel sometimes lack the training needed to make the transition to the new style of supervision." Other problems include the fact that midlevel managers in these kinds of facilities "could benefit from clearer job descriptions and additional training." Finally, it has been argued that "better screening needs to be done of officers for direct supervision facilities" (Zupan and Menke, 1988; Schmalleger, 2006: 377).

Accreditation

Over the past four decades, many jails and prisons at the local, state, and federal levels and in the private sector have engaged in and passed an accreditation process (for example, Freeman, 2000: 332–5; Levinson et al., 2001). "Accreditation is a comprehensive process, incorporating numerous measures and embraces virtually every facet of the organization being assessed" (Champion, 2001: 529). Primarily sponsored by membership organizations such as the American Correctional Association (ACA), these entities send representatives out to correctional facilities to determine whether they are adhering to strict standards and guidelines.[6] In order to carry out this mandate, in 1974, the ACA established the Commission on Accreditation for Corrections (CAC). Recent data on how many correctional facilities are accredited is not publicly available. However, in 2001 there were 1,185 institutions and programs throughout the United States that earned CAC accreditation. Although approximately half of the country's prisons are accredited by the ACA, only 120 of the 3,365 jails have passed the ACA standard (Gibbons and de Katzenbach, 2006: 16, 88). While ACA accreditation is important, keen observers have noted that it is lacking in important standards dealing with the offering of substance abuse counseling and exercise time to prisoners (91). Other experts have noted that although a facility may earn ACA accreditation it still does not mean that the United States Department of Justice may find it in violation of important standards (Friedman, 2014).

Legal suits

In recent times, on account of prisoner litigation and the efforts of several nonprofit organizations – including the American Civil Liberties Union (through their National Prison Project) and Human Rights Watch – attempts have been made to reform jails (Welsh, 1992; 1995; Feeley and Swearingen, 2004). During the late 1980s, almost 33% of all jails in the United States were under court order to improve their conditions (Welsh, 1992). In almost each major city in the United States, local social justice organizations advocate on behalf of jail inmates. In Baltimore, for example, over the course of several years the Public Justice Center, a nonprofit legal advocacy group, was at the forefront of bringing to citizen attention the abuses that have occurred in the Baltimore City Detention Center (that is, the city jail).

In several cases, the federal government has threatened to issue or have implemented consent decrees against jails. This practice enables state and local correctional facilities to be taken over and administered by the FBOP (Federal Bureau of Prisons) unless specified changes are made. No self-respecting warden, commissioner of corrections, or governor likes this situation, so they are under extreme pressure to reform their correctional facilities in accordance with federal guidelines. In 2006, for example, because of court orders, the state of California ceded control of the health care of its prisoners to a federal judge.

In an effort to legitimize the numerous lawsuits the prisoners and advocates have brought against correctional facilities, the federal government passed the Civil Rights of Institutionalized Person's Act (1980). This legislation encouraged prisons to deal on an individual basis with the complaints of prisoners. It ensured that inmates were protected against unconstitutional conditions. It also minimized external interference in the running of prisons and jails.

In 1996, however, Congress passed the Prison Litigation Reform Act (PLRA). "It places limitations on population caps and limits the time periods of injunctions and consent decrees placed on institutions, forces solvent inmates to pay part of the filing fee, and requires judges to screen prison claims to eliminate frivolous law suits" (Bartollas, 2002: 220). This legislation made it almost impossible for the courts to initiate any actions against correctional facilities that were perceived to be overly broad. There is, however, some momentum now, particularly in legal circles, to reform the PLRA and lift the narrow conditions under which prisoners can challenge their conditions of confinement (Gibbons and de Katzenbach, 2006: 85–7).

Preventing those charged from spending time in jail

A considerable number of remedies exist that are supposed to prevent those who are charged and/or convicted of a relatively minor criminal offense from ever entering a jail. These measures typically include a plethora of community-based corrections programs, such as economic sanctions, diversion, pre-trial release, and probation (McShane and Krause, 1993; McCarthy and McCarthy, 1997; Champion, 2002). The following section will discuss these options.

Economic sanctions

There are three basic types of economic sanctions: fines, restitution, and community service. Each is applied to individuals who have broken the law and depend on the person's differing circumstances. Their use also varies from jurisdiction to jurisdiction.

Fines

In the United States, fines are predominantly used as sanctions for minor infractions or crimes, are calibrated to the seriousness of the offense, and are applied to individuals the criminal justice system believes have the ability to pay them. Two of the biggest difficulties with fines are the establishment of the appropriate amount and collection thereof.

As a response to these problems, day fines and enhanced collection procedures have been introduced and, in many respects, are reasonably more effective measures (McCarthy and McCarthy, 1997: p. 140). A day fine is tied to a person's daily salary. This sanction makes "it ... possible to achieve the same relative economic impact on a rich offender as a poor one by taking the same proportion of income and wealth from each individual" (142).

There are five basic difficulties with collecting fines:

1. role orientation;
2. dispersion of responsibility;
3. disincentives;
4. multiple tasks; and
5. enforcement dependence (McCarthy and McCarthy, 1997: 150).

Role orientation refers to the fact that various components of the criminal justice system dislike acting as a collection agency. Dispersion of responsibility relates to the fact that too many branches of the criminal justice system are responsible for administering fees, including money collection and prosecution for non-payment. With respect to disincentives, the organizational entity that collects rarely benefits from the money.

Multiple tasks pertains to the fact that the diverse branches of the criminal justice system are already overtaxed with the work they have, and fine collection is perceived as one more burden.

Finally, with respect to enforcement dependence, it has been recognized that many criminal justice agencies, once they have become accustomed to receiving funding through fines, tend to reorient their mission so that they can continue to secure this money (Miller and Selva, 1994). In order to address the previously reviewed problems, many experts (for example, Morris and Tonry, 1990) advocate the privatization of debt collection. According to these scholars, once it is finally determined that the fines are uncollectible, they can simply be written off.

Restitution and community service

An increasingly popular alternative to fines is the use of restitution, where the person convicted of a crime pays money or provides a service directly to the victim and/or their loved ones. On the other hand, with community service, the individual convicted of the crime performs some sort of work that will benefit the neighborhood, town, or city where the crime was committed. Restitution is typically provided through money, and community service is usually remitted through menial labor – such as raking leaves, painting buildings, maintaining parks, picking up trash, low-skill construction work, washing government vehicles, or cleaning roads or highways – responsibilities that, in most locales, a public works department would normally handle.

The amount of restitution is usually based on the amount of loss (that is, money stolen, replacement value or repair cost of damaged property, medical expenses, income lost, and so on). With this kind of sanction, victims may be involved in determining the appropriate response by the offender. Community service is issued when a specific victim cannot be identified and/or a person is found guilty of so-called victimless crimes.[7] Some individuals sentenced to community service voluntarily fulfill the order; others must report to a community service officer and are supervised while they comply with their obligation.

The kinds of things individuals have been required to do are typically limited only by the creativity of the judge. In some jurisdictions, unusual methods of community service have been implemented. In 1989, five years before he was charged with killing Nicole Brown Simpson, his ex-wife and Ronald Goldman, a waiter (1994), former Buffalo Bills running back O. J. Simpson was allowed to serve as the master of ceremonies for a community organization after he was convicted of assaulting his wife.

Those in favor of restitution and community service think that these sanctions have the potential to help rehabilitate offenders. Sometimes, advocates argue, particularly if victim offender reconciliation is used, the perpetrator can see firsthand the suffering they have caused the victims. Supporters of this sanction also recognize that this is perhaps a rare chance for the criminal justice system to move beyond retributive sanctions toward ones that encourage social justice (Pepinsky and Quinney, 1991; Arrigo, 1998). Others believe that most kinds of community service job details are not going to give those convicted of less serious crimes any valuable skills and simply treat the sanction as some form of bureaucratic ritualism.

Diversion

Diversion minimizes or prevents those accused of a relatively minor crime from being formally charged and/or processed by the criminal justice system. This is also an opportunity for the accused to obtain necessary help or assistance in terms of alcohol, drug, or employment counseling and/or training (McCarthy and McCarthy, 1997: 37). The benefit of diversion to the convicted person includes avoiding the stigma of a criminal sanction. Diversion assists probation and parole agencies by reducing the workload of employees, focusing attention on those probationers and parolees that need more attention, and reducing expenditures of the criminal justice system. Over the years, diversion programs have increased, been improved upon, and been institutionalized by many jurisdictions. In big cities, diversion is most needed because jails and other programs of the local criminal justice system are most likely to be at or over capacity.

Forms of diversion

During the 1960s and 1970s, a number of formal diversion programs were established. Today two types exist: unconditional and conditional. The former are

> programs that remove the offender from the criminal justice process and place no conditions on his or her post diversion behavior. … [the latter are] those that restrict the offender's post diversion behavior, monitor his progress in the community, and provide for reinstallment of prosecution if the conditions of diversion are not met. (McCarthy and McCarthy, 1997: 42)

Conditional programs often require offenders to participate in some kind of treatment. They stipulate that, if the person does not complete the therapy successfully, they may then be formally processed by the criminal justice system (that is, sent to jail).

Unfortunately, some research on diversion suggests that this approach has minimal benefits and may simply add to the cost of corrections. This criticism is especially applicable to how offenders are selected for diversion, rather than the actual programs (McCarthy and McCarthy, 1997: 44).[8]

Drug courts

Since their debut in 1990 in Dade County, Florida, drug courts have spread rapidly across the United States (Douglas et al., 2015). In short, if the arrestee completes a drug rehabilitation program and remains drug free for a year, the charges against them are dropped. Some of these courts focus on treatment, while others channel their resources into the speedy disposition of cases (McCarthy and McCarthy, 1997: 89). There may also be special components.

Typically, the judge, with the assistance of their staff, regularly and closely monitors almost every life change the participant makes. The main goals are reducing recidivism, eliminating substance abuse, and encouraging rehabilitation. This specialization has the added benefit of freeing up the criminal justice system so it can ostensibly focus on more challenging cases (Brown, 2002; Roman et al., 2003).

Although drug courts have increased overall efficiency, one of the largest problems has been the difficulty involved with recommendations for some drug treatment programs. There are typically long waiting lists for these. As a result, the arrestee goes to court and then has a lot of downtime (thus, opportunities to relapse and reoffend) while waiting to be admitted to the drug treatment programs.

It bears mentioning that recidivism is operationalized and measured differently by many researchers and states. Some see it as the person being arrested, others interpret recidivism as a court appearance, some regard it as the criminal charge itself, and others see it as a return to jail or prison.

Alternatives to diversion

Instead of diverting individuals from the criminal justice system, some states have considered the decriminalization of certain acts. There are many victimless crimes on the books that could be eliminated (for example, possession of marijuana, prostitution, gambling, and so on) or the sanctions for these actions could be reduced. Decisions to reduce the penalties are typically decided in a political context, with political parties and well-funded special interest groups often taking opposing positions.

Problems with diversion

There are several difficulties with diversion, including the facts that effectiveness is rarely or poorly measured, and that individuals who are innocent but not yet convicted are often compelled or feel pressured to comply with diversion to avoid the trouble and expense of a prosecution (McCarthy and McCarthy, 1997: 61). Another aspect is that in some jurisdictions with zero tolerance policing or unconditional diversion, the practice of diversion may actually be declining.

Pre-trial release

In general, there are three major types of pre-trial release: bail, pre-booking alternatives, and post-booking releases. Pre-trial release is intended to accomplish several purposes:

1. increased release rates;
2. speedy operations of the criminal justice system;
3. equal justice;
4. encouragement to those who are charged to appear again in court;
5. protection of the community; and
6. minimization of economic costs with maximized benefits (National Center for State Courts, 1975).

Bail

Shortly after being arrested, defendants appear in front of a judge who determines if they can be released on their own recognizance or if they should be granted bail. Posting bail requires the accused to give the court money, a bond, or a title to property (to be held in trust) to ensure that the defendant returns to court on the prescribed date. The money does not have to be theirs. For example, in the late 1990s, John A. Gotti, the head of the notorious Gambino organized crime family, managed to convince his neighbors to post their houses as bail for him. The Eighth Amendment of the U.S. Constitution, however, prohibits courts requiring excessive bail.

Despite the emergence of bail guidelines, judges exercise a considerable amount of discretion in the amounts and conditions they establish in the granting of bail. Judges and magistrates take a number of factors into consideration when they determine whether bail is granted and the amount that it is set at, including:

- the seriousness of the crime;
- the previous criminal history of the defendant;
- the ties the defendant has with the community;
- the need to protect the victim and the community; and
- the presentations and perceptions made by the prosecutor and the defendant's lawyer.

If the defendant on bail fails to show at court, they forfeit the surety, and the judge then issues a bench warrant for the individual's arrest. Regardless, the Constitution does not prescribe a definitive amount for release on bail. This is why many judges, acting out of an abundance of caution, set high bails with defendants (McCarthy and McCarthy, 1997: 77).

Bail agents

In order to keep bail functioning in a cost–effective manner, the criminal justice system depends on bail agents, more popularly known as bail bondsmen. There are more than 15,000 professional bail agents in the United States.[9] Despite their swagger and overzealous reputation, they provide a needed service for those who cannot afford bail. Bail bond offices are typically located close to the main courthouse and city jails. Many are open 24 hours a day, seven days a week, and are noticeable by their large red and sometimes flashing neon signs (Toberg, 1983; McCarthy and McCarthy, 1997: 77).

> Using their own assets or those of an insurance company, bondsmen will provide the surety required for a fee of between 10 and 15 percent. They are licensed by the state, choose their own clients, [and] may set their own collateral requirements. In addition, they may track down and return bail jumpers without extradition and by force if necessary. (Cole, 1994: 405)

To increase the possibility that their clients will show up in court, bail agents – like good criminal defense lawyers – try to maintain regular contact with defendants and try to persuade their family and friends (if known) how important this process is. They may also psychologically prepare their clients for the possible outcome (that is, incarceration). If the defendant fails to appear in court, the bail agent will try to return the person; otherwise, they will forfeit their bond.

Problems with bail

Just like fines, the bail system favors the wealthy and discriminates against the poor; the rich are less likely to feel the deterrent effect of bail. Many people believe that, despite the criteria, getting bail appears arbitrary. Take, for example, financier and billionaire Marc David Rich, who in 1983 was charged with tax evasion, fraud, and "dealing with the enemy." He was indicted, he posted bail, and in 1983 he fled to Switzerland. During the Clinton presidency, Rich's ex-wife Denise gave the Democratic Party several respectable financial contributions, and in the remaining days of the Clinton presidency, she donated money to establish the President's future library.[10] In January 2001, in the last few days that Clinton was in office, he provided Rich with a pardon.[11]

Bail reform

Bail has been modified through reform Acts and guidelines. One of the farthest-reaching pieces of legislation was the Bail Reform Act of 1966, which "created a presumption in favor of release and the imposition of the least restrictive form of pretrial release that would ensure appearance at trial" (McCarthy and McCarthy, 1997: 74). The Federal Bail Reform Act of 1984 expanded the criteria to be used for the release decision to include protection of the community. "This allowed judicial officials, following a hearing, to detain individuals on the basis of the perceived threat they posed to the community" (74). This option, known as preventive detention, is used: if defendants committed a drug felony where there is a possibility of a ten-year sentence; if they used a firearm during the offense; or if they were convicted of a serious crime while on pre-trial release in the five years preceding the current charge. In these instances, they can be denied bail (74).

Another way that bail has been reformed is through the use of guidelines. States use these to ensure a degree of uniformity or consistency in the way they secure the reappearance of defendants. "Bail guidelines were modeled after sentencing guidelines, in an attempt to achieve a more equitable system of determining bail ... bail guidelines create a more visible system of decision-making and hence one that is less subject to abuse" (McCarthy and McCarthy, 1997: 77).

Deposit bail

Initiated in 1964, deposit bail programs allow defendants to post between 5% and 10% of the total amount of bail that is owed. When the defendant returns to court, the amount is returned to the defendant for those who posted the deposit. "Most jurisdictions require that a small sum (usually 1 percent of the total bail amount) be retained by the court to cover the cost of administering the deposit bail system; in other jurisdictions a fee is retained only when a defendant is found guilty" (McCarthy and McCarthy, 1997: 79).

What happens to these federal statutes in the states? Shortly after the federal government makes a legislative change the states follow suit. The federal government often gives the states economic incentives to adjust their criminal codes and sentencing practices to resemble the federal one, for example, through grants.

Nonfinancial pre-trial-release program models

Instead of sending defendants to jail or releasing them on bond, they may be granted a pre-booking alternative, such as a summons or a citation. Post-booking alternatives, on the other hand, may include "recognizance releases or conditional, supervised releases" (McCarthy and McCarthy, 1997: 79).

Pre-booking releases

Summons and citations are notifications defendants are given or receive that order them to either pay a fine (thereby pleading guilty) or appear at a later time in court to answer the charge. In some jurisdictions, the defendant must sign the notification; in others this step is not necessary. In the United States, most people who are issued a citation generally pay the fine or show up to court.

Citations and summons are used with increasing frequency in some states for victimless crimes (for example, the possession of small amounts of marijuana). Pre-booking releases have numerous advantages. They save the courts' and jails' resources. Generally speaking, the person can be released almost immediately after contact with the police.

Post-booking release

Post-booking release, also known as on–recognizance releases and personal recognizance, "provide for the release of a defendant [from custody] prior to trial based on his signed promise to appear for all scheduled court proceedings. No restrictions are placed on the defendant's pretrial conduct and no financial payments are required" (McCarthy and McCarthy, 1997: 80).

There are two basic post-booking releases: "promise to appear" (PTA) and "release on recognizance" (ROR). Both are virtually indistinguishable. In the 1960s, the Vera Institute of Justice in New York City pioneered the ROR method, which "is based on the assumption that judges will grant releases if they are given verified information about defendants' reliability and roots in the community. Court personnel talk to defendants soon after their arrest about job, family, prior criminal record, and associations and then determine whether release should be recommended" (Cole, 1994: 409).

Conditional and supervised pre-trial release

Among the most used nonfinancial means of securing individuals' return to court is the ROR. In order to qualify for this kind of community-based program, defendants must adhere to a number of conditions: reporting on a regular basis to a pre-trial service agency, not committing another crime, and, in the case of a violence-related charge, not having contact with the actual or alleged victim.

In order to coordinate the provision of pre-trial release, most jurisdictions have established pre-trial service agencies. In some locales, these are part of the court system, and in other places, they are part of probation and parole. These organizations supervise those on probation, parole, bail, or ROR. They can also help monitor the individuals and assist them in getting drug and alcohol treatment services, education, training, employment, and other forms of counseling. Pre-trial service agencies may also be responsible for maintaining contact with those people who are on electronic monitoring equipment.

Probation

If an individual is convicted of a misdemeanor (and in the cases of some felonies), judges have the discretion to grant the person probation. In short, the person convicted of the crime is given a jail sentence, but it is suspended if they comply with certain conditions while out in the community. This often means calling in on a regular basis to the probation officer, submitting to random drug (that is, urinalysis) tests, attending some sort of alcohol or drug therapy, participating in job training, holding down a job, making restitution, and so on. (Many of the difficulties with these community corrections programs will be discussed in Chapter 8.) "Almost two-thirds of all convicted offenders serve their sentences on probation ... [it] is designed to keep the offenders in their home community while carrying out the sanctions imposed by the court" (McCarthy and McCarthy, 1997: 96). The number of people subjected to probation has rapidly increased.

Objectives of probation

There are five basic objectives of probation: to protect the community; to carry out the court-ordered sanctions imposed by the court; to assist offenders to change; to support crime victims; and to coordinate and promote the use of community resources in an efficient and effective manner.

Historical basis of probation

Some of the early practices that pre-dated the modern use of probation included releasing those convicted of crimes to members of the clergy, judicial reprieve, and pardon. Over time, probation has evolved into a rather complicated and bureaucratic sanction. Needless to say, probation, like many other community corrections programs, has a number of difficulties: role conflict for the probation/parole officer; the location of community corrections offices; rigid, bureaucratic, or inflexible supervisors; the failure to make a meaningful reduction in recidivism; high levels of work-related stress; violence by probationers and parolees against their officers/agents; overcrowded/overburdened caseloads of probation and parole officers/agents; and lack of adequate funding. (These factors are discussed in greater detail in Chapter 9.)

Starting in the 1980s, the number of people being sentenced to probation increased astronomically. However, the number of probation officers employed to deal with this onslaught did not match the rise. Predictably, we now have a probation crowding problem with not enough personnel to supervise those on this kind of sanction (McCarthy and McCarthy, 1997: 101).

Because probation and parole officers act as both law enforcement officers and social workers, they may suffer from role confusion/conflict. They are often caught between the demands of supervising a large caseload, brokering resources that would help their probationers and parolees live a crime-free existence, and making sure they adhere to numerous conditions of release (McCarthy and McCarthy, 1997: 133–4).

Sentencing guidelines and probation

Several factors affect who is allowed on probation. These vary from state to state, based on the prevailing legislation (McCarthy and McCarthy, 1997: 108). These factors include "the availability of probation services and the judge's perception of the quality of those services can also influence judicial decisions"; "the offender's willingness to accept probation"; and "the judge's perception of the appropriateness of probation for a particular offender" (110, 111). Whether or not the judge feels that probation is appropriate, the recommendations of a pre-sentence investigation (PSI) are prepared by a probation officer or agent (111).

Boot camps

During the early 1980s, in the midst of a tough-on-crime era encouraged by Republican legislators, various states set up military-style boot camps designed to deliver a mental and physical wake-up call to troubled lawbreakers. Started in Georgia and Oklahoma in 1983, over the next 15 years, this program spread to 39 states and targeted both adults and juveniles.

These programs, which are physically separate from larger state correctional facilities, are designed to house inmates from 90 to 180 days. They involve a military or paramilitary regimen, including physical exercise and academic courses to assist inmates pass their GED (General Educational Development test). The original idea seemed to make sense: to put inmates through an intense, military training type of situation, in which their every move was vetted by a drill instructor and a no-nonsense staff; shock them out of their complacency and moral indifference; and reach them before it's too late. Just as the military once practiced psychological "teardowns" of young trainees, boot camp staffs were responsible for working on inmates' psyches, not to mention their behavior and attitudes.

Some individuals who were arrested for less serious misdemeanors and felonies, or those currently serving a sentence behind bars, would be ordered by a judge to spend a brief period of time in the boot camp. If they successfully passed this program, then they would be released on probation or parole. Outspoken politicians and many correctional administrators championed boot camps as a solution to overcrowding, recidivism and, in the end, as a method of achieving a rehabilitative effect.

Scholarly research proved otherwise. During the mid-1990s, a handful of rigorous evaluations sponsored by the Department of Justice's National Institute of Justice (NIJ) and the Office of Juvenile Justice and Delinquency Prevention (OJJDP) were conducted to determine the success of this correctional innovation innovation (e.g., Mackenzie and Souryal, 1991). Unfortunately, these evaluations determined that inductees did no better in terms of recidivism (no matter how it was measured) in the boot camp environment than those inmates who were sent to traditional correctional institutions. Moreover, it does not appear that benefits are accrued in the reduction in prison overcrowding. These conclusions and others led a number of states, including Georgia, to scale back their boot camp experiments.

One key factor that drove this overall reduction in use was the discovery that boot camps, particularly those that served juveniles, were breeding grounds for the abuse of inmates (Hummel, 2002; Bergin, 2013). Routine allegations and confirmations of physical abuse, broken bones, and the dismissal and criminal convictions of a handful of drill sergeants occurred.

For example, in 1999, at a South Dakota juvenile boot camp for girls, Gina Score, an overweight inmate who had been convicted of stealing $25 from a friend died after a forced run. The investigation determined that camp personnel thought she was simply malingering and failed to offer appropriate medical assistance when she collapsed. In January 2006, Martin Lee Anderson, in the Bay County, Florida, Sheriff's Office Boot Camp, was repeatedly beaten by his COs, and he died shortly thereafter. Many other instances of this kind of maltreatment have been recorded, usually the result of a dynamic between inmate and CO. These factors and other problems prompted many states, like Colorado, Florida, and North Dakota, to either scale back their boot camp programs or close them altogether.

As of 2003, there were 50 boot camps still in operation in the United States (Parent, 2003). State departments of corrections (DOCs), juvenile justice advocates, and even the families of boot camp inmates must take bold steps to end this experiment, which has proved to be a failure. State-run boot camp facilities, like chain gangs and so many other debilitating methods of delivering punishment to the wrongdoer, must be closed.

Conclusion

Problems and solutions to jails are ever present. Many of the recommendations, however, have unintended consequences or simply result in ineffective tinkering in the criminal justice system. Although many well-intentioned entities have tried to litigate against the conditions that abound in many correctional institutions, the judicial system has responded primarily by digging in its heels and strengthening the power of DOCs to house inmates in poor living conditions. For inmates, although it is nicer to be housed in a newly constructed facility, like a new-generation jail, changing the design of jails is not radical enough.

Most arrestees awaiting trial or sentencing would rather spend their time out of jail and in the community, but not all individuals released on their own recognizance or out on bail are model citizens. Moreover, certain parts of the criminal justice system are reluctant or unable to vigorously enforce fines and community-based sanctions.

Sometimes inability to cover a fine may simply be a way that an ex-convict "works" or "plays" the criminal justice system in a passive aggressive way. More likely, however, failure of payment may be a reflection of a sanctioned person's financial difficulties or the system's lack of adequate means to collect.

Solutions like intensive probation, electronic monitoring, and increased accountability of community corrections personnel, combined with criminal and civil sanctions for parents and guardians, may be more useful. Undoubtedly, most of these are fraught with problems too.

Another difficulty with many of the more recent community corrections programs is a concern with net widening (for example, Austin and Krisberg, 1981; Cohen, 1985). Although the numerous types of diversion and community-based corrections programs may, on the surface, appear to be benign, they can also have the negative effect of placing more people under the watchful eye of the criminal justice system, leaving them with the lifelong stigma that a criminal charge and conviction produces. This stigma may dissuade employers from hiring them and some educational institutions from allowing them entrance.

Needless to say, federal and state governments, including private foundations such as the Soros Foundation, should increase their grant funding to organizations and individuals who investigate jail conditions and work to improve the conditions therein.

Key terms

Accreditation: A method to determine if a criminal justice agency meets a standard established by a respected accrediting body (e.g., American Correctional Association, etc.).

Bail: The surety necessary to ensure a defendant appears in court. Surety might be cash or property, such as a car, boat, camper, or home. Enables the accused to be temporarily released from custody as long as they exchange surety (i.e., cash, a bond, title to property) to ensure their return to court at a later point in time.

Certification: A method, based on widely accepted criteria, to determine if and identify whether correctional officers have the requisite skills and knowledge to perform their job.

Community service: Individual convicted of a crime performs some sort of work that will benefit the neighborhood, town, or city where the crime was committed.

Consent decree: When the FBOP takes over part or all of a prison system or correctional facility. The FBOP manages the system, facility, or program until it meets identifiable standards or criteria.

Contraband: Items that inmates are prohibited from having while incarcerated (e.g., drugs, cell phones, etc.). Anything (e.g., alcohol, a computer, drugs, or pornography) not authorized for those people on probation or parole to be in possession of.

Deposit bail: Allows defendants to post between 5 to 10% of the total amount of bail they owe to the court.

Discretion: A decision made by criminal justice practitioners to invoke the law/criminal sanction. In the case of the police, it includes the decision to stop, question, search, arrest, and to use deadly force against a suspect.

Diversion: Minimizes or prevents those accused of relatively minor crimes from being formally charged and/or entering the criminal justice system.

Fine: Financial payment made to the courts and/or judge as a sanction in criminal matters.

Eighth Amendment: Prevents those charged with a crime from excessive bail, and cruel and unusual punishment.

Jailhouse snitch: Convicts who give law enforcement or correctional officers (i.e., COs) information they think is relevant or incriminating about other inmates. They hope to receive benefits for this information (that is, lessen his/her sentence or be given special privileges behind bars).

New-generation/direct supervision jails: Introduced in the 1970s, this new housing unit design consists of self-contained units located inside a larger correctional facility. Consists of two floors with cells located around the sides, and a common area on the first floor.

Net widening: The introduction and use of more community corrections programs by the criminal justice system. While keeping people out of jail and prison, it also increased the number of people under the control of the criminal justice system.

Prison Litigation Reform Act: Passed during the Clinton administration. Designed to limit inmate litigation including the number of times a convicted felon could challenge the death penalty against them.

Probation: Process/sentence whereby a judge imposes a prison term on a person convicted of a crime, but then suspends the execution of it for a period of time as long as the offender adheres to certain conditions (i.e., court-ordered sanctions).

Release on Recognizance (ROR): Community based program where defendants must adhere to a number of conditions, such as reporting on a regular basis to a pretrial services agency, not committing another crime, and not having contact with an actual or alleged victim if involved in a violence related charge.

Restitution: Where the person convicted of a crime pays money or provides a service directly to the victim and/or the victim's family.

Role orientation: The disposition that the community corrections officers have. They may emphasize more or less their law enforcement and/or social worker roles.

Warehousing: Incarcerating large numbers of people without any possibility of rehabilitation programs.

Notes

1 In some states, such as Maryland, this can be as long as 18 months.

2 For early research on the jail experience, see, for example, Irwin (1985). He outlined four stages a person incarcerated in one of these facilities will go through: disintegration, disorientation, degradation, and preparation.

3 It may take even longer in prison. Many correctional facilities have only a few phones available to convicts, and a sign-up sheet often regulates their use. It is not uncommon for a prisoner to have to wait a week to make a call, and even then, only when his or her name appears on the time sheet. Inmates are limited to short calls, usually collect calls or those paid for with commissary cards. Convicts are required to give up the phone after only a short time (5–15 minutes); if they linger on past their time and into the next time slot, it will frustrate the next inmate in line.

4 The commissary will be discussed in greater detail in Chapter 5 of this book.

5 See the extended discussion on prison food in Chapter 5 of this book.

6 Although the American Jail Association (AJA) offers certification programs, it does not offer an accreditation program.

7 The expression *so-called* in connection with victimless crimes is used because the victims of these kinds of offenses are often hidden (for example, a family that suffers a loss of income or displacement because of the individual's actions).

8 Some of the diversion models include: alcohol detoxification centers, family crisis intervention units, mediation and counseling following arrest, statutory diversion, treatment Alternatives to Street Crime (TASC), and drug courts.

9 Number retrieved from Professional Bail Agents of the United States website (www.pbus.com) on June 5, 2016.

10 Starting with President Franklin Delano Roosevelt, when American Presidents leave office, they frequently build a library. This helps to preserve and shape their legacy.

11 When individuals are granted a pardon, this means that they are forgiven for the crime that they were convicted of and the sanctions that they were administered are lifted. Pardons are occasionally granted to individuals who have been wrongfully convicted of a crime. Clemency, also known as a reprieve, lessens the penalty for the crime, but the person is still considered guilty of the crime. Commutations involve a reduction in sentence; however, these do not wipe out the charge the individual was convicted of (See extended discussion in Chapter 10).

FOUR

Underfunding

Introduction

It costs U.S. taxpayers approximately $39 billion each year to incarcerate convicts (Henrichson and Delaney, 2012). In 2013, the Federal Bureau of Prisons (FBOP) alone had a budget of $6.445 billion. In 2001, "[s]tates spent $29.5 billion for prisons ... about a $5 1/2 billion increase from 1996, after adjusting for inflation" (Stephan, 2004). Moreover, "[s]tate correctional expenditures increased 145% in 2001 constant dollars from $15.6 billion in FY 1986 to $38.2 billion in FY 2001; prison expenditures increased 150% from $11.7 billion to $29.5 billion" (Stephan, 2004).

The amount of money it costs to incarcerate prisoners varies between the states and the federal system. In 2010, the cost to house an inmate in the states was averaged at $31,286. This ranged from $14,603 (Kentucky) to $60,076 (New York) (www.vera.org/sites/default/files/resources/downloads/price-of-prisons-updated-version-021914.pdf). With respect to federal system it costs an average of $29,291.25 (www.federalregister.gov/articles/2014/05/12/2014-10859/annual-determination-of-average-cost-of-incarceration).

Still, prisoners, correctional officers (COs), wardens, and other correctional professionals are quick to admit that their field is seriously underfunded, and the effects are significant: overcrowding; prematurely released prisoners unsuitable for the community; continuous retrofitting of old institutions; failure to hire the appropriate people to work in the facilities; neglect of proper training for recruits; and scrambling to find money to pay for the renovation of old facilities, the construction of new prisons, and a patchwork of rehabilitative programs.

In the late 1990s, as a result of the passage of the Violent Crime Control and Law Enforcement Act of 1994 (hereafter, Crime Act), American jails and prisons received a temporary increase in funding in the form of grants from the federal government to construct, develop, expand, modify, operate, or improve correctional facilities, including boot camp facilities and other alternative correctional facilities that can free conventional prison space for the confinement of violent offenders, to ensure that prison cell space is available for the confinement of violent offenders and to implement truth in sentencing laws for sentencing violent offenders.

However, starting with the George W. Bush presidency (January 2001), tax revenues from the local, state, and federal governments have been spent on other pressing items. Especially in the wake of 9/11, governments have directed a disproportionate amount of their public safety budgets to law enforcement and cut back on courts and corrections.

Moreover, politicians not wanting to appear soft on inmates refrain from increasing budgets for corrections. The familiar refrain of "corrections must do more with less" is frequently repeated in the legislatures and on the cellblocks, tiers, and wings of jails and prisons. This policy, called fiscal conservatism, is "to be achieved through the development and implementation of cost-minimization strategies (cost containment, controlling building costs, land revenue enhancement) designed to reduce the public tax burden. The increasingly important component of fiscal conservatism is the privatization of correctional services traditionally provided by government" (Freeman, 2000: 106).

Regardless, although the costs of purchasing land and maintaining the physical plant of correctional facilities are high, the biggest expenditure, as with all businesses, is personnel.

Growth in correctional spending

Over the past two decades, budgets for corrections have increased. This is largely due to a greater number of prisoners, occasioned by changes in previously mentioned sentencing laws and practices (that is, "three strikes you're out," truth in sentencing, and the abolishment of parole in several states and the federal system). Other increased costs have been caused by the building out or the construction of new facilities. Finally, the number of convicts with special needs is growing. This includes inmates who are considered seniors, female convicts who have more special needs than their male counterparts, drug-dependent inmates who need special programming, gang members who need more secure housing, and inmates with medical (that is, AIDS/HIV, TB, hepatitis) and mental health issues who may need expensive medical and/or psychological treatment (see Chapter 7).

Jails become the leaders in expenditures

Between 1960 and 1985, spending by state and local governments on corrections was triple the amount that was spent on law enforcement (Ford and Moore, 1992: 2). The increases in correctional budgets have taken place particularly within jails. "[B]etween 1986 and 1990, the annual median operating budget for jails across the nation rose by more than $1 million, from more than $2.2 million to $3.4 million" (2).

Available options

In order to deal with crowding and its economic costs, departments of corrections (DOCs) and the FBOP have taken three approaches: front-end, back-end, or increasing the capacity of facilities (Freeman, 2000: 5). The first strategy usually consists of reducing the number of prisoners entering jails and prisons. The second option involves letting inmates out of correctional institutions much earlier than their proscribed sentence or authorizing the use of legislative caps on prisoner populations in facilities. Lastly, DOCs have increased the size of their facilities or found ways to house more prisoners in the correctional facilities they currently run by being creative with the space they already utilize (5).

Front-end measures

Significant savings can be achieved by preventing suspects or those convicted of crimes from entering the criminal justice system in the first place. Short of teaching people not to commit crimes or training them to take better precautions against being detected or caught, these processes, reviewed in detail in Chapter 3, often include different penalty structures and community-based corrections programs.

Back-end options

The second strategy typically includes the enhanced use of early release options, including parole and other community corrections programs (for example, furloughs). Often early release is arranged through grants of time for good behavior while inside, for inmates who have failing health or are incapacitated by age, or through enhanced transitioning into community corrections programs such as halfway houses. A vast network of residential treatment centers run by private (for profit) and nonprofit entities exist in the United States. "A related mechanism is legislative caps on inmate populations, which are tied to emergency release powers. The caps require the release of inmates when the facility population reaches a certain proportion of capacity, typically 95 percent or higher" (Freeman, 2000: 5). Many prisons now have geriatric cellblocks filled with elderly prisoners, many of them in wheelchairs, on respirators, or in beds hooked up to machines or intravenous tubes that provide fluids and medicine. The inmate population continues to gray, with more convicts serving life sentences and expiring behind the wall. Some prison systems allow elderly prisoners or younger convicts who have been diagnosed to die in a few months to apply for "compassionate release." This release allows a prisoner to go home to die in the company of his or her loved ones. The problem is that few convicts ever make it out the door before they pass away, as the application process may take many months to receive official approval.

Also, it goes without saying that correctional facilities must ensure that their count systems, records, and procedures are properly functioning in order to release inmates when they have completed the time mandated in their sentences. For example, in January 2006, a federal judge granted a $12 million settlement to former inmates of the D.C. jail who "had been needlessly strip-searched after their ordered releases" (Cherkis, 2007) and, in one case, an inmate was held for almost two years more than his sentence permitted. Overdetention is not simply an "inevitabil[ity] due to administrative needs" (Cherkis, 2007). Solutions that have been proffered include processing paperwork in the courthouse rather than in a holding area ("paper orders for each defendant explicitly giving their status") and making sure that "[officers] do not take anyone into their custody without the appropriate paperwork" (Cherkis, 2007).

Capacity expansion

Capacity expansion options are cheaper and the timeliest option, but they are not suitable for all jurisdictions. In some jurisdictions, legal mandates have forced DOCs to build new facilities, renovate existing ones, or modify other buildings for correctional purposes (Ford and Moore, 1992: 6). Wardens and correctional administrators have four options, each with its advantages and disadvantages:

- purchase or lease new land, then build a new facility;
- acquire or lease land with an already existing structure, then assume the costs of renovating it;
- buy or lease land nearby; or
- build an addition to an already existing facility.

Correctional administrators have also managed to increase the capacity of jails through the use of makeshift jails and jail barges.

Constructing an addition to an already existing facility may save money that would otherwise be spent on purchasing or leasing land. Alternatively, locating a satellite or annex jail or prison nearby may alleviate some of the costs associated with transporting staff and inmates (Welch, 1996: 186–7).

Building new structures is risky and very resource intensive (in terms of the time and money required). One alternative is to convert already existing structures – like mothballed government-owned buildings (for example, public schools) – into correctional facilities. Similarly, during the 1980s and 1990s, the New York City Department of Corrections (NYCDC) began to rely on jail barges, reconditioned boats that housed prisoners. These vessels, moored around the island of Manhattan, upset many middle- and upper-class residents, who feared a negative impact on community safety and a decline in their property values. The only remaining vessel is the Vernon C. Bain Center, specifically built to NYCDC specification, at a cost of $160.6 million, that has a capacity of 800 beds.

Unfortunately, both the back-end and capacity expansion responses also have problems. Since both these measures are reactive (the projects cannot be immediately utilized), it takes a considerable amount of time to implement them. For example, it can take a year or more for proposals to be vetted and vendors to submit bids, before the building of a new correctional facility can actually start. Reactive measures also do not force criminal justice planners to reanalyze sentencing practices and/or implement more effective community corrections programs (Ford and Moore, 1992: 6).

Development of cost minimization strategies

There are three basic areas where the costs of jails and prisons can be reduced: "cost containment, controlling the cost of new prison construction, and revenue enhancement" (Freeman, 2000: 110).[1] Some wardens, in an effort to generate additional revenue or offset potential financial setbacks, operate recycling programs. Correctional facilities, as one can well imagine, generate a considerable amount of waste, and some of it can be used to generate income.

Other cost-saving mechanisms include

- reducing the number of inmates;
- decreasing the daily cost of incarceration; and
- controlling the cost of new prison construction.

When facilities are built or renovated, some DOCs have contractors install more energy- (and cost-)efficient technology (that is, better insulation, thermostats, lighting, and so on). Some facilities are capitalizing on solar, wind, and geothermal energy to reduce electricity costs.

Revenue enhancement

Revenue enhancement attempts to develop non-taxpayer revenue sources through the implementation of three strategies: (1) inmate reimbursement; (2) surcharging inmate use of technology; and (3) leasing out unused cells, tiers, and wings. All three strategies can involve the use of inmate labor and varying amounts of interaction with the private sector (Freeman, 2000: 110).

Classification is another way that cost savings can be accrued. In particular, inmates may be sent to a less-secure facility, where it would cost less to house and supervise them. Alternatively, convicts may demonstrate significant change (including being "rehabilitated") and, thus, be amenable to placement on parole (Ford and Moore, 1992: 8–9). The lion's share of a facilities budget is dedicated primarily to personnel. In particular, administrators eat up a considerable amount of money by relying too much on overtime. A correctional manager can address this problem through the judicious use of scheduling, properly timed hiring efforts, and inducements to reduce staff sick time, including buying back unused sick time (Ford and Moore, 1992: 12). This also means making tough choices between mandatory and optimum staffing levels.

Some entrepreneurial sheriffs in small towns have been able to recoup costs, if not provide additional income for their agencies, by leasing out cell space in their jail facilities to the Immigration and Naturalization Service (INS) (Welch, 2002).

Other cost minimization techniques include the use of detailed budgets and requests for proposals (RFPs). A well-developed and thought-out budget can carefully outline the kinds of revenues and expenses that will be incurred and the categories for those elements. This also means that expenditures can be accounted for on a regular basis. A complementary method is the judicious use of RFPs. This is a formalized way through which government entities can get contractors to submit bids to do work, perform a service, or purchase articles (Freeman, 2000: 109–10). Through this process, a more rational approach to contracting out can be achieved, thus minimizing expenses and ensuring compliance with agency directives.

Despite this problem, many states have not cut back on jail and prison spending. The reason behind this counterintuitive response is that most governors and state politicians do not want to appear to be soft on inmates; thus, building a new correctional facility is often seen as being supportive of law and order efforts (Broder, 2003). Moreover, revenue enhancement programs must be viewed critically, because in the past, deplorable experiments, like the convict lease program, were set up under this umbrella. In Georgia, starting in 1868, for example, inmates were leased for $11.00 per year, with the only limitation being to avoid "unseemly cruelty" (a common law limitation that had previously been applied to the treatment of cattle, slaves, and other chattels). The price was not raised even once during all the decades of the convict lease system (and many inmates were never returned to the correctional facilities that they were originally sentenced to). [2]

Legal challenges

There have been numerous legal challenges to the problem of overcrowding. One of the landmark cases was *Bell v. Woolfish* (1979). This Supreme Court case pertained to a prison in upstate New York, where the administration was forced to place two or more inmates awaiting trial in the same cell. The inmates argued that this was a form of punishment and that it was meted out even though they had not been convicted of a crime, thus violating their protections as guaranteed by the Fifth Amendment (that is, due process clause) of the U.S. Constitution. The court argued that the short-term nature of the detention did not violate the law. In 1981, prisoners at a correctional facility in Ohio (*Rhodes v. Chapman*) argued that the long-term nature of double bunking in their facility was unconstitutional. In this case, however, the prisoners were arguing that this qualified as cruel and unusual punishment as forbidden by the Eighth Amendment of the U.S. Constitution. Although supported by the federal district court, the final ruling was overturned by the Supreme Court, which argued that the overcrowding did not qualify as "wanton and unnecessary infliction of pain," a precondition for cruel and unusual punishment to have occurred.

The privatization of prisons as a solution

Perhaps as a result of the fiscally conservative swing at the federal level and many state governments, correctional services have increased their reliance on private enterprise to build, operate, and provide services to jails and prisons. This includes such functions as educational, food, medical, security, and transportation services (Austin and Irwin, 2001: 69–70). There is currently a huge correctional industry in the United States. Companies such as the Corrections Corporation of America (CCA) and The Geo Group (formerly Wackenhut Corrections Corporation) "account for over three fourths of the entire worldwide market" and derive significant incomes from providing local, state, and federal prison services. Moreover, "the total amount of revenues now allocated to private prisons and jails is estimated at $1 billion" (Austin and Irwin, 2001: 65).

Approximately "20 percent of federal prisoners and about 7 percent of state prisoners" are housed in private run jails and prisons (Canon, 2015). Nevertheless, according to Austin and Irwin:

> [T]here are some indications that growth in the use of privatization may be losing its steam and has reached a plateau. ... The stock prices for most of the major firms have dropped substantially in the past year, and there have been a number of highly publicized management problems with several privately operated facilities in Texas, Ohio, and New Mexico. (Austin and Irwin, 2001: 65)

In 1984, the first private prison opened in Tennessee. Since then roughly 150 of these kinds of facilities exist in the United States.[3] A number of entities operate these businesses; however, the most prominent is the Corrections Corporation of America (CCA), a publicly traded company (under the symbol CXW) that sells its shares on the New York Stock Exchange. At one point in time, the CCA stock value soared 1,000 times its price, making its owners and investors "very rich people" (Hallinan, 2003: xvii). Other corporations such as Aramark and Canteen food services have garnered profits supplying correctional services with food. Other things provided by private contractors include linen, medical, educational, and transportation services.

Private prisons are amenable to state correctional planners. They alleviate the stress connected with construction costs, financing, and maintenance. "In 1986, there were just twenty-six hundred privately managed prison beds in the United States. By 1995, there were over sixty-three thousand. States like Tennessee considered privatizing their entire prison system" (Hallinan, 2003: 145). In 2015, according to their website, CCA had 60 facilities located in 20 states (www.cca.com/locations). On the other hand, The Geo Group reported 66 facilities also in 20 states (www.geogroup.com/). Combined they have close to 149,000 beds (Lee, 2012).

Privatization calls into question several ethical, safety, and financial issues. Given that the government is responsible for arresting and adjudicating individuals, is it right for a corporation to profit from the misery of others? In private corrections, the staff often do not have as much training to do their jobs as do correctional workers in state-run facilities. Privatization also makes it harder for the government to control what goes on in corporate-run prisons. Another problem concerns the fact that often after receiving a lucrative contract the provider will "sham" by delivering fewer services or lower-quality items to further enhance their profit margin. Additionally, in the beginning, privatization creates competition that can drive the prices down as companies compete with each other; however, as fewer businesses enter the market, the private companies start increasing their costs to purchasers.

Finally, numerous convicts have suffered under private-run medical care providers. Some (for example, Prison Health Services (PHS)) have continuously run afoul of state inspectors, regulators, and DOCs. Nevertheless, DOCs have regularly renewed their contracts, often taking the position that something is better than nothing. The prison health industry is one area, among others, in the contemporary history of jails and prisons where privatization has failed, and where the function of providing health care must be resumed by the state.

One irony of sorts is that private prisons resocialize the costs when they can no longer achieve their goals. For example, in 1997, after six inmates escaped and went undetected for eight hours, Ed Bradley, former Associate Producer of the award-winning CBS television news magazine *60 Minutes*, did an exposé of the private prison in Youngstown, Ohio. His team discovered that the manual at this CCA facility simply instructed the staff at the prison to "call the local sheriff" if and when the inmates escaped. They simply dumped the problem back onto the state. This prompted Ohio to pass laws attempting (unsuccessfully) to put the burden back onto private prisons to collect their escapees.

Privatization in itself tends to focus so exclusively on profit that the increases in privatization seem due to corporate profit motives, rather than increasing crime waves, state difficulties in building and running their own prisons, and so forth. Thus, privatization of prisons seems only to promote an insatiable profit motive of corporations in an unusual market (market failure?) where more and more dollars seem always to be produced by state legislators.[4]

In short, the reality of prisons these days is that one cannot really talk about a system that is either public or private. We in fact have a hybrid system where selective aspects of the prison are contracted out to the private sector.

Contracting

One means through which prisons have tried to increase their revenues is by contracting with companies (for example, phone companies) that provide services to prisoners for a fee, but then charge above market rates and give the correctional facility a percentage of their income (that is, a kickback). Others seek out private sector companies and provide the labor for them.

One of the more dubious practices in the history of U.S. corrections, as previously mentioned, is the "convict leasing" procedure. The revenues generated through the leases either fund prison programs or are placed back into the correctional facility's general fund. Meanwhile, the jails and/or prisons and the facilities' administration have discretion on how to allocate this money.

In 1947, the Taft-Hartley Act was passed. This prevented prisons from unfairly competing with local industries and labor markets. Almost ever since, before it has been a violation of federal law for state prisons to sell their products in interstate commerce – unless, like the programs in South Carolina and Oregon, they are certified by a federal program known as Prison Industry Enhancement (PIE). This program was created in 1979, and until recently has been all but dormant. In 1998, for instance, 35 states were certified to participate in the program, but, all told, they employed just 2,600 inmates, or about two tenths of 1 percent of the nation's state prison population" (Hallinan, 2003: 149). "Under the provisions of PIE, inmates must be paid the same wages as free workers engaged in similar work. They must also be allowed to keep at least 20% of what they earn. The rest of their wages can be withheld to pay income taxes, child support obligations, room and board charges, and payments due to victim assistance funds" (Hallinan, 2003: 149). Obviously, this kind of program has received ample criticism from organized labor.

Conclusion

Short of abolishing jails and prisons (see, for example, Mathiesen, 1974), there are several means of minimizing underfunding through a combined effort among activists, professionals, and administrators, who can educate and lobby elected officials to spend more on corrections and pass laws that benefit the field. Wardens or senior command staff could apply for state and federal money to improve programs, for example. They could also apply for grant funding and make better use of volunteer programs, like Teach for America and the Inside Out Prison program. We should also encourage jail and prison administrators to use their funding more efficiently.

Additional efforts include supporting the election of those individuals who would make increased funding for jails and prisons their priority. At the state and federal levels, we can work to sanction, dismiss, or better educate and train correctional personnel and management. Correctional administrators should aggressively pursue dishonest or lazy staff. Sanctioning workers when they fail to comply with departmental policies is not easy, particularly because of the blue wall of silence and the strength of CO unions. At the institutional level, solutions include eliminating overtime and ensuring that there are enough trained and qualified staff on which supervisors can rely if someone is sick, on leave, or on vacation,[5] in addition to improving communication between workers and administrators. We need to put an end to business as usual among elected politicians and government workers who approach their jobs in a casual and laissez-faire way.

If more money could be funneled to corrections, then we could implement more evidence based approaches (for example, rehabilitative programs that work) and refrain from poorly thought-out ones (for example, building more prisons, increasing the length of sentences, and so on) based on appeals to emotions. All told, this approach would, in the very least, alleviate the overcrowding problem. Sufficient space in prisons would prevent the diversion of suspects out of the system to probation when they really should be incarcerated. Also, more money funneled into the system would mean higher-quality and happier staff.

Key terms

Back-end measures: Includes parole, early release, good time, and correctional programs such as aftercare.

Capacity: The number of inmates a correctional facility can hold.

Classification: A system for determining the appropriate security level and correctional facility for an inmate.

Compassionate release: When an inmate is dying of a disease and does not have much longer to live, s/he may be released back to the community to be in the care of relatives.

Conditional release: A person is released from correctional custody as long as the individual meets certain criteria.

Design capacity: The number of inmates that a correctional facility was designed to hold (by planners, designers, architects, etc.).

Front-end measures: Preventing suspects or convicted individuals from spending time in a correctional facility. This is usually accomplished through diversion or probation.

Good time credits: Method by which inmates are given time off their criminal sentence if they obey correctional institutional rules, and participate in rehabilitative programs.

Jail barge: Large retrofitted and specially constructed boats that are used as makeshift correctional facilities.

Prison industry enhancement: Partnerships between private industry and correctional facilities.

Privatization: Correctional facilities and services run by the private sector.

Revenue enhancement: Methods where correctional facilities and systems find ways to increase the amount or sources of income to run their facilities and programs. This is often done through charging inmates for health care, food, and special accommodations.

Sham/shamming: In an effort to save costs and increase profits, after a contract is signed, the contractor provides less or lower quality products or services than previously agreed.

Notes

[1] As a result of wardens needing to reduce costs, a sector of the consulting industry now specializes in this activity. This includes a variety of communication modalities such as a monthly newsletter, "Corrections Cost Control & Revenue Report," which specializes in helpful articles on this subject matter (Hallinan, 2003: 12).

[2] Personal conversation with Bradley Chilton, February 21, 2007.

[3] Private entities entered the correctional field about two decades earlier. For example, in 1975 RCA Services contracted with the state of Pennsylvania to run a training school for delinquents in Northampton (Durham, 1993: 33). Since this is a juvenile facility and this book focuses on adults, it is mentioned here only parenthetically.

[4] Personal correspondence with Bradley Chilton, February 21, 2007.

[5] It is recognized that this will be difficult as many COs depend upon the overtime to supplement their income.

FIVE

Prison conditions

Introduction

Conditions inside correctional facilities vary among the federal, state, and local (that is, county and municipal) systems of corrections, between male and female prisons, and among different levels of security. Assessing the state of these environments is difficult, as many firsthand descriptions resemble urban legends, embellished to suit the personal goals of the storytellers. Thus, not all prisons are filthy, have horrible food, and lack rehabilitative programs. Nevertheless, some of the most salient controversial prison conditions are unsanitary living conditions, the absence of adequate health and medical care, poor food, lack of rehabilitative programs, and violence, including sexual assault. These problems often lead to abuse, anger, depression, fear, frustration, and/or violence, not only among the prisoners, but among the correctional officers (COs) too (see Chapter 11). Before continuing, however, it must be understood that these settings are influenced by the powerful effects of the inmate social system and prison subculture (for example, Sykes, 1958; Sykes and Messinger, 1960; Bowker, 1978). These underlying factors exacerbate living and working relationships behind bars.

Health conditions

When individuals are sent to prison, they must worry about catching serious and possibly life-threatening diseases. Correctional facilities are notoriously unhealthy places (McDonald, 1999; Speed Weed, 2001; Murphy, 2003; Wright, 2008; Wilper et al., 2009a; Wilper et al. 2009b). Historically, convicts routinely contracted cholera, yellow fever, and tuberculosis (TB) while doing time – which explains why TB used to be called *jail cough* or *prison fever*. Prisons are typically dirty, lack proper sanitary conditions, are crowded/overcrowded, and have poor ventilation. In situations like this, communicable diseases can quickly spread through the entire inmate population. Diseases are usually transmitted via air or through body fluids, such as semen, blood, and saliva.

Although the administrative corridors may be spotless, the cell house is likely to be filthy. Generally, all the areas of the prison in which the public may enter and where the supervisors have offices are cleaned on a frequent basis. As one progresses to the interior of the correctional facility, behind the security thresholds and into the cellblocks where the prisoners live, the hallways can be dim and dirty, and the lighting and ventilation may also be poor (Ross and Richards, 2002).

Prisons also provide minimal health education. Information that could help convicts is rarely placed on bulletin boards or distributed in the form of memos or pamphlets about how to protect oneself from serious diseases. "The material provided is usually in the form of pamphlets, which are usually beyond the reading level of many inmates."[1] On the other hand, the prison staff typically receive better and more easily accessible information, annual training, and equipment to prevent themselves from getting sick.

The diagnosis of any disease is handled as confidential information. The correctional facility medical staff may not even take the time to do the appropriate tests to isolate the problem, figuring that the minute they give prisoners the bad news, the cons will request medication, an extra expense incurred by the correctional system.

In general, at both the state and federal levels, the provision of medical services in many American prisons is inhumane (Murphy, 2003). There are a number of health concerns, reviewed here from least to most important. [2]

Noise/hearing loss

Prisons are noisy places, with the slamming of cell doors, screaming and yelling, and a constant racket that reverberates off the cement and steel structures. The noise is reminiscent of a crowded transportation hub, concert venue, or shopping center, where the background drone of hundreds of voices may drown out one's own conversation. The noise is so bad that some prisoners suffer hearing damage (Jacobson et al., 1989; Ross and Richards, 2002). There is little that inmates can do to protect themselves from hearing loss, as there is no way to avoid the pandemonium, except to cover their heads with pillows when they are in their cells, sleep with earplugs, or take every opportunity available to be outside in the yard, where the sound dissipates. Hearing loss is especially a problem for older inmates.

Lung cancer

Unsurprisingly, many prisoners smoke. In the past, convicts were allowed to smoke cigarettes or cigars and/or chew tobacco nearly everywhere. Jail and prison cellblocks were typically littered with cigarette butts, and heavy smoke filled the air. Since the late 1990s, correctional administrators concerned with minimizing fires and environmental degradation, and, most importantly, with avoiding lawsuits from prisoners (and COs) who may have developed respiratory illnesses or lung cancer from being forced to breathe secondhand smoke have typically banned cigarettes and cigars from the interior areas of jails and prisons, if not from the complete correctional facility. Today, most institutions strictly forbid both staff and prisoners to smoke inside; all smokers are now required to take their habit outdoors. Some prisons may have designated smoking areas in the yard (Patrick and Marsh, 2001).

Although nonsmokers and smokers attempting to quit may welcome these new institutional rules, many smokers are bitter about the change. For those individuals with a serious nicotine addiction, being locked in a smoke-free environment all day and night, except for the few hours they are allowed to be on the yard, can be very difficult.

Asbestos poisoning

A considerable number of old buildings contain asbestos. It is a relatively inexpensive material that was historically used as a fire retardant, and to insulate heating and air-conditioning systems. In some structures with drop ceilings, the panels that were installed were also made out of asbestos. During the 1960s, it was discovered that asbestos led to life-threatening illnesses such as asbestosis, cancer, and mesothelioma. Since 1978, it has been illegal to use asbestos in residential and workplace construction. In the 1990s, at the East Oregon Correctional Institution, state inspectors noticed that the building had numerous pipes that were coated with highly toxic asbestos. An administrator had the prisoners remove it without any protective gear. The prisoners and COs became sick. When this occurred, the administrators finally turned the task over to a professional asbestos abatement company. Similar incidents have occurred at other correctional facilities throughout the United States (see, for example Carpenter, 2010).

Tuberculosis

Tuberculosis is a lung disease spread in places that are overcrowded with dirty, stale, and stagnant air. Although prisoners routinely (sometimes yearly) have TB tests, if a con has an adverse reaction (red skin marks), they may be told by the medical staff to not worry. If, in fact, a con tests positive for a disease or illness, it is often kept secret, so the sick inmates will not be attacked by fearful prisoners (Bellin et al., 1993).

Hepatitis

Hepatitis is a liver disease spread through blood, semen, bad water, or spoiled meat. Depending upon its strain, in the early stages, cons might not even know they have this ailment. As the illness progresses, the eyes and skin turn yellow (aka jaundice). Hepatitis causes extreme fatigue, and, if it is not treated quickly, it may lead to the deaths of those afflicted. Many individuals from lesser-developed countries, alcoholics, junkies, or other intravenous drug users suffer in varying degrees from this illness. There are several types of hepatitis. The three most common ones range from hepatitis A to hepatitis C (the most debilitating). In its worst iteration, hepatitis C affects sufferers for the rest of their lives. It damages an individual's liver, which is needed to fight infections, get rid of toxins in the body, and store energy (Ruiz et al., 1999).

HIV/AIDS

Acquired Immunity Deficiency Syndrome (AIDS) suppresses the body's ability to fight illness. Not only are homosexuals at risk, but also intravenous drug users, including drug addicts, diabetics, and those who require frequent blood transfusions, like hemophiliacs. AIDS is one of the most highly concentrated diseases among the prison population (Hammond, 1989). A 1994 survey, sponsored by the National Institute of Justice (NIJ), outlined how AIDS was nine times more prevalent in prisoners than in the general population (Hammett et al., 1995). According to a 2005 Bureau of Justice Statistics (BJS) report (Maruschak, 2005), based on a survey conducted in 2003, 1.8% and 2.6% of men in federal and state correctional facilities respectively were HIV positive.

Solutions to poor health/medical conditions

Both prisoners and correctional institutions can minimize the health risks in jails and prisons. Some of these solutions are self-directed, while others involve the intervention of family members, the correctional facility, prison activists, or state or federal governments. Each kind of disease requires its own sort of prevention. With respect to hepatitis, TB, and AIDS, convicts need to avoid coming into contact with other people's blood, saliva, sweat, and semen at all costs, as these could carry any number of infectious organisms.

One method, prison regulations permitting, is for cons to take their personal utensils to the cafeteria. If inmates continue intravenous drug use behind bars, they need to take extra special caution to sterilize any drug paraphernalia and to use condoms if they are engaging in homosexual contact. (Needless to say both these items are contraband.) Otherwise, a trip to the institution may be a good time to get clean.

The most common precaution used by prisoners to maintain or even improve their health is regular exercise – at least walking the yard, possibly jogging, weightlifting, or participating in sports like basketball, handball, or softball (Murphy, 2003). Exercise works off stress, helps a person lose weight, and improves prisoners' health. Some people overcome their addictions to alcohol and drugs, establish a daily routine of exercise, and leave prison in better health than when they arrived. A handful of minimum-security camps may have a tennis court, but cons usually have to wait a long time for the privilege of using it. Also important is educating oneself about food, including learning how to read food labels.

In addition, some prisons allow convicts access to condoms and bleach (World Health Organization, McLemore, 2008). Correctional facilities, however, do not like inmates to have condoms because they believe that these will be used to smuggle drugs and as a means to pursue prohibited activities (especially forced/nonconsensual sex). Although information on selected correctional facilities and states that permit inmates access to condoms exists, no national level data exists on this policy and practice. To date, it appears that New York City, Philadelphia, Vermont, and California supply condoms to inmates incarcerated in their correctional facilities.

It is also important to make sure convicts are not issued the wrong medication or placebos (that is, typically a pill that resembles the proper medication, but has no health benefit) by medical staff. In some facilities, inmates who may previously have held positions as pharmacists, nurses, dentists, or doctors before their convictions may be allowed to stand watch occasionally over the pill/medication line at sick call, where they inspect the prescribed medication provided to prisoners to make sure they are given the right pills (Vaughn, 1997).

When convicts do get sick, the general hope is that it is nothing serious, as the medical services inside correctional facilities are typically limited and substandard (Dabney and Vaughn, 2000). Prisoners who suffer from chronic or acute illnesses are served by an overburdened medical staff, minimal in number, and even if these individuals care to help, they are frequently prevented from doing so by a prison health care system that is underfunded, bureaucratic, and severely limited in the services and medical procedures it is authorized to administer. Prisoners who need costly surgery, expensive medication, or sophisticated medical protocols generally require family and friends to pressure prison administrators. A life-threatening illness, for example cancer, a heart attack, or a stroke, will require outside intervention – possibly a lawsuit or multiple letters, emails, or phone calls from a powerful politician – to get cons transported to a civilian hospital for treatment (Murphy, 2003).

Prisoners who have severe unattended medical problems (or more likely, the family or friends of those incarcerated, if they still maintain contact) should enlist the aid of prisoner advocacy organizations and elected politicians who can contact or write their warden and appropriate members of the state departments of corrections (DOCs) to properly monitor the situation. DOCs should switch to public medical/health providers where the records would be more readily accessible to the scrutiny of the public, news media, and other government oversight agencies. Finally, the federal government, with the assistance of the Centers for Disease Control and Prevention (CDC), should institute nationwide mandatory hepatitis (and other infectious disease) testing and treatment for all jail and prison inmates and those individuals under community corrections supervision.

One of the solutions for minimizing health costs and increasing scope of coverage has been the development and use of telemedicine programs. Since the mid 1990s a number of telemedicine programs have been established in prisons:

> Telemedicine (also referred to as "telehealth" or "e-health") allows health care professionals to use "connected" medical devices in the evaluation, diagnosis and treatment of patients in other locations. These devices are enhanced through the use of telecommunications technology, network computing, video-conferencing systems and CODECs (that is, a system that collapses electronic data so it is easier to transmit). Telemedicine customarily uses two methods to transmit images, data and sound – either "live", real-time transmission where the consulting professional participates in the examination of the patient while diagnostic information is collected and transmitted, or "store and forward" transmission, where the consulting professional reviews data asynchronous with its collection. Many programs employ both transmission capabilities, to maximize efficient use of resources appropriate to the medical services being provided. (www.amdtelemedicine.com)

Although telemedicine is an improvement over the previous method of health care delivery in many correctional facilities (Mekhjian et al., 1999; Magaletta et al., 2000; Morgan et al., 2008; Deslich et al., 2013), it is no panacea as subtle differences in quality of care can occur between face-to-face versus telemedicine modalities.

Another important consideration is that in many jails and prisons, the medical, psychiatric, and dental services are run by private health maintenance organizations (HMOs), like Correctional Medical Services (CMS) (for example, Hylton, 2003). Hylton outlined how CMS "controls the health care of all prisoners in ten states and manages a portion of inmate health care in another seventeen." In general, Hylton provided a convincing portrait of how several important aspects of these businesses are beyond the scrutiny of the average member of the public. Most importantly, CMSs uses a number of clever "accounting practices" to create the impression that their provision of health care is well intentioned, but in reality they do as much as possible to avoid consuming company resources. Regardless of the company used, private HMOs are often beyond the scrutiny of the average citizen.

There are numerous ways that DOCs and the Federal Bureau of Prisons (FBOP) can improve health conditions and the provision of health care behind bars. First, they could switch to public companies, where the records would be more accessible. Some of these strategies were mentioned, almost in passing, in the Commission on Safety and Abuse Report including "end[ing] co-payments for medical care" and extending Medicaid and Medicare to eligible prisoners (Gibbons and de Katzenbach, 2006: 13). "To drive down the costs, legislators pressure corrections administrators to require prisoners to make co-payments for their medical care. While co-payments seem reasonable on the surface, they cost more in the long run by discouraging sick prisoners from seeking care early on, when treatment is less expensive and before disease spreads" (14).

Another recommendation from the Commission on Safety and Abuse (2005–6) was for DOCs to partner with their local public health commissions. According to the report:

> [I]t is disappointing that public health departments have not taken a more active role in ensuring quality health care for prisoners and that county and state executives have not encouraged partnerships between jails and prisons and a broad range of community health-care providers – including public hospitals, local clinics, teaching institution, and doctors and nurses in private practice. (Gibbons and de Katzenbach, 2006: 39)

The commission cited a number of jurisdictions where this takes place, but did not go into great detail. Nevertheless, they did add that

> [p]artnerships with community and public health providers broaden the pool of qualified caregivers who are committed to working in a correctional environment by allowing them to remain connected with community clinics and hospitals, teaching universities, and public health agencies. The partnerships increase the chances that caregivers will have some sensitivity to the particular cultural and language barriers [of prisoners]. (Gibbons and de Katzenbach, 2006: 40)

The commission pointed out a number of advantages to this recommendation including "increas[ing] the odds that people will have clear access to necessary health services after release – sometimes from the very same doctors and nurses who treated them in jail" (41).

Additionally, although there have been calls for mandatory HIV/AIDS testing of prisoners, many civil libertarians, prisoner rights groups, and AIDS activists in the United States and elsewhere (for example, the World Health Organization) have opposed this measure. These groups believe that mandatory testing will lead to prisoners being singled out by both correctional staff and other convicts for victimization in some shape or form (Young, 2006).

Lawyers and prison reform activists have also pressured DOCs to provide better health care. The most significant court case in this policy area is *Estelle v. Gamble* (1976). Here the Supreme Court stated that "deliberate indifference to the serious medical needs of prisoners constitutes the 'unnecessary and wanton infliction of pain' proscribed by the Eight[h] Amendment." It has been noted that because of *Rhodes v. Chapman* (1981), "the level of health care required … is a shifting target. Thus an acceptable standard of health care in 2007 is not the standard that was in place when Estelle was decided" (Wright, 2008: 32). This standard will continue to be fluid into the foreseeable future as well.

Poor food

A considerable amount of controversy surrounds the quality of food in prison. Why? Food holds enormous importance for convicts, not just for its nutritional value but for psychological purposes too (Valentine and Longstaff, 1998; Ross and Richards, 2002: chapter 7). Nevertheless, inmates' perceptions of food quality are often based on what an individual was used to eating on the outside. Indeed, some of the firsthand stories told by cons about meals sound like urban legends or myths, this must be treated cautiously. Moreover, like so many things in the field of corrections, the food differs from one institution to another.

Cafeteria food

Convicts frequently refer to institutional meals as dog food, Ken-L Rations, or Alpo. They are typically served in large cafeterias, also called canteens, or chow, mess, or dining halls. In general, the meals are basic institutional food, like one might receive in hospital or military contexts.[3] On the extreme end of things, the best meals are often served on holidays or when "dignitaries" visit. On these occasions, the kitchen may prepare food of somewhat better quality.

Some facilities have special dietary food lines for those with medical conditions (for example, diabetics) or those whose religion bans the eating of particular foods. For example, the "Common Fare" diet (a simple meal with no pork, no mixing of meat and milk products, and no utensils used in food preparation that have come into contact with pork – for all intents a kosher diet) is often requested for prisoners of the Jewish and/or Muslim faith. Rarely are there strictly vegetarian or vegan meals served in prison (Ogden, 2001). Some correctional facilities integrate the local cuisine into their menu. For example, in the Deep South, catfish, fish heads, corn bread, and grits might be served, while black beans and rice might be more prevalent in Florida than in Texas.

Some days, however, the food is prepared, served, and thrown out with only a small number of cons daring a taste. Occasionally, the fruit and vegetables are or appear to be bruised, overripe, rotten, or canned (Ross and Richards, 2002: chapter 7). And the meat and chicken may seem to be of the lowest quality. Moreover, convicts routinely complain that COs place excrement, rodent parts, and insects in their food (Hassine, 2004). Whether this actually happens is hard to verify.

Prisoners who work in the cafeteria generally eat better and more, as they have greater access to food items. Many also use this job detail to assist themselves with operating an underground/black market business. They may steal food (for example, fruit, vegetables, chicken, and roast beef) and sell it to more financially well-off inmates. Or they may make simple meal items (for example, grilled cheese sandwiches and hamburgers), and sell them in dormitories and cellblocks. Mess hall workers, because of access to yeast, sugar, and fruit, may also be either suppliers to or manufacturers of hooch, moonshine, pruno, or rotgut (that is, alcohol).

The institutional food is often not only of poor quality, but it may also disappear and not even be served in the mess hall. In some correctional facilities, the staff may eat or steal the better food, taking it home to feed their family, pets and farm animals or selling it on the black market (Ross and Richards, 2002: chapter 7). Depending on the prison system, those in solitary confinement may receive "prison loafs," in which the food offered for the day is ground up, placed in a baking pan, and then reheated before being served to the inmates. In FBOP administrative segregation, prisoners eat the same food as those in general population.

Solutions to poor food

In many correctional facilities, the cons who have institutional jobs, a racket, hustle, or access to outside money mailed in, or sent electronically to their commissary account, may buy kitchen food or eat commissary items, which they store in their lockers. In some prisons, well-heeled and -connected prisoners may purchase luxury food items, or food from chain restaurants, like

Pizza Hut or Kentucky Fried Chicken, that are smuggled in by correctional workers (Ross and Richards, 2002: chapter 7).

Most prisons have a commissary, which sells basic items to general-population inmates. These include stamps, food, over-the-counter medication, stationery, hygiene items, clothing, and electronics. In terms of food, the list often contains cheap brands of cookies, crackers, candies, and canned food, like tuna, salmon, and sardines. The commissary account is funded through convict labor earnings, which are placed into convicts' accounts when they work, and through individuals on the outside (for example, family and friends) who deposit money into them.

Depending on the facility, the commissary is located in a hallway and is open either once a week or once a month. Order forms showing which items are for sale and their prices are made available to the convicts. If prisoners can afford to buy food through the commissary, they avoid the dining hall. Prisoners buy food items from the commissary with some kind of plan about how they are going to eat for the next week or month.

The commissary is typically run by an officer who has a few prisoners working for them. Alternatively, an experienced convict whom the prison administration trusts may work it. COs call cons down to the commissary by cellblock. In some correctional facilities, prisoners stand in a very long line leading up to a glass or metal screen window in front of a counter. Alternatively, after submitting the commissary slip, prisoners wait until their number is called.

All prisoners fill out their commissary list, check off what they want, add everything up, put their names and inmate numbers on the forms, and then present their ID or commissary cards (which may be one and the same thing) at the window. The wait depends on several factors, but an inmate can complete their transaction within 45 minutes, on average.

Unfortunately, the items at the commissary are generally overpriced, increasing inmate hostility toward the correctional system. In the FBOP, the profits of the items sold are supposed to be placed in an inmate trust fund. This account is meant to be used for buying recreational items and sports equipment.

In some minimum-security state facilities, convicts who have enough money in their commissary accounts will purchase their meals out of vending machines, heating them up in a microwave oven (Elrod and Brooks, 2003). If these machines are not present inside the facility, then they may be located in a visiting room. The prices of the snack food are seriously inflated. Naturally, there are recurring rumors that vending services are owned by relatives or associates of wardens or by retired COs (Ross and Richards, 2002: chapter 7).

In order to prevent food poisoning, many prisoners skip cafeteria meals that appear risky, and instead supplement their diet with commissary food, vitamins, and large quantities of liquids to flush their systems. Common precautions used by prisoners to protect themselves from bacterial infections are to wash their hands frequently and to eat liberal amounts of hot peppers and salsa, which can be purchased at the commissary. This also works to clear the nasal passages and sinuses, and may help with cold symptoms and allergies (Ross and Richards, 2002: chapter 7).

Physical violence

Violence is endemic to most correctional facilities and has several dimensions. The most common types, psychological and physical, abound in correctional settings (Fleisher, 1989; Bottoms, 1999). Psychological violence (or trauma) is often a precursor to and the effect of physical violence. The first affects the convicts' mental states, and often leads to anger, cynicism, depression, and resistance to authority (Ross, 2010). Physical violence affects the prisoners' bodies and eventually their minds. The following section reviews the different kinds of violence experienced by convicts and briefly discusses the operation of gangs behind bars.

Violence by convicts against themselves

The problem

Occasionally, otherwise mentally stable cons will hurt themselves. This self-injurious behavior includes cutting themselves with sharp objects, pulling their hair out, banging their heads against walls or cell doors, or engaging in dirty protests (that is, smearing feces all over their bodies). Sometimes an older prisoner wakes up one day and decides he cannot "take it anymore." He shakes hands with his buddies and then, during yard time, he walks past the kill zone (that is, prohibited area next to a wall or fence) and is shot to death by one of the COs in the towers. This is called *death by gun tower*.

Another form of suicide is the escape attempt. If convicts try to climb the wall, they will be electrocuted by high-voltage lines or cut by razor wire. More than likely, cons will die on the wall. If, by some small chance, they make it over, odds are they will be shot down by their pursuers. Escaped convicts are usually wanted dead or alive. Or a prisoner may make a spectacular swan dive leap from the fifth-floor tier down to the cement floor below. That is why, among other reasons, in most correctional facilities there is wire mesh extending up from the handrails to the ceilings of the tiers or there is netting between the floors, similar to those found under a circus trapeze.

Other forms of suicide include hanging, overdosing on drugs, slitting wrists and neck, or having sex with an inmate known to be HIV positive. A convict intent on killing themselves might one night drink a considerable amount of prison hooch (alcohol), or ingest whatever drugs they can get, then place a plastic bag over their head, go to bed, and suffocate in their sleep.

If prisoners attempt suicide but survive, they will typically be temporarily locked up in the hole or in the psychiatric unit. The COs typically want prisoners to live, if only because if cons die, there will be an investigation with a lot of questions to answer and copious paperwork to complete. Self injurious behavior is not limited to a handful of prisons, but is widespread throughout correctional facilities in the United States (Smith and Kaminski, 2010, 2011).

The prison infirmary has few medical personnel, and rarely are prisoners taken outside the gates to a civilian hospital; otherwise, there would be an epidemic of cons faking suicide as a ploy to go to a civilian hospital, to facilitate an escape attempt, or to just break the monotony. Cons rarely speak to a psychologist or counselor, and they are usually sent back to the tier when it looks like they have calmed down. If they are in a minimum-security facility, convicts might be taken to a hospital. Here an ambulance can make it into and out of the facility relatively quickly, as compared to a penitentiary.

Solutions for suicidal prisoners

Inmates who are determined by the correctional staff to be suicidal are placed on suicide watch. Typically, the prisoner is removed from their regular cell and moved to a cell or area where they can be regularly monitored, not only by COs but also in some facilities by other convicts, and with the assistance of audio and video surveillance. Additionally, some prisons operate a program known as *suicide companions*, which enables compassionate convicts to receive suicide prevention training to help care for suicide-prone prisoners. Oftentimes, suicidal inmates' clothes are taken away from them, and they are given a suicide gown or smock. In some correctional institutions, this is called a banana or yellow suit or dress (Bruton, 2004: 75–7). The appearance and construction of this garment varies from one institution to another.

Violence by convicts against other prisoners and correctional personnel

There are several kinds of physical violence that cons engage in, including assaults, disturbances, rebellions, riots, and sexual assault (Cohen et al., 1976; Fleisher, 1989). Sometimes the distinctions among these types are difficult to discern because of the fluidity of the actions. The following section attempts to clarify the different kinds of violence and also elaborates on weapons and gangs.

Assaults

Prisoners are frequently beaten, stabbed, or killed in correctional facilities. Despite collection efforts by the U.S. Department of Justice's BJS, data on violence in prison is notoriously unreliable (Gibbons and de Katzenbach, 2006: 25). Nevertheless, in general the higher the security level, the more potential for violence to exist. The most violent convicts are young men serving long sentences; older prisoners may be more dangerous, but they are frequently more logical in their use of violence, which is why they have survived long enough to become older prisoners. Younger prisoners are more inclined than older men to have fistfights (Ross and Richards, 2003). Some of the physical violence is planned; cons might carefully plot out how they will attack or what they will do to a fellow prisoner or CO. Most violence, however, is spontaneous and is the result of some annoyance or irritation. This frustration may start when someone steps in front of a prisoner in a long line, which is perceived as more than a bother. It is a direct challenge. The line-jumper believes or wants to find out if the prisoner behind them can be intimidated.

If the line-jumper gets away with it, they will be back another time, perhaps upping the ante. What bothers many convicts, and is in fact one of their biggest fears, is that once they have decided that they can do "their own time," situations will arise where they will have to prove and/or defend themselves, which will inevitably put them in positions where they will engage in another crime, be convicted (aka *catch another case*), extend their time behind bars, and never go home (Hassine, 2004).

COs (and administrators) need to keep a close eye on all forms of violence in order to respond appropriately. If they overreact, they may have a riot on their hands. The correctional workers generally do not like it when cons fight because it generates onerous paperwork. But some COs have been known to instigate violence, for example, by putting two cons who hate each other together in the same cell and sitting back to watch the fireworks. Meanwhile, jails and prisons experience their share of disturbances, rebellions, and riots (Useem and Kimball, 1989).

Disturbances

Disturbances are low-intensity acts of resistance that have the potential to escalate. Although it may appear that there are no overt reasons for the outburst, they are typically motivated by the low level-frustration or altercation that a convict may have experienced with correctional staff or policies. Usually, they begin with an altercation, then one or more inmates tips over a table in the chow hall or damages institutional property in an outbreak of frustration and anger. If the food in the dining hall is particularly vile that day, the cons may fill up their trays and almost simultaneously throw them on the floor.

A disturbance may start with one con damaging a chair, and then, suddenly, 50 other prisoners are doing the same thing. There is no sanctity to the actions. Cons will indiscriminately destroy a dining hall, turn over a delivery truck that entered the prison, trash a chapel, or trample a bed of newly planted flowers. Some disturbances involve inmates stopping up their toilets so the water overflows into the corridors, making them an unsafe and unsanitary mess. These actions are signs of resistance, indications that inmates have not been totally beaten and still have some fight left in them, and the result of collective frustration and boredom.

Some disturbances are caused by the annoyance of excessive noise. Sound reverberates in cellblocks, which are made primarily of cement and steel. As is often seen in Hollywood films, unhappy prisoners make noise by pounding on metal doors or banisters or screaming profanity at COs. Some cons will not even shy away from throwing human waste products at the guards (known as *sliming*) (Ross and Richards, 2002).

With hundreds of convicts yelling profanities, officers are not going to be in a position to put the whole cellblock in the hole, but they can take away privileges, like yard time, weekly movies, or commissary access, which only enrages the cons that much more. Typically, however, the institution will go into lockdown mode. Few disturbances ever come to the attention of the public. Most DOCs try to avoid responding to news media requests for information on such incidents because they fear the publicity will lead to greater scrutiny of their facility, and create contagion, the spreading of rebellion to additional correctional facilities that hear about it.

Rebellions

Rebellions include work and hunger strikes. A common form of protest in correctional facilities, especially for political prisoners, is the hunger strike. The situation (especially if the media gets involved) has the potential to embarrass the prison authorities. A work strike occurs when convicts refuse to come out of their cells and/or go to the factory, cook, or clean. Without prison labor, administrators cannot effectively and efficiently run the correctional facility. COs (with the help of prison snitches) usually try to identify the ringleaders and will often throw the provocateurs in the hole. The administration then usually transfers the troublemakers to a higher security prison. Work strikes typically end when the cons get hungry and run out of the food stored in their lockers. So the prison, much like big corporations with striking workers, normally waits out the cons. Strikes do not usually last more than a week or two.

Riots

The American correctional enterprise has suffered notorious riots including those at the New York State Penitentiary at Attica in 1971 (Wicker, 1980/1994), New Mexico State Prison at Santa Fe in 1980 (Useem, 1985; Colvin, 1992; Rolland, 1997), the Ohio Correctional Facility Lucasville Prison in 1993, and USP Atlanta in 1995 (Hamm, 1995). The Attica riot resulted in 39–43 dead,[4] including 11 prison employees. Santa Fe left 33 prisoners dead, most killed by other cons, which included murder by blowtorch, decapitation, and dismemberment, as well as beaten, COs being gang-raped and then sodomized with nightsticks and lead pipes (Useem, 1985). The Lucasville riot resulted in 10 dead (Lynd, 2004). Each of these riots included serious injuries to hundreds of prisoners, additional time added to sentences, and tens of millions of dollars of damage to penal institutions. When all is said and done and the riot is put down, life becomes tougher for the surviving prisoners.

Sometimes riots begin when cliques or gangs decide to settle scores by attacking their rivals. Race or ethnic hatred and battles for prison dominance are another reason. Conditions of confinement may be so oppressive that the cons feel that they have no other choice than to retaliate. Long prison sentences, some with no parole and little opportunity for earning "good time" (a reduction in sentence), breed revolt. Riots are not just about COs or workers getting injured or killed; oftentimes, they involve prisoners' attempts to settle old debts.

When a riot is coming, convicts can almost literally feel it in their bones. Prisoners who have been through them before are more skilled at surviving the next one. If experienced cons do find themselves in the midst of a prison disturbance, rebellion, or riot, they try to keep a low profile and not get caught up in the ensuing excitement. Some of the novices will also stay in their cells to avoid the frenzy that runs through the corridors, modeling their behavior after the lifers.

When convicts riot, they typically begin by taking over a tier, cellblock, or part of the prison (for example, cafeteria), with hopes of controlling the whole institution. Even though prisons are made from concrete and steel, this does not mean that innovative cons are incapable of burning them down. They use cleaning fluid, bleach, and floor wax, and then pour it on their mattresses. Once the chemical reactions among these components begin, enough heat is eventually produced for the paint on the concrete to start burning, finally causing the overheated structure of rebar and concrete to collapse. Many roofs are constructed of wood and tar, which will easily go up in flames. Some prisoners will suffer the effects of smoke inhalation, while others will be burned to death in the blaze.

Even though cons can take control of some or even all of a facility on any given day, they cannot hold it for long. The correctional authorities will use a variety of weapons (that is, shotguns, automatic weapons, and so on) and tactics (for example, tear gas, and so on) to retake the facility. If need be, the officers will be supported by local law enforcement, state police, the National Guard, or other military reinforcements. In most riots, more convicts than COs are killed.

Prison riots are doomed to fail. No matter how many COs are taken hostage, beaten, or killed, the uprising will inevitably be crushed by overwhelming force. COs and administrators who survive – or their replacements – will have months, if not years, to take revenge on those who have defied them. This includes pressing administrative and criminal charges against the rioters (Mahan and Lawrence, 1996). Usually, the only time the news media reports on a prison riot is when convicts take hostages or set an institution on fire. In these situations, the news gets out of the prison relatively rapidly, and news organizations cannot ignore the situation as it develops.

Weapons

Many disputes are settled with shanks, homemade weapons made from toothbrushes, pencils, razor blades, broken glass and tape, or any metal, plastic, or wood that can be sharpened and fashioned into either a cutting or a stabbing device. An experienced convict can make a weapon out of nearly anything. For example, a newspaper rolled tight can be used like a knife to thrust at an opponent's vulnerable body parts. Harden this with toothpaste or plaster, and it can be made into a zip gun when it is filled with match heads and a projectile. Another common weapon is a pillowcase filled with soda cans, or a bar of soap hidden in a sock. Prison yard plants and cleaners can also be used as poison, fire accelerants, or explosives, and dental floss can be used to strangle a person (Ross and Richards, 2002: 122).

The solutions

Avoiding fights

Generally, there are a number of rules for avoiding violence in prison. Much of this is embedded as the "convict code" (for example, Sykes and Messinger, 1960; Ross and Richards, 2002: 72). This mainly involves being overly polite, taking your turn, being aware of your surroundings and personal security, and not ratting out another prisoner (that is, becoming a prison informer/snitch). This also means avoiding gambling, drugs, and alcohol.

Con bosses, trustees, and peacekeepers

In some DOCs, the administration has experimented with the use of convicts policing other inmates. Unfortunately, in the more extreme instances, the newly arrived convicts enter a system resembling indentured servitude where the power of the trustee is absolute. Encouraging inmate participation and input in the administration and management of correctional facilities is, in principle at least, a sound idea.

However, the existence of con bosses, prison trustees, or what in California are known as prison *peacekeepers,* is almost always doomed to fail (Marquez and Thompson, 2006). The history of American corrections has numerous examples of prisoners given the power to police other inmates, and in almost all cases, this practice encourages corruption, intimidation, and violence, and reinforces cruel and unusual punishment at the hands of fellow inmates (Dilulio, 1987). In the late 2000s, for example, the California Department of Corrections abolished the prison peacekeeper model and moved to a more impartial method of ensuring inmate compliance and mediation on the tiers, cellblocks, and yards of its prisons.

Separating known enemies or rival gang members

Correctional facilities are obligated to ensure that inmates who have difficulties that have led to or may lead to violent encounters with each other are not kept in the same cell or cellblock. Oftentimes, this potential challenge is identified during classification (see Chapter 6). But scores are not only settled by individuals who know each other. Occasionally, there is a contract set up for the assault or murder of another inmate. If the facility was aware of this, then moving one of the two individuals from harm's reach would make sense.

Reducing the possibility of riots

Given the devastating effects of riots, it is understandable that experts have conducted research on how to best resolve them. Useem et al. (1995), for example, conducted an in-depth study concerning how major riots in U.S. prisons were successfully ended. They place these into three stages: pre-riot, actual riot, and post-riot. Before this kind of violence takes place, prison administrators are advised to ensure that their prisons have a riot plan that includes "command structure with well-defined lines of authority," clear instructions on the use of force and weapons, interagency cooperation that specifies each agency's responsibilities, and proper training. In order to "prevent and deal with riots," the correctional facility must provide adequate supervision of staff in connection with "security practices," "ensure security of the physical plant and equipment," encourage staff to pay attention to "false clues" and to communicate this information to superiors, and use a combination of force, negotiations, and strategies that range from immediate use of force to waiting until inmate leaders are ready to negotiate. Unfortunately, similar research has not been conducted on the convict side of the equation. Finally, prison officials also have to provide opportunities for inmates to blow off steam, like yard time, a gym, or a library. This may quell some tendencies to engage in violence including riots.

Correctional officer violence

The problem

The prison staff periodically uses physical violence, including less than lethal force (for example, pepper spray and TASER guns) against convicts (Pratt et al., 1999). COs are allowed by law to use force when life and property are in peril. Additionally, most correctional systems require their officers to be trained in and to follow the "continuum of force" model, a range of appropriate responses to inmates who are uncooperative and disobedient, including physical presence, verbal commands, and show of force through officer presence. Within this model, violence should be the last resort rather than the method of first choice.

When officers do beat convicts, it is often out of retaliation, because they have attacked an officer or have instigated work strikes, riots, or escape attempts. Occasionally, COs have been accused and convicted of torture (Kerness and Ehehosi, 2001). When staff violence does occur, the perpetrators try to be discreet in their actions in order to minimize witnesses. If force is necessary, it often takes place when the COs have power in numbers. In the FBOP, for example, each institution has a Special Operations Response Team (SORT) (pejoratively referred to by inmates as the *goon squad* or Ninja Turtles). This group typically consists of five officers and one lieutenant. They are used when inmates refuse to get out of their cells, in what is typically called a cell extraction. The most important question with respect to violence by COs is: How frequently is it used, and is it done in an indiscriminate manner? Unfortunately, empirical research on this behavior is scant.

COs do not need to use violence to get convicts to follow orders, rules, procedures, and policies. They typically achieve their authority through five bases of power (that is, legitimate, coercive, reward, expert, and referent). The two most important ones to motivate prisoners are legitimate and expert power (for example, Hepburn, 1985). Most often, COs will avoid using violence if they can. To begin with, most prisoners are in better physical condition than most COs. Additionally, there is a strong likelihood that other inmates will come to the assistance of the inmate being beaten.

Moreover, violence creates extensive ill will that is remembered for a long time. Instead, COs will rely on threats and other nonphysical shows of power. Unlike the violence inflicted by the cons on each other, most CO violence is more subtle. If they dislike an inmate, COs, either alone or in a group, may engage in several disrespectful actions. These include:

- *Denying privileges.* COs may refuse convicts access to the telephone, trips to the infirmary, or they may strictly control the amount of toilet paper they can use or when they can get a new roll.
- *Confiscating possessions.* COs will take correspondence from and pictures of loved ones, including children, partners, or spouses, as well as sheets, clothing, food, and legal papers.
- *Destroying belongings.* This may include tearing up mail, artwork, books, and educational material (usually under the guise of a cell search).
- *Playing with the temperature.* Prisons can refuse to turn up the heat in the winter or leave the air conditioners off in the summer.
- *Placing inmates who hate each other in the same cell.* COs can move inmates who hate each other into the same tier, cellblock, or cell. Convicts may be moved into cells with individuals that the COs know are sadistic or have a vendetta against the person in question. This situation may lead to an assault or homicide. Although the CO may have to account for this "error in judgment," there is always the possibility they will use the defense of plausible deniability.
- *Repeatedly tossing (searching) cells.* Cells can be frequently searched and/ or this can be done when it is most inconvenient for the prisoner. In the middle of the night, while prisoners are sleeping, COs may turn beds over, dumping prisoners on the floor. The COs might drag convicts to the floor, handcuff them, and go through all their personal effects while searching for weapons and contraband items (Kalinich, 1986).[5] And, in the process, the con might be hurt; their head or other parts of their body may hit the walls, doors or bars on cells.
- *Repeated strip-searching of inmates.* Strip searches, ostensibly used to detect drugs, weapons, and other forms of contraband, can be another form of intimidation. If they want, COs can order inmates to be searched numerous times a day (Ross and Richards, 2002).
- *Frequently transferring inmates to different facilities.* Often referred to as diesel therapy, some inmates frequently ride the prison bus or van for weeks on end from one institution to another. In these situations, they do not eat or sleep well, and their health often deteriorates.

Solutions

Increasingly over the years, DOCs have been sensitized to and have started training their officers in the previously mentioned use of force continuum. This specifies when and how correctional force can be applied to inmates. In general, this method allows officers to use force only after all other methods have been exhausted. Also the proper training of officers in the use of force has had some effect on lessening excessive force against inmates. Having a use of force policy that is handled through a grievance procedure is a viable solution to conflict resolution. A considerable amount of use of force by COs reflects the fact that the senior management is not being appropriately attentive or simply looking the other way when problems arise (Hemmens and Atherton, 2000).

Over the past three decades, as a partial solution to this problem, many DOCs have begun using video surveillance technology to monitor both inmate and prison officer activities. This equipment is purported to be fail safe. However, creative COs can find places to assault inmates where no cameras have been located. Additionally, if a cell extraction is about to be performed, COs will often videotape it in case the inmate initiates a legal suit where the procedures are called into question.

Regardless of the perpetrator or victim, we also need better mechanisms to capture the data on violence behind bars (Gibbons and de Katzenbach, 2006: 13). In fact, just like the practice in some daycare centers in the United States, surveillance may act as a deterrent if webcams are installed in selected parts of the prison and families are allowed access to see what is going on from a remote location.

Passive aggressive behavior

Prisoners have several creative ways to resist authority. Many of these methods, in prison slang called *slow playing,* are similar to what a child going through the "terrible twos" stage may do when they get stubborn. One slow playing approach is to comply with direct orders but to do so very slowly or poorly. For example, when an officer tells a group of cons to paint a corridor, what under normal circumstances should take a day may end up requiring a week. In other words, convicts carry out the order in such a manner as to anger the officer. Alternatively, inmates might ignore an officer and pretend to be hard of hearing. This typically frustrates the officer (Lerner, 2002).

At other times, convicts may refuse a CO's direct order, such as to get out of their cells. In this case, the COs might perform a cell extraction. Most forced removals involve the participation of a number of COs wearing riot gear and the occasional use of less than lethal weapons, like pepper spray. These procedures are also now commonly carried out with one of the COs videoing the event, in case an inmate files a grievance or initiates a civil suit for damages incurred during this procedure.

Another more involved action is for prisoners to file writs, motions, lawsuits, and class action suits. Administrators and officers consider jailhouse lawyers to be some of the most dangerous people in prisons because they know how to write legal motions and bring them before a court. At the very least, even if the convicts are denied satisfaction through legal proceedings, they may succeed in tying up the DOC's resources, possibly intimidating and embarrassing the prison authorities, and communicating with the outside about the conditions of confinement (Thomas, 1988).

In most lockups and prisons, COs are quick to state that the majority of inmates do not get into trouble as a result of following the rules. The problem population comprises approximately 1% of the prisoners in an institution. When there is an incident, such as a stabbing on a tier, COs cannot place all of the suspects on administrative segregation (aka *the hole*). COs can try to investigate the incident, but rarely can they prove the identity of the culprit/s.

Gangs

Some jails, prisons, and penitentiaries appear as if they are literally run by gangs (Stastny and Tyrnauer, 1982; Camp and Camp, 1985). Even if convicts want to "do their own time" and be left alone, there are strong pressures to join a gang for self- and mutual protection. In situations like these, unaffiliated individuals are subject to routine victimization, and they may not be able to defend themselves. Gang members may coerce, extort, or steal material possessions or services from convicts. Sometimes this is done when inmates conduct a cell invasion, by running en masse into the victim's cell and grabbing anything of value (Hassine, 2002).

Prison gangs typically coalesce around race, ethnicity, nationality, and neighborhood. One of the most common distinctions is among the African American, Hispanic, and white gangs that dominate many correctional facilities. Gang members basically "hang together." This means eating as a group in the cafeteria, walking the yard together, pumping iron (lifting weights), and sticking close to each other at work assignments or in housing units. The loners – the inmates lacking social skills or friends and/or suffering from a mental illness – and those who are physically weak are vulnerable to being physically attacked or preyed upon (American Correctional Association, 1993; Ross and Richards, 2002).

The different types

A number of ethnic and race-based prison gangs exist (American Correctional Association, 1993). In these milieus, there is often considerable diversity. In terms of the African American gangs, prisons have been havens for members of the Black Guerrilla Family, the Bloods, the Crips, and the Vice Lords. Hispanic and Latino gangs have included the Neta and Latin Kings, which are predominantly Puerto Rican and Hispanic, and the Mexican Mafia and La Nuestra Familia, which are mainly Mexican American. White gangs include the Aryan Brotherhood, Dirty White Boys, Hells Angels, and Outlaws. Some, like the Colombians (many of whom are affiliated with the drug cartels), are multiracial, which makes trying to identify groups based solely on skin color difficult. Nonetheless, the gang members often share similar mannerisms, language, and styles of dress.

Most of these organizations have long histories. Gang membership often evolves and spreads geographically. In the California institutions, some of the Blue Bird Gang and Hells Angels of San Quentin (motorcycle gangs) eventually evolved into the white supremacist Aryan Brotherhood. The black gangs of the 1970s, like the Crips and the Bloods, first started in Los Angeles. They soon spread to other cities in California, then made their way across the Midwest to the East Coast, where they became established in New York City, Boston, and Philadelphia (Moore, 1978).

The public in general think that gang members are teenagers and young adults, but gangs, in fact, include all different age groups, ranging from junior gangsters and gang warriors (that is, "gang bangers") to older gang members (Klein, 1997). These groups also include "wannabes," associates (that is, family or friends who are loosely connected to the members), and auxiliaries (that is, girlfriends and wives, etc). A few senior members may even manage established legitimate businesses that employ high-powered accountants and lawyers, and they may have the resources to buy judges, politicians, and their way out of prison. Ultimately, gangs are a form of organized crime (Lavigne, 1989). Gangs also vary based on their level of sophistication.

Some gangs exist primarily for economic gain (focusing on business activities, like selling drugs, theft of goods, and extortion), while others are formed for mutual self-protection, and some gangs are more violent than others. Prison gang culture is often an extension of street life into the penitentiary. Traditions learned in the ghetto or barrio are often "imported" into correctional facilities (Irwin and Cressey, 1962).

Gang affiliation will typically depend on the region of the country in which convicts have to do time. For example, in Illinois and New York, a disproportionate number of Hispanic gangs, such as the Latin Kings and the Vice Lords, or black gangs, such as El Rukin and Black Gangster Disciples, are part of the criminal element. In Florida, you may see Puerto Rican gangs like the Nietas and 27s. In California and Texas, correctional facilities house the Mexican Mafia, Texas Syndicate, Texas M, and Texas Family among other gangs. Much like political parties, gangs have different factions or divisions. In the Mexican organizations, for instance, there are both urban and rural components.

Joining a gang

Gangs recruit new members on the street, in jails and in prisons, and they have colonized many state and federal penitentiaries (Hagedorn, 1988). A gang may serve as a surrogate family providing social and emotional needs for its members, both on the street and in prison. In fact, some members refer to their gang as their family.

Joining a gang carries many obligations and responsibilities, including participating in feuds, revenge, and retaliation against rival factions. These conflicts may extend from the "hood" to the penitentiary and may last for years. One important aspect of all gang affiliations is respect. Young people who

Exhibit 5.1

Film

American Me (1992)

The Hollywood movie (released in 1992) portrayed the problems of contemporary Mexican American prison gangs, in particular the Mexican Mafia (MM), also known as *La eMe* or (eMe for short), how they operated, the power struggles inside the group, and how they coped with drugs, family, and prison life. Based on the true story of Santana (played by actor James Edward Olmos), a young Mexican American individual who rises from juvenile street criminal to respected leader of an East Los Angeles gang that had members both in well-known California prisons such as Folsom State and in the barrios of the major urban centers in California. During his first incarceration in juvenile hall, Santana kills a rapist and garners the respect of his fellow inmates. He starts La Clique (the gang) as an emerging adult, and the group quickly gains power and competes against other Mexican and Chicano gangs, White supremacist gangs, and the African American gangs. In prison, members are recruited, sell drugs, and in some instances are obligated to kill traitors or liabilities. Loyalty to the gang is placed above family obligations. A considerable amount of activity in the film takes place around the prison yard, in the cells, and beyond the watchful eyes of the COs.

grow up in inner-city neighborhoods want to be respected and not "dissed" (Anderson, 1999). And the way respect is usually displayed in the ghetto and barrios is through style (for example, Ferrell, 1993; Ferrell and Sanders, 1995; Miller, 1995), by the clothes you wear, the money you spend, the car you drive, and the violence you engage in. In the prisons, gang members are recognizable by the ways in which they carry themselves, including altering their uniforms and sharing their food and contraband, and by the individuals they hang out with in the chow hall and yard (Bourgois, 2002).

Gang members often expect to go to prison. When they go to a correctional facility, they try to make themselves comfortable. This means that they want new uniforms that are sharply pressed and as many amenities that they are allowed to have in their cells. Some want a locker full of cigarettes and commissary food. Some want nothing more than to watch sports channels like ESPN every day, all day.

How they work

Gangs are organized to carry out business, not only on the street, but also in prison. They are heavily involved in bringing contraband into the penitentiary. These items typically include alcohol, cell phones, cigarettes, condoms, currency, drugs (that is, dope), tobacco, tattooing materials, and nicotine patches. These are components of the "inmate economy" and are used for exchange.

Gangs employ a variety of methods to get contraband into prisons. One way is to have visitors bring the prohibited items into the visiting room. Another method is to throw them over the wall or fence in a tennis ball or to use slingshots to propel the projectile. Another method is airdrops, in which drugs are released from small airplanes or drones that fly over the institution at night (Ross and Richards, 2002).

Gang members may also recruit or coerce COs to bring contraband into prison. They may compromise the COs by threatening to report any deviant or illegal behavior they observe or hear about. This includes seeing them drinking alcohol on the job, appearing intoxicated, doing drugs, or having sex with a prisoner. Alternatively, a convict may successfully threaten an officer's family by finding out where they live. Still, some COs – because they are paid so little or want to make extra money – smuggle contraband into the institution (see, for example, Toobin, 2014).

In many prisons, it is not uncommon to find that some gangs focus heavily on sports betting. Since the standard currency in prison is a carton of cigarettes or postage stamps, this is usually the minimum bet placed. On the other hand, convicted dope dealers, who are used to "living large" and having a lot of money, may bet $10,000 to $20,000 on a game. The loser will need to have the money sent in from the outside. If they are lucky, their partner, relative, or friend will arrange to have the money put on their commissary account. Then they will be required to go to the commissary and purchase items on a regular basis to pay off their gambling debt. Alternatively, if someone owes $1,000, they may have a buddy on the street pay it to the gang on the outside (Ross and Richards, 2002).

Finally, a gang may convince new members or wannabes (who do not have a criminal record) to apply for a job as a CO with the state DOCs. Some jurisdictions appear so desperate to hire and have such low qualification requirements that they will employ anyone who does not have a felony conviction. If hired, the person then acts as the go-between to smuggle drugs and other forms of contraband into the prison (Hagedorn, 1988). In short, gangs typically increase the amount of violence behind bars and compromise inmate and CO safety.

Solutions

Many prison systems have tried to implement gang prevention programs. Most DOCs educate COs in how to identify gangs (Gaston, 1996; Valentine and Schober, 2000; Boyd, 2009; Winterdyk and Ruddell, 2010). According to Ruddell et al., (2006), "[t]he types of interventions that a jail or prison develop are likely to depend on the number of organizational characteristics, such as size of the facility, the internal and external resources that the institution can draw on, and the nature of the gang problem" (36). The following outlines some of the more common approaches to gang management.

During classification, for example, DOCs try to determine membership and, if possible, to separate gang members from the general population so that they do not threaten other inmates, by sometimes placing them in administrative segregation (Fong, Vogel, and Buentello, 1992). "Texas has gone even further in its attempts to control gangs. Managers have designated gang intelligence officers in each prison who gather gang-related information and identify gang members and leadership. Active cooperation in the sharing of information with other" criminal justice jurisdictions minimizes gangs' ability to recruit new members, and organize behind bars (Freeman, 1999: 70).

Other options are to place gang leaders in Supermax prisons, where they will have no or minimal contact with fellow inmates.

Gang treatment and rehabilitation is another option. Occasionally, DOCs institute these kinds of programs. For example, in 1993, the Hampden County Correctional Institution in Massachusetts tried the following. After segregating gang members, the DOC then put them through a cognitive training program (Toller and Tsagaris, 1996a; 1996b). In some state prison systems, like those in New York, programs led by inmates have been implemented. The Alternatives to Violence Program (AVP), which started in 1975, is run by lifers who hold workshops and teach younger inmates about the causes of violence, how it can escalate, and how to avoid it.

Sexual assault

Most people who are sent to prison fear being raped (Lockwood, 1980; Rideau, 1992; Human Rights Watch, 2001). Undoubtedly, there is both consensual and coerced sex in prison. These practices are also complicated by male prostitution. Nevertheless, sexual assault is rarely about physical attraction or gratification; it is about violence, politics, power, and business. Some convicts routinely and habitually exploit others sexually. When in prison, some convicts or groups of cons try to coerce fish (the new arrivals), using fear and/or violence to force them into sexual submission. Surrendering puts a fish at the mercy of the violent thugs. If new cons resist, this stance may become a source of challenge for rapists, while victims may risk serious injury (and they might be raped regardless) or even be killed.

Solutions

Experienced prisoners suggest that, in the long run, for physical safety and psychological peace of mind, resistance is the best course of action. Cons must demonstrate with tough talk and threatening behavior that they are prepared to defend themselves and that anyone who assaults them will pay a price. Most sexual predators generally make cost–benefit calculations and will almost always go for the easy mark rather than the hard target. One of the solutions for individuals who are raped or fear being sexually assaulted, especially if they are homosexuals, is to place them in administrative segregation. This action has a number of advantages and disadvantages. One of the drawbacks is the fact that once sent there they will get labeled, and if they want to eventually return to a regular cellblock, they will have a difficult time not appearing like a pariah.

Some of the means through which prison systems deal with cons' pent-up sexual frustration and alienation are the use of extended family visits/conjugal visits and furloughs (Lockwood, 1980). Another strategy is stiffer sanctions. These practices may not, however, stem the problem of prison rape. Again, these are token programs, available in few institutions and for only a handful of prisoners.

Conjugal visits

Few prison systems allow conjugal visits. If they are permitted, it is only for prisoners with no *shots* (that is, disciplinary reports) who are living in minimum-security correctional facilities and who are *getting short* (within a year of release) (Hensley et al., 2002; Hensley et al., 2002). Typically, a conjugal visit may last eight hours, one day, or a weekend if it involves family and children. Conjugal visits are allowed in nine states.

> [The very first] program began in South Carolina in the late 1800s. In 1918, the Mississippi State Penitentiary at Parchman, initially an all-black penal farm, began allowing wives to visit. But for half a century, only those two states allowed conjugal visits. Then, in 1968, they were joined by California. Other states soon followed, and in 1980 Washington State, for the first time, allowed wives to spend the night in its prisons. (Hallinan, 2003: 133)

In the Washington state program, "Twice a month they come for a visit, which takes place in one of six trailers on the reformatory grounds. The trailers are essentially fully furnished mobile homes intended, as much as possible, to mimic an apartment in the outside world. There are bedrooms, bathrooms – even a small kitchenette for family meals" (135).

Hallinan adds, "There is little statistical evidence that family visitation programs work, largely because they have gone unstudied . ... In the absence of statistics, the only way to judge the program is through anecdote and experience" (Hallinan, 2003: 134). The results of what little research has been done on the effect of conjugal visits are divided with respect to their impact on both homosexual behavior and sexual assaults in prison (Hensley et al., 2002; Hensley et al., 2002). Still, most correctional facilities have discontinued conjugal visits, so the prisoners must make do with what sexual relief they might get by breaking the visiting room rules (Ross and Richards, 2002).

Furloughs

Some prisons grant furloughs, which enable prisoners to go home for a couple of days to be with their spouses and families. Convicts can be either accompanied by COs or unaccompanied. A furlough is a temporary release of an inmate from a facility. A few correctional institutions for women actually maintain a residence on the grounds so mothers can spend a weekend with their children, but no men are allowed.

Stiffer legislation and sanctions

Since the passage of the Prison Rape Elimination Act (PREA) of 2003, the federal government is taking the issue of male rape in prison more seriously. The $60 million that was earmarked for this Bill enabled the Department of Justice's BJS to conduct a two-year survey, which was administered in state and federal prisons, concerning the pervasiveness of sexual assault. One of the results of this initiative was a report produced by the Washington, D.C.-based Urban Institute (Zweig et al., 2006), which involved a survey and analysis of state correctional administrators to determine what sorts of programs or changes they had implemented in the area of rape prevention in correctional facilities. The authors of the report found initiatives in the areas of policy development, prevention, investigation and prosecution, victim services, staff training, incident documentation, collaboration with other entities, and opportunities for additional funding. Since then additional research, training and technical assistance, grants to states, and "the development of national standards for the prevention, investigation and prosecution of prison rape" have occurred (Smith, 2008). Implementation of PREA, however, has been slow at best (Thompson et al., 2008).

Supermax prisons as a solution to prison violence

Over the past decade, correctional systems at the state and federal levels have introduced or expanded the use of Supermax prisons (Suedfeld, 1974; Rogers, 1993; Kurki and Morris, 2001; Toch, 2001; Ross, 2007). These facilities – also known as Special (or Security) Handling (or Housing) Units (SHUs) or Control Handling Units (CHUs) – are stand-alone correctional institutions, or wings or annexes inside an already existing prison. They are known for their strict lockdown policies, lack of amenities, and use of prisoner isolation techniques. Escapes from Supermaxes are so rare that they are statistically inconsequential.

Supermax prisons in the United States

Since the 1990s, almost every state in the United States has either a stand-alone Supermax facility, or has it as an annex, wing, or tier of an existing correctional facility. Not only do the individual states have these kinds of units, but in 1994, the federal government opened its first Supermax prison in Florence, Colorado, and the facility was dubbed the "Alcatraz of the Rockies" (Ross, 2013b). Supermax prisons are a result of the recent growth in incarceration that has occurred throughout many of the world's advanced industrialized countries (Toch, 2001)

Part of the reason for the proliferation of this kind of correctional facility is the conservative political ideology that started during U.S. President Ronald Reagan's administration (1981–9). During the 1980s, as a response to the increase in the public's fear of crime, a progressively punitive agenda guided criminal justice and led to an increased number of people incarcerated in all types of prisons. This approach was continued by Reagan's Republican successor, George H. W. Bush (1989–93). Originally designed to house the most violent, hardened, and escape-prone criminals, today's Supermaxes are increasingly used for persistent rule-breakers, convicted leaders of criminal organizations (for example, the Mafia) and gangs, serial killers, and political criminals (for example, spies and terrorists) (for example, Suedfeld et al., 1982; Barak-Glantz, 1983; National Institute of Corrections, 1997; Riveland, 1998; Lovell et al., 2000; Neal, 2002; Bruton, 2004). In some states, the criteria for admission into a Supermax facility and the review of prisoners' time inside are very informal or even nonexistent.

Number of convicts in Supermax facilities

The number of convicts being sent to Supermax prisons is growing. The Supermaxes, maintained by the FBOP in Marion, Illinois, and Florence, Colorado, for example, "incarcerate approximately 1,500 people" (www.bop. gov/locations/weekly_report.jsp, July 20, 2007), including such infamous criminals as "Unabomber" Ted Kaczynski and Oklahoma City bombing co-conspirator Terry Nichols. Nevertheless, only a fraction of those incarcerated in state and federal prisons are sent to a Supermax facility. In 1998, approximately 20,000 inmates were locked up in this type of prison, representing less than 2% of all the men and women who are currently incarcerated across the country.

Conditions of confinement

One of the more notable features of all Supermax prisons is that prisoners are typically locked down 23 out of 24 hours a day. Other than supervision by COs, inmates have virtually no contact with other people (fellow convicts or visitors). Access to phones and mail is strictly and closely supervised or restricted. Supermax prisoners have very limited access to privileges such as watching television or listening to the radio.

Supermax prisons also generally do not allow inmates to either work or congregate during the day.[6] In addition, there is absolutely no personal privacy; everything the convicts do is monitored, usually through a surveillance camera that is continuously on. Communication with the COs normally takes place through a narrow window in the steel door of the cell and/or via an intercom system. Although cells vary in size and construction, in general, they are 12 by 7 feet in dimension. A cell light (called a nightlight) may remain on all night long, and furnishings consist of a bed, a desk, and a stool made out of concrete, and a stainless steel sink and toilet. Despite these simple facilities and the fact that prisoners' rehabilitation is not encouraged (and is next to impossible in these conditions), Supermax prisons are more expensive to build and run.

In Supermaxes, inmates rarely have access to educational or religious materials or services. Almost all toiletries (for example, toothpaste, shaving cream, and razors) are strictly controlled (Hallinan, 2003). When inmates are removed from their cells, they typically have to kneel down with their backs to the door. Then they are required to place their hands through the slot, a 12-by-8-inch hole in the door, and are then handcuffed.

Effects of Supermax incarceration

All told, the isolation, lack of meaningful activity, and shortage of human contact take their toll on each prisoner's psychological well-being. Supermax inmates often develop severe psychological disorders, including delusions and hallucinations, which may have long-term negative effects (Grassian, 1983; Grassian and Friedman, 1986; Haney, 1993; Haney and Lynch, 1997; Zinger et al., 2001; Briggs et al., 2003; Gibbons and de Katzenbach, 2006: 54–6).

It is difficult for reporters and scholars to gain access to prisoners, COs, and administrators. Correctional professionals are reluctant to talk with outsiders for fear that they may be unnecessarily subjected to public scrutiny. Likewise, we do not have comprehensive psychological data on individuals kept in these facilities. Fortunately though, numerous reports have documented the effects of this kind of incarceration. The conditions inside Supermax prisons have led several corrections and human rights experts and organizations (for example, Amnesty International and the American Civil Liberties Union) to question whether these prisons are a violation of (1) the Eighth Amendment of the U.S. Constitution, which prohibits the state from engaging in cruel and unusual punishment, and/or (2) the European Convention on Human Rights and the United Nations' Universal Declaration of Human Rights, which were established to protect the rights of not only people living in the free world, but also those behind bars. Supermax prisons have plenty of downsides, and not just for the inmates. Some people have suggested that Supermax facilities are simply part of the correctional industrial complex (for example, Christie, 1993/1994). Most of the Supermaxes in the United States are brand new or nearly so. Others are simply freestanding prisons that were retrofitted. According to a study by the Urban Institute, the annual per-cell cost of a Supermax is about $75,000, compared to $25,000 for each cell in an ordinary state prison (Mears, 2006).

We have plenty of super-expensive Supermax facilities – two thirds of the states now have them. But they were designed when crime was considered a growing problem, and now we have a lower violent crime rate that shows no real sign of a turn for the worse. However, as good as these prisons are at keeping our worst offenders in check, the purpose of the Supermax is in flux.

Cracks in the armor

No self-respecting state director of corrections or correctional planner will admit that the Supermax concept was a mistake. And one would be wrong to think that these prisons can be replaced by something drastically less costly. However, correctional experts are beginning to realize that just like a shrinking city that finds itself with too many schools or firehouses, the Supermax model must be made more flexible in order to justify its size and budget.

One solution is for these facilities to incarcerate different types of prisoners. In May 2006, for example, Wisconsin DOC officials announced that over the past 16 years, the state's Supermax facility in Boscobel – built at a cost of $47.5 million (in 1990) and with a capacity of 500 inmates – has consistently stood at 100 cells less than its capacity. It now houses maximum-security prisoners – serious offenders, but a step down from the worst of the worst. This shift in policy increases the utility of the Supermax and perhaps justifies its expense.

In the history of the Maryland prison system, for instance, there have been two Supermax prisons. The very first Supermax was called the Maryland Correctional Adjustment Center (MCAC), otherwise known as the Baltimore Supermax. Although planning for this institution had been on the books since 1972, the state lacked the finances to go ahead with this decision. Both the stabbing to death of Officer Herman Toulson in 1984, and the state recognizing that it had difficulty controlling inmates who were disproportionately violent, particularly those who had life sentences, were the needed catalysts for accelerating the allocation of funds for the construction of MCAC (Mears, 2006: 15–16). Construction began in 1986 and the facility was opened in 1989 (16). MCAC was located among the other downtown correctional facilities, including the City Detention Center, Central Booking, the Penitentiary, and the Diagnostic Center.

Modeled after the USP Marion, the first modern federal Supermax, it housed Maryland's worst criminals. With a capacity for 288 inmates, the Supermax opened at a cost of $21 million. Over time, MCAC evolved into a complex institution, housing not only the most incorrigible of Maryland's inmates, but also the state's death row and federal pre-trial detainees. In the fall of 2003, the Supermax had 13 death row inmates. The prison also had a contract with the U.S. Marshals to hold federal detainees.

In 1994, Federal investigators tried to get access to the prison but were repeatedly denied. During that time, approximately 70 convicts were transferred out. The Department of Justice (DOJ) threatened to sue the Maryland Division of Corrections (MDOC). The DOJ was finally allowed inside in May and June of 1995 (Gavora, 1996). In response to the DOJ investigation, the therapeutic model returned. The MDOC sent staff to the Colorado State Penitentiary in Canon City to study their Supermax program in order to make changes.

In 2010, in addition to the reasons listed above, complaints regarding continuous incidents of disorder, staff problems, and costs increased. MCAC inmates were transferred to the North Branch Correctional Institution, the state's new Supermax facility near Cumberland, Maryland. MCAC was renamed the Chesapeake Detention Facility, and although it is still owned by the government of Maryland, it now houses federal pre-trial detainees.

Converting cells is one approach to dealing with a lack of appropriate inmates for Supermaxes but not the only one. Other ideas include building more regional Supermaxes, jointly administered by neighboring jurisdictions, and filling them by shifting populations from other states. This would allow state DOCs to completely empty out a given Supermax, and then close it down or convert it to another use. There is also the possibility that some elements of the Supermax model could be combined with the approaches of traditional prisons, creating a hybrid that could serve a wider population. However, different types of prisoners would have to be kept well away from each other, a logistical problem of no small concern.

Prison litigation

Beginning in the 1960s and running throughout the last four decades, there has been an increase of lawsuits brought forth by/against correctional facilities and prison systems. Relying on different amendments to the U.S. Constitution, prisoners, activist lawyers, and judges have passed numerous important legal reforms concerning prison conditions and practices. Referencing notions of civil rights based in the First, Fourth, Fifth, Sixth, Eighth, and Fourteenth Amendments, prisoners in state facilities have won important victories.

Several landmark cases have been passed including, *Trop v. Dulles*, *Guthrie v. Evans* and *Ruiz v. Estelle*. These success stories, however, do not mean that the practice of corrections is in step with judicial mandates. Why? Many policies and practices that have been banned are, for one reason or another, still in practice to varying degrees (Chilton, 1991: chapter 8).

Moreover, efforts to remedy prison conditions, by using the legal system, have been challenged at the federal level through the passage of legislation such as the Prison Litigation Reform Act (PLRA) (1996). This law is an attempt to frustrate the courts' ability to provide relief to prisoners, correctional institutions, and systems. The PLRA states that the courts "shall not grant or approve any prospective relief unless the court finds that such relief is narrowly drawn, extends no further than necessary to correct the violation of the federal right, and is the least intrusive means necessary to correct the violation of the federal right" (18. U.S.C. para. 3626a(1)A)

Conclusion

Inmates feel the brunt of prison conditions. Most people do not willingly go to jail or prison because they fear having to live for an extended period of time in the terrible conditions inside. The general public believe that harsh prison conditions are appropriate to serve as deterrents and punishments for individuals who engage in crime. However, if anything reigns true about deterrence and prisons, it is that the empirical findings are specious.

Likewise, prison administrators' willingness to allow the news media access to correctional facilities reflects the extent to which they believe that they are doing a proper job and that their prisons may act as a deterrent to potential criminals or delinquent youth entering the system.

Key terms
Acquired Immunity Defense Syndrome (AIDS): Contagious disease that suppresses the body's ability to fight illness. Passed through bodily fluids. Prevalent in homosexuals, drug addicts, diabetics.

Cell extraction: When correctional officers unannounced and forcefully remove an inmate from his/her cell typically to search the cell for contraband.

Commissary: Sells basic items to prisoners such as food, clothing, stationary, toiletries. Money for items is taken from the prisoner's account.

Conjugal visit: Temporary visit of spouse (and family) on correctional facility premises.

Dirty protest: An inmate spreads his own feces all over his body. COs (and other prisoners) are then reluctant to touch the inmate. This is particularly difficult in the context of a cell extraction.

Furlough: Prisoners allowed to go home for a short period of time to be with spouse or family.

Hepatitis: Liver disease spread through bodily fluids, bad water, or spoiled food. May cause skin and eyes to turn yellow. Left untreated can cause death of person infected.

Kill zone: Prohibited part of a prison where inmates are not allowed. If convicts are discovered there, they will be shot.

Slow playing: When an inmate complies with direct orders from a CO but does it very slowly. This may frustrate the officer.

Suicide by escape: When an inmate attempts to escape knowing full well that this action will lead to his death.

Supermax prison: Stand alone correctional institutions or wings or annexes inside already existing correctional facilities. Known for their strict lockdown policies and practices, lack of amenities, and use of prisoner isolation techniques.

Tuberculosis (TB): A lung disease spread in places that are overcrowded with dirty, stale, and stagnant air.

Notes

[1] Personal correspondence with Miguel Zaldivar, June 2007.

[2] These problems are compounded when inmates are disabled and have special medical needs, like wheelchair-accessible ramps.

[3] Some scholars have argued that the food, in terms of nutritional value, is better than what many of the people in poorer countries eat.

[4] Reports vary on the number of people who died.

[5] Contraband typically includes cell phones, illegal drugs, money, and weapons, but because of recent changes, cigarettes, nicotine patches, and all tobacco products (including chewing tobacco) are also now banned.

[6] There are some exceptions, as a few Supermax prisons allow inmates to congregate during yard time.

SIX

Classification/risk assessment[1]

Introduction

Officially, prison systems use classification systems (aka *designation*) as a means to assign inmates to different security levels. Typically, the hard-core violent convicts serving long sentences are assigned to maximum-security prisons, the incorrigible prisoners serving medium-length sentences are sentenced to medium-security prisons, and the relatively lightweight prisoners serving short sentences are sentenced to minimum-security camps, farms, or community facilities. In higher security correctional facilities, inmates spend more time in cells, and there is more scrutiny over their activities. In lower security facilities, prisoners have more privileges, including free time, privacy, recreational amenities, and longer visitation hours.

Before 1980, most of the nation's prisons and jails used "subjective classification," which relies heavily on the judgment and hunches of line officers. Since then, every prison system has shifted, at least as a matter of policy, to "objective classification." These standardized and automated classification criteria "place greater emphasis on fairness, consistency, and openness in the decision-making process" (Gibbons and de Katzenbach, 2006: 29).

For some convicts, the decision where they will be sent is already made before they enter a correctional facility. In the federal system, judges may only make designation/security/ programming recommendations – only the Federal Bureau of Prisons (FBOP) can make a final designation or other correctional decision, under the constitutional separation of powers doctrine. Depending on sentencing guidelines and one's criminal history, a decision is made with respect to what security level would be most appropriate for a given convict. Where a convict is sent depends on a number of factors. Typically, the Division of Probation and Parole prepares the presentence investigation (PSI) report. In order to complete the document, the designated probation or parole officer reviews a number of factors relevant to the convicted person's circumstances, including age, education, work and criminal history. The resulting report makes a recommendation where the person should be sent, and is given to the judge and shared with the defense attorney and prosecutor. Concurrently, some well-heeled and high-profile defendants (for example, Bernie Madoff, Martha Stewart, and so on) or their loved ones may employ the services of sentencing consultants. These professionals can be located through membership organizations like the National Alliance of Sentencing and Mitigation Specialists, and the National Association of Sentencing Advocates. For a hefty fee, these specialists will prepare a report that recommends where a client should be sentenced. The defendant's attorney then gives this to the prosecutor with the hope that the judge will be influenced. The judge may or may not adopt the recommendation. In fact, they may completely ignore it regardless of the source.

Another important distinction is between external and internal classification systems. The former consists of decision-making processes used by state departments of corrections (DOC) regarding an inmate's "custody level that will determine where the prisoner will be housed" (Austin, 2003: 2). The latter refers to the judgment that is made when a convict reaches a correctional facility with respect to the "cell or housing unit, as well as which facility programs ... the prisoner will be assigned" (2).

Classification of inmates serves many functions for the DOCs and the individual correctional institutions. In general, this process determines the facility and security level to which a person will be assigned. This may facilitate the rehabilitation of the person, and protect convicts and correctional officers (COs) from being hurt by an inmate who should be at a higher-security correctional institution (that is, one does not want the wrong person in a facility). Classification also saves taxpayer money because sending too many prisoners to higher security prisons, which are more costly to operate, drains the DOC's scarce resources (Clements, 1996; Austin, 2003).

Typically, classification occurs at intake in a facility also commonly called the fish bowl, reception center, and/or receiving and departure.

Correctional treatment is generally assumed to begin with the classification process. Classification procedures are conducted in reception units located within the prisons or special reception and classification centers at another location. Classification committees, reception-diagnostic centers, or community classification teams sometimes perform these processes. The purpose of classification varies among institutions, but basically it is expected to help with inmate management or treatment planning efforts (Allen and Simonsen, 2001: 245).

Classification officers and case managers are typically civilians, called noncustodial personnel, who usually hold university degrees. In the FBOP, classification is done by case agents. Classification was formerly done by regional designators operating from each regional office, but this task has now been consolidated in the new central center in Grand Prairie, Texas. Although

---

Exhibit 6.1.

Classics in corrections

Patricia van Voorhis' *Psychological Classification of the Male Adult Prisoner* (1994)

This is the most well-known book on prisoner classification. The researcher examined five different classification systems, using the FBOP-approved psychological test and tracking the outcomes of a specific group of prisoners for six months. Van Voorhis discovered that

> there are compelling psychological differences among inmates
> with regard to their experiences of the prison environment. These
> differences influence most of the important aspects of prison life,
> including communication and interactions with others, participation
> in prison programs, stress, fear, and vulnerability, as well as the
> difficulties inmates pose to others. ... These differences can be
> identified systematically. (261)

Since the publication of this book, these classification tools have been integrated into other more popular systems including, LSI-R, LSI-SV, AIMS, and AICS.

---

intake procedures differ, convicts typically arrive scared, hungry, exhausted, and wearing handcuffs, belly chains, and leg irons. Standing in line, they are ordered to strip, are searched and then sprayed or dusted with delousing chemical, issued institution-approved clothes, and finally ordered to submit to a battery of medical and psychological examinations administered by COs, who are easily confused with medical staff. Convicts call this *kicking the tires*.

The new prisoners may spend weeks or months at the reception center, housed in cells or dormitories. Eventually, they are ordered to a classification meeting where an officer announces their official security level and prison assignment. Some time later they are transported to their new home – a penitentiary, prison, or camp. In many systems, classification is a two-part process. The first one selects the specific correctional facility. Once an inmate is transferred there, it is then determined which program best suits them (for example, work, counseling, academic or vocational, or special treatment) (Allen and Simonsen: 288).

Depending on the correctional system, prisoner classification is typically reviewed one or more times a year. In the FBOP, this is called a *team meeting*. A prisoner with a major disciplinary report may be reclassified very quickly, and transferred to administrative segregation (the hole), or cuffed and transported to a higher security prison. To no surprise, being reclassified to lower security takes more time, is rarely initiated by staff, and may require repeated requests by the inmate and/or their attorney.

FBOP prisoner classification

Classification levels

The number of classification levels varies from one correctional system to another and is subject to change based on a number of factors, including overcrowding and new facilities coming on line (that is, being built and completed). In order to get a sense of the complexities of classification, the FBOP classification levels are reviewed below. The FBOP has five levels, referred to as an "inmate classification system," which serves to variably segregate, protect, punish, and reward prisoners.

This is a "classification ladder," with high security in the federal system at the top and minimum security at the bottom. As prisoners complete their sentences and get "short" (which means a year to release), they might be moved to minimum-security camps or community custody. Unfortunately, most men and women move up the ladder from minimum to medium, or medium to high, rather than down. Few medium- and high-security prisoners ever make it to the camps. The classification designations have changed over the years to accommodate the growth in FBOP prisons and population. The old system had six security levels, with 6 to 5 being maximum, 4 to 2 being medium, and 1 being minimum. USP Marion (the first Supermax penitentiary) was the only level 5 institution. U.S. penitentiaries were level 5 (for example, USP Atlanta, USP Leavenworth, USP Lewisburg, and USP Lompoc); the federal correctional institutions ranged from 2 to 4 (for example, FCI Talladega, FCI Sandstone, and FCI Oxford), and the federal prison camps were 1. Security levels 2 to 6 were "in" custody, which meant inside the fence or wall. Level 1 was "out" custody, which meant they were federal camps that had penetrable security fences. Level 1 community custody referred to prisoners in camps who were eligible for community programs – work assignments or furloughs.

In the 1990s, the FBOP collapsed these six security designations into five: high, medium, low, minimum, and administrative (equivalent to high security, but reserved for detention centers with a mix of pre-trial detainees and inmates, and Federal Medical Centers (FMCs)). The FBOP prisoner population is approximately 10% high (USP), 25% medium (FCI), 35% low (FCI), and 25% minimum (FPC), with the balance not assigned a security level. Many of these unclassified men and women are in administrative facilities (medical or detention), transit, or are being held in local jails or private prisons.

Administrative refers to Administrative Detention Max (ADX) Florence (CO) (the highest security prison in the country), FTC Oklahoma City (a medium-security transport prison), and the FMCs (which may be maximum, medium, or minimum security).

The central inmate monitoring system

FBOP staff must check the Central Inmate Monitoring System (CIMS) before any prisoner is reassigned to a new cellblock, dormitory, or prison. CIMS is a computer system that tracks nine special categories of inmates:

1. "Witness Security" prisoners are government informers who have testified, are testifying, or will testify in court cases.
2. "Special Security" prisoners are prison snitches cooperating in internal investigations
3. "Sophisticated Criminal Activity" prisoners are those inmates identified as being involved in large-scale criminal conspiracies, for example, organized crime, drugs, or white collar. They may be men or women who are targets of the federal Racketeer Influence and Corrupt Organization (RICO) or Continuing Criminal Enterprise (CCE) prosecutions, which carry life sentences (Richards, 1998: 133). Many of these convicts are suspected of being connected to major drug smuggling organizations, or they have refused to plead guilty, cooperate, or inform on other persons.
4. "Threats to Government Officials" prisoners have been convicted of writing letters, making phone calls, or issuing verbal remarks that convey the intent to do bodily harm to public officials.
5. "Broad Publicity" prisoners are those inmates involved in high-profile cases.
6. "State" prisoners are inmates serving state sentences who were transferred into the federal system because they were "difficult".
7. "Separation" prisoners are those who have been moved to another institution because they are government witnesses, institutional snitches, gang leaders, or persons in danger of being killed or killing someone else.
8. "Special Supervision" prisoners are police, judges, and politicians who are provided protective privilege (Richards and Avey, 2000). These men and women are usually designated to camps (because they may be unnecessarily victimized or killed in a penitentiary).
9. "Disruptive Groups" prisoners may include members of organizations, such as street or prison gangs and political groups (for example, Black Panthers and Communists).

Regardless of the sophistication of this listing, convicts may not know they have been singled out for such attention.[2]

The problems with classification

There are several difficulties with classification (Clements, 1996). Some of these challenges are in connection with the instruments that are used, while other problems are related to the process. In terms of the instruments, many experts have suggested that the classification instruments that are used to make determinations have suffered from issues of reliability and validity. Factors typically used for determining potential for misconduct, such as drug and alcohol abuse, escape attempts, length of sentence, severity of sentence, or amount of time left in sentence, are not useful (Austin, 2003: 5). Austin notes that "although prison classification and other risk assessment instruments are now common, there is a disturbing trend that suggests that many of these systems were implemented without first being properly designed and tested" (2).

Alternatively, the classification *process* has numerous challenges, including the following: overcrowding prevents the timely transfer of inmates to suitable programs; correctional facility labor is prioritized; female prisoners are hampered by the lack of appropriate institutions; quantitative assessments are too narrow; inmate files are typically incomplete; participation in prison programs is a bad measure; disciplinary matters have a disproportionate effect on allocation; and classification may be used for unofficial purposes.

Overcrowding frustrates the process

Although in principle, classification is a valuable tool, it is frustrated by correctional facility conditions. Unfortunately, the best-laid plans often fail. One of the most problematic concerns is crowding/overcrowding. This prevents inmates from entering the educational, counseling, and vocational programs and facilities that would be best suited for them (Allen and Simonsen, 2001: 246).

Institutional job details take precedence

The day-to-day demands of running an institution and "available vacancies" often overshadow classification decisions (Allen and Simonsen: 246, 288). A convict may need more formal education so they are assigned remedial classes, but since, for example, a prisoner is a baker, and the kitchen is short of qualified personnel for that day or week, kitchen duty may be assigned instead. Other examples include:

> [A]n inmate may genuinely want to learn welding. If the welding class is filled, ... but there is a vacancy in the furniture shop, the

inmate may be assigned to the furniture shop; no effort would be made to offer additional welding instruction. Also, inmates will often be assigned to a maintenance operation, such as food service or janitorial work that is unlikely to conform to their own vocational ambitions. (288)

One of the major complicating factors involves logistics:

Institution personnel may genuinely wish to provide the recommended program for an inmate; however, the need to keep the institution going inevitably shapes decisions. Personnel may rationalize maintenance assignments on the basis that many inmates need the experience of accepting supervision, developing regular work habits, learning to relate to co-workers, and the like. All of that may be true, but the treatment staff members are no less frustrated than the inmates are when prescribed programs are ignored. (Allen and Simonsen: 289)

Women prisoners suffer the most

Women make up less than 10% of the prison population (see Chapter 7). They are usually confined in one or a few correctional facilities in each state. These prisons may hold female prisoners classified for different security levels in various sections of the same institution. Exceptions include the large states and the FBOP, where women with different security levels may be imprisoned in separate institutions. In any case, the steady increase in the incarceration of females may result in the further differentiation of women's prison.

Quantitative measures are poor indicators

There is an implicit belief that better data and statistical analysis will somehow improve things for prisoners and correctional staff alike. The problem is that convicts and COs are different constituencies, often with competing concerns. The inmates want less restrictive classification (minimum or medium security) in which they might have better living conditions (that is, more time out of cell, less restrictive family visits, better access to programs, and less violence). In comparison, prison staff may want prisoners to be housed in more restrictive environments (that is, maximum security, control units, segregation) where they are "locked in" and have little freedom of movement, thus giving the COs more control and less exposure to potential assault and injury.

Inmate files are incomplete

"Inmate files" (which usually include PSI reports, criminal offenses, and institutional reports) should not be the sole determinant of classification decisions. Simply analyzing inmate files and observing classification hearings does not allow for the exploration of the full dimensions of an individual convict's character. Ethnographic or qualitative research, on the other hand, can be used to get a better understanding of the complex issues involved (Ross and Richards, 2002; 2003).

Participation in prison programs is a poor indicator

Using prisoner participation in prison programs as a measure is problematic. Activities (that is, work, vocational training, education) include custodial responsibilities (that is, washing dishes, mopping floors, cleaning bathrooms), duties that masquerade as training (that is, cooking, mowing lawns, hoeing fields, tending crops, painting and repair), and basic education programs (ABE (Adult Basic Education), GED (General Educational Development)). Few of these activities elicit prisoner enthusiasm or are considered real opportunities to learn new marketable skills or knowledge. *Positive program participation* is usually defined by prison staff as an instance in which the convict showed up, did not refuse direct orders, and made a good show of pretending to work or study. In many institutions, existing programs are very basic and do not serve many prisoners. They seem to exist mainly to silence external critics, fulfill state mandates, and occasionally provide public relations benefits to the news media. Often, when the correctional budgets are cut, the helpful programs that do exist are the first to be terminated.

A more important problem (Berk et al., 2003) occurs when a prison system no longer expects its prisoners to participate in programs, as they may no longer exist. Most U.S. prison systems do not pretend to provide vocational or educational programming. Prison administrators limit their responsibility to operating orderly institutions, while trying to control contraband and violence, and preventing escapes. The way many DOCs have solved this situation, although incredibly expensive and controversial, is by building high-security institutions (for example, Supermax prisons) and filling them with reclassified prisoners.

Disciplinary reports are often circumspect

Classification consists of reviewing any "disciplinary actions" (aka *disciplinary reports*) and "demonstrations of positive participation in an inmate program." COs routinely issue "write-ups" (also called *shots* or incident reports in the

FBOP, *115s* in the California Department of Corrections, or simply *tickets* in many prison systems) every chance they get. Prisoners housed in crowded/overcrowded cellblocks or dormitories may collect minor tickets for petty infractions or major tickets for defending themselves against predatory or aggressive individuals. Many convicts claim disciplinary committees rule against convicts without affording them due process rights. In response to contacting the news media or calling a congressional office to complain about staff or the lack of medical services, a convict may be given tickets, get dragged to the "hole," be reclassified, or eventually be shipped out to the penitentiary or Supermax.

Using disciplinary reports as the primary criterion for the reclassification of prisoners may lead to the construction of more maximum-security prisons. It costs more to house prisoners in high-security correctional facilities, and as previously mentioned, prisoners who serve time in these institutions suffer more psychological problems and are less prepared for release.

Classification may be used for unofficial purposes

Classification may unnecessarily load up high-security prisons with lower socio-economic class minorities, where tension and ultimately more violence occur. African American, Hispanic, Latino, and Chicano prisoners are more likely to be "young" and gang affiliated, and to collect bad conduct "tickets." The FBOP and many states have struggled for years with schemes to "racially balance" institutions (Henderson et al., 2000). Like school busing programs, they transport prisoners from institution to correctional facility, trying to somehow racially integrate prisons as dictated by policy directives and Supreme Court decisions.

Depending on the prison system (including the budget, number of institutions, population counts, and level of disorder), prisoners are shuffled from one institution to another. These transfers may or may not reflect official classification schemes. When a given prison is bursting at the seams, with prisoners sleeping in hallways, three to a one-person cell, or on bunk beds arranged in recreational areas or classrooms converted into makeshift dormitories, official policy is frequently ignored, and busloads of prisoners are transferred to whichever facility has empty beds. This is commonly referred to as *population override*.

Solutions

As argued earlier, classification has numerous problems. Many of these are connected to a prison bureaucracy that is "resistant to change and partly to the poor environment for change provided in the prisons themselves" (Allen and

Simonsen, 2001: 247). Moreover, "[s]everal states have abandoned classification reception–diagnostic centers as counterproductive because the centers raised inmate and staff expectations above the level of possible achievement. The treatment model has a place somewhere in corrections, but not, it seems, in high-security prisons" (247). Nevertheless, approximately five measures can be marshaled in the hope of improving the classification process.

First, *have prisoners actively participate in the classification decisions.* Convicts are rarely asked to comment on prison policy and procedure. If they do, they are typically subject to recrimination. While prisoners may not be considered stakeholders (Berk et al., 2003), convicts should become more involved in the decision making.

Second, *hire more qualified personnel* to deal with the large number of cases. This also means that these staff should be better educated and trained, and accommodations should be made by the respective organizations that enable them to obtain advanced training. As Austin states, "unless there are strong staff training and monitoring components, these instruments will fail to perform as designed. Using what are largely psychometric tests, staff responsible for conducting assessments should be certified to perform such tests" (Berk et al., 2003: 3).

Third, *increase the number of correctional professionals* responsible for classification. This way decision making can be shared among more people. The idea here is that more sets of hands and eyes should help improve the entire process.

Fourth, *provide enough time for the professionals to properly investigate each case.* This means that classification should be done more frequently and over a long enough period of time during which the convicts can be observed and interviewed in different settings.

Finally, *increase the pay for classification officers.* This would make the job task more attractive to correctional professionals.

Until these strategies are experimented with or implemented, correctional personnel will simply be going through the motions.

Conclusion

In the United States, massive numbers of people are incarcerated on a daily basis, and there is a belief that better classification procedures will minimize our problems with incarceration. At the very least, these may save the taxpayer the increased costs of housing prisoners in more restrictive settings.

The point is that classification includes additional factors that may not be amenable to statistical number crunching. The research teams or even the prisoner may not even know some of these variables.

Nevertheless, as long as the classification of prisoners is based entirely on outdated measures of individual behavior (that is, criminal offense, conduct inside correctional facility, gang affiliation), without reference to the bigger structural issues (poverty, racial discrimination, the war on drugs) that have created the boom in the prison population, or to prison programming that could lower the rate of disciplinary reports and predictable parole failure, very little will change.

Classification determines if an inmate fits any special needs categories, including health, physical, or mental disabilities, and even addictions. Ideally, this process should lead to rehabilitation, which in turn should reduce recidivism. Classification should result in savings for the DOCs and ultimately the taxpayers. Last but not least, it should also protect correctional workers from being victims of physical violence.

Key terms
Central Inmate Monitoring System: Name of the information system used by the FBOP to keep track of inmates within their facilities.

Disciplinary reports: Documents the kinds of infractions inmates engage in.

Fish bowl: Inmate and CO name for place where inmates who have just come into the correctional system are held for observation.

Kicking the tires: Inmate term for a classification meeting.

Population override: Where the correctional facility goes over its official rated number of places.

Pre-sentence investigation: Report prepared by a probation or parole officer and given to a judge that reviews a number of factors relevant to the convicted person's circumstances including their criminal history. It makes a recommendation where the person should be sent. The document is given to the judge and shared with the defense attorney and prosecutor. The judge may or may not adopt the recommendation.

Prison camp: A minimum security correctional facility.

Racketeer Influence and Corrupt Organization (RICO) Act: A law that allows the federal government to provide harsher penalties and engage in civil suits connected to ongoing criminal organizations (e.g., gangs, organized crime, etc.).

Risk assessment instruments: Help correctional professionals determine the degree to which an individual convicted of a crime will reoffend and their potential to be rehabilitiated.

Security level: Based on the dangerousness of inmates. Includes Supermax, maximum, medium, and minimum correctional facilities. As the conditions move from Supermax to minimum they are more relaxed at less secure facilities.

Shots: Also known as a ticket. Disciplinary action, issued by a CO, that forces an inmate to administrative segregation.

Team meeting: A classification meeting held at the end of an inmate's stay in the fish bowl, or held once a year to determine if the current security level an inmate is in is appropriate.

Notes

[1] This chapter builds upon Richards and Ross (2003).
[2] CIMS is legally outlined by 28 C.F.R. 524.72 and USDOJ–FBOP statement (P.S.) 5180.04 Central Monitoring System (August 16, 1996).

SEVEN

Special populations

Introduction

Most correctional personnel and administrators recognize and know that certain kinds of inmates may need different facilities, policies, and programs. Often the state departments of corrections (DOCs) and Federal Bureau of Prisons (FBOP) are viewed as lagging behind in their approach toward these groups, and only when there is some sort of crisis are they forced to change. This chapter identifies these special populations, outlines the challenges they face in correctional institutions, and advances some solutions. In particular, this analysis focuses on problems connected to LGBTQ prisoners, the mentally ill, those suffering from HIV/AIDS, the graying prison population, and women behind bars.[1]

Lesbian, gay, bisexual, and transgender (LGBTQ) inmates

According to McNamara (2014), "LGBTQ [LGBT and queer] inmates suffer disproportionately compared to other detainees in many ways." This is experienced in three areas: "sexual and physical abuse'" "discriminatory visitation rights'" and "limited access to any sexuality-related literature." He suggests that:

> The primary method prisoners can use to challenge abusive prison officials and discriminatory policies is a civil action for deprivation of rights, claiming that state officials have deprived them of their Eighth Amendment right to be free from cruel and

unusual punishment and their Fourteenth Amendment right to equal protection under the law.

He then suggests that "claims are extremely difficult for prisoners to win because the parameters of their rights are largely undefined."

In terms of sexual abuse and physical violence, LGBTQ inmates are more likely to be victims of these two types of abuse. Whereas 3.5% of heterosexual males reported being sexually victimized, 34% of bisexual and 39% of homosexual men indicated sexual victimization (Beck and Johnson, 2012).

> In prison, LGBTQ inmates are frequently targeted for physical and sexual assaults due to their size or stature; "feminine" characteristics, such as long hair or a high voice; unassertive, unaggressive, or shy demeanor; or having been convicted of a sexual offense. Prisoners possessing any one or a combination of these characteristics typically face an increased risk of sexual abuse. (McNamara, 2014)

Because of narrowly defined criteria of who a family member is and how prison officials interpret them, LGBTQ inmates are often prevented from having their friends visit them.

More specifically, transgender inmates have a higher vulnerability to "social exclusion," "discrimination," "inadequate and inconsistent medical treatment," and "sexual assault" (Edney, 2000: 239). According to Edney, "Part of the susceptibility of transgender prisoners to sexual assault in the prison setting is the excessively masculine nature of the prison environment" (331). In classification, prison authorities fail to distinguish between the sex and gender of incoming prisoners and thus send them to facilities based on their birth assigned genders or genitalia. One of the most common solutions that correctional facilities take once a transgender inmate is victimized is to place them in protective custody or isolation. This only exposes the prisoner to greater psychological deprivations and unequal treatment.

Solutions

Increasingly, some advocates for transgender prisoners (see, for example, Scott, 2012) have argued, based on the Due Process clause of the Fourteenth Amendment, that they should be housed in facilities based on their self identified genders and not on their genitalia. Unfortunately correctional policies and practices in the United States are slow to heed this argument.

Mentally ill inmates

Problems

Given the number of inmates who are suffering from mental illness, some observers may legitimately question whether the mentally ill are a separate special population in correctional facilities. In particular, according to the most recent Bureau of Justice Statistics (BJS) report (James and Glaze, 2006), approximately 45% of federal convicts, 56% of all state prisoners, and 64% of jail inmates are suffering from some sort of "mental health problem." This accounted for 1,264,300 individuals. According to the study, "mental health problems were defined by ... a recent history or symptoms of a mental health problem" (1). The primary diagnosis is depression and/or some sort of psychotic disorder (for example, suffering from delusions or hallucinations).

Predictably, the symptoms are highest among jail prisoners, and less pronounced when one moves to the state and federal systems: "The high rate of symptoms of mental disorder among jail inmates may reflect the role of local jails in the criminal justice system . ... Among other functions, local jails hold mentally ill persons pending their movement to appropriate mental health facilities" (James and Glaze, 2006: 3). More specifically, mental health problems are "more common among female, white and young inmates" (5). In terms of care, some convicts with mental health problems receive 24-hour supervision in a special housing or psychiatric unit, while others are only provided with some sort of counseling or drug therapy (that is, psychotropic medications).

Whether the number of prisoners who have some sort of mental health problem or illness is increasing is difficult to determine because comparable statistics have not been kept for a lengthy period of time. In 1998, for example, approximately 283,800 inmates were determined to be "mentally ill" (Ditton, 1999). As mentioned earlier, 1,264,300 of all federal, state, and local inmates in 2005 suffered from some kind of mental health problem. Although the terminology for this affliction may not be exactly the same, it would seem that the number was 4.5 times greater in 2005 than it was in 1998.

Statistics aside, correctional workers, administrators, and prisoners generally agree that there has been an increase in the number of people with mental health problems being sent to and living in U.S. jails and prisons. This is often because the mentally ill are turned away from mental institutions or are too challenging for the traditional mental health facility (Gibbons and de Katzenbach, 2006: 46; Testa, 2015). Most DOCs and the FBOP are not equipped to "handle these inmates. Line officers are not trained to deal with the idiosyncrasies of these individuals introduce[d] to the prison environment. Furthermore, the FBOP lacks the mental health professionals to treat these inmates."[2] The mentally ill end up making greater demands on staff time, are frequently manipulated and victimized by other convicts (Blitz et al., 2008; Crisanti and Frueh, 2011), and often end up in administrative segregation for their own protection and/or for the safety of staff and inmates.

In addition, there are not enough skilled staff who are responsible for these inmates' well-being. One only needs to take a look at the DOC's and FBOP's websites to notice that there is a desperate need for mental health professionals (for example, psychologists, psychiatrists, social workers, and so on). Not only are correctional officers (COs) and administrators poorly equipped to deal with these individuals, but so are the inmates. The inmates may not have the necessary patience to live and work with mentally ill individuals, who are in great danger of being ridiculed, harassed, and/or attacked.

Most of the time, the mentally ill are medicated – sometimes heavily – and they seem to walk the halls in a zombie-like state. It is acknowledged that "the presence of counseling personnel and services is often uneven, fragmented, or inadequate" (Arrigo, 2005: 595). "The majority of inmates receiving therapy/counseling and medications [a]re housed in facilities without a mental health specialty" (Beck and Maruschak, 2001: 4). One of the problems is that many of the mentally ill are sent to solitary confinement – a punishment whose issues were outlined in Chapter 4. Arrigo reminds us that "[i]n those instances where treatment is uneven, absent, or otherwise ineffective, questions remain about whether the correctional milieu is itself responsible for breeding and sustaining long-term mental illness and dysfunctional behavior" (2005: 593). Moreover, in solitary confinement mentally ill inmates' psychological condition may worsen.

Solutions

Finding appropriate solutions for housing, managing, and treating mentally ill prisoners depends on the onset of the mental illness, the individual's response to medication and/or therapy, the inmate's level of functionality, and the availability of housing alternatives. Indeed, there is a range of places in which mentally ill convicts can be detained. In the United States, however, there are only 12 facilities whose "primary function (identified by the largest number of inmates) was mental health confinement" (Beck and Maruschak, 2001: 4). As mentioned earlier, most inmates "receiving psychotropic medication were in general confinement or community-based facilities" (4).

In short, those suffering some sort of mental illness should be shifted to secure facilities in which licensed and competent mental health professionals can properly assess, monitor, and provide them with appropriate therapy to stabilize and hopefully improve their conditions. Other suggestions include using better screening on intake and making sure that licensed and skilled mental health professionals (and not simply COs) are making the decisions about what kinds of facilities would best house these inmates (Gibbons and de Katzenbach 2006). Other practices include a variety of different forms of diversion (See Chapter 3), which can also involve crisis intervention training for law enforcement officers, mental health courts, and drug courts (Testa, 2015).

The graying prison population

Problems

Over the past three decades, the average age of prisoners has increased. "Between 1995 and 2010, the number of state and federal prisoners aged 55 or older nearly quadrupled (increasing 282 per cent), while the number of all prisoners grew by less than half (increasing 42 per cent)" (Human Rights Watch, 2012).[3] The higher average age of prisoners can be tied to longer and harsher sentences, as well as to the fact that Americans on the whole are living longer. The graying prison population means that older inmates need special medical treatments, procedures, prescriptions, and medical supplies. "Elderly men in prison have a high incidence of respiratory and heart problems, diabetes, depression, poor circulation, arthritis, bladder problems, Alzheimer's, Parkinson's, and hypertension" (Crawley, 2005: 354). These kinds of inmates have "specific health and mobility needs" that require "significant financial, regime, and indeed, health and safety implications in the prison environment" (354). This easily becomes a financial burden to the correctional system. "Health-care costs comprise 10 to 20 percent of prison operating costs and are the fastest-growing item of corrections budgets, due in large part to an aging prison population that requires greater and more expensive medical attention" (Welch, 2004: 457).

Solutions

A considerable debate exists regarding how to competently and fairly deal with an increasingly elderly inmate population. Solutions range from providing specialized facilities to early release (Soderstrom and Wheeler, 1999). In particular, "[o]lder inmates are less interested in GED (General Educational Development) classes and other educational programs and more interested in learning how to secure Social Security benefits upon their release. Preparing them to return to the community might be the most pressing problem facing the correctional system" (Welch, 2004: 458). Anything the jails and prisons can do to help them with this reality may be the best solution for the graying prison population.

Another solution is to encourage DOCs and the FBOP to utilize compassionate release. According to Price (2005) this practice "is appropriate when circumstances unforeseen at sentencing make continued incarceration unjust, and when no other adequate legal mechanisms exist to effect sentence reduction" (150). In reality, the procedure, though publicly supported by many state and federal guidelines, is rarely used.

HIV/AIDS

Problems

There is a sizeable population of inmates in state and federal prisons and jails that are afflicted with HIV/AIDs. According to the Centers for Disease Control and Prevention, "In 2010, there were 20,093 inmates with HIV/AIDS in state and federal prisons with 91% being men." More specifically, "Among state and federal jurisdictions reporting in 2010 there were 3,913 inmates living with an AIDS diagnosis." They add that in the context of jails, both African American men and women (compared to whites and Hispanic/Latinos are disproportionately diagnosed with HIV) (Anonymous, 2015). This population faces numerous risks both to themselves and others incarcerated and working in the same facilities. Some of these issues include a shortage of AIDs/HIV-related information and resources inside correctional facilities in terms of awareness, prevention, testing, and treatment. Also the rapid turnover of prisoners, especially in jails, can frustrate adequate provision of resources to inmates who are sufferers of AIDs/HIV. Likewise there is the issue of privacy. It is not in the patients' interests to disclose the information to others for fear of ostracization and/or victimization.

Solutions

A number of solutions to the identification, education, and treatment of HIV/AIDS patients in jails and prisons have been advanced (Hammett et al., 1999; Welch, 2004: 450–6). To begin with, and as previously mentioned in Chapter 4, there are arguments both for and against mass screenings of all inmates in correctional facilities. Advocates say that this would allow convicts who are HIV positive or have AIDS to get the treatment they so desperately need. Opponents point out that rarely can the information be kept secret, and then the patients' confidentiality will be breached. It is generally understood that once inmates are behind bars notions of privacy almost always take a backseat to institutional safety and mass screening may make better sense.

Clearly, better education and training of both correctional workers and inmates is fundamental to minimize the spread of AIDS and to reduce irrational fear connected to the disease. Proper medical care, especially the administration of the drug Zidovudine, more popularly known as AZT, which curtails the development of HIV/AIDS, is advocated. Also integrating those with AIDS into the general population rather than segregating them has been found to be helpful to minimize stigma and other forms of social isolation. Other suggestions include distributing condoms among consenting homosexuals in prison, and providing access to long-term hospitalization, which would help ease the pain and suffering related to this illness.

As mentioned earlier, one of the solutions offered by the National Commission on Safety and Abuse in Prison is to partner with local public health departments. The report, however, did not provide a strategy on how to accomplish this task. Additionally, there are a number of nonprofit organizations that provide free information and counseling to prisoners who have HIV/AIDS or suspect that they may have been infected. One of them, for example, is the Osborne Association, located in New York's Bronx neighborhood. Prisoners can call this organization collect and receive information on the disease, as well as on preventive measures (www.osborneny. org/programs.cfm?programID=3).

Women

Problems

As of 2013, there were 2,13,700 women incarcerated in jails and prisons in the United States (Glaze and Kaeble, 2014: 6). This represents about 10% of all convicts. Women are typically sentenced to jail or prison for frequent convictions for petty crimes (for example, shoplifting), possession of drugs, small-scale drug dealing, embezzlement, credit card fraud, writing bad checks, and homicide. Recent statistics suggest that the categories of crime for which women are serving time in state facilities indicate that 34.8% of convictions are for violent crimes, 30.0% property related, 29.1% connected to drugs, and 5.3% public order offenses (Harrison and Beck, 2006: 9).

Over the past two decades, female convicts have been found to be typically single, between 25 and 34 years old, and struggling to survive poor economic circumstances. Most are minorities, have never finished high school, and have multiple children. In terms of racial breakdown, 50% are African American, 36% White, and 16% Hispanic. According to profiles that have been developed, the average female inmate probably dropped out of school somewhere around the ninth grade because she became pregnant and had no one to take care of her child. She never acquired a formal education that would allow anything more than a low-paying, service-sector job such as that of a hotel maid or kitchen staff. She periodically, if not totally, depends on public assistance. When the inmate was younger, she was most likely sexually abused; she has a history of being physically abused by men, dating back to her teenage years. She uses alcohol and/or drugs, and has been arrested numerous times (Ross and Richards, 2002: chapter 11).

Because of the war on drugs, stiffer mandatory sentencing guidelines, and the widespread acceptance of women as legitimate criminals, a considerable number of women have entered the prison system in the past two decades. Since 1983, it is estimated that the number of women has grown by 344%, as compared to 207% for men.

Women are less likely to have a history of engaging in violent crime. When they do kill, however, the victims are usually their fathers, husbands, boyfriends, or children; rarely do they commit an act of violence against strangers. And despite the fact that today more women than ever before are being charged with serious drug felonies, they typically serve as accessories rather than principal actors.

Most states have numerous prisons for men and at least one facility for women. Nearly every state has at least one women's prison. However, some of the more sparsely populated states – which might have a total of only 50 female convicts – end up shipping them to a neighboring state or housing them in separate wings of county jails.

Men do time in facilities with security levels ranging from minimum to Supermax. Because there is usually only one women's prison in an entire state, all the security levels are typically contained within the same institution. Therefore, most female prisons, at the state level, resemble minimum-security camps. About one-fifth of women are incarcerated at coed facilities where they live in separate units; the only contact with members of the opposite sex is in vocational, educational, and recreational settings (Pollock-Byrne, 1990; Owen, 1998).

There are no maximum-security or Supermax federal prisons for women in the United States. The highest security correctional facility for women, at worst, resembles a medium-security prison for men. For example, the Federal Prison Camp in Lexington, Kentucky, houses 400 female prisoners, yet has no fence or gun towers. At the same time, some women housed there are serving life sentences. Although women's prisons typically have fences, they have less razor wire and fewer detection facilities. Correctional systems do not erect sophisticated security because they do not expect these women to escape and commit additional crimes. Even though it would be relatively easy to break out of such a facility, escapes from women's prisons are rare events. If more women in correctional custody attempted escapes, one can be sure that state and federal planners would install additional security features. This does not mean that life behind bars for women is easy.

Five of the most important problems that women face that are qualitatively different than those that men encounter include sexism, violence by COs against inmates, child custody while behind bars, pregnancy, and release.

Sexism

The criminal justice system (and jails, prisons, and community corrections, by extension) is disproportionately sexist. Typically, this means that if there is some sort of vocational training, it tends to be sex-role based. For example, female convicts might be trained as office assistants, cosmetologists, seamstresses, and domestic servants. According to Welch, "some of these programs are self-defeating. For instance, some states require a license to work in cosmetology, and such licensing is denied to ex-inmates. Moreover, cosmetology and clerical work are 'pink-collar' jobs, which are generally low-paying and often considered dead-end employment" (2004: 178). According to Owen (2005):

> [R]ehabilitative programs for women offenders are typically based on generic programs that make few gender distinctions. ... For example, women's prisons are deficient relative to men's prisons in educational and vocational programs they offer. Men's prisons typically provide a greater variety of such programs and training for more skilled (and better compensated) occupations. (1054)

Violence

In the nineteenth century, most female prisoners in the United States were not separated from the men, inevitably leading to physical and sexual abuse. Even when they were confined in a separate wing of a coed facility, women were vulnerable to abuse by male administrators, correctional workers, and prisoners. A number of female reformers championed the cause of female inmates, and by the twentieth century, many states and the federal government had established prisons solely for women that were increasingly staffed by women.

Over the past two centuries, conditions have improved for female prisoners. Historically, the sexual abuse of female prisoners by male staff members is common (Human Rights Watch, 1996). These incidents include "sexual abuse, sexual assault, sexual harassment, physical contact of a sexual nature, sexual obscenity, invasion of privacy, and conversations or correspondence of a romantic or intimate nature" (Owen, 2005: 1052). In most states, any sexual relations between prison staff and inmates is considered by law to be sexual assault. In short, there is no such thing as consensual sex between prisoners and COs. Hundreds of correctional workers have been fired and/or indicted and convicted of sexual assault charges resulting from their coercion of female prisoners. "Conservative estimates for the rate of sexual victimization of women in prison indicate that nearly 30% will experience some form of unwanted sex while confined" (Arrigo, 2005: 595).

Some state prison systems, like that of Georgia, have implemented tough "no touch, no contact" policies. In these settings, men are not allowed to supervise female convicts. If a man enters the unit, an announcement, almost like a warning, of "man [or male] on range" can be heard. At some federal prisons for women, hotlines allow female prisoners to make complaints if they have been sexually abused. This is sometimes a public relations exercise simply designed to garner support from the wider public and to show them that something is being done about this problem. It has been said that when incidents of such abuse come to the public's attention, state correctional systems will have their public relations department representative cover for the bureaucracy's intransigence. Even today, there are a number of states that have not outlawed staff–inmate sex.

Maintaining custody of children

Many female prisoners are mothers who may feel that their children have been abandoned to the makeshift care of relatives, social service agencies, foster homes, or put up for adoption. Many women lose legal custody of their children when they are adjudicated as "bad mothers."

Some female prisoners were great mothers before they went to prison, but because of their crimes, their children have been legally removed from their custody. Incarcerated mothers frequently worry about worst-case scenarios; for example, her spouse divorces her while she is in prison, remarries, moves to another state with the children, and becomes difficult to locate. Most female convicts who have had their children taken away are consumed by remorse about their criminal behavior.

The situation is made worse by laws such as the Adoption and Safe Families Act passed in 1997. Originally designed to "to keep abused or neglected children from languishing in foster care while their biological parents, often drug-addicted, tried to kick their habit," the law has become a tautology of sorts. In short, the simple fact that a mother was incarcerated for a specific period of time is interpreted as grounds for determining abuse (Cohen, 2006a). Additionally, "[i]nmates often can't attend a hearing on whether their parental rights should be terminated. In some cases they aren't even informed about those hearings, which may be held hundreds or thousands of miles away" (1). The United States is "the only nation that routinely moves to terminate the parental rights of incarcerated parents whose children are in foster care" (Cohen, 2006b: 1).

Giving birth behind bars

Many women enter prison while pregnant and give birth to their children while serving time. According to BJS data, as many as 6% of the women entering state and federal prisons are pregnant. There are no reliable statistics on the number of pregnancies that result in termination, miscarriage, or birth. Worse, some female prisoners are raped by COs while incarcerated and then forced to give birth to the offspring. When a prisoner goes through childbirth, many times she is handcuffed and transferred to a civilian hospital. The cuffs are not taken off during either labor or delivery. With luck, a relative will take in the baby. More likely, the baby will be turned over to foster care or put up for adoption (Amnesty International, 2001).

A very small number of correctional facilities may allow a mother to care for her newborn in prison for a short time. For example, larger jails, like Rikers Island in New York City, have neonatal centers. But babies of incarcerated mothers are usually only allowed to stay if the female prisoner will be released shortly, perhaps within a few weeks, so neither she nor her baby will be a burden on the system.

Some people mistakenly believe that a pregnant woman can be absolved from a prison sentence. Contrary to what may have taken place during earlier times in American history, when it comes to sentencing a woman, carrying a child does not provide any protection for a woman from being sent to jail or prison, nor does it serve as an excuse for immediate release.

Reintegration of women

After their release from correction custody, many female prisoners who are also mothers immediately begin searching for their children. Like their male counterparts, they leave prison with little money, no place of their own to live, and no job. They usually stay with relatives or complete their sentence in halfway houses. Some of these facilities are fairly depressing and are usually located in economically depressed and unsafe neighborhoods. Pass by one of these on a hot summer day, and you will see women parolees congregating on the front steps while cars filled with leering men cruise by looking for new girlfriends. Other female parolees remain isolated inside the house, frightened of the pimps and dope dealers who frequent these neighborhoods. Most of these women will return to a life of dependency that includes social service agency handouts or the games of the street.

Solutions

Correctional officers, administrators, and planners must avoid being sexist in the way they treat women behind bars and upon release. It is hoped that the additional number of female COs and administrators will have an impact on this problem, but there is scant reliable empirical research on this process in this context. This would go a long way in increasing appropriate vocational programs. Also the DOCs need more funding for facilities and programs in which female inmates can not only give birth to, but raise their infants. Additional mechanisms that would encourage conjugal visits by family members may lessen the pain and suffering women may feel when they are cut off from their loved ones.

Conclusion

Many of the solutions to special populations rely on letting public health and community service agencies take a larger role in providing critical services to inmates. Increasing prisoner and correctional awareness and training can also go a long way in improving the lives of prisoners. This is easier said than done as correctional agencies' budgets are typically relatively small and their ability to do outreach is often hampered.

Key terms
Adoption and Safe Families Act: Passed during the George W. Bush administration which makes it easier for the government to declare a mother unfit so that her child can be put up for adoption.

AZT: Drug used to treat AIDS.

Graying of prison population: The tendency for the correctional facilities in the United States to have older prisoners.

Psychotic disorder: One of the most debilitating psychiatric disorders. Usually accompanied by hallucinations and delusions.

Special populations: Inmates who require special facilities and programs that significantly differ from the general population (i.e., mentally ill, graying prison population, women, and those with HIV/AIDS).

Notes
[1] Every few years, the Department of Justice, through the Bureau of Justice Statistics, conducts two corrections-related surveys (that is, the "National Prisoner Statistics" and the "Deaths in Custody Reporting Program") that result in different publications. Where possible, data for this chapter comes from these sources.

[2] Personal correspondence with Miguel Zaldivar, June 2007.

[3] Unfortunately this is the most recent national-level data on this topic that is currently available.

EIGHT

Rehabilitation

Introduction

One of the major goals of the correctional sanction is rehabilitation. This objective generally refers to a collection of programs and practices used to retrain convicts so they stop engaging in crime. In order to understand prisoner rehabilitation, we must first know something about its historical, philosophical/ideological, and programmatic origins and implications.

Historical legacy

Rehabilitation of prisoners is not a new concept or a recent process. We can probably date rehabilitation back to the "ancient understanding of lawbreaking [which] advocated corporal punishment as to 'beat the devil out' of the criminal – literally and figuratively" (Welch, 2011: 78). Eventually this model, which quickly drifted into a mode of punishment rather than rehabilitation, became prominent. It was not until the Enlightenment that prominent thinkers (for example, Beccaria, Bentham, and so on) were able to convince power holders that this model was not successful at achieving its ends, and would be better served by the creation of correctional facilities.

In America, one of the first prisons, the Walnut Street Jail in Philadelphia, established by the Quakers (aka the Society of Friends) in 1790, was an attempt to change the ways of criminals. This facility originated the *silent and separate* system, which the rest of the Pennsylvania prisons, such as Eastern State Penitentiary (built in 1821) and Western Penitentiary (built in 1826), adopted. Walnut Jail administrators believed that if prisoners were kept in separate cells furnished with Bibles, they would have time to reflect on their sins and transgressions and, when they were eventually released, be morally upstanding citizens.

131

Later, as the country grew in population, a competing corrections philosophy and practice developed at the prison in Auburn, New York (built in 1818). The administration of this prison believed that a military regime, where convicts lived and worked together but remained silent, would have a rehabilitative effect on them. This alternative was called the Auburn, New York, or *silent but congregate system*.

The rehabilitation movement also had adherents in the reformatory movement, which can be traced back to the first juvenile reformatory established by Zebulon Brockway in New Jersey in 1876. At that time, correctional planners also introduced the so-called medical model to corrections. Prisoners were considered to be sick and, thus, afforded various treatments to return them to health, including drug therapy and psychotherapy.

Ideological/philosophical context

Not only does rehabilitation have a historical context, but it also has ideological origins and implications. Liberals and radicals generally favor rehabilitation, whereas conservatives place more emphasis on punishment and community safety. This is probably why in U.S. political history, Democrats prefer correctional innovations and programs to help convicts and ex-cons, whereas Republicans scale back these kinds of initiatives and disproportionately focus on punishment and public safety. Most of the decline in public support for rehabilitation occurred in the late 1960s and early 1970s, and has remained fairly stable since then (Cullen, 2006).

Experts and opinion leaders from both ideological camps have been critical of rehabilitation for different reasons. Conservatives have argued that rehabilitation does not work. Liberals, on the other hand, claim that the introduction and use of more community corrections programs (with rehabilitative objectives) by the criminal justice system cause net widening (that is, a process whereby an increase in the number of sanctions available to those who are convicted of a crime leads to more people falling under the control of the criminal justice system) (Austin and Krisberg, 1981). Although those convicted of minor crimes are kept out of jail and prison, this policy increases the number people under the control of the state.

Programmatic realities

Analysts have delineated the context of rehabilitation into three areas: changing how prisoners respond to their environment, altering their motivations, and changing their lifestyles (Alleman, 2002: 25–37). Unfortunately, most jails and prisons devote scant resources toward these goals. Thus, we are left with human warehouses, where little attention is paid to rehabilitation and treatment, or to providing prisoners with opportunities to better prepare themselves for a law-abiding life.

This reality has a disproportionate effect on juveniles who are brought under the watchful eye of the criminal justice system. Rehabilitation, whether as part of institutional corrections or as an option under the community-based part of corrections (for example, probation and parole), is complicated and, in many respects, almost impossible to implement and administer. To ensure rehabilitation, the correctional system needs to closely evaluate inmates and place them into programs that best assist them. This typically occurs at classification and can significantly impact rehabilitation.

The current state of rehabilitation

A generation ago, one aspect of the correctional focus was on attempting to alter and/or influence convicts' attitudes, behaviors, and improve their employability in anticipation of their eventual release. A quarter-century of experiencing a high rate of recidivism (caused primarily by technical violations) has put this approach in disfavor. Today's emphasis is on protecting the public by locking up criminals and ensuring that they serve most, if not all, of their sentences. Today's jails and prisons typically prioritize punishing individuals convicted of criminal charges and attempting to increase public safety, not rehabilitation.

Largely motivated by the Attica Riot (1971), a considerable amount of scholarly attention has been focused on figuring out how to improve corrections. One noticeable piece of research was a report popularly credited to Robert Martinson, titled "What Works? – Questions and Answers about Prison Reform." It was the product of a long-term study, under the directorship of Douglas S. Lipton and administered by the New York State Division of Criminal Justice, to determine how to best rehabilitate offenders.

The document synthesized 231 English-language studies, published between 1945 and 1967, on attempts to rehabilitate prisoners. The report, which was 1,484 pages long, was originally blocked from publication, because the findings ran counter to what the state was planning (that is, a series of rehabilative programs). After some legal maneuvering, Martinson managed to get a summary printed in the spring 1974 edition of the journal *Public Interest* (Hallinan, 2003: 33–6). In short, he concluded that "with few and isolated exceptions," the rehabilitative programs "had no appreciable effect" on recidivism. If you look closely at the longer study, what he was really saying was that across categories of intervention (for example, counseling and probation), no modality seemed to work reliably (more often than not). Nevertheless, many interested parties have interpreted Martinson's statement to mean that rehabilitation efforts have absolutely no influence on convict recidivism.

Although some scholars, like Palmer (1975), pointed out that 48% of the studies that had recidivism data in Martinson's study showed positive treatment effects, Martinson's findings were welcomed by conservatives at the time, who had finally found an expert, with scholarly bonafides, to support their claims and efforts. For the historical record, Martinson later recanted his position on rehabilitation programs in a 1979 article published in the *Hofstra Law Review*:

> But whether they work – and how well they work – depends on the conditions under which they are applied. ... By 1979, though, few people wanted to listen. The movement away from rehabilitation and toward punishment was well on its way – propelled, in large measure, by Martinson's original article. Conservative politicians and academics had seized upon the article and used it to bolster arguments for longer and more punitive sentences. (Hallinan, 2003: 36)

This was the state of affairs despite the accumulation of good social science data on rehabilitation (for example, Cullen and Gendreau, 2000; Andrews and Bonta, 2006). Finally, to support the conservative approach toward prison confinement, in 2001, Congress (under Representative Dick Zimmer (R)) passed the No Frills Prison Act, barring such amenities as televisions and coffee pots in Federal Bureau of Prisons (FBOP) cells.

Most Americans and selected correctional practitioners are in favor of rehabilitation (Flanagan and Caulfield, 1984; Cullen et al., 1988; Cullen and Gendreau, 1989; 2000; Cullen et al., 2000; Kifer et al., 2003). More specifically, support for rehabilitation is strongest for juveniles and less so for violent inmates. In general, Americans support both treatment and punishment, which they do not see as irreconcilable approaches. Finally, we now have a growing body of knowledge on what works with convicts (mainly cognitive-behavioral programs with high-risk convicts, preferably delivered in the community and followed up with aftercare and employment). How one implements these programs is, of course, another story. Regardless of how we tinker with the programs, correctional settings are typically suboptimal environments for the rehabilitation of inmates.

Vocational training

There are several kinds of vocational training that convicts receive; however, these are bounded by job availability, work assignments, hourly rates, and the types of jobs available behind bars (Gerber and Fritsch, 2001). The following section reviews these issues.

Job availability

In jails and prisons, the distinction between vocational training and working a job is often blurred. So called good and/or meaningful jobs in prison are in short supply. Getting a decent assignment and avoiding bad work details is important for maintaining prisoners' morale and earning some meager wages to place in their commissary accounts. When preferred jobs are not present, there are often make-work duties; these are typically boring cleaning, gardening, and other manual labor jobs. Working makes it easier for convicts to do their time. Nevertheless, prisoners do more than make license plates, street signs, and mailbags. Prison industries at both the state and the federal levels are a vital part of the national economy, producing thousands of different products and providing services marketed all over the United States. These products include office furniture, clothing, printing services, textiles, electronic parts, and vehicle services. The primary consumers of these products manufactured by prison industries are state and federal government entities.

Convicts may also work for private contractors doing telemarketing, providing banking and credit card services, making airline and hotel reservations, and managing state lotteries. So the next time you receive one of those annoying phone calls from some stranger trying to sell you magazines, home repairs (or improvements), home equity loans, or vacation packages, keep in mind that this may very well be a convict calling from prison.

Work assignments

Not everybody in prison has a job. There are never enough work assignments for the whole population. Some inmates spend the whole day in their cells, venturing forth only to go to meals, to visit the library, or to participate in some sort of recreation, like working out with weights or playing handball. In an institution of about 2,000 prisoners, 400 (20%) of the convicts will be working in the prison industries (factory), 100 (5%) will be in the kitchen, another 100 (5%) will be mopping floors, another 100 (5%) will be doing maintenance work (plumbing, carpentry, air-conditioning repair, painting) and groundskeeping (cutting grass, planting flowers, shoveling snow), 200 (10%) will be in GED (General Educational Development) classes, 50 (2.5%) will be in drug treatment classes, 200 will be in the hole (usually 10% of the prison population can be found in the hole at any one time), and 200 (10%) will be on medical leave, laid up in their cells, or in the infirmary with diabetes, heart problems, bad backs, or other problems. The rest of them, over 30% of the prison population, are confined to their housing units, with absolutely nothing productive to do (Ross and Richards, 2002).

In order for a facility to function at all, convicts must do almost all the menial labor. They may work in the kitchen preparing meals, or spend years sweeping, mopping, and waxing corridor floors, or in the laundry washing massive amounts of clothing, sheets, and towels.

Inmate pay

Just because inmates may have a work assignment does not mean they will be paid. The institution is under no obligation to compensate prisoners for their labor. In fact, many prisons around the country do not pay their convicts anything. Departments of Corrections (DOCs) budget very few funds for inmate pay. The reason why they pay prisoners anything is so they can buy small things from the commissary or pay for telephone use.

The lack of money in a commissary account can often make an inmate feel desperate. There is usually a waiting list of a couple of years for the positions in the prison industries, because that is the best way for convicts to make money. In any event, inmate pay for general labor is very low, typically a few dollars a week. To the authorities, work for convicts is a privilege, not a right. In prison, even bad jobs are hard to get.[1]

Types of available jobs

Vocational training generally means kitchen duty, maintenance work, or groundskeeping, which is supervised by correctional officers (COs) who provide little instruction to the inmates. Although these are officially called vocational programs, the convicts know that these are work assignments. Unless convicts are "physically or mentally challenged" (that is, mentally ill or suffering from a mental disability), washing dishes eight hours a day, seven days a week, can hardly be called vocational training. This labor will not lead to a better job on the outside.

Although the FBOP runs UNICOR (also known as Federal Prison Industries), which exists to simultaneously train inmates and produce needed products for the federal government, there may be a two-to-three-year wait for jobs. Recognizing the problems inherent to their training opportunities, some prison systems have incorporated the private sector into their job training. Selected businesses may believe that it is in their economic self-interest to establish premises in a correctional facility. A limited number of inmates are then allowed and paid the prevailing wage, and a portion of their salaries is deducted to pay for things like fines, restitution, child and family support, taxes, and sometimes room and board. Oregon is a case in point. "[T]he state's inmate work program is run as a for-profit business under an assumed business name, Inside Oregon Enterprises. It … leases inmates to companies in need of labor. Although the inmates must be paid market wages, employers do not pay benefits" (Hallinan, 2003: 144).

One popularly-known employer of convict labor is the Oregon-based clothing manufacturer Prison Blues (www.prisonblues.com). Started in 1989, this company produces blue jeans, yard coats, work shirts, and related apparel. The "tough guy" image, besides the fact that prisoners make the clothing, has helped the clothing line's widespread popularity among some consumers. There is apparently a long waiting list among inmates at Eastern Oregon Correctional Institute for these manufacturing jobs.

Education

Most prisoners typically and desperately need to upgrade their formal education. In some correctional facilities, the majority of inmates are high school dropouts. In prison, however, opportunities for receiving some form of formal education are in short supply and are dwindling (Taylor and Tewksbury, 2002).

The setting

Typically, prisons may have an education section or department that occupies a floor or wing of a building. This may include a small library and a few classrooms, and is usually staffed by teachers, COs, and convict clerks, with a range of certifications, training, and ability. The utility of the program depends as much on the skills of the officers or teachers, as the determination of the individual prisoners (for example, Fisher-Giorlando, 2003; Tregea, 2003). The quality of educational programs generally varies based on the security level. Most maximum-security or Supermax prisons' educational programs are limited to the Adult Basic Education (ABE) certificate, which is generally understood to be an eighth-grade education, and the GED certificate, that is basically a high school diploma.

Difficult to pursue

Most convicts are lucky to receive basic instruction that could lead to the achievement of a GED. The education programs are mostly inadequate. Very few resources (staff, space, and so on) are devoted to "inmate education," and prison administrators rarely support higher education." Many wardens, even those who publicly portray themselves as dedicated to rehabilitation, see outside instructors as potential threats to the security and smooth running of the institutions. Convicts taking college classes also may be subject to frequent cell searches and disciplinary transfers to administrative detention (solitary confinement) or other institutions. This disrupts their ability to regularly take classes.

Some wardens may consider educated convicts to be a threat to their authority, since these individuals may be more knowledgeable and skilled, and may appear more credible than other prisoners, particularly in their communications with outsiders (for example, the news media and oversight agencies). In short, educated inmates may report on poor prison conditions, corruption, and incompetent administrators. Then again, on the other hand, educated convicts may be easier to deal with because they may distrust rumor, and respond better to reason, facts, and empirical support.

The Violent Crime Control Act (aka the Crime Bill), passed in 1994 during the Clinton Administration, cut funding for postsecondary correctional education to prisoners. Up until the summer of 1995, Federal Pell Grants were available for prisoners in both state and federal prisons, as a means of paying college tuition for courses taught inside prisons or by correspondence. This benefit was not without its problems. Occasionally, some inmates applied for the grants, but never received the support because they were transferred to another correctional facility. Alternatively, prisoners sometimes applied for Pell Grants, but the education office at the prison, and not the individuals themselves, actually received the funds, which could be spent by the institution on anything that could be even vaguely interpreted as educational (for example, basketballs, pencils, and flower gardens). Those who serve time no longer have to worry about the hassle of Pell Grants, because the grant program has been canceled. As if to add insult to injury, in 1998 the Drug Free Student Loan Act was passed, which denied student loans or work-study programs to individuals who had been convicted of drug offenses, whether this was at the misdemeanor or at the felony level.

Solutions

In every jail or prison, there are a dedicated group of inmates, many of them college educated, some of them former teachers, who tutor other men for their ABE or GED. Many DOCs and the FBOP emphasize the need for prisoners to complete these basic educational requirements. Meanwhile, there are multiple opportunities for self-education and sometimes formal education.

Self-education

Numerous possibilities exist for inmates to educate themselves, not only by reading appropriate books, but also by participating in informal classes with other prisoners.

Convicts who are literate often have more free time to read than they have ever had in their lives.[2] They generally have two options. On the one hand, they can borrow the worn, tattered, and outdated books in the prison library. Oftentimes, the classics are missing. Even amid volumes of so-called trashy fiction, prisoners will always find a few worthwhile books. On the other hand, since inmates rarely have access to well-stocked library collections, prisoners often need to ask outsiders to purchase books from publishers or bookstores and then mail them into the prison. In communications with outsiders, convicts sometimes ask for the classics and college textbooks. This reading material can help convicts prepare themselves if they are planning to go to school upon eventual release (Richards, 2004). Some prison libraries have access to inter-library loan, to receive books from other libraries throughout the state.

Prisoners sometimes organize semiformal classes on a wide range of topics. Men convicted of white-collar offenses teach many of these, including entrepreneurial subjects like writing business plans, applying for small business loans, and operating a company. Many convicts are foreign born. Thus, it is relatively easy to find a tutor to help inmates learn a foreign language. Also worth noting are the instructions by jailhouse lawyers in writing administrative remedies, writs, motions to court, and appeals. Such classes taught by convict volunteers are unofficial, with no financial or material assistance coming from the prison authorities.

Formal education

Considerable academic research clearly demonstrates that higher education is the single most effective means to lower criminal recidivism rates (Tregea, 2003; 2014). Simply stated, prisoners who complete a year or more of college courses while incarcerated are much less likely to violate parole or be returned to prison on a new conviction. Nevertheless, formal classes, beyond the GED, with rare exceptions, are not available in jails and prisons. Most correctional systems do not have postsecondary education offerings. The only institutional program worth taking may be a computer repair class, operated on contract by an outside corporation. Convicts may enjoy learning about computer architecture and program languages, but most of the teaching is devoted to remedial math classes. Some inmates may actually learn enough basic algebra to pass the computer course exams. Unfortunately, this unique prison program is often discontinued when the funding expires.

Occasionally, cash-strapped or entrepreneurial local institutions of higher learning might offer introductory college-level courses. These programs are often dependent on the resources, and the predicted and actual financial incentives that the educational institution receives in addition to the whims of the warden. In any event, these programs only serve a few dozen prisoners at a time and only those who can somehow scrounge up the funds to pay the tuition. The college or university often terminates the program when it discovers that the convicts cannot afford the courses and/or when they lose patience with the bureaucrats who manage the correctional facility. Alternatively, a DOC may be so slow with the payments that a school may decide that it is not economically viable to continue (Ross and Richards, 2002).

College credit by correspondence

As most prisons do not offer college courses or actively support prisoners who pursue postsecondary education, one alternative is for prisoners to take self-paced college classes by correspondence. Most of these university programs do not have admission requirements and do not require a GED or high school diploma to begin classes. Many of these programs have been operated by for profit colleges and universities with questionable track records (Ross, Tewksbury and Zaldivar, 2015). Almost every correctional facility has a small group of prisoners who take these classes by mail. They usually hang out in the main prison library or law library where it is quiet, and they might have access to typewriters and copy machines.

The time it takes prisoners to complete a course of studies depends on several factors: the time limits established by the correspondence school; the inmates' funds to pay for courses, books, and stamps; scholastic ability; determination; the conditions of confinement, including access to the internet;[3] and distractions. Convicts have to figure out how to pay for the college credit courses and what classes to take. Inmates may use the meager amount of money they earn inside the prison, or ask for outside help (for example, family or friends) to pay for courses. Prisoners also need to have the prison case manager, counselor, or free world friend make arrangements to pay the university. Another idea is to have outside family or friends pay for the first course, and then reimburse them later and/or when the prisoner is released.

Typically, inmates are subject to many security restrictions that complicate their efforts, including no more than a handful of books in cells, limited use of typewriters or computers and copy machines, and regulated mail procedures. Some mail, coming and going, is opened, read, and copied by COs. In years past, books mailed to convicts from friends and families typically had the covers ripped off by prison employees to prevent the entry of contraband into the institution.[4] Now the only way convicts can receive books is from a reputable publisher or bookseller.

College credit courses are not for everybody. Prisoners, just like first-year students on college campuses, have a high rate of failure. On the other hand, inmates have lots of time to read, room and board is provided, and depending on the conditions of confinement, there may be few distractions. Cons who fail to complete a course of studies while incarcerated may finish college degrees at universities when and if they are released from jail or prison. Meanwhile two well-publicized alternative educational programs exist: Inside-Out and Inviting Convicts to College.

Inside-Out Prison Exchange Program®

College students, some pursuing bachelor degrees in criminology and criminal justice, take university-level classes in prison alongside incarcerated students, formally known as the "Inside-Out Prison Exchange Program: Examining Social Issues through the Prism of Prison." Piloted in 1997 by Lori Pompa, an instructor in the Department of Criminal Justice at Temple University, with the support of the Philadelphia Prison System and Temple University, the program now boasts over 20,000 "inside" (incarcerated) and "outside" (campus-based) students having participated in the experience.

In 2002, Pompa, Inside-Out's founder and Executive Director, received a year-long Soros Justice Senior Fellowship to expand Inside-Out nationwide. In 2004, she stated, "After relatively limited outreach, 75 instructors have expressed interest in being trained in this approach. The first Training Institute, scheduled for mid-July 2004, was attended by 20–25 instructors from a dozen different states" (www.temple.edu/inside-out/). Since then, a total of 700 instructors from 45 states in the US and nine other countries have taken part in the intensive, seven-day, 60-hour Inside-Out Training Institute.[5]

The program incorporates the pedagogy of community-based learning (that is, a kind of pedagogy that takes campus-based students out of the classroom to learn, as equals, alongside a group of community partners). Pompa says:

> This unique educational experience provides dimensions of learning that are difficult to achieve in a traditional classroom. At its most basic level, Inside-Out allows the "outside" students to take the theory they have learned and apply it in a real-world setting, while those living behind the walls are able to place their life experiences in a larger academic framework.[6]

The Inside-Out Prison Exchange Program®

> ... was established to create a dynamic partnership between institutions of higher learning and correctional systems, in order to deepen the conversation about and transform our approaches to issues of crime and justice.... This semester-long course provides a life-altering experience that allows students to contextualize and rethink what they have learned in the classroom, gaining insight that will help them to better pursue the work of creating a more effective, humane and restorative criminal justice system. At the

same time, Inside-Out challenges men and women on the inside to place their life experiences in a larger social context, rekindles their intellectual self-confidence and interest in further education, and encourages them to recognize their capacity as agents of change – in their own lives as well as in the broader community. [The students meet] once a week ... through which 15–18 undergraduate students and the same number of incarcerated men or women attend class together inside prison.

All participants read a variety of texts and write several papers; during class sessions, students enter into dialogue about issues in small and large groups; and, in the final month of the class, students work together on a class project. Crucial to the Inside-Out pedagogy is the powerful exchange that occurs between "inside" and "outside" students.[7]

"Inviting Convicts to College" program

In 2004, Professors Susan Reed, Chris Rose, and Stephen C. Richards, criminal justice professors at the University of Wisconsin-Oshkosh (UWO), coordinated the first "Inviting Convicts to College" program in two state prisons (Rose et al., 2005; Richards et al., 2006; Richards and Ross, 2007). On a weekly basis, pairs of undergraduate student teachers visit two medium and maximum-security prisons and teach the *Convict Criminology* course. The university students learn to teach by writing their course syllabi, giving lectures, administering examinations, grading their own class of prisoner-students, and receiving internship credits in return. The prisoners get a free education that is relevant not only to their backgrounds, but also possible future careers.

The curriculum is composed of one free noncredit college course that includes two required books, *Convict Criminology* (Ross and Richards, 2003) and *Beyond Bars* (Ross and Richards, 2009). *Beyond Bars* is about getting out of prison, a favorite subject of all convicts. *Convict Criminology* includes eight chapters authored by former prisoners who were or are now university professors. The texts seek to inspire the prisoner-students to plan on attending colleges and universities upon completion of their prison sentences. Prisoner-students discuss the readings and write papers. Part of the course is devoted to teaching inmates how to transition from prison to college, including completing college admissions and financial aid forms.

Upon finishing the course, the prisoner-students receive a certificate of completion from the university. Students often show the letters notifying them of their acceptance to college to their fellow convicts, and this, in turn, has inspired more prisoners to take the course. Some convicts' "release plans" may include attending college or university.

The "Inviting Convicts to College" program includes a number of innovative ideas. The classes are free because undergraduate or graduate students teach them. University departments that include student internship programs may find this model an attractive idea for placing students as classroom instructors in prisons. Deploying students in this fashion means that universities do not incur the expense of reassigning faculty to teach these classes. The use of student interns as instructors helps keep university and departmental costs to a minimum. The faculty members, in turn, supervise a number of internships, including multiple placements of student interns in different prisons. This model is relatively easy to implement, thus making it easily employed at no expense in many correctional facilities across the country.

As of May 2016, the program has now been running for 12 years, with a total of 48 semester courses.[8] The student interns have been supervised by professors Michael Lenza, Stephen C. Richards, and Chris Rose. The courses are very popular with both prisoners and the university student-teachers. Many of the convict students exited prison to enter college or university. Some of the student-teachers went on to attend graduate programs. Both prisons report having long waiting lists of prisoners interested in taking these courses.[9]

Summary

A prison record and a GED provide men and women released from prison with few long-term career prospects other than minimum-wage jobs, but college courses may improve this outlook. After getting out of prison, one possible path for former inmates is to go to college (Ross and Richards, 2003). As a former prisoner, ex-cons are already institutionalized. If they chose and/or qualify, then dormitory living and its bureaucratic rules may be easy for them to deal with. Considering ex-cons usually emerge from behind bars without a job, have no income, and have not typically paid taxes in years, they can sometimes even qualify for nongovernmental student loans and possible grants.

Faith-based programming

As mentioned earlier, during the past four years in U.S. prisons, there have been attempts made to integrate more religious programming (primarily Christian) and to get faith-based communities involved in prisoner re-entry programs. This may include the promise of housing, meals, and work once a prisoner is released. Although there is a long history of religious communities' involvement with prisons, this current iteration can be traced back to the time when former President George W. Bush was governor of Texas. He allowed the Prison Fellowship Ministries (led by Charles W. Colson, a former convict, who had done time because of his role in the 1971 Watergate break-in scandal) entrance into the Texas Department of Corrections to run a program called InnerChange Freedom Initiative, which was "a Bible-centered prison-within-a-prison where inmates undergo vigorous evangelizing, prayer sessions, and intensive counseling" (Kleiman, 2003). To date, there have been few evaluations of the success of this program or others. One particular study, produced by the University of Pennsylvania's Center for Research on Religion and Urban Civil Society, touted Colson's program as a success, but the study was severely criticized for selection bias (Kleiman, 2003). Meanwhile, several such programs have fallen under the watchful eye of civil libertarians because of allegations of using state funds for religious purposes (Henriques and Lehren, 2006).

Therapy in prison

Many prisons operate a variety of alcohol and drug treatment programs. Too often, staff or inmates who are unqualified run the programs. "Departments of corrections frequently encourage inmates to establish self-help programs. These are run primarily by the inmates themselves and often express ethnic and cultural goals. Self-help groups meet in the evenings and on weekends. They usually are required to have a staff sponsor and to establish governing bylaws and procedures" (Bartollas, 2002: 314). Needless to say, there are many problems with drug treatment behind bars (Austin, 1998). Some of the more successful programs are Alcoholics Anonymous (AA) and Narcotics Anonymous (NA). These programs, sometimes with the assistance of outside volunteers, teach and support prisoners in a "twelve-step program," which involves both psychological and lifestyle changes. There is a certain continuity within these programs, and when prisoners are released on parole, their officers may require them to attend these meetings and/or one of the conditions of parole may be to attend AA/NA (Austin, 1998). In fact, many individuals in AA/NA are ex-cons. Cognitive-behavioral programs are consistently found throughout US prisons and are designed to address and modify the patterns of thought that some have argued contribute to criminality. In brief, "The therapy assumes that most people can become conscious of their own thoughts and behaviors and then make positive changes to them. A person's thoughts are often the result of experience, and behavior is often influenced and prompted by these thoughts. In addition, thoughts may sometimes become distorted and fail to reflect reality accurately" (Clarke, 2010). In general, the scholarly research seems to indicate that this treatment modality is effective with both juvenile and adult inmates, and can minimize recidivism (Landenberger and Lipsey, 2005). Anger Management Programs, on the other hand, have been found to be of questionable utility (Terry, 2003: 160–83). Once again and unfortunately, in the recent get-tough era, state governments have cut back funding for competent therapy programs.

Not to be forgotten are a myriad of therapy-like programs such as Shakespeare in prison, yoga, dog training, girl scouts in prison, that can both decrease inmate stress while behind bars, and assist them to forge positive links to the outside world and possibly assist with reentry.

Boot camps

Other solutions for rehabilitation have been the creation of boot camps in state-run facilities (Armstrong et al., 2002). As mentioned in Chapter 3 of this book, also known as shock or intensive incarceration, these types of programs started in Georgia and Oklahoma in 1983. Essentially these programs, which, based on the most recent research, are currently operating in approximately 39 states and are separate from the main facility, last a maximum of 120 days and involve a military or paramilitary regimen.

> Most are residential facilities for juvenile delinquents or adult criminals with military style structure, rules, and discipline. Boot camp programs are expected to reduce prison crowding and related costs. They are also intended to reduce recidivism and antisocial behavior. Finally it is commonly believed that they can deter individuals from future offending while also helping to rehabilitate them through the imposition of discipline. (Odo, Onyeozili, and Onwudiwe, 2005: 79)

Unfortunately, rigorous evaluations have discovered that inductees do no better in the boot camp environment than those sent to traditional correctional institutions (Armstrong et al., 2002: 126). Moreover, it does not appear that benefits are accrued in the reduction in prison space (overcrowding) (Mackenzie and Souryal, 1991).

Second Chance Acts

Toward the end of the Clinton Administration (1990s), a handful of criminal justice experts (for example, Petersilia, 2003) and well-placed USDOJ (U.S. Department of Justice) officials (for example, Travis, 2005) argued that because of the numerous people who were incarcerated for long sentences under the War on Drugs (ca. 1971–present), both the federal and state DOCs and numerous communities would soon witness an increasing number of prisoners returning to society. More importantly, the U.S. criminal justice system and the communities to which these ex-cons would return were ill-prepared for this effect. This phenomenon, labeled prisoner re-entry, employs "the use of programs, practices, and strategies targeted at promoting the successful re-entry of prisoners back into the community" (Swanson et al., 2010: 61).

Why is prisoner re-entry important? Approximately 7.65 million people are released from jails and prisons each year. And about 97% of all incarcerated will be returned to the streets, most of whom are ill-equipped to re-enter "normal life" (Petersilia, 2003), while about two thirds of all inmates who leave America's correctional facilities will be rearrested and sent back to prisons. In order to prevent this cyclical process, it has been argued that we need:

- appropriate and better programs that help prisoners to readjust;
- programs that should be run by both the profit and nonprofit sectors;
- a public that must be more involved in the reintegration of prisoners;
- more coordination;
- more resources to be allocated to successful programs;
- the involvement of faith-based communities; and
- evaluation mechanisms to determine how successful these measures are.

This new-found awareness has led to an increase in research and advocacy on re-entry and to calls for legislation that could provide resources to organizations, both profit and nonprofit, to help ex-cons transition back into the community. Although various administrative efforts in this direction occurred during the George W. Bush administration, one of the major accomplishments between 2001 and 2009 was the drafting and passage of the Second Chance Act.

During the formative years of the Bush administration, the USDOJ created the Prisoner Re-entry Initiative. "Designed as a cooperative effort among several federal agencies, it funds state re-entry programs. In addition, Bureau of Justice Assistance grants are awarded to state departments of corrections for developing prerelease services for prisoners transitioning back home" (Swanson et al., 2010: 61).

The Second Chance Act of 2007[10]

In January 2004, President George W. Bush, in his first State of the Union address, signaled his intent to push for funding for a Prisoner Re-entry Initiative. The original Bill, the Second Chance Act of 2007,[11] was initially tabled in Congress in the spring of 2005 by Senator Danny Davis. Numerous hearings were held on the Act, and several people and organizations testified on its behalf, including several state governors who, over the past two decades, have felt the pinch of the massive increase in their prison populations. The Act had a rather long and tortuous history, but it was finally passed and received appropriate funding.

In general, the Second Chance Act (H.R. 1593) received considerable bipartisan support, including endorsements from over 200 organizations. Both liberal (for example, the American Bar Association, the Children's Defense Fund, the National Association for the Advancement of Colored People-NAACP, and the National Council of La Raza) and conservative organizations (for example, the American Conservative Union, the Christian Coalition, the Family Research Council, and the National Sheriff's Association) endorsed the bill. Yates (2009: 133–6) declared that proponents argued for the bill on economic, crime control, and compassionate grounds.

Despite this support, there was some pushback by selected members of Congress. For example, on December 6, 2006, Senator Tom Coburn (R-OK) put a hold on the Bill. He argued that "there is no federal role in prisoner re-entry," and that his state was doing perfectly fine in minimizing recidivism and reintegrating ex-offenders back into society. According to Yates (2009), the criticisms could be boiled down to the following issues: fear of unequal competition between those who currently have both state and federal money, and new entities entering into the market; fears that once the federal government started funding the program it would lead to increasing government subsidies in this policy sphere; and a perception that prisoners were somehow being given a privileged status (compared to other needy segments of society), distinguished by their ideological position.

In April 2008, President Bush signed the Second Chance Act of 2007 (H.R. 1593) into law. The Bill in its final version is "designed to ensure the safe and successful return of prisoners to the community." The Act, earmarked at $65 million, was intended to help state and county re-entry initiatives, fund community and faith-based groups to deliver services to ex-convicts, and encourage drug treatment programs. Finally, it was aimed at ensuring adequate housing, work, substance abuse counseling, mental health treatment, and support for families and children.

The need for this Bill was fairly self-evident. At the time of its passage, it was commonly acknowledged that communities must take an active role in the reintegration of prisoners. More coordination at the federal level was necessary, and money needed to be appropriated to determine how successful these programs are.

In December 2009, "the Senate approved an appropriations bill for fiscal year 2010 that provides $114 million for prisoner re-entry programs administered by the Department of Justice, including $100 million for Second Chance Act grant programs and $14 million for re-entry initiatives in the Federal Bureau of Prisons. The House of Representatives passed the bill (H.R. 3288) on Thursday, December 10, 2009."

Shortly after the passage of the legislation, in 2008, a number of Requests for Proposals (RFPs) made their way to the Office of Justice Programs, more specifically the Bureau of Justice Assistance, which is responsible for administering these programs.

This initial RFP was issued in the spring of 2009. In that year, there were three funding mechanisms:

- FY 2009 Second Chance Act Mentoring Grants to Nonprofit Organizations (worth 10 million dollars);
- FY 2009 Second Chance Act Adult and Juvenile Offender Re-entry Resource Center (worth 2.2 million dollars); and
- FY 2009 Second Chance Act Prisoner Re-entry Initiative Program (demonstration grants) (worth 7.7 million dollars).

In 2009, the Bill was up for reauthorization. It was relabeled The Second Chance for Ex-Offenders Act of 2009 [H.R. 1529]. In 2010, three new RFPs were released (with submission dates of June 10, 2010):

- Second Chance Act technology careers – To provide technology career training to individuals in state prisons, local jails and juvenile residential facilities; and
- Second Chance Act Evaluation and Educational Improvement Grants - To evaluate and improve academic and vocational education for incarcerated adults and juveniles, and then recommend to the USDOJ the best practices for such educational programs.

The grants were targeted toward "[states], units of local government, territories and federally recognized Indian tribes; and other public and private entities." Up to $750,000 per applicant was allowed for the first grant and $2.5 million was available for the second. As of this writing, the awarded grants have not yet been subject to scientific evaluations. This will happen in due course and the money for this will in all likelihood be channeled through the National Institute of Justice.

In March 2009, President Barack Obama signed into law an appropriations Bill that provides $25 million for Second Chance Act programs, with $15 million in grants for state and local re-entry projects, and $10 million for nonprofit mentoring and transitional services for the remainder of the fiscal year. For 2010, the President requested more than $200 million for re-entry programs, including $100 million for Second Chance Act programs administered by the USDOJ and $112 million for those overseen by the U.S. Department of Labor (CCA, 2010). In 2010 and 2011, funding to support the Act was continued with $100 million the first year, and $70 million the second. Although a new Second Chance Act (that is, The Second Chance for Ex-Offenders Act of 2011 (H.R. 2065), which was aimed at the expungement of ex-felons' criminal records, was introduced in Congress, it failed to progress pass the committee stage. In September 2015, the Fair Chance Act (S. 2012) was introduced in Congress by U.S. Sen. Cory Booker (D-NJ) and U.S. Rep. Elijah Cummings (D-NJ-7). The legislation strives to increase work opportunities for ex-felons, including outlawing federal agencies and their contractors from asking potential candidates if they have ever been convicted of a crime (that is, ban the box).

Conclusion

Most jails and prisons fail to adequately rehabilitate inmates, but this should not come as a surprise. The emphasis in jails and prisons is disproportionately on punishment, and the external benefit is supposed to be community safety. Still, as this chapter has outlined, there are opportunities for both administration- and convict-led efforts for prisoners to improve themselves. Also important are the numerous programs either run or assisted by outside volunteers. These exist in prisons like Graterford, Angola, and San Quentin. They help with health, literacy and job skills for prisoners.

One must guard against the perception that treatment effects are too idiosyncratic to allow for the implementation of programs with broadly positive effects. Although there are "responsivity" issues (individuals react differently depending on how a treatment is delivered), there is growing evidence (as noted earlier) that most people convicted of a crime are generally responsive to cognitive-behavioral interventions (Andrews et al., 1990).

Meanwhile, periodically, well-meaning individuals and organizations gain access to prisons and, with the blessing of the warden, senior correctional personnel, or the DOC, manage to get their "rehabilitative" programs implemented. Unfortunately, this "correctional quackery" often suffers from poor science. Their beneficial claims are based on anecdotal rather than empirical evidence. It is also difficult for such programs to compare the advantages of their experiment to other programs around the country. For example, it would be useful to know how the acquired skills and experiences transfer to something that is tangibly useful on the outside (Latessa et al., 2002).

> Understandably, some rehabilitation programs work better than others, but no program works all the time – or even most of the time. The best success rate for the programs is only about 20 percent, and even this figure can be misleading. Different programs measure "success" in different ways. For some, success means a complete halt to criminal activity. The inmate, after his [sic] release, never again has a brush with the law. For others, an inmate may

be considered rehabilitated if the "rate" of his criminal activity declines: He may be rearrested (or reconvicted or reimprisoned) and still be considered "rehabilitated" so long as he is not rearrested as often as he might have been had he not participated in the rehabilitation program. The consensus is that programs that work best tend to be those that teach so-called life skills like balancing a checkbook and those that stress family involvement. (Hallinan, 2003: 133)

Key terms

Boot camp: Military like, short-term stay correctional facility. Started because some legislators and correctional practitioners believed that inmates lacked discipline, and this method would best assist them.

Correctional quackery: Quick fix rehabilitative programs and practices that have been introduced in the field of corrections.

Faith-based programming: Using the skills and resources of religious communities, especially evangelical Christian communities, to help in the reform of convicted felons.

General Education Development (GED): High School Equivalency test.

"Inside-Out Prison Exchange" program: Program that brings college level students into the local prisons to take a class with inmates. Administered by Temple University.

"Inviting Convicts to College" program: Developed by the University of Wisconsin-Osh Kosh professors. Students teach prisoners using the book *Convict Criminology*. Upon graduation students are given a certificate and then assisted in applying to university.

Jailhouse lawyer: Inmate, sometimes with formal legal training, who assists other inmates in the preparation of legal documents and processes.

Net widening: The recognition that over time instead of closing jails and prisons or through the process of decriminalization the criminal justice systems comes up with new ways to monitor and sanction individuals who break the law. Also includes the expansion of probation and parole to include things like urine tests, etc.

No Frill Prisons Act: Passed in 1994, barring such amenities as televisions and coffee pots in FBOP cells.

Rehabilitation: Programs and practices used to change convicts so they stop engaging in crime.

Responsivity: How well an individual responds to different kinds of treatment based on how it is delivered; there is growing evidence that most offenders are generally responsive to cognitive-behavioral interventions.

Second Chance Act: Federal legislation passed in 2008 which provides additional resources to states and private entities to help prisoners make the transition back to the community.

Technical violation: When an individual on probation or parole fails to abide by the conditions of their sentence.

Notes

[1] For a review of current pay rates of prisoners in state and federal systems see, for example, www.prisonpolicy.org/prisonindex/prisonlabor.html.

[2] This presupposes that they are relatively literate. As many studies have demonstrated, reading and writing abilities among prisoners are very low.

[3] In most correctional facilities, inmates are not allowed internet access, however they may be able to access www.corrlinks.com, which they can use for e-mail. Alternatively, sometimes a link to a particular online educational interface can be arranged on an individual basis.

[4] The staff are concerned about drugs (for example, sheets of LSD, heroin, or cocaine), weapons (for example, razors or hacksaw blades), or money being hidden in a cloth, cardboard, or paper cover.

[5] Personal correspondence with Lori Pompa, August 19 2016.

[6] Personal correspondence with Lori Pompa, August 3, 2007.

[7] Downloaded December 3, 2015.

[8] Personal correspondence with Professor Stephen C. Richards, July 16, 2007 and May 13, 2016.

[9] Email conversation with Professor Christopher Rose, September 1, 2015.

[10] This section draws on Yates (2009: 111–55).

[11] The Second Chance Act of 2007 can easily be confused with H.R. 1529, the Second Chance for Ex-Offenders Act of 2009, which concerns the expungement of criminal records for criminals.

NINE

Overburdened community corrections system[1]

Introduction

Community corrections consists of a number of different types of programs and sanctions for individuals who have either been charged with or convicted of a crime, or who have served jail or prison time but are still under the supervision of the criminal justice system. As reviewed in Chapter 3, there are various community corrections options including prerelease, supervised release, probation, intermediate sanctions, parole, and mandatory release. The problems experienced by community corrections are not only for the agencies and officers, but also for the individuals who are awaiting their trials, people who have been convicted of a crime but have been sentenced to probation, inmates who are released from jail or prison on parole, and their families and loved ones. Over the past decade, this non-institutional approach has encountered or experienced numerous problems. These difficulties continue to occur, even after repeated criticisms during the 1980s and 1990s claimed that community corrections programs were too lenient, and that tougher sanctions and forms of control needed to be implemented (for example, Morris and Tonry, 1990).[2]

Community corrections now stresses programs that make probationers and parolees more accountable, and protect the public better. These gains, however, have come at a cost. Probation and parole officers/agents spend a considerable amount of their time writing reports, receiving training, going to court, attending probation and parole revocation hearings, and talking with program providers, all of which take time away from actually supervising their caseload.

The emergence of prisoner re-entry as a new policy concern

At the tail end of the Clinton Administration (1990s), a handful of criminal justice experts (see, for example, Petersilia, 2003) and well-placed USDOJ (U.S. Department of Justice) officials (see, for example, Travis, 2005) argued that because of the numerous people who were incarcerated for long sentences under the War on Drugs (ca. 1971–present), both the federal and state departments of corrections (DOCs) and communities would soon experience an increased number of prisoners returning to society. More importantly, the U.S. criminal justice system and communities where these ex-cons will return are ill-prepared for this effect. This phenomenon labeled "prisoner re-entry" is "the use of programs, practices, and strategies targeted at promoting the successful re-entry of prisoners back into the community" (Swanson et al., 2010: 61).

Why is prisoner re-entry important? Approximately 7.65 million people are released from jails and prisons each year. And about 97% of all incarcerated will be returned to the streets, most of whom are poorly prepared to succeed (Petersilia, 2003), and about two thirds of all inmates who leave America's correctional facilities are rearrested and sent back to prisons. In order to prevent this recycling, it has been argued that we need:

- appropriate and better programs that help prisoners to readjust;
- programs run by both the profit and nonprofit sectors;
- involvement of the public in the reintegration of prisoners;
- more coordination;
- more resources to be allocated to successful programs;
- involvement of faith-based communities; and
- evaluation mechanisms to determine programmatic success.

This new-found awareness has led to an increase in research and advocacy on re-entry, and in calls for legislation that would provide resources to organizations, both profit and nonprofit, to help ex-cons transition back into the community. Although administrative efforts during the George W. Bush Administration addressed these initiatives, one of the major accomplishments between 2001 and 2009 was the drafting and passage of the Second Chance Act.

During the formative years of the Bush administration, the USDOJ created the Prisoner Re-entry Initiative. "Designed as a cooperative effort among several federal agencies, it funds state re-entry programs. In addition, Bureau of Justice Assistance grants are awarded to state departments of corrections for developing prerelease services for prisoners transitioning back home" (Swanson et al., 2010: 61).

The problems

Several difficulties confront the modern practice of community corrections (for example, Finn and Kuck, 2005). These include: role conflict; the location of community corrections offices and social service providers; rigid, bureaucratic, or inflexible supervisors; the failure to make a meaningful reduction in recidivism; high levels of work-related stress; violence by probationers and parolees against their officers/agents; overcrowded/overburdened probation and parole officers/agents; lack of adequate funding; and the growth of a prisoner re-entry complex.[3] The following provides a review of these challenges.

Role conflict

One of the problems for some probation and parole officers is that they suffer from role conflict (for example, Goffman, 1959). On the one hand, they perform some of the duties of social workers; on the other hand, they are law enforcement officers. "The majority of officers used to see themselves in the counseling role. Personal involvement in the supervision of offenders was emphasized" (Bartollas, 2002: 132).

During the 1970s, the reintegration model emphasized probation officers as resource brokers instead of counselors. Increasingly, their role as law enforcement officers is stressed (Hemmens and Burton, 2003). Why? Historically, many community corrections workers earned degrees in the fields of social work, psychology, and sociology. Now they are disproportionately drawn from individuals with community college diplomas or university degrees in criminology and criminal justice. These factors combined mean that, compared to past practices, probation and parole officers are more likely to violate (that is, charge and/or rearrest) probationers or parolees who do not comply with their court-sanctioned requirements. In sum, over time, the probation/parole officer role has shifted its focus to public safety functions, emphasizing surveillance, control, and ensuring that their charges comply with the numerous court-mandated orders (West and Seiter, 2004; Bonta et al., 2008).

Location of community corrections offices and social service providers

Although some probation and parole offices are located in or next to courthouses, most of the agencies, as well the facilities that are established to help ex-cons (for example, residential treatment centers and halfway homes), are situated close to or within the parts of towns where the probationers and parolees live (Hipp et al., 2011). These neighborhoods are typically poor or economically depressed. On the one hand, it makes sense to locate community corrections agencies and social services agencies that assist them in these neighborhoods. Rent and land are relatively cheap in these parts of the city, allowing typically cash-strapped probation and parole departments to take advantage of these cost savings.

Additionally, it is easier for probationers and parolees to access these programs, since they are not required to hop on a bus or subway, and spend half a day traveling across town or downtown just to speak to their officer or agent. Also it must be understood that probation and parole offices and related services experience a lot of community backlash, particularly in middle-class residential areas or upscale commercial parts of a city, as a result of their office location. Many landlords refuse or are reluctant to rent to probation and parole agencies. Residents and business owners argue or worry that probationers and parolees will commit new crimes close to these locations, or will in some manner negatively affect property values.

On the other hand, arguments can also be made that locating community corrections offices and related services in poorer parts of town only contributes to the cycle of poverty and crime that these communities experience. In short, the offices are often located in poorer areas because the communities in more upscale neighborhoods generally complain that they do not want ex-cons wandering in their streets and back alleys, or into commercial establishments. Needless to say, where a probation and parole office is located is a major, real challenge for probationers and parolees in rural parts of states and places without access to adequate public transportation. Consequently, it would stand to reason that the number of technical violations for failures to report would be higher in these situations.

Rigid, bureaucratic, and/or inflexible supervisors

An additional difficulty that has plagued community corrections is that officers/ agents routinely complain about unnecessarily rigid, bureaucratic, and/or inflexible supervisors. Many administrators forget what it was like when they were line parole or probation officers. "The overall pattern of probation in the late 1980s and 1990s showed much defensiveness on the part of administrators and little tolerance for innovation" (Bartollas, 2002: 141). A corollary problem is that advancement possibilities for probation and parole officers are limited. Administrators seem to remain in their positions for long periods of time, and when a few positions open up, there is considerable competition.

Failure to make a meaningful reduction in recidivism

One of the effects of an overburdened community corrections system is the high rate of recidivism. But recidivism, as was previously discussed, is a complex phenomenon that is difficult to define and measure (Austin, 2003). Moreover, because of the human element, there is only so much a probation or parole officer can do to help a probationer or parolee to change their attitudes and behavior. This is perhaps why most community corrections agencies try to shy away from using the term recidivism, and evaluate the progress of their clients in terms of whether they have *successfully met the conditions of the supervision.* In the end, these factors contribute to a considerable amount of stress on the part of the officers, and this leads to job burnout and high turnover rates.

High levels of work-related stress

Almost all of the problems with community corrections have led to increased levels of psychological and physical stress on probation and parole officers and related correctional staff (Finn and Kuck, 2005). Undoubtedly, the amount of stress varies based on the job detail and the kinds of individuals the community supervision workers are responsible for. It also depends on the maturity level, the work attitudes, and the experience of the probation and parole officers. This challenge has been recognized not only by workers and management, but also by the federal government. During the mid-1990s, the National Institute of Justice (NIJ), for example, funded a series of studies examining stress in this job category (for example, National Institute of Justice, 1998). Most of the sources of stress are embedded in the following discussion.

Violence by probationers and parolees

Few probationers and parolees like going to the community supervision office or welcome visits by their officers. This is especially true if there is a possibility that their status (that is, probation or parole) will be revoked and their freedom to live in the community (that is, outside a correctional facility) is in peril. According to Finn and Kuck (2005), somewhere "between 39 and 55 percent of officers have been victims of work-related violence or threats" (1). Supervision means that many officers make home and work visits in poorer and more dangerous parts of a city, county, or state. This puts them in contact with all sorts of unsavory elements of society, and the risk of victimization, particularly assaults, is greater in these environments.

Overcrowding/high caseloads

The number of people in community corrections depends on a variety of factors including the population of the state, "differences in sentencing philosophies, and the availability of probation resources within the state" (McCarthy and McCarthy, 1997: 108). It stands to reason, however, that if a significant number of people are being sent to correctional facilities and these places are overcrowded, then community corrections will be utilized for those individuals when judges and parole boards deem them suitable for this sanction.

The majority of individuals sent to jail and prison will eventually be released back into the community (aka *re-entry*), and many will serve the balance of their sentence on parole. The simple result is that there are too many people for probation and parole agencies to handle, and funding has not increased proportionally to the number of individuals on probation or parole needing supervision.[4] In short, this translates into higher caseloads than normal. Overcrowding means that there is more planned and unexpected paperwork and deadlines (Finn and Kuck, 2005).

Lack of adequate funding

As in the case of institutional corrections, budget cuts and increased numbers of people on probation and parole have meant that over the past two decades community corrections agencies have had to do more with less. In turn, staff are frequently stretched too thin, and the utilized facilities and offices, like those of many inner-city public services in the United States, are dilapidated, shoddy, or in need of renovation, and equipment is either broken or technologically outdated. Although some money is recouped by charging probationers or parolees for services like urine tests, electronic monitoring (EM), and house or work visits, this funding source is clearly not enough.

Most states, like Maryland, charge a supervision fee of approximately $40.00 per month for everyone under probation and parole. In many state systems, community corrections workers put in a couple of years, and, if they are appropriately qualified and lucky, they then transfer out to the federal parole system where salaries and benefits are higher and working conditions are significantly better. Increasingly, money is being cut for community corrections. This means that when the lion's share (typically 85%) of the agency's budgets goes for salaries and fringe benefits, little money is left for meaningful programs for the people who need it the most, in particular convicts who have been released who have few resources at their disposal.

Exhibit 9.1

Classics in corrections

Richard McCleary's *Dangerous Men: The Sociology of Parole* (1978)

An ex-convict and current professor of Sociology and Criminology at the University of California–Irvine, McCleary provides an in-depth account into the minds and actions of parole officers. This early ethnographic study outlines the positive and negative aspects of working as a parole officer. McCleary (1978/1992) develops a useful typology of ex-cons on parole. According to the author, a dangerous ex-con is one who cannot be influenced by the parole officer, thus increasing the likelihood of having their parole revoked. The study also looks at the working conditions for and decision-making of parole officers, in particular the relationships they have with their co-workers and supervisors, and the types of individuals who are attracted to this kind of position. Since the book has been written, there have been several changes in the DOCs, and in community supervision. This include the kinds of policies, practices, and laws that probation and parole officers must administer.

The introduction and growth of the prisoner re-entry industry (PRI)

Predictably, both activists and concerned citizens are worried about not only the problem of prisoner re-entry, but its wider implications. The concept of the PRI was first made public and given scholarly attention in the summer 2010 special issue of *Dialectical Anthropology*, which contained a handful of articles that dealt in whole or in part with this issue. The authors of the piece introducing the special volume, in manifesto-like style, state that "the next step in the expansion" of the Prison Industrial Complex is the PRI. Thompkins et al. claim, "Beyond the privatization of prisons and prison services, there has been a much broader and less noticeable expansion of the 'Prisoner Re-entry Industry' (PRI)" (2010). These writers add:

> In scope, the PRI now parallels the prison system itself in its political-economic spread. ... These institutions exercise a kind of super-authority, allowing for the continued recommitment of released prisoners to the custody of the prison industry and/or continued post-prison supervision. And with the staggering rates of incarceration (and thus release), the PRI has come to control an increasing proportion of the domestic population. (Thompkins et al., 2010)

The authors note the economic importance of the PRI, commenting that it "feeds both the profits and the growing influence of the PRI" (Thompkins et al., 2010).

Ducksworth, another contributor to the special issue, commenting on the growth of the PRI, maintains that "what began as a legitimate social need has now developed into a major federal, state, and county initiative that includes both the private and the public sector; with many of the not-for-profit agencies taking on the characteristics of the for-profit entities. And all seem to be making money!" (2010). He suggests that there are many problems with the PRI, but singles out two for discussion. The first is society's inability to know when re-entry ends. In short, Ducksworth is suggesting that we may be keeping ex-prisoners in re-entry programs too long, extending their punishment and control under the guide of "helping prisoners re-adjust to the outside world." Even if an individual's prison time was far in the past and their behavior since then has been exemplary, the reality is that the stigma of being an ex-con remains with that person for the rest of their life. The second area for criticism is "the professionalization of the industry." Ducksworth states that much like former drug users and abusers make good drug counselors, the persons who are best suited to help an ex-prisoner are those who have been through this experience as well: "an equipped, skilled, and committed former offender is usually far better able to assist another former offender through the transition phase than someone only intellectually exposed to the experience" (2010).

Meanwhile, some of the research included in the special issue addresses how well these private service providers are performing (Kleis, 2010). Kleis, for example, states that "Parolees, like other populations directly impacted by the PRI, have become targets of exploitation and coercion by those individuals and social institutions of control which has resulted in the development of the PRI, and a para-prison system" (1). Other research (Speck, 2010) looks at how well ex-cons do when they go to work in human services' organizations. Speck, for instance, points to the historical legacy of the war on poverty when, through grants made available during the Johnson administration, an increasing number of people began working for the human services sector.

Admittedly, criticizing the re-entry movement is not easy. Many well-respected and well-meaning individuals work hard not only as parole officers, but as administrators of programs trying to help ex-cons. Also, many of these people and the organizations they work for expended considerable resources in order to pass the Second Chance Act. In short, their hearts are in the right place. Those taking up the challenge of criticizing this aspect of re-entry must be careful not to bite the hand that feeds them, and this, in part, may have tempered the criticism and analysis of the *Dialectical Anthropology* authors.

The rendering of the prisoner re-entry complex and the comparisons with the Prison Industrial Complex (PIC) are not without criticism. According to

Ross (2011), although the PRI concept makes intuitive sense, as the current literature and critique stands, it has eight distinct drawbacks including:

- it does not recognize that privatization of re-entry is an old concept;
- it fails to take into consideration the net-widening thesis;
- writers make unsupported claims and there is some conceptual confusion connected to the PRI concept;
- no attempt is made to determine the amount of money that private re-entry-related organizations earn;
- the role of faith-based community organizations is ignored;
- privately run halfway houses are omitted;
- the Second Chance Act is missing from discussion; and
- most importantly, the critics may be overstating the case.

In short, the opportunities to make money in the re-entry field are almost endless. However, the recent scholarly research to date that examines the existence and growth of the PRI suffers from a number of shortcomings in terms of documentation, breadth, and overgeneralization. This state of affairs, however, does not mean that the PRI is wrong, but the scholarship should be interpreted as the start of a conversation and not an end in itself.

Solutions

In order to deal with the overburdened community corrections system, important changes have been implemented. The following discussion reviews the most salient of these initiatives. These innovations include community corrections officers carrying weapons, utilizing private-sector therapeutic communities, user fees for probationers/parolees, redistributing the workload, new classification levels, enlisting faith-based communities, experimenting with techno-corrections, and specialized caseloads.

Carrying weapons

It goes without saying that most people who are under probation or parole are hostile to community corrections workers. Officers are sometimes in jeopardy of being assaulted or killed (Parsonage and Bushey, 1989; Parsonage, 1990). Since the late 1980s, some states and the federal probation system have permitted community corrections workers to carry guns. Most jurisdictions are now allowing probation and parole officers to carry weapons as well (Camp and Camp, 1999). Likewise, some community corrections workers (for example, in Maryland) are now wearing body armor when they effect arrests or go into situations that they believe are dangerous, and in some jurisdictions arrests of probationers and parolees are now only done by municipal and state police officers instead of by probation and parole officers.

Residential programs/therapeutic communities

Part of the solution for overburdened community corrections also includes the use of residential programs or therapeutic communities. Similar to halfway houses, these typically nonprofit organizations train and counsel ex-cons. Some are run by government corrections departments while others are administered by private self-help organizations. One of the most respected private initiatives is the San Francisco-based Delancy Street Foundation. On average, Delancy Street participants have served four terms in prisons, have 18 criminal convictions, and have been substance abusers for ten years (Mieszkowski, 1998). "Today the foundation has 1,500 full-time residents in five self-run facilities around the United States – including a spectacular 350,000-square-foot complex on San Francisco's waterfront, and a rural ranch in San Juan Pueblo, New Mexico" (Mieszkowski, 1998). When the residents leave, they are expected to have two marketable skills that they learned through this program. Its graduates have become "lawyers, doctors, small business owners, restaurateurs, mechanics, contractors, and salespeople." In sum, many of these private programs have been met with praise, especially because they have a visible impact on recidivism.

User fees for probationers and parolees

Increasingly, in order to deal with the additional financial burden that has been placed on community corrections offices, probationers and parolees in some jurisdictions are now being charged user fees (for example, for urine tests) – a nominal amount these individuals, under supervision, must pay for partaking in this sanction. Needless to say, this is an imperfect solution. Ex-cons struggling to find gainful employment end up saddled with extra financial obligations that cut into their meager earnings (Bronner, 2012). No wonder that in some jurisdictions, ex-cons refer to probation and parole officers as collection officers.

Redistributing the work

Caseload standard

In the past, an ideal caseload for probation and parole officers was between 35 and 50 adults (American Probation and Parole Association [APPA]).

no empirical evidence shows that this range is ideal or that it is regarded as such any longer. In practice, caseloads vary widely (Vetter and Adams, 1970). *The Corrections Yearbook: 1999* reported that the average caseload of adult probationers was 124. Caseloads ranged from 54 in Wyoming to 352 in Rhode Island. Intensive supervision probation caseloads average 25 offenders, ranging from 9 in Arizona to 51 in Rhode Island. (Cromwell et al., 2002: 128)

Over the past three decades, different "ideal numbers" have been proposed. In 1973, for example, the President's Commission on Law Enforcement and Administration of Justice (National Advisory Commission on Criminal Justice Standards and Goals, 1973) recommended that probation/parole caseloads should be 35 clients per officer. They argued that

> [h]igh caseloads, combined with limited training and time constraints forced by administrative and other demands, culminate in stopgap supervisory measures. 'Postcard probation,' in which clients mail in a letter or card once a month to report on their whereabouts and circumstances, is an example of one stopgap measure that harried agencies with large caseloads use to keep track of their wards. (Schmalleger, 1999: 350)

Additionally, most probation and parole agents work for small agencies administered by a handful of managers (351).

Across America, there is a considerable range with respect to the number of cases assigned per officer. In one recent survey, officers in Arkansas supervised 154 individuals, whereas those in Wisconsin were responsible for 51 (Cromwell et al., 2002: 129). "[T]he average [number of] face-to-face contacts between officer and probationer was 18 in 1998. Offenders under intensive supervision averaged 114 contacts per year" (128).

Workload standard

Caution, however, must be exercised, as

> not every offender needs the same type or amount of supervision to achieve the goals of probation or parole. There are a number of proven and accepted methods for determining the type and amount of supervision, but the key is that in order to be most effective and efficient, there must be varying amounts of supervision provided to offenders. (APPA)

The APPA

recommends a "workload standard" instead of a caseload standard. It does not make sense, the APPA argues, to count every case as equal. A case requiring maximum supervision effort may require, for example, four hours of the probation or parole officer's time per month. A medium supervision case may require two hours per month to effectively supervise. A minimum supervision case may only require one hour or less per month of the probation or parole officer's time. ... Depending on the makeup of the caseload, the officer could effectively and efficiently supervise 30–40 maximum supervision cases, 60 medium cases, and as many as 120 minimum cases. In practice, caseloads contain offenders at every level of supervision need. The ideal caseload then is calculated by determining how many hours are available to the officer and adjusting the caseload to account for the various supervision requirements of the persons being supervised. (Cromwell et al., 2002: 128)

Workload versus caseload standard

The workload standard takes into consideration the fact that probation and parole officers have other duties beyond supervising clients. These may include writing pre-sentence investigation (PSI) reports and traveling across or around a large geographic region (Cromwell et al., 2002: 128). Occasionally, probation and parole officers working in large states like Texas supervise a caseload that is spread out over 300 miles. Alternatively, there may be community corrections officers who have caseloads in large inner cities that are confined to 12 city blocks (128). In sum, it is very difficult to set an ideal caseload number, but the workload standard helps managers and researchers make better comparisons among probation and parole officers and helps administrators better apportion the workload to make things fairer among employees (128). It must also be understood that some probation and parole officers have mixed caseloads including probationers and parolees.

In Maryland, for instance, the Division of Parole and Probation currently operates with only intensive and standard (aka *minimal*) levels of probation. Sometimes, however, the "standards" consume more time than the intensives.

Another issue is that, in some cases, the interim between actual in-person contacts might stretch for weeks, and this can lead to a lackadaisical approach to handling probationers and parolees. This practice has been pejoratively labeled *postcard probation*, in which officers and parolees/probationers will chiefly communicate through the mail, and rarely by phone or in person.

Starting in 2001, some jurisdictions have introduced kiosk technology. With this system, pretrial, probationers, and/or parolees, have their fingerprints scanned and this is electronically compared to the ones on file. They are also asked a series of questions and may receive instructions electronically from their community supervision officers (Ogden and Horrocks, 2001).

PSIs written by other community corrections professionals

One of the biggest problems with probation is that in many offices the individual who is supervising probationers is the same person writing up the PSI. Rarely is this recognized as a conflict of interest, although it should be. Why? Because the impact of these recommendations will affect an office's workload. So, for example, if a division needs more individuals to supervise, PSI writers might simply recommend probation. If a probation office is overwhelmed, then a writer may favor incarceration (Czajkoski, 1973; Campbell et al., 1990). This is part of the reason why the task of writing PSIs is being increasingly taken out of the hands of probation officers and given to other correctional professionals. In Maryland, for example, parole agents no longer write PSIs, investigators do. And the investigators do not supervise offenders.

New classification levels

Workloads have also been coupled with the development of new classification levels. These are typically broken down into intensive, medium, or minimum supervision. Most of these categories are modeled after the Wisconsin Classification System, or the National Institute of Corrections (NIC) Model Probation Client Classification and Case Management System (Bartollas, 2002: 128). This approach may help decrease the burden on probation and parole officers.

The enlistment of faith-based communities

Undoubtedly, there is a prisoner re-entry problem/challenge (Petersilia, 2003). This has been recognized at different levels of government. State and federal correctional services are worried about the increasing number of individuals who are being released from jails and prison, and they fear that there are not enough resources in the community to manage this population. At the federal level, former President George W. Bush acknowledged the challenge of prisoner re-entry in his January 20, 2004, State of the Union Address. Bush outlined how he intended to utilize faith-based groups to help the federal government successfully manage the re-entry of prisoners into the community. According to Bush, "This four-year, $300 million initiative will provide transitional housing, basic job training, and mentoring." Although religious groups (particularly Christian-based) have historically been involved in rehabilitating prisoners, to date no unbiased evaluations have been done on the current faith-based initiative. At the time of this writing, there are numerous popular media accounts of these initiatives, but evaluations looking at a comprehensive array of these unique programs using social scientific methods do not exist. Instead, the evaluations are of local or state-based programs that are scattered around the country and appear somewhat idiosyncratic in terms of their findings.

Techno-corrections

During the 1980s, specialized technology improved, enabling more inmates to be released from jails and prisons and to be supervised out in the community (Fabelo, 2000). Methods include electronic monitoring (EM) systems and pharmacological treatments. In general, EM involves a tracking device (like a wrist or ankle bracket) worn by the probationer or parolee, and it is sometimes combined with home confinement. It consists of a control computer, a receiver, and a transmitter. Communication can be established through a landline, cell phone, or satellite. If probationers/parolees leave a proscribed area or enter into a prohibited one, a signal is emitted to their designated probation or parole office. The community corrections office then asks the probationers/parolees to get in touch. If the probationer/parolee does not respond in a specified period of time the community supervision center attempts to locate them.

Electronic monitoring use has grown considerably since 1986 from a first test group of approximately 95 individuals in Florida to about 70,000 individuals monitored by local, state, and federal entities. But EM is not without its difficulties. During the 1990s, reports surfaced that cited problems with the devices and the practice of using EM (Corbet and Marx, 1991; Hoshen et al., 1995). These included technical difficulties (that is, "bugs") with the equipment, substantial up-front costs, the cost of running the system effectively, and community reaction to criminals who are on EM. In particular, members of the public often do not feel comfortable when they see individuals wearing EM devices, and do not believe that EM does an adequate job tracking people released on probation or parole. Although both the equipment and protocols for its use have improved, recent evaluations of EM outline a number of problems with these devices that still exist (Kilgore, 2013).

Nevertheless, one variant of EM is the Secure Continuous Remote Alcohol Monitor (SCRAM), an ankle bracelet that analyzes a person's sweat for the presence of alcohol in the bloodstream. It is increasingly being used as a condition of probation or parole in several jurisdictions in the United States. SCRAM was introduced in 2003; by summer 2007, its manufacturers claimed that 40,000 individuals had used the device. Part of the reason behind the rise in popularity of this sanction and control is because it has been sported by various well-known American celebrities, like actors Lindsay Lohan, Tracey Morgan, and Michelle Rodriguez (Zumbrun, 2007).

Another kind of techno-correction approach involves the use of drugs. Since the mid-1990s, states such as California, Florida, Georgia, Texas, and Wisconsin require men convicted of sexual offenses with minors, when released from prison into the community, to register with the local police and be chemically castrated. These individuals receive shots of Depo-Provera, a drug that lowers the body's production of testosterone and hampers the sex drive (Fabelo, 2000). As for how long men are on this drug, it depends on the terms and conditions of their release. It could be from as long as they are on parole/probation to the remainder of their life.

Electronic monitoring and drugs are not supposed to offer a solution to overburdened community corrections programs, but they decrease the need to personally monitor those individuals on the probation or parole officer's caseload.

Specialized caseloads

The probation and parole profession has recognized that ex-cons (with similar criminal convictions) can benefit by dealing with specialist probation and parole officers. This group includes probationers and ex-cons that have alcohol and substance abuse problems, dangerous offenders, sex crime offenders, and those who have mental health issues (Cromwell et al., 2002: 130). Thus, there has been increasing specialization among probation and parole officers, and the system benefits through more efficient case management.

Rhine et al. (1991) reported that "by 1990, specialized parole caseloads were being used in 25 states."

> Fourteen states were using specialized caseloads for sex offenders, 12 for drug offenders; 10 for offenders with mental disabilities, five for 'career criminals,' and 2 for violent criminals. Specialized caseloads for DWI ... offenders were established in Texas in 1983 and now exist in virtually every medium-to-large probation department in the nation. Although few empirical studies have been conducted of the efficacy of specialized caseloads, anecdotal evidence supports the concept. (As quoted in Cromwell et al., 2002: 130)

Addressing the privatization of community corrections

In order to properly understand the role of privatization in the recent initiatives in prisoner re-entry, a responsible critique needs to do the following:

- recognize that privatization of re-entry is an old concept and process, and must be adequately integrated into a critique;
- understand just how the expansion of re-entry processes can contribute to net widening;
- ensure that claims about the downsides of re-entry are properly argued;
- rigorously determine the amount of money private re-entry-related organizations earn;
- examine the role that faith-based organizations and privately run halfway houses have in re-entry;
- determine just how much the Second Chance Act has contributed to expanding re-entry; and
- make sure that claims are based on empirical and not anecdotal evidence.

Conclusion

Through the implementation of sound policies and practices, coupled with the professionalization of probation and parole, along with rigorous empirical research, we may be able to minimize the problems of the overburdened community corrections system. But this is extremely difficult in an environment where government cutbacks exist, and an increasing number of people are being incarcerated and/or placed on community corrections programs each day. Finally, the community corrections system needs more resources – particularly funds to be earmarked to this vital service, trained professionals who are capable of doing a proper job, and more emphasis on rehabilitation rather than on simple reporting requirements.

Key terms

Caseload standard: The number of probationers/parolees that a community corrections officer is expected to supervise.

Depo-Provera: A drug that acts to lowers the body's production of testosterone and hampers the sex drive. Sometimes given to male sex offenders upon release from a correctional facility.

Electronic monitoring: A tracking device worn by the probationer or parolee, which consists of a transmitter, receiver, and computer. Allows the DOC to monitor the whereabouts of individuals.

Postcard probation: Clients send in a letter or a card once a month to report on their whereabouts and circumstances.

Presentence investigation: A step in the sentencing process whereby the probation officer does a detailed investigation of the individual who hasn't been accused of committing a crime.

Prisoner reentry: Term used to describe the contemporary practice of releasing prisoners from jail and prison through mandatory release and/or parole and assisting them back into society.

Recidivism: Term used to provide a measure of four alternative kinds of interrelated actions/behaviors: convicts committing another crime; convicts being arrested; convicts convicted of a crime; and convicts returning to jail or prison.

Role conflict: When individuals (e.g., parole or probation officer) assume two different conflicting roles, such as social worker and police officer.

Technocorrections: Specialized technology that allows for the possibility of keeping more inmates out of jail and prison and instead supervised in the community.

Therapeutic community: Facilities where participants live, eat, and are provided with ongoing counseling. This may be one-to-one or in the context of a group.

Workload standard: Organizing a probation/parole officer's caseload based on the individual specifics of a case and the amount of time it takes to properly supervise the person.

Notes

[1] An earlier version of this chapter benefited from the comments of Ginger Duke-Miller, Ernest Eley, Mike (Lee) Johnson, Alicia Peak, and Dana Valdivia.

[2] One of these innovations was the use of intensive probation.

[3] Although most jurisdictions use the terms "probation" and "parole" to refer to different periods of the criminal sanction, with probation being a front-end option and parole a back-end option, the FBOP uses probation, as in probation officers, to describe the job classification of someone who supervises an individual who has been released from prison into the community and is still supervised.

[4] This chapter does not review the problems faced by residential treatment centers. For an analysis of some of these, see, for example, Bartollas (2002: 112–13).

TEN

Crowding/overcrowding

Introduction

If you are a criminal justice practitioner, inmate, or former inmate, and/
or pay attention to the news, then it should come as no surprise that U.S.
jails and prisons are severely crowded and overcrowded. In some facilities,
four prisoners are sleeping in cells originally designed for one person. Other
correctional institutions have converted their halls, recreational areas, and
classrooms into dormitories with double and triple bunking. "By 1980,
two-thirds of all inmates in this country lived in cells or dormitories that
provided less than sixty square feet of living space per person – the minimum
standard deemed acceptable by the American Public Health Association, the
Justice Department, and other authorities. Many lived in cells measuring
half that" (Hallinan, 2003: 97). Fortunately, most of these situations are
only temporary and after a while a jurisdiction must look for longer-term,
lasting alternatives to the shortage of cell space. Many experts might say that
underfunding is the biggest problem facing corrections.

If the correctional departments at the municipal, regional, state, and
federal levels had more money, then new facilities would be built, more and
better qualified correctional officers (COs) would be hired, and overcrowding
would no longer be an issue. This presupposes that the money would be spent
properly and that qualified persons could be hired and trained throughout the
ranks. Regardless of this chicken-and-egg problem, there are several causes of
the overcrowded conditions in our jails and prisons (Bartollas, 2002: chapter
18).

Overcrowding is recognized as a problem by a wide cross-section of
individuals with expertise in the corrections field. This reaction is not simply
that of well-intentioned do-gooders; among those who advocate reducing
overcrowding are state and federal judges. However, the Supreme Court
has overruled the sentiments of these jurists. The Court argued in *Bell v.
Wolfish*, 99 S. Ct. 1861, 1875 (1979), a landmark overcrowding case, that the

Constitution does not provide for the "one man, one cell" ethos. They argued that if states wished to put two men in a cell designed for one, they were free to do so. Likewise, the Supreme Court added, in *Rhodes v. Chapman*, 101 S. Ct. 2391, 2400 (1981), that the Constitution does not guarantee inmates "comfortable prisons."

It should be understood that this problem varies from state to state and between the state and the federal systems. Nevertheless, crowding/overcrowding is not an either-or situation. There is considerable nuance in determining whether a facility is crowded or overcrowded. In order to assess whether crowding or overcrowding exists, the corrections field has developed three complementary standards: a facility's *rated capacity*, *operational capacity*, and *design capacity*.

The first figure is the number of prisoners or beds a facility can handle as judged by a qualified expert who is responsible for making this determination. The second approach refers to the number of inmates a correctional institution can accommodate given the staff, programs, and services available. The final benchmark is the number of convicts that the original planners, designers, or architects envisioned that the facility would be able to house (McKinnon, 2004: 656; Schmalleger, 2006: 366). In general "[r]ated capacity estimates usually yield the largest inmate capacities, while design capacity ... typically shows the highest amount of overcrowding" (Schmalleger, 2006: 366). Jail and prison administrators and the secretaries of each state DOC selectively use these standards to suit their individual short-term purposes.

What many analysts fail to consider is that the total number of jails is decreasing. Newer and bigger jails are being built to address overcrowding; however, capacity has not kept up with the actual numbers of inmates (Allen and Simonsen, 2001: 168). This can be represented by a simple fraction: number of institutions/cells. If, in the construction of big facilities, the number of cells decreases, then administrators have an overcrowding problem. If, on the other hand, the number of cells increases, then the situation is better for the prisoners and staff.

Crowding/overcrowding leads to many, if not most, of the other problems facing the correctional system including:

1. hostility, anger, and violence by convicts toward other inmates and COs;
2. compromised security for both convicts and staff – in particular, it fuels gang activity (Hallinan, 2003: 98–100);
3. ability to follow through with classification plans;
4. rehabilitation taking a backseat to the demands of running a safe and secure institution;
5. strain on the infrastructure and equipment of the institution and on the services that are provided to inmates. Things break down more often because they are overused – like a lock that opens and closes all day long or that has been abused by frustrated cons. Inmates typically take their

aggression out on other inmates, correctional staff, the building, and the equipment; and

6. pressures to build more facilities.

Causes

There are several interrelated reasons that have led to the problem of overcrowding. These include moratoriums on the death penalty, zero tolerance policing, the aging prison population, the closing of correctional facilities, demographic shifts, the increased costs of running jails and prisons, public and political apathy, and new sentencing laws.

Moratoriums on the death penalty

In some states (that is, Arizona, Colorado, Ohio, Oklahoma, Oregon, and Washington[1]), where they have put a moratorium on the death penalty, this shift has led to a slight increase in the prison population. Inmates are now afforded multiple appeals. They typically start with the statewide system, and, when the state appeals are exhausted, they move on to the federal courts. Prisoners given the death penalty typically have to wait a little over seven years before their sentences are carried out. In the meantime, those sentenced to death and their lawyers usually appeal their sentences on a variety of grounds. However, this number is marginal. Alternatively, in some states where there is a long wait on death row, there is an overcrowding problem.

Zero tolerance policing

Likewise, the use of zero tolerance policing (in jurisdictions where law enforcement officers are not allowed to use discretion) has been argued to increase the number of people behind bars. Much has been discussed about zero tolerance policing (for example, Dennis, 1997), the notion that in some jurisdictions, parts of a city, or with some types of crime, police officers are required to stop, question, search, issue a citation or a summons, or arrest an individual if they believe the individual has committed a crime. Zero tolerance policing typically takes place in the context of the policing of hot spots, and High Intensity Drug Trafficking Areas (HIDTAs). It minimizes an officer's ability to use their own discretion.

The aging/graying prison population

As previously reviewed, the population of prisoners 55 years and older is increasing. This is not simply because the elderly are committing more crime. The tendency of inmates to live longer means that more individuals are being housed in correctional facilities. In some prison systems, institutions have been specially created for the elderly. As people age, they typically need more health care and specialized facilities. The Federal Bureau of Prisons (FBOP) runs six Federal Medical Centers (that is, FMC Carswell (TX), FMC Lexington (KY), FMC Devens (MA), FMC Butner (NC), FMC Rochester (MN), and MCFP Springfield (MO)). Overall, the problem is more acute in states that have life without parole sentencing practices (Flynn, 1992).

The closing of correctional facilities

Albeit a rare occurrence, states periodically close jails and prisons. This type of action – often opposed by most COs and their unions – usually only takes place after numerous attempts by the state to renovate one or more correctional facilities, or to appropriate funds to purchase land and build a new facility have been made. This explains why so many older and deteriorating jails and prisons are still operating. Exceptions do occur though. For example, in March 2007, the State of Maryland finally closed the House of Corrections located in Jessup. Over the past decade, the 128-year-old prison, pejoratively referred to as *The Cut,* had experienced several officer stabbings. The 800 inmates were dispersed to different facilities throughout the state.

Demographic shifts

In general, the number of people convicted of committing crimes has increased over the past few decades. This is largely due to shifting birth rates, which started approximately 18–35 years ago. This is seen as the population at risk, because crime is usually a young person's activity. That group is a direct result of the baby boom following World War II, which clogged the school systems of America in the 1950s and 1960s and has now affected yet another area – urban crime. That group is also the one with the highest unemployment rate, and in time of general underemployment, will continue to commit crime out of proportion to its size (Allen and Simonsen, 2001: 243).

Increased costs of running a facility

Over time, because of the professionalization of COs, union pressures, legal suits, and other factors, it has become more expensive to run a jail or prison. Enormous resources are required to efficiently and legally operate correctional institutions. Conterminously, governments are freezing the budgets of jails and prisons, or are imposing budgetary cutbacks. Underfunding means that jails and prisons must generate more money from other sources or simply do without. Correctional planners often assume that costs will be saved if prisoners and functions are consolidated in the same physical building. Through this increased use, however, facilities deteriorate, causing health and safety issues for convicts, COs, and correctional administrators alike. If conditions become too unsafe, because of the threat or reality of successful lawsuits or public outcry, inmates are transferred to other existing jails and prisons. Unless regular maintenance, upgrading, and planning are done, correctional institutions are disproportionately at the whim of each and every subsequent warden, state director of corrections, and state legislature.

Political and public apathy

Politicians, political candidates, and the public have become apathetic about allocating more funds to corrections if that means improving prison conditions or rehabilitative programs. It is easier for convicts to remain "out of sight, out of mind." Most people believe that those who are incarcerated are guilty and that they are getting their just deserts. And no politician who appears to be soft on crime is likely to be elected or reelected. On the other hand, elected representatives are frequently actively writing and passing laws to increase penalties for criminal behavior. However, they are rarely cognizant of (or unwilling to publicly admit) the unintended consequences of their activities. Likewise, as reviewed in Chapter 2, the public is generally poorly informed, and plagued with all sorts of myths about both who is incarcerated and what goes on behind bars. Thus, they remain apathetic (Ross, 2000c: chapter 7).

Sentencing laws and practices

The growth in correctional populations is attributable to a number of previously reviewed factors, including severe sentencing laws (for example, the crack versus cocaine sentencing disparity, three strikes you're out, mandatory sentencing) and practices, and the fact that the federal government and many state governments have abolished parole, thus forcing inmates to stay longer in their correctional facilities. The Sentencing Reform Act of 1984, in particular, put an end to parole at the federal level, reducing good time, mandatory minimums, and determinant sentencing. Similar initiatives were then implemented in several states. In addition to the aforementioned mandatory sentencing laws, Congress passed Aimee's Law in 1999. Named after Aimee Willard, a university student living in Philadelphia, who was raped and killed by a Nevada state parolee, this law holds states financially liable if they release an inmate and that person commits another felony in a different state. The "release states" are now obligated to pay any arrest, prosecution, and imprisonment costs incurred by another state, in addition to $100,000 to the victim's family. Thus, states are now under the obligation to either successfully rehabilitate the individual or prevent them from release (www. congress.gov/bill/106th-congress/house-bill/894).[2] Given that rehabilitation is almost impossible behind bars, there is a tendency to keep inmates locked up for longer periods of time. All told, this situation prevents states from releasing more inmates (see Exhibit 10.1).

Exhibit 10.1

Causes and effects of crowding/overcrowding

Causes	Effects
Demographic shifts	Increased wear and tear
Underfunding	on prison facilities
Changes in sentencing	Security of facilities is
Closing correctional	compromised
facilities	Increased violence
Increased costs	Rehabilitation is curtailed
Moratoriums on the death	
penalty	
Zero tolerance policing	
The aging/graying prison	
population	
Political and public apathy	

Solutions

By far the most frequent solution proposed by state and federal correctional planners to the problem of crowding and overcrowding has been the construction of new correctional institutions, which cost millions of dollars each. Understandably, estimates on the cost of new jail and prison construction vary.

Some reports place the average cost to build one bed space for a prisoner at $54,000. This figure, however, does not include the amount of money the state or FBOP needs to finance the construction of a correctional facility, nor to feed, clothe, and "rehabilitate" inmates. The increase in the number of jails and prisons built has forced many states into debt.

> California, for example, between 1980 and 1990 spent more than $5 billion building new prisons. ... Across the nation, prison construction has outpaced the construction of new schools. Moreover, while construction addresses overcrowding, it has no impact on reducing prison populations and may actually contribute to growing incarceration rates. ... Critics argue that the construction strategy is based upon an "If you build it, they will come" philosophy; that is; the more prisons that are built, the more inmates will be found to fill them. (McKinnon, 2004: 657)

Meanwhile, it appears as if there is always a budget crunch within state DOCs. As a response, officials often cut overtime for officers and try to reduce benefits, and this often results in compromises to officers' safety. Correctional facilities need to be more creative in developing methods of staffing and maintaining the institutions, and funding programs for inmates. Nevertheless, how have local correctional systems dealt with the problem of overcrowding?

The ten solutions most often used include:[3]

1. purchasing abandoned buildings (for example, motels);
2. using manufactured housing units (for example, trailers);
3. erecting tents;
4. using jail barges;
5. renting spaces from other jurisdictions;
6. placing prisoners under house arrest;
7. using electronic monitoring;
8. double and triple bunking;
9. shipping inmates out of state; and
10. relying on private prisons to pick up the slack.

Sometimes it takes an innovative leader to deal with the problem of overcrowding. For example, in the 1990s, shortly after the new jail was opened in Kings County in Seattle, WA, and it almost immediately became filled to capacity, the manager invited senior representatives from different local criminal justice agencies to meet once a month at a local restaurant to help him manage this problem. These informal and informational conversations led to a concerted effort among judges, police officials, and prosecutors to either lessen the number of people going to jails or hold the jail population constant (Coleman, 1998).

Other ways to get out of prison

With the exception of escaping and/or death, there are three other basic legal ways individuals can get out of prison: commutation, amnesty, and pardon. All of these fall under the broad category of clemency. The final issue discussed is prison abolition.

Commutation

Commutation is when the executive (that is, President, governor, or board of pardons) reduces the sentence of a person convicted of a crime. This practice can occur before the individual enters a correctional facility or during the time, the person is incarcerated. Often the reduction is made "based on time already spent in jail and prison and results in almost immediate release of the petitioner" (Allen and Simonsen, 2001: 614). These kinds of executive actions are often controversial. In the spring of 2007, for instance, President George W. Bush commuted the prison sentences of his Chief of Staff, Vice President Dick Cheney, and White House insider I. Lewis (Scooter) Libby for obstruction of justice, perjury, and making false statements to federal investigators.[4]

Pardon

In general, a pardon "nullifies an original sentence and can occur while an offender is incarcerated, or while on parole or probation. A pardon can also be issued after a full sentence has been completed, or even granted posthumously" (Thomas, 2005: 135). There are two basic types of pardons: full/absolute or conditional. The first "applies to both the punishment and guilt of the offender" and eliminates "the existence of guilt in the eyes of the law. It also removes his or her disabilities and restores civil rights. The conditional pardon generally falls short of remedies of full pardon, is an expression of guilt, and does not obliterate the conviction" (Allen and Simonsen, 2001: 700).

Pardons are also acts of the executive. At the federal level, these can be granted by the President, and at the state level, it is the governor who has the power to bestow pardons. In both instances, these individuals review cases after a pardon board has vetted them. In general, there are three reasons for pardons: "(1) to remember a miscarriage of justice, (2) to remove the stigma of a conviction, and (3) to mitigate a penalty. Although full pardons for miscarriages of justice are rare … some individuals [have] been released from prison after it has been discovered that he or she was incarcerated by mistake" (Cole, 1994: 668–9).

Amnesty

Amnesty is a form of pardon typically "granted to a group or class of offenders." In the United States, amnesty is frequently given after wars "to soldiers who deserted or avoided service." This is typically done to curry favor with potential voters (or constituencies) in upcoming elections (Allen and Simonsen, 2001: 614). For example, in 1977 under President Jimmy Carter, Vietnam veterans who had evaded the draft or deserted were offered amnesty (Baskir and Strauss, 1987). Similarly in 1997, President Bill Clinton "gave amnesty to qualified Central American aliens residing in the United States" (Thomas, 2005: 135).

Prison abolition

No sooner was the first prison constructed than there were calls for its reform. One of the most radical positions has been the prison abolition movement, which "want[s] to either eradicate whole elements of the current punishment system or bring an end to it entirely. They also advocate for a variety of alternatives" (Greene, 2005: 2). In the forefront of this movement are "activists, ex-prisoners, academics, religious actors, politicians, inmates and their families" (2). The modern origins of prison abolition started during the 1960s in Scandinavia and soon spread to other Western countries. In the United States, the prison abolition movement began in 1976 with the help of Quaker and prison minister Fay Honey Knopp, who established an organization called the Prison Research Education Project and later authored the well-known book, *Instead of Prison: A Handbook for Abolitionists*. In 1981, the Canadian Quaker Committee for Jails and Justice started advocating prison abolition, and in 1983, the very first International Conference on Prison Abolition (ICOPA) was held in Toronto (Ross, 1983). Since then, the organization has evolved, including a name change, substituting the words "circle" for "conference" and "prison" for "penal," so that the organization is now called the International Circle on Penal Abolition.

NIMBY

Often, when it comes time to locate or build a jail or prison, correctional administrators and planners have difficulty finding an ideal spot. Local residents are typically not happy with a facility being built so close to where they work or live, or to where their children go to school. This phenomenon is usually referred to by its acronym NIMBY (that is, Not In My Back Yard), which alludes to citizens' concerns about the negative effects, especially safety and/ or the impact on their property values. Often, the neighborhoods in which correctional facilities are housed are the poorer ones. In 1998, in Washington,

D.C., for example, the Corrections Corporation of America (CCA) purchased 42 acres in Anacostia, the historically impoverished southwest part of the city, in order to build a much-needed prison for the District. In part as the result of the corporation having been criticized for the way it had run its prison in Youngstown, OH, residents of Ward 8, where the parcel of land was located, were upset with the decision to build the facility there, mounting a spirited campaign against its construction (Thompson, 1998: B1, B9). Locations such as this one make sense for developers of jails and prisons. It is often comes down to economics, since the land in such locations is cheaper. Needless to say, the D.C. government never approved CCA's plans for the jail.

Then again, many economically depressed communities either lack a political voice to prevent the construction of a nearby jail or prison, or are all too happy to have correctional facilities be built in or relocated to their town, city, or region. For example, an archipelago-like group of correctional facilities, including the city jail and state prison buildings with various security classifications, has been established in an impoverished section of downtown Baltimore. Various businesses that are dependent on the existence of the correctional facilities (for example, store front bail bonds operations) have sprung up almost next door. The nearby residents of this section of town are typically transient and thus rarely participate in local politics.

On the other hand, some local or regional bodies lobby their elected and appointed officials to attract a new jail or prison. This was true in Florence, CO, where during the early 1990s, the residents bought land and donated it to the federal government for building a Supermax prison. Similar situations exist. As portrayed in Michael Moore's *Roger and Me*, shot in Flint, MI, the residents lobbied the state government to have a new prison situated there to pick up the slack from a faltering economy, largely caused by the closing of the local General Motors plant (1989). Similarly, in Weed, CA, "supporters of a proposal to build a prison in their town have held prison rallies and barbeques to raise money to hire a public relations expert to argue their case to state officials" (Welch, 1998: 110–11). Although many constituencies assume that these new correctional facilities will spur local economic growth, this accepted wisdom has been called into question (Hooks et al., 2004).

Conclusion

In many states that have determinant sentencing, the DOCs engage in a process known as *collective incapacitation*. With this approach almost all of those charged with a criminal offense that involves jail or prison time complete their entire sentences behind bars. In systems where there is *selective incapacitation*, on the other hand, only those individuals that a judge determines will benefit from incarceration or that they believe are becoming career criminals will be placed behind bars (Schmalleger, 2006: 367). Regardless, both of these practices contribute to the increased number of people incarcerated.

Several factors are taken into consideration when a new jail or prison is built, including the conditions of existing nearby institutions, the cost of maintaining the old ones, demographic shifts, cash flow, and other economic uncertainties. Although many people advocate rehabilitation programs, like drug treatment, higher education, and vocational skills, it is difficult to realistically provide them if there is overcrowding (especially when long waiting lists develop for popular and needed programs).

Policies and practices in connection with life sentences should be reexamined (Liptak, 2005). It must be understood that for one reason or another, some people who are given a criminal sanction do change, while others, no matter how long the sentence or severe the punishment is, may never mend their ways. Notwithstanding, over the past three-and-a-half decades, U.S. state and federal prison populations have grown at exponential rates. This makes it difficult to implement rehabilitative programs. It also makes the job of a CO and other correctional workers more dangerous. Parole boards and sentencing commissions must reexamine the purpose, intent, and effects of life sentences and governors should start reviewing cases for executive clemency. Overcrowding will be a dominant problem in the U.S. correctional system for the foreseeable future.

Key terms

Aimee's Law: Named after Aimee Willard who was raped and killed by a parolee. Forces states to be financially liable if they release an inmate and that person commits another felony in a different state.

Amnesty: A form of pardon typically "granted to a group or class of offenders."

Capacity: The number of inmates a correctional facility can hold.

Career criminals: Repeat offenders who commit a disproportionate amount of crimes.

Clemency: Subsumes pardon, commutation, and amnesty.

Collective incapacitation: A tendency to incarcerate everyone who is convicted of a crime no matter how minor the crime.

Commutation: When the executive (i.e., president, governor) or a board pardons or reduces the sentence of a person convicted of a crime.

Conditional release: A person is released from correctional custody as long as the individual meets certain criteria.

Design capacity: The number of inmates that a correctional facility was designed to hold (by planners, designers, architects, etc.).

Jail barge: A way of housing inmates on reconditioned ships. Popular in New York City during the 1990s. Boats would be docked around Manhattan (i.e., NYC) and moved if neighbors complained.

NIMBY (not in my backyard): The idea that residents or property owners in an area do not support having correctional facilities built near their homes, places of work, or children's schools.

Operational capacity: The number of inmates that can be effectively handled based on the amount of prison staff, programs, and services available.

Pardon: "… nullifies an original sentence and can occur while an offender is incarcerated, or while on probation or parole" (Ross, 2008: 157).

Prison abolition: The goal of a social movement dedicated to eradicating parts and/or the entire current punishment system (i.e., jails, prisons, and other correctional facilities) in the United States and elsewhere.

Rated capacity: "… the number of prisoners or beds a facility can handle as judged by a qualified expert who is responsible for making the determination" (Ross, 2008: 152).

Selective incapacitation: Only individuals who may become career criminals or who would benefit from incarceration receive jail/prison sentence as determined by a judge (Ross, 2008: 159).

Zero tolerance policing: The aggressive enforcement of one or more criminal laws in a particular jurisdiction, or during a specific time period; no discretion is allowed on the part of the officer.

Notes

[1] Death Penalty Information Center, June 13, 2016, www.deathpenaltyinfo.org/node/5829.

[2] After a comprehensive search the author was unable to find any evaluations of the effectiveness of this law.

[3] Readers are reminded that these may differ from practices that are advocated (e.g., decriminalization, sentencing reform, etc.).

[4] Background details surrounding this incident are portrayed in the fictional movie *Fair Game* (2010), starring Sean Penn and Naomi Watts.

ELEVEN

Death penalty

Introduction

The death penalty, also known as capital punishment and/or execution, is the most extreme form of criminal sanction that the criminal justice system can implement. Due to a multiplicity of reasons, the death penalty is one of the most controversial actions that the state can employ against its citizens. This is particularly important in the cases of juveniles, of those who suffer from diminished capacity (for example, mental retardation), and of wrongful convictions. In the United States, the death penalty is administered to those individuals who have engaged in capital or extremely serious crimes. Although not all states have the death penalty, the federal government and the majority of the states (31) do. The only jurisdictions that do not have the death penalty (20 in total) are Alaska, Connecticut, District of Columbia, Hawaii, Illinois, Iowa, Maine, Maryland, Massachusetts, Michigan, Minnesota, Nebraska, New Jersey, New Mexico, New York, North Dakota, Rhode Island, Vermont, West Virginia, and Wisconsin. Additionally some states where death penalty laws exist do not have any convicts on death row. For example, since 1996, Kansas, New Hampshire, New York, and Wyoming have lacked death row convicts.

California, Texas, and Florida are the states with the highest number of death row inmates. Since 1930, there have been over 4,300 executions, and since 1977, Texas has led the way in executions (approximately 144). Do you notice any commonalities among those states that are pro–death penalty? In general, the conservative southern states (where the Republican party is strong) are more likely to advocate the death penalty than the northern ones.

Just because a person is waiting on "death row," so named because of the long hallway where the inmates' cells are located, does not mean that a prisoner's sentence has been commuted. Prisoners given the death penalty typically wait a little over seven years before their sentence is implemented

(Mays and Ruddell, 2015). In the meantime, their cases are often appealed on a number of grounds. Sometimes, a governor may intervene and commute a sentence to life without parole (LWOP). Despite the numerous stays of execution, most death row inmates are eventually killed.

Analysts have discovered three basic disparities within the context of the death penalty: race, gender, and jurisdiction. Although jurisdiction was discussed already, most death row convicts are African-Americans and male. Additionally, about half of all death row inmates have never been married, and about 25% are widowed, divorced, or separated (which may be explained by their partners' low confidence that they will ever be released and resume a relationship). Fewer than half of death row convicts have a high school education, and over half are between the ages of 20 and 39. Few death row convicts are women; approximately 44 women remain on death row (Mays and Ruddell, 2015).

There are five ways that those on death row can "meet their maker." The most prominent is through lethal injection, with 27 states promoting this option. Otherwise the death penalty is administered through gas chambers (7 states), hanging (4), and firing squads (3). Prisoners are often given a choice between lethal injection or one of the other forms. Since 1977, most people (406) have been killed through lethal injection. The use of the electric chair has declined either because states have declared it to be cruel and unusual punishment or because other ways of execution have been deemed preferable. The last person to be put to death in the federal system was Louis Jones, Jr. (March 18, 2003).

Arguments for and against the death penalty

Both those who advocate and those who oppose the death penalty have put forward a number of arguments to support their positions (for example, Mays and Ruddell, 2015: 252; Welch, 2011: 325–8). These two dichotomous arguments are outlined below

A. Why is the death penalty appropriate?
1. It deters people from committing crimes that would result in the death penalty (specific and general).
2. It satisfies retributive tendencies.
3. It lessens one more threat to the world by eliminating an individual who is dangerous.
4. It brings the community together.
5. It is a matter of tradition.
6. It reflects the belief that LWOP is more costly than the death penalty.
7. It avoids vigilante-style responses to crime and criminals.
8. It reduces crowding/overcrowding.

Exhibit 11.1

Documentary

Mr. Death: The Rise and Fall of Fred A. Leuchter, Jr. (1998)

This documentary, by Errol Morris, focuses on the rise and fall of Fred Leuchter, a self-taught engineer who became an expert on execution devices. Leuchter claimed that his services were used to improve the electric chair and gas chambers at different prisons in the United States. This work later brought him to the attention of Holocaust deniers like Ernst Zundel. Zundel and his cohorts persuaded Leuchter to examine the gas chambers at the Auschwitz concentration camp. Leuchter eventually produced a report, which was discredited based on the questionable scientific methods he used. His actions and report ultimately ended his career as a consultant with various state departments of corrections. Throughout the movie, Leuchter demonstrates how he does not seem to know much about actual historical events, as reflected in the fact that he doubted the reality of the Holocaust. The movie also shows how an intense focus on improving the technology of death (that is, methods by which we put people to death) can reveal how some people are divorced from the moral and ethical questions involved in the application of this state sanction.

B. What is wrong with the death penalty?

1. It is a cop out. It is more punishing for the individual to spend the rest of their lives behind bars.
2. Innocent people are sometimes sentenced to jail/prison, but when you sentence them to death, there is no reversal of the decision.
3. There are ethical/moral arguments against it.
4. It creates anger and sadness for the family of the individual sentenced to death.
5. It costs the state too much money (for example, legal proceedings).
6. It does not deter individuals from committing capital crimes.
7. It frequently violates the Eighth Amendment against the imposition of cruel and unusual punishment.
8. It is expensive/wastes limited resources/taxpayers' dollars.
9. It costs more resources than if an individual is sentenced to LWOP.[1]

Most scholarly research indicates that the death penalty does not serve as a deterrent for individuals convicted of committing a capital crime (Nagin and Pepper, 2012). This, however, does not prevent the average person from believing that the death penalty prevents others from committing crimes and that the death penalty is a form of payback and/or just deserts (Champion, 2005: 346–7; Welch, 2011: 339–40). Some suggest that the reason why we should consider LWOP is not based on humanitarian grounds but that the death penalty is the easy way out and a long prison sentence will be hard on the body and psyche and force the prisoner to reflect on a daily basis on the harm they have caused to the victim's family and loved ones. This is mostly an assumption rather than something born out by empirical research. Also, those who put forward this argument erroneously assert that incarceration is an easy punishment to endure. Closely connected to the deterrence debate is the possibility that executions can lead to increased violence (Bowers and Pierce, 1980). Referred to as the brutalization theory, an increasing amount of research has been marshaled to examine this process. Several contradictions and unusual stances are present in the death penalty debate. For example, there is a strong connection between those who are pro-life (and thus, anti-abortion) and those who support the death penalty. The underlying argument here is that it is wrong to take the life of an innocent child based on the sanctity of human life, but once a person has been given a chance (and failed miserably), it is okay to kill them. Likewise, some anti-death penalty activists are happy to dismiss the drawbacks of the death penalty, when the perpetrator is a notorious serial killer (for example, Ted Bundy), a mass murderer (for example, Pol Pot), or a terrorist (for example, Osama bin Laden) (Champion, 2001: 331).

A general history of the death penalty

The death penalty is typically used for individuals who have committed a crime that the community thought was gravely serious. In the past, however, people were sentenced to death for almost any crime, including arson, assault, burglary, counterfeiting, horse theft, pick pocketing, piracy, rape, robbery, slave rebellion, and sodomy (Bedau, 1982: 6).

Over time, in most advanced industrialized and Western democracies, many of these crimes (for example, slave rebellion) have ceased to exist, the penalties have lessened, and in many cases, first-time offenders of less serious crimes have received probationary sentences. On the other hand, treason and murder are still crimes that are typically punishable by death.

In previous centuries, people were put to death in a variety of "appalling," agonizing, and by today's standards, highly unusual ways, including but not limited to: boiling in oil, beheading, breaking on the wheel, burning to death, burying alive, crucifixion, drowning, flaying, impaling, pulling apart, the rack, given over to lions and other wild animals, and sawing in half (Bedau, 1982; Foucault, 1977).

The invention of jails and other detention facilities is one major cause for the decrease in the use of the death penalty. Although prisons have been around since the creation of castles and other similar types of fortifications, it was not until the Enlightenment (in the eighteenth century) that there was a rapid expansion in the construction of jails and prisons. The building of correctional facilities allowed societies to punish lawbreakers without killing them.

Another change that has occurred in the administration of the death penalty is the now private nature of the executions (Bedau, 1982: 22). Until relatively recently, in terms of human history, almost all executions were public (for example, public hangings, the use of the guillotine, and so on). For the convict and their loved ones, this was a humiliating affair, but the leaders of many countries (or political units) hoped that public executions would deter people from committing similar acts. According to Welch (2011):

> Eventually executions were brought behind the closed doors of the prisons. ... It has been suggested that over time the executions placed the monarchy in an unfavorable light since such brutality became viewed as excessive. Paradoxically, these displays of "justice" undermined the legitimacy of rulers. ... By moving punishment to the prison, offenders would be kept from receiving public sympathy". (322)

Despite the various intentions, social scientific research has determined that the death penalty is not an effective deterrent. Why? Most people who commit homicides do not think very carefully about costs and benefits before they commit their crimes.

Furthermore, we now have prisons where we can incarcerate society's wrongdoers for lengthy periods, and the death penalty is not only a viable sanction in many states, but also a controversial political issue. In particular, no self-respecting politician wants to appear soft on crime, and thus, elected officials are very careful when they are campaigning for election or reelection to not position themselves against the death penalty if they think they might lose votes.

A history of the death penalty in the United States

During colonial times, individuals were rarely put to death, as they provided economic benefits to the community.

> King (2003, 947-949) outlined how three procedural protections limited the use of the death penalty in colonial Virginia. First, persons convicted and given the death penalty could have a higher

court review in their case. The reluctance to use the death penalty is evidenced by the high number of convictions that were "set aside" for various technical reasons. Second, convicts sentenced to death were able to ask for benefit of clergy ... In addition, persons sentenced to death had the ability to seek pardons. Unlike the executive clemency today ... [g]ubernatorial pardons were commonly granted. (Mays and Ruddell, 2007: 253)

Exhibit 11.2.

Film

Dead Man Walking (1995)

This commercial movie (directed by Tim Robbins), based on the real-life story of Sister Helen Prejean (played by actor Susan Sarandon), focuses on her attempt to assist Matthew Poncelet (played by actor Sean Penn), who was sentenced to death in the State of Louisiana, and appeal his sentence. Poncelet and an accomplice were convicted of the brutal death and rape of a young girl and murder of her boyfriend. Poncelet never shows remorse, but insists on his innocence until just before the execution. Through the course of her work, Prejean meets not only Poncelet's family, but also the families of the two victims. The families of the victims, other members of the community, and her supervisors, are not happy with Sister Prejean. Poncelet loses his appeal, after which he asks Prejean to be his spiritual advisor. She tells him that he cannot be redeemed until he tells the truth. Minutes before his execution, he confesses to the crime and apologizes for his actions. The movie allows the viewer to develop a modicum of sympathy towards Poncelet, and brings a window into the lives of the perpetrator's and victims' families. The families of the victims did not appear to get any satisfaction from the death of Poncelet.

Benjamin Rush, one of the signers of the Declaration of Independence, basing his insight on Becarria (1738–94), a famous Italian jurist and one of the earliest advocates of abolishing the death penalty, argued "scriptural support for the death penalty was spurious; the threat of hanging does not deter but increases crime; when a government puts one of its citizens to death, it exceeds the powers entrusted to it" (Bedau, 1982: 8).

Over time, states started to drop certain offences as capital crimes. "For instance, in 1961, Nevada dropped train wrecking from its list of capital crimes, and Illinois repealed the death penalty for dynamiting. On the whole, however, many more capital statutes have been added during this century than have been removed, and considerable publicity has surrounded these additions" (Bedau, 1982: 13).

Furman v. Georgia (1972)

One of the most important steps in the death penalty in the United States occurred in the 1970s. This was a result of the famous case *Furman v. Georgia* (1972), which ruled that the application of the death penalty is arbitrary and capricious. In particular, it was argued that the death penalty violates the Constitution's Eighth Amendment against cruel and unusual punishment. According to Welch (2011), "the decision was based, in part, on narrow considerations. In particular, state statutes were unconstitutional because they did not offer judges and juries any guidelines or standards to determine death sentences" (335). Thus, the administration of the death penalty was temporarily banned in the United States. Because of this decision "more than 600 prisoners on death row had their sentences commuted to life imprisonment" (335).

Gregg v. Georgia (1976)

This decision was not welcomed by most pro-death penalty states (particularly those in the South). Advocates worked hard to find a legal loophole to reinstate the death penalty, and within four years, Georgia reworked its criminal code to allow for the death penalty. "In 1976, the U.S. Supreme Court ruled on *Gregg v. Georgia* ... in that it decided that capital punishment is not, in itself, cruel and unusual punishment. The cornerstone of *Gregg* was that the conditions and procedures of death sentences be clearly established" (Welch, 2011: 337). Thus, in 1976, the death penalty was reintroduced in many states.

The current way that the death penalty is applied in the United States

Each state has different rules with respect to how the death penalty is applied (for example, exactly when and who may be present during the execution). More "humane" ways to put people to death have also been developed.

Over the past century, one of the biggest challenges for the states has been finding a relatively safe way of killing people that was "pleasant" for the witnesses. That is why there has been so much experimentation with the way we execute people.

The way we put people to death has changed from hanging, to firing squad, to electrocution, to gas chamber, and to lethal injection (mid-1980s), the final of which is a three-drug cocktail that puts the individuals to sleep, paralyzes them, and then stops their hearts. Practices like the gas chamber are very dangerous to witnesses and very resource intensive.

In the United States, the death penalty was once applicable for a whole host of crimes, but now it is only used for murder. In short, the crime has to be a death-eligible homicide in order for the death penalty to be applied.

Many states have repealed their death penalty legislation. In recent times, some governors (for example, George Ryan Sr., governor of Illinois) opposed to the death penalty have commuted the sentences of many individuals to LWOP. In 2003, Ryan, just before leaving office, commuted the sentences of 167 inmates to life in prison.[2] Another development in the history of the death penalty has been the cases adjudicated by the Innocence Project in which exculpatory DNA evidence was collected, leading to the release of individuals who were incarcerated on death row.

Liebman and colleagues (1999) reported that fewer than 6% of all persons sentenced to death are actually executed. In many cases, inmates live on death row for decades before their execution. With few inmates being executed, death row populations have swelled, although the number of persons condemned to death has been decreasing in sharp contrast to the growing jail and penitentiary populations (Mays and Ruddell, 2007: 251).

Another reason why some individuals have been spared the death penalty is jury nullification. This occurs when a jury is sure that the accused committed the crime, but it does not like the penalty. As a result, the jurors acquit the person of the crime.

Additionally, there have been Supreme Court cases that have ruled that the death penalty should not be used against juveniles and the mentally retarded.

Death penalty in other countries

Around the world, the only other countries besides the United States that have the death penalty are Iran, Iraq, Japan, Peoples Republic of China, Saudi Arabia, Singapore, St. Kitts & Nevis, Taiwan, and North Korea. With the exception of Belarus, all of the nations belonging to the European Union have rejected the use of the death penalty. Although there is no single reason why, the European states are typically concerned that governments tend to wield too much power. This sentiment allegedly dates back to the legacy of Nazi Germany and the other fascist regimes that operated during World War II. Amnesty International reports that by 2015 102 countries have "completely abolished the death penalty" (www.amnesty.org/en/what-we-do/death-penalty/, June 13, 2016).

That is why some states refuse to extradite people wanted by the U.S. criminal justice system, if they might be sentenced to the death penalty. If this is the case, there is protracted negotiation between the U.S. Attorney and the country where the individual has sought shelter (or escaped to).

In the case of extradition proceedings, one of the following can happen. An individual is identified as wanted in the United States, and a warrant is issued for their extradition. Once the individual is in custody, they can waive extradition or fight it. Either a public defender in that country or a private attorney will take on the case and legal motions are filed back and forth to prevent the speedy extradition of the individual. When the person is finally extradited they are done so with the proviso that if convicted the harshest sentence they might receive is LWOP (Ross, 2011c).

Conclusion

The death penalty has been abolished in European Union countries and in most advanced industrialized democracies. The United States remains out of sync with these advanced industrialized democracies. This situation presents a contradiction because the United States purports to be a leader in human rights and equality, although this controversial legislation remains on the books. So, why do anti-death penalty activists work so hard? They do not want to take a chance that the wrong person might be executed, even if this means the penal system has to spend considerable resources keeping them incarcerated.

Key terms

Benefit of clergy: In the past, individuals who were convicted of a crime were allowed to either be supervised by the Church or join the clergy instead of being incarcerated or given the death penalty.

Brutalization theory: "… the use of the death penalty as a punishment by the state deadens people's respect for life and thus increases the incidence of homicide" (King, 1978: 683).

Extradition: Legal method and process by which a country transfers a suspected or convicted criminal to another country, regulated by treaties and other international laws.

Furman v. Georgia (1972): Famous Supreme Court death penalty related case arguing that this sanction was arbitrary and capricious. It led to the temporary suspension of use of the death penalty in the United States.

Gregg v. Georgia (1976): Famous Supreme Court death penalty related case "that decided that capital punishment is not, in itself, cruel and unusual punishment" (Welch, 2011: 337). This led to Fuhrman v. Georgia being overturned.

Guillotine: Originating in France, this tall frame like contraption contained a thick, heavy, and angled blade, suspended in grooves and tracks by a rope. When triggered, the blade would behead the person who was placed there. Used frequently during the French Revolution.

Innocence project: Investigates allegations of wrongful convictions and educates the public about miscarriages of justice.

Lethal injection: Most popular way that the death penalty is applied in the United States. Consists of a three-drug cocktail that puts the individual to sleep, paralyzes them, and then stops their hearts.

Life without parole: Sentence given to a person convicted of a felony, typically one that is death eligible. Convicts given this kind of sanction are required to spend the balance of their life locked up in a correctional facility. In the United States, this sanction is no longer applicable to juveniles who have committed felonies.

Note

[1] The option of LWOP has been criticized by numerous anti-death penalty advocates, who claim that this type of sentence is worse than the death penalty (Wright, 1991; Villaume, 2005).

[2] In September 2006, Ryan was convicted of a number of white collar crimes and was sentenced to federal prison.

PART III

Challenges for correctional officers and administrators

TWELVE

Hiring standards, requirements, practices, and training

Introduction

Working as a correctional officer (CO) is not easy. Several challenges must be addressed for a person choosing this profession. In order to better understand these difficulties, this chapter reviews the number of COs working in the United States, their basic demographic characteristics, their motivations for working in this field, the process of getting hired, educational requirements, age restrictions, the pay, and the training that COs receive.

Number of correctional officers in the United States

Over the past four decades, the number of COs hired by federal, state, and local correctional systems has increased but not at a level commensurate with the number of people being incarcerated. What does this mean? In short, correctional systems increasingly have to do more with fewer employees.

According to the U.S. Department of Labor, Bureau of Labor Statistics (BLS), COs held about 469,500 jobs in 2012 (www.bls.gov/ooh/protective-service/correctional-officers.htm). The BLS adds:

> Employment of correctional officers is projected to grow 5 percent from 2012 to 2022, slower than the average for all occupations. Although budget constraints and a falling crime rate will require fewer workers, job openings will continue to become available because the dangers associated with the job cause many to leave the occupation each year.

About 16,000 CO jobs were in Federal correctional institutions, and about 15,000 jobs were in privately owned and managed prisons. (www.bls.gov/oco/ocos156.htm).

Demographics

The numbers of male, female, and visible minority COs vary from state to state, and different jurisdictions (that is, local, state, and federal). According to the Bureau of Justice Statistics:

> Male employees outnumbered female employees by a ratio of 2 to 1. Among correctional officers and custody staff working in direct contact with inmates, men outnumbered women by a ratio of 3 to 1. The largest difference in staff by gender was among correctional officers in federal facilities. In federal facilities, 87% of correctional officers were men and 13% were women. The smallest difference – 52% men and 48% women – was among the total workforce in private facilities. In state operated facilities, about 74% of correctional officers were men and 26% were women. (Stephan, 2008)

One of the fastest growing segments of this population are women and nonwhites.

A number of reasons have contributed to the increased number of women and minorities in the field of corrections, including the passage of the Civil Rights Act of 1964, which prohibited discrimination in hiring based on race and ethnicity; the 1972 amendment (Title VII) to this Act, which made it illegal in the hiring and firing processes to discriminate based on race, color, religion, sex, or national origin; and numerous civil suits by minorities and women, which have backed up this legislation.

Clearly, female COs experience the job differently than men (Zupan, 1986; Pogrebin and Poole, 1997; Lawrence and Mahan, 1998; Farkas, 1999). The issues concern discrimination, stress, and the way female COs relate both to male prisoners and to fellow COs.

Getting hired

Most jails and prisons will accept applications from individuals who are U.S. citizens between the ages of 18 and 21 years, who have completed high school or obtained its equivalent education (for example, GED (General Educational Development)), who have not had any felony convictions, and who have had at least two years' work experience (service/correctional-officers.htm).

The Federal Bureau of Prisons (FBOP), in particular, wants its recruits to have either an undergraduate degree or three years' experience in a field delivering "counseling, assistance, or supervision to individuals." They also must be in good health and meet the requirements of "physical fitness, eyesight, and hearing" (www.bls.gov/ooh/protective-service/correctional-officers.htm).

Although "14 percent" of US correctional systems "do not include pre-employment elements in their hiring practice" (Hill, 2007: 12), typically, those wishing to work as a CO:

1. fill out an application with the relevant municipal, county, state, or federal agency;
2. sit for a written test, complete a paper-and-pencil psychological examination (like the Minnesota Multiphasic Personality Inventory (MMPI) test or California Personality Inventory (CPI)), perform a physical test, and are subjected to a urine (that is, drug) test;
3. submit to a criminal background investigation;
4. have a medical exam;
5. perform a physical ability/agility test;
6. have a face-to-face psychiatric test; and
7. have a personal interview (Freeman, 2000: chapter 12).

This last step is often the most important, as seasoned human resource personnel suggest that the suitability of the candidates is best disentangled during the face-to-face interviews. Upon acceptance, officer recruits will undergo some sort of in-class training either at the institution where they will work or at a state training academy/facility.

Age restrictions: problems and solutions

Most correctional systems require their candidates to be between the ages of 18 and 21. Many COs get into the field at a relatively early age. Some correctional professionals worry that younger recruits are more immature, and might be susceptible to being manipulated or corrupted by convicts under their watch. At least by 21, the person has matured more, graduated from high school, had a number of life experiences, and possibly experienced the challenges and rewards of marriage and parenting and/or the frustration of being unemployed, married, or divorced.

Educational requirements: problems and solutions

There is considerable variability with respect to the educational requirements that states have for hiring recruits. In eight states the only educational requirement necessary to be hired is a GED (Hill, 2007: 13). In 1999, in 22 (42 %) states, a GED or high school diploma was considered adequate to qualify for CO employment. Only 16 states (31.4 %) required a high school diploma or its equivalent for CO work. In 1997, 38 states indicated that their current correctional staffs had less than 30 units of college credits. The greatest emphasis on college education was among the Midwest prisons (Sechrest and Josi, 1999: 54).

Pursuing and earning a college diploma or university degree is usually thought to be the more professional approach. Research is not clear just how much a diploma or degree helps criminal justice practitioners. However, correctional administrators see having an education beyond a high school diploma as a stepping stone to entering middle and senior management positions. At the very least, it helps narrow down the pool of potential candidates (Champion, 2005: 489, 493).

Some correctional professionals argue that having a four-year degree means that officers will have a better understanding of the job. This presupposes that the courses that COs take are specifically geared to the profession, dealing, for example, with operating facilities, supervising different inmates, writing reports, public speaking, and working with diverse cultures. The classes offered to correctional workers should be evaluated on a continual basis in order to keep up with the constant changes in the field. There should also be some sort of advisory board that consists of Department of Public Safety representatives, COs, and administrators, to decide what information is taught, how it should be delivered, and how students should be evaluated.

Many correctional professionals claim that a two-year diploma from a community college is sufficient for entrance into the profession. But what if applicants' degrees are in supposedly unrelated fields like computer science? Should they be denied entrance as prospective candidates, or will they be able to find a proper position with a department of corrections (DOC)? All of this is debatable as people from all kinds of subject fields become successful COs. Moreover, institutions of higher learning and the courses they offer are not all created equal; thus those that emphasize critical thinking skills would be preferable. Other difficulties arise due to the shifts that COs are expected to work. It is not easy for those who wish to continue their education to go to classes held at times they have to work or should be sleeping, particularly when a supervisor asks them to stay late and/or do a double (that is, two shifts back to back). There also need to be programs in place where DOCs and the FBOP give tuition remission to COs so they can pursue higher education.

Moreover, it is recognized that training geared specifically to COs is insufficient. Frequent complaints about training include that it is either too short or does not emphasize the right kinds of knowledge or skills to be truly useful. COs and administrators are well aware of recruits who, after making it through the academy, quit after one day or week on the job. They argue that if the recruitment and training were more realistic about the field of corrections, then this problem would be mitigated. A final difficulty is that many people do not want to be COs because of the numerous myths and misconceptions people have heard about the field.

Pay: problems and solutions

Salaries for correctional workers vary considerably based on the type of institution an officer works at, their seniority, and whether the employee works for the federal, state, or municipal correctional services, or for a private company, like Corrections Corporation of America (CCA) and the GEO Group, Inc. On the one hand, if, for example, officers are employed by a local jail in an economically depressed part of the country, their hourly rates may very well be just a little higher than the minimum wage. If, however, a person works for the federal system, they may make an amount that is comparable to what someone may earn as a federal law enforcement officer (for example, Federal Bureau of Investigation, Department of Homeland Security, and so on). Nevertheless, according to the *Corrections Compendium* survey administered in 2004, "The minimum starting wage in New Jersey is $45,549. Top wages for the entry-level category were reported by Wisconsin as $50,759, Colorado as $52,368 and Nevada as $53,390" (Hill, 2007: 12). More recent information from the Bureau of Labor Statistics (2014) reports that the highest average salaries for COs can be found in the state of New Jersey with COs earning an average wage of $71,600 (www.bls.gov/oes/current/oes333012.htm). In general, given the educational requirements (typically a high school diploma or GED), the entry-level salaries are very good compared to other fields that individuals might be employed in. This also does not include the money they can make working overtime, nor benefits.

Finally, in terms of benefits, more than half of correctional systems have a cafeteria plan. Other kinds of benefits include "cost-of-living increases, merit increases, paid holidays and vacation days, sick days, personal days, retirement pay, health insurance, dental insurance, disability pay, and life insurance" (Hill, 2007: 12). Additional benefits include "longevity bonuses, flexible spending accounts, shift and weekend pay differentials, meal allowances ..., uniforms and uniform cleaning services, hearing aid benefits, prescription drug plan" and early retirement plans" (13).

Availability of jobs: problems and solutions

In order to attract appropriate recruits, correctional systems engage in a number of practices including job/career fairs, stipends for postings in rural locations, signing bonuses, finders' fees, networking with high school counselors, and all manner of advertising (Hill, 2007: 12).

Some correctional facilities have difficulty staffing positions. The supply and demand for COs varies from one DOC to another. In some places, jobs go unfilled, with COs regularly being asked to work overtime. The need to fill CO spots is also dependent on a number of factors including, but not limited to, the health of the local economy and the labor market, the proclivity for individuals to move in search of new employment (that is, some people, particularly young adults with minimal family commitments, are more willing to take a job somewhere else), the attrition rates (that is, turnover in personnel) in DOCs, the mobility of the general population, the speed with which DOCs can adequately train new recruits, and changes in the prison population.

Meanwhile, correctional supervisors throughout the United States habitually ask COs to work additional shifts. Though less an issue today than it was a decade ago, one problem area concerns mandatory overtime. COs forced to work doubles get overtired, are prone to accidents and sloppy paperwork, and thus cannot do their jobs properly. Meanwhile, overtime eats into already stressed budgets. Furthermore, legislators are reluctant to increase budgets for DOCs, simultaneously believing that criminals deserve their just desserts and fearing that any increase in correctional spending will be used to improve "nonessential" prison conditions (which they are opposed to). With respect to COs, many legislators feel that they already receive too many benefits (Allen and Simonsen, 2001: 363).

One of the more recent innovative ways to hire COs has been through the federal and state Job Corps programs. According to the U.S. Department of Labor:

> the Job Corps is a no-cost education and vocational training program administered by the U.S. Department of Labor that helps young people ages 16 through 24 get a better job, make more money, and take control of their lives. At Job Corps, students enroll to learn a trade, earn a high school diploma or GED and get help finding a good job. When you join the program, you will be paid a monthly allowance; the longer you stay with the program, the more your allowance will be. Job Corps provides career counseling and transition support to its students for up to 12 months after they graduate from the program. (http://jobcorps.dol.gov/about.htm)

For the time being, however, this program, is limited to one particular geographic location.

Operating since 2002, with its first class in 2003, the Gary Job Corps Training Academy Program (in San Marcos, Texas) trains candidates to work in prisons operated by the Texas Department of Criminal Justice. Alternatively, students are eligible to work in one of the many private prisons in the Lone Star State. Since its opening, the program has trained 95 students with 20–5 graduating each year. The Job Corps programs are similar to the police cadet programs that were started during the mid-1990s, which were introduced in the wake of the community policing movement (Nink et al., 2005).

According to the Bureau of Labor Statistics, the federal agency that tracks employment-related data

> Employment of correctional officers is projected to grow 5 percent from 2012 to 2022, slower than the average for all occupations. Although budget constraints and a falling crime rate will require fewer workers, job openings will continue to become available because the dangers associated with the job cause many to leave the occupation each year. (www.bls.gov/ooh/protective-service/correctional-officers.htm)

The study cautions that the increasing

> demand for correctional officers will stem from mandatory sentencing guidelines calling for longer sentences and reduced parole for inmates, and from expansion and new construction of correctional facilities. However, mandatory sentencing guidelines are being reconsidered in many states because of a combination of budgetary constraints, court decisions, and doubts about their effectiveness. Instead, there may be more emphasis on reducing sentences or putting offenders on probation or in rehabilitation programs in many states. As a result, the prison population, and employment of correctional officers, will probably grow at a slower rate than in the past. Some employment opportunities will also arise in the private sector, as public authorities contract with private companies to provide and staff corrections facilities. (United States, 2006: 359)

Training: problems and solutions

There are considerable differences with respect to how and where CO candidates are trained. At a minimum, "Federal, state, and some local departments of corrections, as well as some private corrections companies, provide training based on guidelines established by the American Correctional Association. Some states have regional training academies that are available to local agencies" (www.bls.gov/ooh/protective-service/correctional-officers. htm#tab-4).

Initial formal training may occur at a state-run academy, while the balance of knowledge, skills, and training is delivered at an actual correctional facility. At the academy and/or at the correctional facility to which they are assigned, CO candidates "receive instruction in ... self-defense, institutional policies, regulations, operations, and custody and security procedures" (www.bls.gov/ ooh/protective-service/correctional-officers.htm#tab-4).

Although on the job, recruits will typically serve out a probationary period, and are then subjected to random drug testing. Officer "trainees typically receive several weeks or months of training under the supervision of an experienced officer" (www.bls.gov/ooh/protective-service/correctional-officers.htm#tab-4). In the Federal Bureau of Prisons (FBOP), recruits "must undergo 200 hours of formal training within the first year of employment, including 120 hours of specialized training at the Federal Bureau of Prisons residential training center" at Glynco, GA (www.bls.gov/ooh/protective-service/correctional-officers.htm#tab-4).

The entire process is typically expensive for the state and federal correctional systems. Thus, they try to weed out unsuitable candidates early on in the process to prevent the expenditure of additional costs of hiring (Conover, 2001). Unlike most police departments, some correctional agencies will have their new hires go directly to the job, and, after a probationary period working on a tier or cellblock, will then send them to the training academy. This is because many DOCs have been in the awkward position of putting people through the expense of the academy only to have the recruit quit after they discover firsthand the challenges of the job.

Most DOCs separate recruits into different groups, give them specialized training, and then move on to the next cohort of new hires. This approach relies on the understanding that the majority of the new employees will learn the bulk of their duties through on the job experience and not in a classroom setting. The administration hopes "that recruits will learn general job responsibilities, procedures for carrying out these responsibilities, practical skills for task performance, and something about the expectations of supervisors" (Champion, 2005: 488). Nonetheless, many recruits feel that these training sessions did not properly prepare them for their jobs. At the very least, there are basically two types of training for recruits: preservice and in-service.

Preservice

Based on the 1995 American Correctional Association (ACA) *Vital Statistics*, COs at "more than half of the agencies surveyed had to complete at least five weeks of pre-service training before they could begin working as officers. In many systems the combined length of time spent in basic and on the job training exceeded 25 weeks."

> [Preservice training] consists of both classroom instruction and on-the-job experiences. Probationary periods for correctional staff averaged 9.5 months, with a low of 3.8 months in Wisconsin to a high of 18 months in Utah. Most DOCs have 12-month training programs. In 1988, the training hours for most new correctional officers averaged 232 with 42 in-service hours. Vermont had the lowest number of required training hours with 40; Michigan required 640 training hours. ... During the 1990s, the average probationary periods for state and federal correctional officers increased from 8 months to 9.5 months. (Champion, 2005: 493)

A lot of this depends on supply and demand conditions.

What these figures neglect is the content of the courses, including the subjects covered, the method of instruction, exercises the recruits are trained or educated in, and the instructors' qualifications and abilities. Subjects include first aid, the law, policies and procedures, and the conducting of proper searches.

There is no empirical evidence which suggests that higher levels of education makes better COs (Burke et al., 1992: 174).

> Generally, more education for officers is instrumental in gaining them managerial positions. Thus, those officers who aspire to middle-level or upper-level management in prison settings would probably benefit from acquiring an advanced degree. Some officers have reported that having a higher level of education enables them to understand inmate culture better and to resolve inmate-officer conflicts more effectively. (174)

When top-level prison managers seek additional education and training, it underscores the importance of continuing education, as well as improving the image of COs in their respective institutions.

Part of the need for training correctional personnel has been met by colleges and universities (Stinchcomb, 2000). An increasing number of brick-and-mortar institutions of higher learning and online educational institutions are offering two-year associate degrees in corrections. Some of these require internships or practicums working in actual or simulated jail or prison facilities.

Exhibit 12.1

Classics in corrections

Ted Conover's *Newjack: Guarding Sing Sing* (2001)

This book, published in 2001 by Ted Conover, a well-known and respected investigative reporter, tells the story of the process he went through in order to become a CO. It takes us from the academy where he was tear-gassed to working in different sections of Sing Sing, the infamous New York State maximum-security prison, including rotations in solitary confinement, the gym, and the psych ward. Conover wrote about some of the deviant folks in the system, both other COs and inmates. He also told of how his family and he were affected by his job; in particular, Conover became disproportionately short-tempered around them.

Conover was basically thrown into the experience and had to rely on his own instincts to do the job. Like his fellow officers, he appeared to be totally unprepared for the new work experience. He discovered that every correctional professional in Sing Sing worked in a different manner; there was little uniformity among the people enforcing the rules in the facility. This state of affairs frustrated Conover and his colleagues.

In-service

In addition to the formal training that recruits may receive in advance of their job, when they are actually working as COs, they may get some sort of in-service training, the frequency of which can vary from correctional institution to institution and from state to state. This also includes periodic instruction in new rules and regulations. Many skills need to be periodically updated like cardiopulmonary resuscitation, first aid techniques, and cell search procedures. And when new developments occur, like the threat of HIV/AIDS, new methods are implemented in the care and treatment of inmates suffering from these ailments (Freeman, 2000: 316–20): These protocols must be integrated into the training too.

Extracurricular education

Many COs attend community colleges and universities in pursuit of a diploma or a degree. They typically enroll in programs in criminology or criminal justice, and may also take classes in psychology and sociology, or even a foreign language. Similar to convicts, it is not necessary to attend a formal class somewhere. Because of their flexibility, there are several correspondence and/or online courses offered by universities and associations, like the ACA, that are available to COs. Another strategy is what is called "cross-training – temporarily working in correctional fields that are not your own" (American Correctional Association, 2004: 63). Alternatively officers may be seconded to another correctional institution where they will acquire additional job-related skills and experience that they can utilize when they return to their original facilities. Employees can find out about these opportunities through their work networks or through organizations such as the ACA, American Jails Association (AJA), and American Probation and Parole Association (APPA). Regardless, like many fields, much of learning to be a CO is done on the job by observing more senior officers and modeling their behavior.

Professionalism

Closely connected to the issue of training is that of professionalism. Over the past 80 years, corrections, much like the fields of law and medicine, has adopted rigorous standards for the training and certification of workers. This change is largely a reflection of the recognition that in order for COs to do their job properly they need specialized knowledge, skills, and training. These aspects generally include conducting searches, controlling and restraining convicts, writing and speaking effectively, providing proper medical and emergency care, transporting prisoners, self-defense, and the use of a variety of weapons (for example, firearms and chemical weapons). Many of these policies and practices are contained in standards, which are specified by state DOCs and national accrediting bodies, like the ACA (Farkas, 1990; Stinchcomb, 2000).

Certification

As mentioned earlier, a handful of membership organizations (for example, ACA) have started to certify COs. "A fundamental concomitant of accreditation is certification, which involves a review and evaluation of an individual's credentials and capabilities as they relate to his or her current correctional functions" (Champion, 2001: 529). This means that the members will have to know a specific body of knowledge, adhere to certain moral and ethical standards, and be tested on a periodic basis to maintain their certification. Other options are for individual states to develop a certification process and have COs licensed by these entities.

Conclusion

Entry requirements to the field of corrections are similar to those found in other types of criminal justice and law enforcement jobs. The demand for qualified correctional personnel is high, but the competition is not as stiff as that found in other law enforcement positions. In general, working in a correctional facility is less desirable than parole or probation, municipal police, or state patrol. For the amount of education required, however, the pay is respectable.

Other issues need to be taken into consideration. These include the current and future needs among COs, the FBOP, and DOCs. Given changes in demographics in the United States, there is a strong need for bilingual officers, particularly those who can speak Spanish.

Criminals who are incarcerated in jails and prisons these days are also probably better educated and knowledgeable in the ways of the institution than they once were. Some of these people can be quite dangerous. For example, if a convict has a trade (for example, electricity or plumbing), knows a lot about this aspect of the jail or prison structure, and gets a job in the facility, they could wreak havoc with the day-to-day operations of the institution. So COs who come into the institution should be relatively versed in looking out for these potential threats.

It is difficult to make the job of a CO more attractive. Certainly, paying candidates more money would be a step in the right direction. Treating COs better, properly training recruits and those who are on the job, and educating the public might minimize turnover and attract suitable candidates to the profession. Additionally, trying to better educate the public (as alluded to in Chapter 2) about the realities of corrections would minimize the myths and might prevent individuals from quitting shortly after being hired.

There is considerable variability with respect to the educational and work history background required for suitable recruits. Each state and the federal system have their own requirements for COs. Some mandate a high school education. Others require that applicants not have a criminal record, including misdemeanor convictions. Some DOCs are more lax and are willing to accept recruits who have been convicted of some misdemeanors. Many people enter the field of corrections with only a GED, while others come in with a community college diploma. Still other recruits possess a university degree. Although initially resistant to recruits who have an advanced education, as more members among their ranks have bachelor's and higher degrees, correctional administrators are now requiring this kind of advanced education at least for middle management positions.

Finally, jail and prison personnel receive training through a wide spectrum of programs. These include courses offered by a centralized state correctional facility, on-the-job classes, and in-service courses. Multiple opportunities exist for entrance into the profession and new methods for training recruits are experimented with on a regular basis.

Key terms

California Personality Inventory: One of two major personality tests typically used in hiring practices. Detects the presence of major mental illnesses.

Certification: Specific body of knowledge or skills that individuals may be required to know and master. Those required to obtain certification must do so on a regular basis.

Minnesota Multiphasic Personality Inventory: One of two major personality tests used in hiring practices. Detects the presence of major mental illnesses.

Newjack: A new recruit into the New York State Department of Corrections.

Professionalism: Knowledge and skills that are specific to a particular job. This is embedded in standards produced by the state or some accrediting agency.

Smug hack: The notion that correctional officers are uncaring and gruff in their manner.

THIRTEEN

Working conditions

Introduction

Many correctional officers (COs) are unhappy with their jobs. This is largely because of perceived and actual poor working conditions and the low status accorded to their profession by the wider public. Most people do not plan to pursue careers in corrections (Gibbons and de Katzenbach, 2006: 65–75). They start working in jails and prisons for various reasons, including having long stretches of unemployment, having poorly paid service jobs, and their unions going on strike with no hope in the immediate future that matters will be resolved in an expeditious manner (Lombardo, 1989).

Many officers also feel that they cannot leave their CO positions to find better paying jobs – a situation, often referred to as the golden handcuffs. Although a correctional worker may dislike his or her current job, the relative pay (compared to other occupations the individual is qualified for) is typically good enough to rule out the option of quitting. Meanwhile, other semi-attractive jobs do not offer competitive pay, seniority, or similar working conditions and benefits, so the officer stays put.

Nevertheless, these working conditions can lead to stress, cynicism, burnout, and CO deviance. The following chapter reviews these problems and some suggested solutions.

The problems

Correctional workers cite numerous issues about their working conditions that cause them difficulties (Gibbons and de B. Katzenbach, 2006: chapter 4). These problems include boredom, shift work, under-staffing, prisoners' bad attitudes, diseases, and violence.

Boredom

One of the chief complaints COs cite is boredom. This is one of the reasons why many do not like to talk about their work with their spouses or significant others, family, or friends. Some suggest that the unchanging routine of their jobs (for example, standing around, observing inmates, filling out forms, doing counts at specified times, and so on) makes COs lazy. Other observers have even argued that a considerable amount of CO abuse can be attributed to the officers' boredom (Ross, 2013c). On the other hand, working as a correctional professional does offer more variety than, say, working on an assembly line.

Rotating shift work

Corrections, like many other criminal justice careers or first responder jobs (such as firefighters and emergency medical technicians), usually involves rotating shift work. This kind of schedule can take its toll on a person's physical and mental health. Individuals required to work in this manner nearly always feel deprived of sleep, which may lead to irritability, poor eating habits, weight gain, and stomach ulcers. Scheduling quality time with a spouse or significant other and children is difficult, as is making time for routine visits with the doctor or dentist. It is also difficult if you are the primary caregiver in a family. This rotating schedule also means that, for some shift workers, regular exercise is not easily manageable, as most gyms are not open around the clock. This complaint is by no means universal, as some COs actually look forward to the fact that every few weeks they will be rotating the time that they work. The change can break up the monotony or boredom inherent in the job, and this may psychologically help correctional workers get through the week.

Under-staffing

Due to a lack of funding and/or budget deficits, many correctional facilities are forced to operate with a less-than-ideal number of officers. Some individuals work more than one post, doing different tasks. Although this can break up the monotony, it can equally result in inefficiency and a tendency to take shortcuts to get the job done. To be sure, many officers are able to work doubles and earn time-and-a-half pay, thereby paying off the loans for their house or car earlier – but this comes at a price. Officers who push themselves in this way may suffer psychological and physical consequences, and are often tired and irritable. Another aspect is compromised safety when inmates become unruly and officers need to respond. Officers need to be mentally alert to the changing dynamics of the institution and be able to make split-second decisions, all of which is hampered if an officer is overtired and irritable.

Inmates' bad attitudes

Although inmates may not threaten or use violence against correctional workers, many, regardless of the consequences, frequently harass, insult (using condescending language or gestures), and verbally abuse COs. Moreover, COs are always under the watchful eye of the inmates, and every mistake is pointed out to them. This is especially true during count, the practice that ensures that the tier, wing, and/or correctional facility has the requisite number of inmates it was assigned. If an officer or group of officers miscounts the number of prisoners, they are likely to be berated by the inmates. Sometimes, as an ultimate act of disrespect, convicts may toss urine and feces at COs. At any given time, the number of inmates for which a CO is responsible can be overwhelming. Such treatment and working conditions frustrate most conscientious workers and contribute to high levels of stress, fatigue, and burnout.

Life-threatening illnesses

Jails and prisons are notoriously unhealthy places in which both prisoners and COs have been known to develop serious medical illnesses. Those who spend time in a correctional institution, whether as inmates, as COs, or as administrative personnel, must be concerned about the reality of contracting a serious – and possibly fatal – disease or illness (for example, TB, AIDS, and hepatitis). Not only is this because correctional workers may come into contact with inmates' blood, saliva, or other bodily secretions, but there is also the potential of contracting lung cancer from secondhand smoke and hearing loss because of the constant racket on the cellblocks and tiers. It is not simply COs and administrators who are in danger of catching a disease themselves, they also risk spreading it among family members and other loved ones. Prisoners' medical records are confidential, and the prison's medical staff may not take the time to do the appropriate tests to isolate the problem/person and implement a medical plan.

A significant problem with many contagious diseases, however, is that a cure depends on early detection – which becomes more difficult in a correctional setting, where medical services are usually rationed out (Murphy, 2003). If, in fact, a convict tests positive for a serious illness, the condition is likely to be kept a secret because the prison authorities do not want the convict to be attacked by fearful prisoners or improperly handled by ill or poorly informed COs. Also, unless the convict is in the infirmary or hospital under treatment, the prison administrators do not want COs to treat them any differently. In most facilities, individuals suffering from highly contagious diseases are terminally ill and placed in segregation.[1]

The possibility of violence

The threat of physical violence from inmates is always present. Not only does this occur on a daily basis, but also the possibility of being assaulted or killed is heightened in the context of disturbances, strikes, and riots. There are many opportunities for aggression to occur, and inmates can be quite creative with respect to the places where they may assault a CO and the things they can use as weapons. Riots, strikes, and disturbances can and may break out at any time, and the atmosphere is continuously unsafe (for example, Hallinan, 2003: 105–13) (see Exhibit 13.1).

Exhibit 13.1

Classics in corrections

Lucien Lombardo's *Guards Imprisoned* (1989)

In 1989, Lucien Lombardo, a former prison teacher at New York State's Auburn Correctional Facility and now a professor at Old Dominion University, published *Guards Imprisoned*. The study is the product of a series of interviews Lombardo conducted with COs at the Auburn prison. While dated, the book outlines the numerous roles that COs take on in managing and running a typical prison. He explains some of the problems that each type of officer encounters on the job.

Lombardo concludes that "[p]eople become correctional officers because they want stable jobs with steady pay and good benefits. Indeed, 60 percent of the officers interviewed reported that the pay and job security are the 'best' things about the job 'for the work we do' or 'for the education [level] we have attained'" (177–8). It wasn't the nature of the work that attracted them; accepting this job was a way of avoiding less attractive work or of escaping a workplace strike situation. Lombardo's interviews found that most officers were dissatisfied with their jobs. Approximately 25% said that there was absolutely nothing satisfying about their jobs. Many even compared their jobs to prison sentences.

Solutions

Numerous solutions can be implemented to improve COs' working conditions, including overcoming boredom, battling the negative effects of shift work, addressing under-staffing, dealing with inmates' bad attitudes, precautions against diseases, and avoiding becoming a victim of violence. The forming of correctional unions, an additional solution, will be discussed in Chapter 15.

Overcoming boredom

Correctional workers who can "think outside of the box" often look for more exciting positions within an institution or create additional tasks for themselves in an effort to make their days go by more quickly and/or to strengthen their résumés for the possibility of job promotion. Volunteering for special assignments is also another option. Some COs try to work as many night shifts as possible in order to avoid the boredom of the days and to sneak in time to do schoolwork, and when they have to work the day shift, they will volunteer for escort details (that is, transporting prisoners around or out of the institution) in order to get out of their assigned tier or wing and/or facility as much as possible. External escorting allows COs to get outside of the facility and away from the watchful eyes of other inmates, co-workers and supervisors. Sometimes these escort duties can occupy a whole morning or afternoon, or an entire shift.

Battling the negative effects of shift work

For those who are married, cohabiting, and/or have school age children or others they must care for (for example, elderly or sick relatives), it sometimes helps to have a spouse or significant other who has the same routine. This is why sometimes COs are in relationships with partners who also work shifts (for example, nurses, other first responders). Over time, because of seniority, it is easier for correctional workers to get the shifts that work best for them. Certainly, good communication with one's spouse (or significant other) will minimize the constant stress regarding coordination that always crops up.

Overcoming under-staffing

Not having enough officers to work a tier or cellblock can be most properly addressed by the COs' union. It is in the best interests of the union to have as many workers as possible. That way more dues are collected from each and every worker. If a grievance is filed in connection with under-staffing, and/or scheduling and no remediation is in store, the situation may lead to possible lawsuits and a court battle between the department of corrections (DOC) and the union.

Dealing better with inmates' bad attitudes

Although COs have the power to sanction (for example, write up inmates, also known as giving them a shot) prisoners who violate institutional rules, seasoned correctional professionals learn to ignore or not take seriously convicts' provocative communications and behavior. Alternatively, they have developed strategies to deflect threats or challenges through a combination of tough talk and humor. Otherwise, better training of COs in conflict resolution can sometimes de-escalate volatile situations (Christian, 1998).

Better training of COs in conflict resolution techniques

Some COs, either because they were never properly trained or because of cynicism developed during the job, are not good at de-escalating violence. Although the importance of developing conflict resolution skills is often stressed, sustained programs in the U.S. correctional training settings is rarely documented and/or analyzed (Cornelius, 1988).

Precautions against diseases

Many COs spend a lot of time worrying about and doing things to prevent themselves from being infected. Thus they take a number of precautions to minimize their exposure to contagious diseases. The prison staff have better access to information, memos/directives, procedures, training, and protective equipment than convicts. Most correctional personnel avoid coming into contact with blood and bodily fluids at all costs, as they could carry any number of infectious organisms.

Typically, they just tell an inmate to clean up a mess if they discover it. Otherwise, some COs now wear protective (for example, Nitrile) gloves, wear surgical masks while cleaning up blood or physically handling prisoners, and use hand sanitizer after handling inmates. A common precaution is also to practice good personal hygiene through frequent hand washing with antibacterial soap. Some correctional institutions should administer free vaccines to their employees. In this environment, it is especially necessary to take the appropriate amount of time to properly screen inmates during classification or intake (Gershon et al., 2005).

Some experts have argued that COs should be made aware of the health status of all inmates they supervise, rather than having a blanket or universal caution against all prisoners. Advocates of this position suggest that the officers' lives could be in jeopardy at any time, or that illnesses could affect their health and safety. Moreover, infected officers might unknowingly spread diseases among their family members and other loved ones. It is also understood that, once sentenced to prison, arrestees lose a considerable measure of their privacy and that these critical health issues should be made public – at least to the COs and administrators.

Administrators, on the other hand, might argue that once COs know this kind of information, they may consciously or unconsciously refuse to assist infected inmates or give preferential treatment to non-infected convicts. This information may also stigmatize the infected convicts among the other inmates. The debate about revealing the health status of prisoners and who specifically should know is not easily resolved; no matter which side prevails, few people will be happy. In a more general sense, departments of corrections should, to the extent possible, abolish the contracting out of medical facilities and services.

Approximately 20 states use private Health Maintenance Organizations (HMOs) (Kutscher, 2013), which are relatively unaccountable to the public. If this practice was eliminated or better monitored, it might go a long way in improving the health not only of inmates, but of COs too (Siever, 2005; Gibbons and de Katzenbach, 2006).

Avoiding becoming a victim of inmate violence

In terms of violence, COs take many precautions. Most try to stay constantly aware, even hyper-vigilant, of their surroundings in their workplace. They learn to be on guard for any swift atmosphere changes on the tiers, which often signal that something serious is about to occur. The most common precaution used by COs to maintain or even improve their health, work off stress, and lose weight is regular exercise: walking, jogging, weight training, or playing sports like basketball, handball, or softball. Not only will exercise, plenty of sleep, and a proper diet help keep a correctional worker alert and help them deal better with potential attacks, it may also help minimize stress. The correctional institution may allow its workers to use the facility's gym after hours and/or negotiate better terms with local private fitness centers.

Increasingly, state DOCs are requiring or enabling (financially) officers to purchase stab-resistant vests. This kind of protective gear minimizes the damage of an attack via a knife or sharp object to the body of the CO. The vests do not, however, protect the officer's face, neck, or legs. Correctional officers also need to avoid defining their lives singularly by their role at the workplace. Regular doctor's visits are a must to keep their health in check and to make sure that their panels of immunizations are up to date.

Burnout

Most helping professions (for example, social workers and educators) and those involving shift work lead to some sort of burnout. Burnout includes most of the following attributes: emotional exhaustion, depersonalization, and reduced personal accomplishment, all of which can occur among individuals who do "people work" of some kind; a progressive loss of idealism, energy, and purpose as a result of work conditions; a state of physical, emotional, and mental exhaustion marked by physical depletion and chronic fatigue, feelings of helplessness and hopelessness, and the development of negative perceptions of self-worth and negative attitudes toward work, life, and other people (Champion, 2005, quoting Maslach, 1982).

Burnout "signifies a reduction in the quality or effectiveness of an officer's job performance. ... Debilitating reductions in effectiveness are often accompanied by higher recidivism rates among probationers and parolees, more legal problems and case filings from officer/inmate interactions, and greater labor turnover among correctional officers" (Champion, 2005: 498).

Some of the factors that contribute to or mediate burnout are age, sex, and years on the job, as well as:

> self-esteem, marital status, and degree of autonomy and job satisfaction function. ... The social support system is made up of others who perform similar tasks and the frequency of contact with these people for the purpose of sharing the frustrations of work. These factors form a mosaic from which stress stems. Stress is manifested by physiological, psychological, and/or emotional indicators. Burnout may result; one important consequence of burnout may be labor turnover. (Champion, 2005: 498)

It should be understood that although most criminal justice practitioners encounter stress and potential burnout, the amount varies based not only on the individual, but also on the situation. Probation and parole officers experience stress differently. "In contrast to probation-parole offices, state prisons are more austere, controlled, and stress-provoking environments" (Carlson et al., 2003: 279).

Stress

Stress is a normal "physical and mental reaction to a demanding situation or event" (American Correctional Association, 2004: 78). In general, there are two types of stress: positive and negative. The former is healthy and the latter is unhealthy for body and mind. When a person experiences stress, a fight or flight reaction occurs. "The body readies itself to do whatever is necessary for survival (either fight or run away) by: increasing the heart rate, tensing muscles, dilating the pupils, making breathing faster and deeper, raising blood pressure" (American Correctional Association, 2004: 78, 79).

For some people, the stresses of modern life are often insurmountable. Many households cannot get by financially without both partners working. This also means that some people find it difficult to balance the competing demands made upon their time. As in most helping professions, COs can work long hours and may be subjected to a considerable amount of stress.

Over time, stress takes its toll on COs' physical and mental health. If not addressed, stress typically leads to serious medical problems, like heart disease, high blood pressure, strokes, circulatory problems, stomach ulcers, urinary problems, and loss of interest in sexual activity. It can also contribute to burnout, "loss of care and concern about one's profession that result[s] from continued and unresolved stress" (American Correctional Association, 2004: 81).

Moreover, "[s]uppressed anger or burnout may be expressed through: irritability, hopelessness, emotional over-reactions, intensely negative attitudes toward people, rigidity or 'going by the book'" (American Correctional Association, 2004: 81).

Sources of stress

The sources of stress for COs are found in many shift work jobs including those that require workers to

> rotate among various posts and duty hours, ... come in early or stay late, drop what convicts are doing to help out another officer, ... called in on a day you weren't scheduled to work. These disrupt your sleep patterns and family life, often creating more tension. ... Doctors say that it is not the amount of stress that causes health problems; [i]t is the way a person deals with stress that really matters. Therefore, what COs need to learn to do is manage the stress they have in their lives. They need to find productive, socially acceptable ways of releasing it so that it doesn't harm them. (American Correctional Association, 2004: 82)

The subject of stress among COs has been researched on several occasions. The findings are complicated and somewhat contradictory (Brodsky, 1982; Honnold and Stinchcomb, 1985; Lasky and Strebalus, 1986; Lindquist and Whitehead, 1986; Cheek and Miller, 1993). One way that researchers have examined stress is through life expectancy and other quality-of-life measures. Cheek (1984), for example, said that COs have a life span of 59 years (whereas the national average is 75). They also have a divorce rate that is twice the national average and have higher rates of suicide, alcoholism, heart attacks, ulcers, and high blood pressure. These figures are now outdated and do not take into consideration the kinds of people who become COs. In other words, is it the working conditions or the individuals who want to work in the field that presents a selection bias? No one knows for sure. It is also important to understand that the sources of stress differ between managers and workers (Weinberg et al., 1985). In sum, stress can manifest itself in constantly being late for work or meetings, calling in sick, absenteeism, prisoner abuse, irritability, and feelings of hopelessness. If stress is not minimized, not only does it have an effect on the individual employee, but also it can affect the ability of an institution to operate effectively and efficiently.

The federal government takes an interest

Under Title XXI of the Violent Crime and Law Enforcement Act, Congress established a Law Enforcement Family Support program. The funding of solicitations for research was handed over to the National Institute of Justice (NIJ). There were three objectives to this program namely:

> To develop, demonstrate, and test innovative stress prevention or treatment programs for state or local law enforcement and/or correctional personnel and their families; to conduct research on the nature, extent, causes, and consequences of stress experienced by COs and their families, or to evaluate the effectiveness of law enforcement and/or correctional officer prevention or treatment programs; and to develop, demonstrate, and test effective ways to change law enforcement or correctional agency policies practices, and organizational culture to ameliorate stress experienced by law enforcement and COs and their families (National Institute of Justice, 1998).

Although the majority of the research was directed toward police officers (for example, Finn and Esselman Tomz, 1996), many of the findings were applicable to correctional workers too. Utilizing interviews with close to "100 people, including mental health practitioners, law enforcement administrators, union and association officials, and almost 50 line officers and family members from both large and small agencies," (xiii) the report provides detailed information on initiatives including planning, structuring programs, staffing options, dealing with confidentiality, and a variety of different services to minimize stress.

Turnover

"Burnout and stress occur among correctional officers, especially during the first year of their duties." During this time "[t]urnover rates are as high as 38 percent in some jurisdictions, such as Arkansas." "Between 1990 and 1998, turnover among correctional officers ranged from a low of 9.6 percent in 1991 to a high of 14.9 percent in 1998 ... 20 percent of all entry-level correctional officers left before completing their probationary period" (Champion, 2005: 498). DOCs need to hire individuals who have the appropriate educational background and personality for the job. This is not an easy task. In order to minimize job turnover, a number of suggestions have been advanced. One of them is using more senior and respected officers as mentors.

Solutions to burnout and stress

Correctional administrators must be vigilant about the sources of stress and how they are caused, and they should try to implement procedures to minimize the unsettling effects of stress (Champion, 2005: 499). COs "often say that their supervisors focus only on the negative aspects of work performed. When supervisors provide only criticisms of work improperly done and leave unrewarded work of good quality, the morale of personnel suffers greatly" (499). One way to reduce stress is to allow correctional workers to contribute to the decision making of their unit through some kind of participatory management. This is often referred to as participative management/total quality management (reviewed in Chapter 14).

In sum, maintaining physical health through regular exercise, ample recreation, eating a healthy diet, sufficient rest, not smoking, restricting alcohol use, engaging in deep relaxation (for example, yoga, transcendental meditation, tai chi, and so on), and taking vacations on a regular basis can help alleviate burnout and stress. Some of these solutions would be aided if the correctional institution provided a well-equipped gym or discounts at a nearby gym or health club.

Conclusion

Working conditions for COs are almost similar to living conditions for prisoners. Understanding how COs operate and think in this unique environment may help minimize stress, burnout, and turnover. COs must remain aware and vigilant to take responsibility for their own safety and health and not rely on the DOC to do it for them. A number of practical solutions for minimizing burnout found in other law enforcement and helping professions can be applied to the field of corrections. If properly utilized by both corrections officers and administration, these measures can minimize health concerns, encourage better on-the-job performance of personnel, and reduce turnover.

Key terms

Burnout: When officers' effectiveness and performance reduces based on accumulated stress and boredom in the job.

Cross-training: When a correctional worker temporarily works in a correctional position that is NOT their own.

Escorts: COs transport prisoners around or out of the correctional institution on doctors' visits, court dates, etc. For COs, this is a convenient way to get out of the facility as much as possible.

Golden handcuffs: Officers feel that they cannot leave the field of corrections to find a better paying job.

Helping profession: Includes teachers, social workers, and first responders.

National Institute of Justice (NIJ): Research arm of the United States Department of Justice.

Rotating shift work: An absence of permanent shifts, where employees will work for a short period of time—days, evenings, and night shifts.

Stress: Physical and mental reaction to a demanding situation or event.

Turnover: How often an institution has people who quit their jobs, or who are fired, leaving positions vacant.

Note

[1] Legislation regarding privacy of inmates is complicated and discussed in greater detail in the following factsheet "Corrections, Law Enforcement & the Courts Health Insurance Portability and Accountability Act of 1996 (HIPAA)" (www.nga. org/files/live/sites/NGA/files/pdf/FACTSHIPAAHYBRID.pdf) (downloaded, December 5, 2015).

FOURTEEN

Correctional officer deviance[1]

Introduction

Although numerous definitions of deviance exist, at the very least, deviance is an action or behavior that violates generally accepted norms (Adler, 2005). Deviance is the foundation from which many of society's policies, practices, and laws are developed. Policies, practices, and laws are usually written because entities (from organizations to countries) codify certain acts of deviance. Deviance can and does occur in all workplaces, and in all jobs, occupations, and professions.

Since the 1960s, numerous scholars have outlined various acts of deviance in certain jobs, occupations, and professions. From adolescent workers (Ruggerio et al., 1982) to doctors (Morrow, 1982), a steady stream of research and analysis of deviance has been published. Some of this work has examined deviance in the criminal justice professions. Unfortunately, the majority of this analysis has focused on the deviant actions of police officers (for example, Barker and Carter, 1994; Kappeler et al., 1994), and by comparison, little work has been done on correctional officers (COs). Thus, there has been a paucity of definitions of deviance (sometimes labeled "misconduct") as applied to COs.[2]

More common are definitions of corruption. According to McCarthy (1996), corruption includes "the intentional violation of organizational norms (that is, rules and regulations) by public employees for personal material gain" (231). Such behavior would subsume theft, smuggling contraband, embezzlement of money from the correctional facility or inmates, theft of property, and misuse of authority (232). Although a respectable start, this definition conflates deviance with corruption. Instead, perhaps a more generic definition would suffice. In the field of corrections, deviance is generally considered inappropriate work-related activities in which COs may engage.

Although some COs commit acts of deviant behavior, rarely do introductory textbooks and scholarly articles on corrections tackle this subject at any great length.[3] Authors and researchers might briefly mention violence or excessive force by COs, but rarely do they conduct research or write anything about less visible deviant behaviors, such as theft, corruption, or sexual assault.

Many correctional agencies and the American Correctional Association (ACA – the largest organization representing COs) have codes of ethics or standards of conduct – "dos" and "don'ts" – which are taught to recruits and selectively reinforced by veterans and administrators of correctional organizations. Nonetheless, systematic analyses of compliance with and breaches of these standards are rarely attempted. A closely related term to deviance is "corruption." Identifying and finding appropriate remedies to deviance can be difficult. Public officials (such as COs and administrators) may engage in morally reprehensible and/or ethically questionable behavior (for example, accepting free meals from contractors), but it is hard to empirically determine when and how this conduct is sanctioned. This type of action may even occur with a supervisor's knowledge, an eventuality that calls into question whether, in fact, norms are actually being violated.

When a news story describing an incident of alleged or real CO deviance is brought to the public's attention, an organization's legitimacy is typically challenged, and this can prompt some sort of official investigation. The controversial behavior will typically be compared to existing norms, policies, and practices, and one of three things will commonly happen: the administration may publicly announce that it will no longer tolerate the controversial behavior; the administration might increase enforcement against rule breakers; or the rules and regulations will be changed to reflect current practices.

Responding to CO deviance becomes difficult in the cases in which nearly all of an organization's workers have violated an existing policy or practice over a considerable period of time and the supervisors and administrators have knowingly failed to take any meaningful remedial action. This is a situation in which a norm has not been violated, but a policy or practice has been.

As alluded to earlier, the discussion about deviance is intimately tied to the study of ethics. Clearly, COs face many temptations on the job, and deviant acts inevitably take place. The frequency of such occurrences, however, is generally a matter of speculation. Interest in deviant behavior has increased over the past decade, largely because of well-publicized inquiries that have occurred in the field of corrections and the allegations of abuse in connection with Baghdad's Abu Ghraib prison (Hersh, 2004). In fact, the National Commission on Safety and Abuse in Prisons (Gibbons and de Katzenbach, 2006) selected aspects of CO deviance as one of its major areas of investigation. Finally, because of the difficulty in obtaining reliable and comprehensive evidence, the extent of deviance perpetrated by COs is unknown, and no comparison of this type of deviance with that engaged in by law enforcement personnel, for example, or other professionals yet exists.

Given the lack of current scholarship in this area, this chapter briefly reviews the academic research that has been conducted on the problem of CO deviance.[4] It then outlines the most dominant kinds of documented deviance and official/state-initiated solutions that have been proposed and, in many cases, implemented.[5] This information is organized into a typology that could be used for further analytical purposes. The author concludes with recommendations on how this chapter's findings could be utilized to better improve the field of corrections.[6] Although some scholars of jails and prisons have provided causal explanations of selected aspects of CO deviance (for example, Worley and Worley, 2013), no such attempt is made here.

The scholarly literature on CO deviance

To date, some activist-produced publications (for example, Human Rights Watch, 1996; 2001) and practitioner-based periodicals (for example, *Corrections Today*) have reviewed selected aspects of CO deviance; however, a definitive body of scholarly literature about this behavior does not exist. Most typically, the studies concentrate on subcomponents of this phenomenon or related issues, such as CO power (for example, Hepburn, 1985; Stichman, 2002; Stojkovic, 1984). Research focusing on the subcomponents of CO deviance has examined a variety of issues: racial and sexual discrimination and/or harassment (Britton, 1997; Camp et al., 2001); CO corruption (McCarthy, 1996; Worley and Cheeseman, 2006); and excessive force and/or violence by COs (Cohen et al., 1976; Bowker, 1980; Marquart, 1986; Hemmens and Atherton, 2000; Hemmens and Stohr, 2001). The topic of CO deviance is also embedded in complementary concepts, such as inmate boundary violations (Marquart et al., 2001), and in larger issue studies that concentrate on professionalization as a solution to problems with COs (Farkas, 1990; Stinchcomb, 2000), selection procedures (Stinchcomb, 1988), and CO leadership (Stojkovic and Farkas, 2003).

In broad terms, two major types of CO deviance exist: the abuse of power and corruption. The abuse of power is typically covered by studies of CO violence and of inmate victimization. Bowker (1980) produced what is considered by many scholars to be the most thorough treatment of CO deviant behavior. Though his research is outdated, he looked specifically at the victimization of prisoners by COs. Assessing the general handling of this subject matter, Bowker noted that "the treatment of the subject is superficial in that incidents tend to be mentioned only in passing (or as part of a polemical piece of writing), and they are not presented or analyzed in any great detail" (143). He also pointed out that incidents of deviance "tend to be recorded factually" and not placed into a theoretical context:

> [The] quality of the reporting of incidents is often difficult to determine. Reports are usually limited to the views of one of the participants or observers, with no corroboration from others. Even when reports are written by social scientists, they usually consist of second- and third-person accounts derived from interviews rather than direct observation by the scientists. (143)

Finally, Bowker (1980) challenged the variable definitions pertaining to victimization experiences. He organized victimization into three types: physical, psychological, and sexual. Although this perspective provides a foundational framework for research, the concept of deviance is more encompassing.

Corruption, which typically involves an attempt to achieve a personal economic gain, is given less attention in the scholarly writing on COs. One of the most important treatments of this subject, however, is Sykes's (1958) classic and controversial book *The Society of Captives*. In this publication, Sykes argued that most COs are, upon occasion, susceptible to corruption. He offers three major explanations for this behavior: correctional workers develop friendships with prisoners; they engage in reciprocity; and simply engage in "default" actions (for example, COs may be either lazy or overcommitted, or they are unable or unwilling to spend the necessary time that is required to properly do their jobs). In its day, this book's conclusions were judged as relatively controversial, inspiring a number of research studies about COs' working conditions and relationships with inmates. During the 1960s and 1970s, some (for example, Irwin, 1970; Irwin and Cressy, 1962) questioned the efficacy of the functional model as portrayed by Sykes. In order to build upon this literature and place it into some sort of conceptual framework, the components of CO deviance and the possible solutions to the acts of misconduct are outlined. In addressing both issues, a typology that will have heuristic possibilities is advanced.

Types of CO deviance

Based on multiple sources,[7] 15 primary types of deviance engaged in by correctional workers can be identified. This type of behavior includes but is not limited to: improper use of agency equipment and property; failure to fulfill the required duties of the job; mishandling/theft of inmate property; drinking alcohol on the job; accepting gifts from inmates and contractors; discrimination; abuse of authority; sexual relationships with inmates; smuggling contraband; theft; unnecessary violence against prisoners; general boundary violations; and sexual harassment of fellow COs. Most of these deviant behaviors are interrelated and self-explanatory, but the following section reviews each activity in detail. The processes can be further broken down into three categories depending on the target of the deviance (that is, the institution, inmates, and fellow COs). Although in reality all three groups of behavior are interrelated, for clarity's sake, this outline will leave the categories separate.

Deviance against the institution

Improper use/misuse of agency equipment and property. Multiple opportunities exist for COs and administrators to take advantage of their organizations' resources for personal benefit and/or use. This includes acts as simple as using photocopy machines (for birthday party invitations, recipes, school-related texts, and so on), stealing office supplies and equipment (for a part-time business, home use, and so on), and borrowing equipment (such as vehicles when theirs is in the shop). At other times, because of boredom, anger, or frustration, COs may break equipment, or they may use equipment against other COs as a practical joke (for example, pepper spraying someone in the bathroom).

Using corrections equipment (or machines, for example, walkie talkies, metal detectors, and so on) in a manner in which it was not intended (including "monkey-wrenching" or purposely breaking equipment/machines) is a frequent occurrence in factories and the industrial sector (Abbey, 1975). Many of these instances are acts of low-scale, uncollectivized rebellion, a reflection of frustration with poorly functioning or maintained equipment/machines, or of difficulties with the management of an institution. Additionally, if equipment/machines do not work properly, there may be a tendency among workers to further damage them, either as a demonstration of their discontent or as a means to compel the administrators to finally replace the faulty equipment/machines.

Purposely shirking one's duties. Periodically COs fail to perform their duties for other reasons than incompetence or an inability to remember. Such deliberate behavior could extend to: falsifying log entries when failing to do their rounds and/or when coming in late or leaving early; playing cards and/or computer games; using smart phones for personal business; watching television and/or listening to the radio (for example, during a sporting event broadcast); recreational reading; sleeping; leaving an assigned area without authorization; refusing to respond to prisoners' and/or fellow officers' requests because of general laziness; and taking longer breaks and lunch hours than given. In addition to ripping off a facility by not enhancing its value through one's labor, this can effectively compromise the security and safety of other officers.

Theft of correctional facility property. Institutional food is typically not only of poor quality, but some of it may also disappear even before being served in the mess hall. In some penitentiaries, staff may occasionally eat or steal the better food. They may take it home to feed their farm animals or their pets, or they may sell it to others. Additional items of value may also mysteriously disappear and make their way into the correctional workers' possession (Ross and Richards, 2002: chapter 12).

Abusing sick time. Although correctional employees are allowed to use sick time when they have a legitimate reason, as in many other institutions, reports of abuse of sick time periodically surface. Part of this deviance depends on the documentation personnel are required to submit to their supervisors and the diligence of supervisors in reviewing this kind of behavior (Worley and Worley, 2011).

Accepting gifts from inmates and contractors. Occasionally, inmates (or their friends, families, and associates), because of camaraderie or in hopes of ensuring a future favor, try to give COs gifts. Likewise, contractors and suppliers to the facility or department of corrections (DOC) may give COs gratuities or discounts on goods or services. The hope is that if their products or services are needed, these vendors will be favored. These gratuities are typically frowned upon by the senior administrators and accrediting bodies. Accepting gratuities may eventually (depending on the situation) lead to corruption and/or the preferential treatment of inmates and contractors. This prevents the institution from dealing with the vendors in an unbiased fashion. Decisions regarding possible contracts may be made based on personal relationships rather than the contractor/vendor who can give the best-quality service at a reasonable cost. And, during the lifetime of the contract, personal relationships may mitigate a CO complaining when there is poor service.

Deviance against inmates

Abuse of authority. COs have a considerable amount of power while on the job (Clemmer, 1958). They can write up (submit negative reports about) inmates they do not like, or they can humiliate convicts in front of others. Other kinds of abuse include confiscating inmates' possessions, destroying their belongings, playing with the thermostat settings, arbitrarily denying privileges, placing inmates who hate each other in the same cell, repeatedly tossing (searching) cells, repetitively strip-searching inmates, and frequently transferring inmates to different correctional facilities. Alternatively, COs can give some inmates housing or jobs that are more desirable, or more access to entertainment (for example, television) and sports privileges. All combined, these kinds of actions are often referred to collectively as the abuse of authority. "[This] frequently involves one, or all, of the following activities: the acceptance of inmate payoffs for special consideration in receiving legitimate prison privileges ... ; the acceptance of inmate payoffs for special consideration in obtaining or protecting illicit activities ... and extortion" (Freeman, 1999: 350).

Mishandling/theft of inmate property. Inmates' possessions come in and out of a facility either when convicts are transferred to an institution or when friends and family mail or bring items to the prison. Inmates routinely complain that COs steal or damage their items. One recurring reason for this behavior is connected with the fact that, in the normal course of doing their jobs, officers must ensure the safety of the institution and prevent contraband from coming into the jail or prison. That is why, for example, COs are typically required to remove the covers of hardcover books and search inmates' personal effects at intake and during cell searches (Worley and Cheeseman, 2006).

Discrimination toward inmates. The U.S. jail and prison system has experienced a long history of discriminatory behavior directed toward certain racial and ethnic minority inmates (especially African American and Hispanics), and toward those who are homosexual, lesbian, and transgender (Souryal, 2009). This can range from the kinds of amenities they are provided to being singled out for violence/excessive force.

Violence/excessive force against prisoners. The prison staff can and do use violence against convicts. They are allowed by law to use force when life and property are in peril. Nonetheless, two major concerns arise from the use of force: How frequently is force used, and is it done in an indiscriminate manner? Most often, officers will avoid using violence if possible, since it creates ill-will that the prisoners are not likely to forget. Instead, correctional workers rely on threats and humor to motivate inmates to comply with directives. When officers beat inmates (not to be confused with excessive force), this is often precipitated by the latter having initiated or followed through on an attack or instigating work strikes, riots, or escape attempts (Kerness and Ehehosi, 2001; Pratt et al., 1999).

Unlike the deadly violence that convicts inflict on one another, most acts of violence committed by COs are psychological. If the officers want to remind a prisoner about who is in charge, they might destroy that convict's mail, refuse to turn up the heat, deny telephone privileges, or toss the prisoner's cell more frequently than normal. In the middle of the night, while a convict is sleeping, COs may overturn a bed, dumping them onto the floor. COs do not usually take the time to politely wake up an inmate; rather, the officers might drag them to the floor, handcuff them, and rummage through their personal items to search for weapons, drugs, or other contraband items. An officer who wants to particularly anger an inmate might confiscate pictures of loved ones, sheets, clothing, food, and legal papers.

Strip searches, ostensibly used to detect drugs and weapons, are another form of intimidation and violence. COs can order an arrestee to go through this humiliating act numerous times a day on the cellblock, in the cafeteria, outdoors, or when entering or exiting the visitation room. A prisoner may be forced to stand naked outside in a snowstorm, regardless of the danger of frostbite. This might even happen below the gun tower, with M-16 or AR-15 rifles and shotguns pointed in the prisoner's direction.

Sometimes, in medium and maximum security prisons, when the COs think an inmate may have contraband hidden inside his or her rectum, a strip search will include a finger wave. Similar to a doctor conducting a prostate examination, the CO or medical professional (for example, nurse) will insert a gloved finger in the rectum – but the correctional worker is much less likely to be as gentle as a doctor. It must also be remembered that staff do not necessarily have to inflict violence on an inmate themselves; they can often convince another prisoner to do it on their behalf (Cohen et al., 1976; Hemmens and Atherton, 2000; Hemmens and Stohr, 2001).

Sexual relations with or assault of inmate.[8] Over the years, a long history of the sexual abuse of female convicts by male staff members at the women's prisons has been documented (Marquart et al., 2001; Worley and Worley, 2011). In most states, sexual relations or inappropriateness between prison staff and convicts is considered by law to constitute sexual assault or rape. Consensual sex between the keepers and the kept does not exist. Over the past two decades, hundreds of COs have been fired and/or indicted and convicted on sexual assault charges (Human Rights Watch, 1996; Moss, 2008; Stewart, 1998).

Some state prison systems, like Georgia's, have implemented tough "no touch, no contact" policies. In these situations, men are not allowed to supervise female convicts. If a male enters the unit, COs are instructed to announce "man [or male] on range." At some federal prisons for women, administrators have installed hotlines through which female prisoners can make complaints if they have been sexually abused. Sometimes this is a public relations exercise designed to garner support from the wider public by publicizing that something is being done about this problem. Nonetheless, several states have still not outlawed staff–inmate sex to date.

Although female sexual relations with inmates occur (for example, Worley et al., 2010), historically sexual relations with prisoners have been more of a problem with male correctional employees than with female correctional workers (Beck et al., 2007). However, news stories of male-on-male and female-on-female sexual relations are occasionally reported. For example, in 2000, Garrett Cunningham, while incarcerated at the Luther Unit of the Texas Department of Criminal Justice, was repeatedly raped, not by a fellow inmate but by a CO. Stories about female officers abusing male inmates are rare, as it is often perceived that male prisoners are the beneficiaries in this kind of behavior.

Deviance against other COs

Drinking on the job. COs who come to work under the influence of alcohol, drink on the job, use prescription or over-the-counter drugs in a manner in which they are not prescribed or illegal drugs that impair their judgment, are unable to properly respond to the demands of their work. They threaten not only their own safety, but also that of their fellow COs. Alcohol use is often part of the CO subculture. Drinking is usually done for camaraderie, social bonding, and stress relief. Using illegal drugs, or using prescription drugs in a manner in which they were not intended, may set COs up for charges of corruption (that is, they are the first to be suspected of smuggling contraband into the facility), regardless of the means by which the substances were obtained.

General boundary violations. Boundary violations include "actions that blur, minimize, or disrupt the professional distance between correctional staff members and prisoners" (Marquart et al., 2001: 878). This type of conduct, including inappropriate relationships, disregards the typical roles of COs as supervisors and guardians, and inmates as individuals who are to follow orders. This kind of deviance can be further demarcated into general boundary violations which are "'unserious' framebreaks committed by employees who accepted from inmates, or exchanged with inmates, ... drinks, food, craft work or materials, or wrote letters to prisoners" (883). Boundary violations upset the power relations between COs and the inmates.

Discrimination. Correctional workers and organizations, like most people, should be cognizant about discriminating based on age, race, ethnicity, sexual preference, and national origin. This kind of discrimination can occur in the hiring of potential COs and the treatment of inmates. Starting in the 1960s, a series of lawsuits were brought on behalf of women who applied to be COs. This coincided with massive changes due to the 1964 Civil Rights Act. These steps helped pave the way for the increased hiring and promotion of women in the corrections field (for example, Zupan, 1992). Discrimination against women as COs does not simply end with hiring and promotion, but it can also be detected in "tokenism, differential treatment by male supervisors and administrators, and opposition by male co-workers" (330). Discrimination also takes on particularly ugly forms in the occasional news media story about COs being members of radical right wing organizations, such as Aryan Nations or the Ku Klux Klan (Camp et al., 2001).

Sexual harassment of fellow correctional workers. Both male and female officers and administrators may engage in sexual harassment directed toward each other. This may include repeatedly asking fellow workers for dates, inappropriate touching, and stalking. Sexual harassment can also be exhibited in the creation of a hostile work environment by bringing pornographic magazines to work, displaying pornographic materials on the job, objectifying other individuals, and making comments about body parts (Britton, 1997; Savicki et al., 2003; Stohr et al., 1998; Worley and Cheeseman, 2006).

Smuggling contraband. Contraband is brought into prisons with the help of a variety of individuals, including COs (Kalinich, 1986; Lankenau, 2001). These items vary from institution to institution, from state to state, and typically include alcohol, cell phones, cigarettes, condoms, currency, drugs, nicotine patches, tobacco, and tattooing materials. These are often components of the "inmate economy" and are frequently used for exchange. Correctional workers who bring in such items may have been compromised (for example, an inmate or group of convicts may have damaging information on a CO that can be used against them), or they may see these opportunities as additional ways to supplement their income.

Summary

By far the most dominant acts of CO deviance are targeted against other officers. While on first pass, actions such as drinking on the job may put an officer at risk and damage the reputation of the institution, they primarily put other COs at risk.

Exhibit 14.1

The legacy of correctional officer deviance in Florida's Department of Corrections

Correctional officer deviance occurs throughout American jails and prisons on a regular basis. One of the states that has recently and semi-frequently been in the public spotlight regarding correctional officer violence towards inmates and corruption has been Florida. Many of these controversial incidents have been kept quiet behind closed doors. Needless to say, a series of beatings leading to the death of inmates under questionable circumstances have made their way to the news media and garnered negative public attention and public inquiries. Some of the more infamous incidents have included the death in 1999 of Frank Valdes, a death row inmate, who was beaten to death by correctional officers. Another incident involved the scalding to death in 2012 of prisoner Darren Rainey. In 2006, corruption extended all the way to the Secretary of Corrections office, when James Crosby, then Secretary, and his colleague were convicted of illegally using convict labor. A number of reasons have been put forward regarding why this has occurred, including the blue wall of silence among correctional officers, a culture of CO violence, and the remote nature of the prisons and how this mitigates public scrutiny of what occurs inside the nearby correctional facilities (see Reutter, 2016).

Types of solutions to CO deviance

There are at least 17 methods by which CO deviance can be minimized, curtailed, or controlled. These mechanisms are drawn from both the corrections and public administration literature. Solutions can be divided into three categories based on the point of implementation in the career/work pattern of a CO: preservice, in-service, and continuous.

Under the first category are included:

- conducting thorough background investigations on applicants;
- proper and thorough training; and
- certification.

The following actions fall within the second category:

- participative management/total quality management (TQM);
- • using power appropriately;
- reporting malfunctioning or broken equipment in a timely manner;
- exposing waste and violations of rules; and
- the use of ombudsmen and ethics committees.

Under the last group of solutions we have:

- realistic alternatives to selective contraband and banned inmate behavior;
- cultural awareness – diversity and gender sensitivity training;
- accreditation;
- proper employee evaluation;
- random drug, criminal background, and credit checks;
- better leadership;
- the creation and use of internal affairs units;
- sanctions; and
- professionalism.

Before reviewing these mechanisms, however, it must be understood that the act of reporting deviance is not as simple as it may sound.

Impediments to reporting deviance

In principle, corruption, violence, or violations of rules should be reported. However, this is easier said than done. COs, like police officers, have to deal with the powerful effects of the occupational subculture, the so-called officer code (Kauffman, 1988), especially the "blue wall of silence" which means that coworkers will generally not reveal potentially harmful information about fellow correctional workers because this action may frustrate teamwork or mutual protection from inmates while on the job. Clearly, no CO relishes the thought of being in a dangerous situation and not being able to count on having backup. Thus, COs are very careful about reporting acts of deviance among their fellow officers. Officers that do reveal the wrongdoings of fellow COs, supervisors, or correctional facility administrators are often referred to as whistleblowers.

Categories of solutions

Preservice

Conducting thorough background investigations on applicants. Before hiring a CO, most jurisdictions conduct a thorough examination of potential candidates. Most jails and prisons consider applicants who are U.S. citizens, between the ages of 18 and 37, who have completed high school or obtained its equivalent education (for example, General Education Development), have not had any felony convictions, and have had two years' work experience (www.bls.gov/ooh/protective-service/correctional-officers.htm#tab-4). The Federal Bureau of Prisons (FBOP), in particular, wants its recruits to have either an undergraduate degree or three years' experience in a field delivering "counseling, assistance, or supervision to individuals." Applicants also must be in good health and meet the requirements of "physical fitness, eyesight, and hearing" (www.bls.gov/ooh/protective-service/correctional-officers. htm#tab-4)

Typically, those wishing to work as a CO:

1. fill out an application with the relevant state or federal agency;
2. take a written test and a psychological examination (like the Minnesota Multiphasic Personality Inventory test or the California Personality Inventory), perform a physical test, and submit to a urine (that is, drug) test;
3. submit to a criminal background investigation;
4. have a medical exam;
5. perform a physical ability/agility test;
6. have a face-to-face psychiatric test; and
7. have a personal interview. (Freeman, 1999: chapter 12)

This last step is often the most important, as seasoned human resource personnel are responsible for determining the suitability of potential candidates through face-to-face interviews.

Proper and thorough training. COs should be given proper training not only in the skills and knowledge of the job, but also in the ethics, rules, and regulations of the position. Despite this objective, considerable differences with respect to how and where CO candidates are trained exist across the country. At a minimum, DOCs design their training based on "guidelines established by the ACA and the American Jails Association. Some States have regional training academies that are available to local agencies" (www.bls.gov/ooh/protective-service/correctional-officers.htm#tab-4). Initial training may occur at a formal state-run academy with the balance of knowledge, skills, and training being delivered at an actual correctional facility. At the academy or at the correctional facility to which they are assigned, CO candidates receive instruction in self-defense, firearms, "institutional policies, legal regulations, and operations, as well as custody and security procedures" (www.bls.gov/ooh/protective-service/correctional-officers.htm#tab-4). Increasingly courses on integrity and ethics are being taught to rookies (Stewart, 1998: 83). While on the job, recruits typically serve out a probationary period and are subject to random drug testing. "Officer trainees typically receive several weeks or months of training in an actual job setting under the supervision of an experienced officer" (www.bls.gov/ooh/protective-service/correctional-officers.htm#tab-4). In the FBOP, recruits "must undergo 200 hours of formal training within the first year of employment. They also must complete 120 hours of specialized training at the U.S. Federal Bureau of Prisons residential training center at Glynco, GA, within 60 days of their appointment" (www.bls.gov/ooh/protective-service/correctional-officers.htm#tab-4).

The training process is typically expensive for the state and federal correctional systems. Thus, they try to weed out unsuitable candidates early in the process to prevent the expenditure of additional hiring costs (Conover, 2001). Unlike most police departments, some correctional agencies require their new hires to start immediately on the job; after a probationary period of working on a tier or cellblock, the new employees are then sent to the training academy. This alternate course was developed when various DOCs were placed in awkward positions after authorizing the costly training of new recruits only to have the new hires quit after experiencing the monotony and fear attendant to their jobs. Most DOCs separate recruits into different groups and provide them with specialized training, before moving on to the next group of new hires. This approach relies on the understanding that the majority of the new employees will learn the bulk of their responsibilities through experience and not in a classroom setting. The administration hopes "that recruits will learn general job responsibilities, procedures for carrying out these responsibilities, practical skills for task performance, and something about the expectations of supervisors" (Champion, 2005: 488).

Certification. The certification of COs, including requiring them to learn a specific body of knowledge, to adhere to certain moral and ethical standards, and to undergo periodic testing for certification renewal, may decrease the possibility of deviance (Levinson et al., 2001). A small number of membership organizations (for example, ACA) have recently started to certify COs. Among other options, individual states could develop certification processes and have COs receive licensure through designated certification entities, such as the ACA or a state regulatory agency. The national prison commission made the following suggestion:

> Treat criminal justice professionals just like doctors and lawyers, by making their employment conditional upon a valid license or certification. Half of the states in the country, however, lack a formal process for certifying qualified corrections officers and decertifying those who violate the law or rules of professional conduct. Additionally, there is no national-level mechanism that exists to record and share such information among local jurisdictions and states. Thus, dangerous officers can find employment in different facilities and systems because their past behavior is not known to new employers. (Gibbons and de Katzenbach, 2006: 71–2)

The commission also recommended the creation of a national correctional officer data bank to prevent and/or minimize the ongoing employment of problem COs.

In-service

Participative management/TQM. During the 1980s and 1990s, correctional facilities, inspired by the private sector, introduced new opportunities for line staff to contribute to the formation of institutional policies and practices. This process, called TQM, has been evaluated through an array of select experiments. Most evaluations have suggested that historically TQM existed in name only and that it competed with an older paramilitary approach to managing correctional personnel. TQM is often no more than a buzzword used to describe techniques that are intended to encourage employees to become more involved in the decision-making process. When it is properly utilized, TQM is not simply window dressing (Freeman, 1999: chapter 11). To the contrary, it can actually help the corrections system to act on the input of workers (Slate and Vogel, 1997; Slate et al., 2001; Stinchcomb, 1998).

Using power appropriately. The general public may presume that correctional facilities, administrators, and officers are, by nature, authoritarian (Freeman, 1999: chapter 9). This impression, influenced by the mass media depictions of COs, derives from the numerous rules that inmates must follow and from the fact that infractions typically lead to some sort of administrative action or even physical action on the part of the COs. The stereotypes about officer authoritarianism do not mirror reality. COs do not have the resources to sanction each inmate. They recognize that, in general, they are outnumbered and that forcing convicts to do things against their will most likely backfire.

In order to accomplish their jobs, COs must make appropriate use of their power. Hepburn (1985) categorized five kinds of power: legitimate, coercive, reward, expert, and referent. The most useful types are legitimate and expert power; the worst type is coercive. By law, COs are empowered to do certain things. They know the policies and procedures of their institutions better than anyone else and can help guide inmates through their daily routines. In terms of expertise, COs should know the institutional rules better than the prisoners; this creates a context in which each CO can work effectively. Hepburn concluded that effective COs inspire prisoners' cooperation through a complicated set of rewards and punishments. Some of the privileges include periodically ignoring the rules, overlooking violations, granting choice job assignments, and writing favorable reports. The problem with this kind of exchange relationship is that it has the potential of being taken to the extreme. For example, a CO may smuggle in contraband or encourage illegal behavior on the part of the convicts.

Reporting malfunctioning or broken equipment in a timely manner. In order to minimize the likelihood of being blamed for malfunctioning or broken equipment and to insure inmate and personal safety, COs should inform the proper individuals in their correctional institutions in a timely fashion about equipment issues. Timeliness is especially important if the problems are tied to safety-related equipment. If the administration is slow to fix or replace broken equipment, then correctional workers can often file a report through a union representative (for example, shop steward). Such reluctance to deal with broken equipment can spark cynicism about the organization at large.

Exposing waste and violations of important rules. Although the "blue wall of silence" among correctional workers is ever present, most training manuals advise recruits to report infractions to their immediate supervisors. This is easier said than done because of the ramifications a correctional worker might experience if they report coworker infractions. When considered from various perspectives, there are rational-sounding arguments for both reporting violations and remaining silent. It is relatively painless for outsiders to take the moral high ground and to cite the whistleblower legislation that currently exists in some states and at the federal level. However, one should consider the complications that arise when the deviant individual in question is a CO's immediate supervisor or when the reporting CO has previous acts of misconduct that they want to hide or keep hidden.

Most COs are naturally timid about reporting the deviance of coworkers. Those who choose to remain silent often do so out of fear of retaliation from fellow officers and administrators. Once COs consider a colleague to be a snitch, that individual may find themselves without the necessary support in dangerous situations. One major deciding factor comes into play when COs anticipate that not reporting their colleagues' deviant behavior may later wind up implicating themselves; in such a case, a CO may feel a stronger obligation to inform appropriate-level superiors of an infraction. From a strictly moral or ethical point of view, the failure to report an act of deviance can be almost as bad as committing the act in the first place. Most DOCs stress that employees have a duty to report infractions. Some ways are better than others for the reporting of violations of norms, policies, and practices. Face-to-face or confrontational situations are rarely the best means and methods of communication. The more experience COs have, the greater the odds will be that they will discover and utilize ways to report wrongdoings so that they will not be caught in an undesirable situation in the future. Sometimes, this may mean talking to the offending person in private. On the flip side, once the deviant behavior has been reported, management may attempt to blame the incident (that is, pass the buck) on the workers and to deny responsibility for its own failure to manage or lead.

The use of ombudsmen and ethics committees. Occasionally, correctional facilities or DOCs have ombudsmen who on their own or with their staff investigate abuse and cut through the red tape for prisoners, their loved ones, and correctional workers. An additional mechanism to serve as a check on correctional work is the use of ethics committees, which consist of groups of "every level of management, union representatives, and community representatives" that review complaints against COs (Freeman, 1999: 354). A similar function is conducted by an inspector general who acts as in-house quality control in large government organizations.

Continuous (that is, starts in preservice and continues during in-service)

Realistic alternatives to selective contraband and banned inmate behavior. Many problems connected with the banning of some contraband items (for example, tobacco, nicotine patches, and cell phones) can be solved though alternative policies and practices than those that currently exist. Correctional facilities are not health institutions, thus the complete elimination of the possession and use of tobacco is, in many respects, overzealous. Thus, having designated places where smoking is allowed (for example, in the yard) may be preferable to a complete ban on tobacco-related products. Likewise, the abnormally high financial costs incurred by inmates associated with telephone use, in addition to strict rules on access, may in fact contribute to the increased smuggling of cell phones into prisons. Likewise the numerous incidents of inappropriate contact between inmates and COs, sometimes initiated by inmates for one reason or another, might be lessened if the ability and practice of conjugal visits were liberalized.

Cultural awareness – diversity and gender sensitivity training. In order to minimize acts of discrimination against inmates and fellow officers, many correctional institutions require employees to take cultural diversity and gender sensitivity training. This is often carried out by an employee of a state DOC who makes the rounds of each individual correctional facility. Sometimes the instructor provides lectures on relevant topics, while at other times, they may use group activities (for example, scenario development) in order to teach COs the implications of their actions and to present various methods for diffusing workplace problems (Freeman, 1999: 67).

Accreditation. In order to improve the working conditions at jails and prisons, correctional managers and officials can seek accreditation by the ACA, which has developed standards that have been agreed upon by recognized experts. Accreditation helps ensure that an organization remains current and functions to the best of its ability. The accreditation process requires prisons to submit voluntarily to inspections by the ACA, representatives of the media, scholars, or possibly a board appointed by a governor; this is a complex relationship, but it typically leads to improvements in a facility's programs and infrastructure. COs commonly do not like working in institutions that have practices, rules, and regulations that do not appear to make sense. These protocols may have seemed logical to previous administrations, but they may appear inappropriate, silly, or antiquated in comparison to current practices and conditions.

Proper employee evaluation. Most correctional facilities assess their employees' performance. These evaluations provide many benefits, including preventing COs from engaging in deviance or crime and providing discipline for employees who have engaged in periodic deviance. Performance evaluations can be as simple as a written report, in which a supervisor checks off items on a list, or as complicated as a process of negotiation between a boss and an employee. Performance appraisals are also mediated by union regulations and are often tied to bonuses and pay raises (Latham and Wexley, 1981).

Random drug, criminal background, and credit checks. Since the dawn of using urine tests and criminal background and credit checks as a condition for screening applicants for employment, an increasing number of professions use this practice as a method to protect the integrity of their employees and their institutions. The field of corrections is no different. Not only should COs be subject to random post-hiring drug testing, but in order retain their good standing, COs should be subject to periodic criminal and credit checks. This kind of evaluation serves as a deterrent for COs who may engage in various questionable behaviors. Simultaneously, correctional facilities should provide free (psychological and financial) counseling, and be willing to supply referrals to well-qualified professionals and agencies in the community that can offer treatment/assistance for employees who need it. In addition to random drug, criminal background, and credit checks, correctional institutions would be best served if, as in many jurisdictions, close cross-gender supervision was eliminated. A reduction in corruption, violence, and inappropriate relationships (including ones of a sexual nature) might be achieved if the number of strategically placed video cameras that exist in facilities was increased. Although one might argue that both inmates and COs will find spaces where closed circuit television is not present, this practice will serve as a deterrent.

Better leadership. Better leadership is critical to the minimization of deviant behavior among COs. Not only is it necessary for managers and wardens to have the appropriate qualifications for their leadership positions (such as, relevant experience and education), but also they must also evaluate situations from a broad perspective and should not be authoritarian. Administrators must be able to motivate a team. They also need to be proactive and not simply reactive. "Effective correctional leadership involves a set of practices that acknowledges both the internal and external environment of corrections" (Freeman, 1999: 236–7). One must keep in mind that a distinction exists between managers and leaders. Managers usually help workers perform their daily tasks, including processing the appropriate paperwork, whereas leaders see the bigger picture and plan for the organizational mission. The correctional field needs administrators who are not simply managers but who are leaders who can help their organizations move forward and deal with both planned and unanticipated changes (Riveland, 1997; Stojkovic and Farkas, 2003).

The creation and use of internal affairs units. Most DOCs have developed mechanisms to investigate allegations of officer or administrator wrongdoing. The relevant oversight is provided by entities that go by a variety of names, including offices of inspector generals, offices of professional responsibility, and departments of internal affairs. Once a complaint is launched, these offices usually collect evidence that substantiates the complaint or exonerates the accused. In some DOCs, if evidence of wrongdoing is found, an office will take this information to the institution's warden or to the state's commissioner or secretary of corrections for further action (that is, dismissal, sanction, and so on). In various jurisdictions, the internal affairs authorities have the power to arrest the accused officer (Bell, 2002; Freeman, 1999: 356–7).

Sanctions. Depending on the severity of the deviance, an internal investigation may be opened, and typically the CO in question will appear in front of an in-house disciplinary board. This unit can recommend dismissal, transfer, docking of pay, or retraining. If the matter is of a criminal nature, then formal criminal charges can be made through the local district attorney. In such an instance, the officer is typically allowed to be represented by a lawyer or a representative of his or her correctional union. The message from such proceedings is that the administration is not satisfied with business as usual.

Professionalism. Professionalism exists in many jobs and the field of corrections is no different. Professionalism attempts to demonstrate to both individuals who have chosen to work in the field of corrections, and others (that is, the general public, news media, and legislators), that not anybody can be a CO, but there is a specific body of knowledge that both recruits and seasoned veterans should know at different stages of their career. Member organizations like the American Correctional Association and the American Jails Association promote professionalism through the dissemination of publications, training, conferences, and the establishment and monitoring of accreditation standards. Professionalism also impacts policies on hiring, salaries, and working conditions. Professionalism can serve as a deterrent to correctional officer deviance.

Not all solutions are as important as others. Methods to reduce CO deviance require resources. Cash-strapped correctional facilities and DOCs must make cost–benefit decisions regarding where they want to invest to prevent and properly respond to CO deviance. In general and historically, proactive measures (that is, those that are taken before the individual becomes a sworn officer) are believed to be better for the correctional system as a whole. But DOCs must also implement processes and safeguards that are universally agreed upon to be useful throughout the CO's employment in the field. It is expensive to recruit and train COs, and instead of weeding out the COs who engage in deviance on the job, it may be in the best interest of the institution to have procedures in place to reinforce their employees' commitment to integrity. In this case, accrediting bodies and CO unions can been useful in monitoring and insuring that COs commit to professionalism.

Conclusion

COs' deviance leads to a breakdown in inmate–officer and officer–officer trust. This perception has a wide audience and may contribute to a decrease in public confidence in correctional facilities' ability to do their jobs (for example, Mancini and Mears, 2013). When this trust is lost, it is rarely reasserted, and when it is, an incredible amount of time is required to reestablish it. If levels of deviance are high, a facility cannot work at an optimal level and cannot successfully implement meaningful rehabilitative programs. Both COs and managers must be conscientious in their efforts to prevent themselves from participating in deviant behavior and to insure that they deal with incidents in a timely fashion.

In order to build upon this research, it might be interesting to examine how COs, other correctional workers, correctional administrators, convicts, and ex-convicts feel about the seriousness of not only the types of deviance described in this chapter, but also the solutions suggested here.[9] In this case, perhaps an exploratory study administered to each of these groups of individuals might highlight similarities and differences among these diverse groups and point the way to solutions that are realistic. In short, this framework should serve as the basis for further theory building and possible model development.

Key terms

Blue wall of silence: The idea that officers will not reveal potentially harmful information about a fellow CO because it may result in lack of teamwork or mutual protection from inmates while on the job.

Boundary violations: Actions that blur, minimize, or disrupt the professional distance between correctional staff members and prisoners.

Deviance: Attitude, opinion, action, or behavior that violates generally accepted norms.

Guard subculture: Informal rules and standards shared by COs. Also a means of transmitting work related information to other COs, such as, do not rat out another CO.

Leader: Creates or shapes the vision for a group or organization. Helps to motivate participants/members to accomplish the group or organization's goals.

Manager: Helps workers perform their job including processing the appropriate paperwork, time sheets, etc.

Monkey wrenching: Purposely breaking or destroying equipment either to speed up management buying a new one or out of a sense of frustration or boredom.

Norm: Generally accepted attitudes, opinions, and behaviors.

Power: Ability to influence others actions. In a correctional context, Hepburn (1985) identifies five types that a correctional officer can use.

Retribution: When a person or organization seeks to redress a perceived or actual wrong committed against them.

Total Quality Management (TQM): Techniques that encourage employees to become more involved in the day-to-day decision-making and planning in work-related environments.

Notes

[1] This chapter builds upon Ross (2013c). Accordingly, thanks to Nancy Hogan and Eric Lambert for comments on earlier versions of this work.

[2] Although this analysis is mainly tailored toward prisons and COs who work in them, many of the actions that are identified occur in jail settings too.

3   There are some exceptions to this observation. Freeman (1999) and Phillips and McConnell (2005), who have written prison administration texts, have separate chapters that look at the problem of ethics in correctional settings. Likewise, there has been some fledgling work done on correctional ethics at every level of the penitentiary (for example, Kleining and Smith, 2001).

4   Research on prison administrators, and probation and parole officers is relevant; however, this chapter is restricted to the work that explicitly focuses on correctional officers.

5   Thus, this chapter ignores prisoner- and prison activist-initiated solutions. For a review of prisoner resistance, see, for example, Ross (2010).

6   It has been suggested that in order to proceed, it might be helpful to either derive these controls from the scholarly literature on deviance by law enforcement officers or to compare them the latter with police officers. However, the author argues that although both work in the criminal justice system, there are significant contextual differences mitigating this approach.

7   This is based on a review of scholarly research, news media reports, informal conversations with both inmates and correctional workers, and it is informed by the writer's close to four years of work inside a correctional facility. Where appropriate, the author has attempted to cite scholarly sources.

8   A closely related act of deviance is having sexual relations with the wife, husband, boyfriend, or girlfriend of the inmate.

9   See Stohr et al. (2000) and Worley and Worley (2011) for examples of this type of research.

FIFTEEN

Officer pay and workload

Introduction

A considerable amount of research has been conducted on correctional officers (COs). Most findings suggest that they "are alienated, cynical, burned out, stressed but unable to admit it, suffering from role conflict of every kind and frustrated beyond imagining" (Welch, 1996: 137). It is not a profession that many people choose as their lifelong career. Most individuals go into corrections seeing it as a temporary job, thinking that they will spend at the most one or two years in a correctional setting, but over time, it ends up being a career.

Some correctional workers see their jobs as a sentence, much like one handed down to a person who is convicted of a crime. As the argument goes, the only good thing about the COs' sentence is that they can go home at the end of their shifts. Historically, COs have not been paid well nor have they received many benefits. One of the biggest drawbacks is that there is approximately a 16% turnover of COs each year "and [this] is higher where the pay is lower" (Gibbons and de Katzenbach, 2006).

Over time, however, with the advent of unionization and professionalization, this situation has improved, although there are still discrepancies in salaries among states and between genders (Mallicoat, 2005). Another relevant issue is professionalization, which started with the requirement of wearing uniforms and possessing a specific body of knowledge. One of the most significant, if not symbolic, changes was during the nineteenth and twentieth centuries from using the job title "guard" to CO.

Correctional officers' work in transition

In 1991, Crouch argued that over the past two decades, the work of COs has changed largely because of "(1) an emphasis on rehabilitation, (2) changes in the size and composition of inmate populations, and (3) judicial intervention" (as cited in Welch, 2004: 137). Although the last two components are important, the first no longer applies.

Guard subculture

Crouch and Marquart (1980) suggest that the subculture developed by COs "is vital to the occupational socialization of the recruit. Rookies listen to, observe, and imitate ranking officers. Moreover, the presence of the guard subculture teaches rookies the following: (1) how to perceive inmates, (2) how to anticipate trouble, (3) and how to manage inmates" (Welch, 2004: 139).

The guard subculture idea is not without its critics. For example, Klofas and Toch (1982) and Klofas (1984) suggest that there is so much variability among COs, their superiors, and inmates that the guard subculture argument does not carry much weight as an explanation for correctional officer behavior.

Pay/benefits

During the first half of the twentieth century, COs' salaries were very poor. Over the past five decades, through the passage of labor laws and professionalization, the hourly pay rates have improved. Nevertheless, wages vary based on the region, the state, and the system (state or federal) a CO works in, as well as gender. In some states, COs may not make much more than minimum wage. On the other hand, the best-paid COs work for the Federal Bureau of Prisons (FBOP). "As the workforce has become increasingly professionalized, with college-educated staff who claim to possess special expertise in the area of 'corrections,' salaries and status have increased correspondingly. ... If you factor in overtime, this could mean that COs make what amounts to be a middle class income" (Austin and Irwin, 2001: 98).

There are significant pay differentials between female and male COs. Male COs are generally paid better than women. In 2002, according to the U.S. Bureau of Labor, female COs only made 78.6% of their male counterparts' salaries. Moreover, few management positions are held by female COs. True, some women work as captains, lieutenants, and wardens, but these ranks are typically occupied by men. This is even the case in female-controlled correctional institutions run by female wardens. Women are found working more in state facilities than they are in the FBOP. The compensation is increasing in prisons for COs – both male and female – and one of the most important reasons is unionization. According to the Bureau of Labor Statistics, "The median annual wage for correctional officers and jailers was $39,040 in May 2012" (www.bls.gov/ooh/protective-service/correctional-officers.htm).

Unionization

Starting in the 1940s, COs have attempted to gain more control of their work environment. They have achieved this through the interrelated processes of seeking professionalization and unionization (Welch, 2004: 145). CO unions started in the mid-twentieth century, and about 50–70% of all COs are now unionized. What do these unions do? Like most others, they try to improve wages, benefits, and working conditions for their membership.

At this point, many criminal justice jobs have either become unionized or the workers are governed by rules established by professional associations. In addition to a desire for better pay, benefits, and working conditions, one of the reasons why correctional workers have unionized is because they believe that both jail and prison administrators, and the judicial system, have abandoned them as a result of court decisions that have been passed in support of convicts' rights (Welch, 2004: 145).

In addition to joining unions, COs have become members of professional organizations like the American Correctional Association (ACA). This entity "offers training and networking opportunities and speaks for the field in national forums" (ACA, Professionalism in Corrections: 10). The ACA also has a code of conduct that members must abide by if they want to be in good standing.

Unions can minimize the turnover rates of COs. How can this be? If the workers get more money, benefits, and better working conditions, it minimizes COs' reasons for quitting. Several different unions represent state and federal correctional workers. According to Page, "prison officer unionization has taken root in more than half of the United States and that more than one-third of all American prison officer unions are independent (i.e., unaffiliated with the both the American Federation of Labor and Congress of Industrial Organizations and the Change to Win coalition" (2011a: 7–8). In Maryland prisons, for example, some of the unions representing COs include the Communications Workers of America (CWA) and the American Federation of State and Municipal Employees (AFSME). In some states, CO unions have become very powerful. One of the most powerful is the California Peace Officers Association, which has been very successful in lobbying the legislature, establishing and encouraging a correctional building program, and influencing sentencing practices (that is, making them longer and harsher, thereby ensuring jobs for all their membership) (Page, 2011a; 2011b). Even so, because COs' jobs, like law enforcement ones, are essential service positions, they are typically not allowed to strike. So what do they do to exert their will? They go on "job actions," sickouts, or suffer "the blue flu."

Blue flu occurs when most of the COs in a facility call in sick. This means that the institution is short staffed, which typically puts the correctional facility into a state of crisis. Meanwhile, inmates still need to be supervised and fed. Unless noncustodial personnel can be easily shifted around, management is forced to rely on scab (nonunion) labor (and in most states, this results in a violation of labor laws). Sometimes recruits can be rushed through the corrections academy (which is also a poor option). Alternatively, the warden and senior personnel temporarily suspend their administrative duties and work the tiers. Thus, correctional administrators grudgingly have to assume the responsibilities of directly supervising the inmates.

When this happens, convicts end up spending more time in their cells and get increasingly frustrated with the conditions. When they are out of cell, there may be a greater possibility of inter-inmate violence and more contraband flowing around the institution because proper and/or frequent searches are not being conducted. No self-respecting warden, superintendent, or commissioner of corrections wants this to happen for a prolonged period. This process forces management's hands to quickly conclude labor negotiations by making concessions.

Professionalization

COs have responded to criticisms about their work through professionalization. This usually encompasses the development of specialized knowledge and skills, an occupational culture, a code of conduct, and the capability of sanction by the group (Vollmer and Mills, 1966). In short, this typically means increasing the educational and training requirements needed to work in correctional facilities. Many of these rules and regulations have been developed and promoted by the ACA. It is also important for correctional institutions to be accredited. Policies and practices that are present in an institution should not simply be there because of past practice. Many policies are no longer applicable or are simply a function of the whims of some administrator/s over a decade ago.

Most people who have been in the working world for a while realize that a considerable number of the rules and regulations in organizations are silly, irrelevant, antiquated, and illogical. This perception may exist because one may not have enough experience with the rationale behind the origins of the rules, or it may be that no one to date has challenged their inclusion and use in the daily routines. In sum, there are countless irrelevant and/or ineffective rules that are still present in policy manuals and taught in correctional officer training academies.

Summary

Surveys of the American public consistently show that few people ever consider working as COs. COs are also perceived to be relatively unintelligent and poorly paid, and are thus referred to in derogatory terms, such as bulls, cops, hacks, knuckle draggers, and screws. This is largely because correctional work is a low-prestige job and perceived to be highly dangerous. This can be explained by the company that they must keep, the paramilitary structure of the work place, their pay, and media and popular culture presentations of COs.

Correctional workers frequently complain that the rules are always changing so that neither they nor the convicts are certain how things should function. COs are also frustrated about a number of significant Supreme Court cases that have curtailed their power. Some are nostalgic about "the good old days" when convicts were more respectful and COs' orders went unquestioned (Cole, 1994).

Conclusion

Being a CO is similar, in some respects, to being a dentist. Both professions perform a valuable service, but few people want to be under their care or supervision. Despite reasonable pay expectations and decent social standing, interactions with dentists are frequently avoided or postponed.

Compared to many jobs, COs earn a decent wage for the amount of education required by their position. Most departments of corrections do not require recruits to have an education beyond high school. The better jobs in administration generally require candidates to have a minimum of a bachelor's degree. The higher up you go, however, the greater the preference for advanced education. Undoubtedly, unionization and professionalization have improved work conditions, salaries, and benefits for COs, but the fact remains that few people want to enter this profession.

Key terms

Blue flu: Because COs are not legally allowed to strike, in order to press their demands COs at one or more facilities call in sick all at the same time.

Guard subculture: An informal and unwritten means for transmitting job-related information to rookies and other COs. It is also a means of socializing rookie COs into the norms of the profession and workplace.

Unionization: Process of bringing a union in to a workplace.

SIXTEEN

Management and administration

Introduction

Although many correctional officers (COs) and correctional administrators believe that in any given correctional facility inmates are the biggest challenge, in many institutions both inmates and COs think that the administrators (particularly those at senior levels) are the biggest problem sources. In part because of the paramilitary nature of prisons, wardens and senior management are often seen as autocratic, poorly trained, and ineffective (Freeman, 2000).

The history of corrections is replete with stories of wardens making decisions with minimal consultation with their staff. For example,

> To protect his authority, the autocratic warden created disunity in the prison community in that the formation of groups of either prisoners or guards was never permitted. The wardens' intelligence system ensured that neither guard nor prisoner could trust anyone. The paramilitary model of management, with its military terminology, downward flow of communication, rigid rules and regimentation, and impersonal relationships, further protected the wardens' absolute power and helped maintain an orderly, neat, and secure institution. (Bartollas, 2002: 259)

"Many wardens complain that they spend far too much time in their offices, coping with memoranda and urgently required reports. They say that they are too busy to inspect their cellblocks from one week to the next" (Bartollas, 2002: 259). Despite these claims, numerous wardens have been very hands-on in their engagement, making significant changes not only in the institutions that they manage, but also in their state departments of corrections (DOCs) (for example, DiIulio, 1987).

Over time, the way that wardens relate to their subordinates has changed:

The majority of bureaucratic wardens of the 1970s used participatory management. Many wardens of the 1980s chose the control, consensual, or responsibility model to manage their correctional facilities. The wardens of the 1990s and first decade of the twenty-first century viewed themselves as professionals and team players dealing with institutional problems in innovative ways. (Bartollas, 2002: 261)

How do COs who aspire to be wardens one day reach this position? The training of professionals to properly and effectively manage and lead correctional institutions inevitably takes place both on the tiers and cellblocks of correctional facilities and in the classroom. On-the-job training gives correctional administrators the opportunity to learn to deal with different situations that might arise unexpectedly and to develop a repertoire of problem-solving strategies. On-the-job training also facilitates mentoring by superiors, who will hopefully adequately supervise, support, and mentor correctional managers and leaders, thereby passing on the appropriate career-relevant knowledge and techniques.

In addition to on-the-job training, it is recognized that formal education in the classroom setting is essential for training effective correctional managers and leaders. Students and instructors in college- and university-based criminal justice programs and state correctional training facilities need relevant and high-quality learning materials to help them understand the field of corrections and prepare for careers in this field. Many of these classes are taught using existing college-level textbooks (Ross, 2008b). Another aspect to keep in mind is that within both the state and the federal correctional systems, promotions usually result in COs and administrators being moved to different institutions. For those who work in a state system, this could mean a relocation to a facility that is reasonably close to where an individual originally worked, however in the Federal Bureau of Prisons (FBOP) a transfer might involve a different part of the country.

The problems

Effectively managing correctional staff is frequently a challenge for most administrators. The biggest difficulties lie in the area of inability to manage one's time, failing to delegate, staff selection, developing COs and managers, and staff retention.

Inability to manage one's time

Most people have difficulty managing the tasks that they need and want to accomplish. We waste a phenomenal amount of time doing things that are often pleasurable but not important, and many of us are constant procrastinators and avoiders. This perception rings true with correctional managers and leaders, whose typical weaknesses include failure to delegate, not planning and determining priorities, overplanning and overorganizing, too many in-person meetings, too much time on the telephone or with email, meetings, paperwork, and personal habits (Phillips and McConnell, 2005: 87–90).

Failing to delegate

Many managers are reluctant to delegate tasks to subordinates and/or when they do delegate, it is done poorly, often in such a way as to guarantee that the person or team now responsible for the task fails (Phillips and McConnell, 2005: chapter 6). Delegation goes beyond a simple job description. "Delegation is both a process and a condition. It is, in part, the act of assigning work to an employee, a process that generally is well understood. But consideration of delegation often stops at this point" (65). There are strong psychological reasons why managers and leaders avoid delegation, yet the advantages of delegation are numerous. According to Phillips and McConnell, "Delegating certain tasks can free up more time to concentrate on true supervisory activities" (67) and delegation "help[s] subordinates learn and grow, rather than acting in a manner that holds them back" (68). They add, "When a manager delegates, employees get a taste of greater responsibility and perhaps some decision-making experience. They are likely to take more pride in what they do, reflect higher morale, both individually and as a department, and exercise more individual initiative" (68).

Selecting the appropriate staff

Corrections has always suffered from an inability to attract and retain suitable officer candidates to do the job. "The problem is tied to the public's notion of penal institutions, as well as to the comparably less favorable aspects of the job" (Ford and Moore, 1992: 10). Managers typically rise up through the ranks from either the custody or programming sides of the institutions. Rarely do they come in from private industry, and these individuals often suffer from tunnel vision, an inability to think outside the box.

Development of COs and managers

In most DOCs, rising up through the ranks usually is done through competitive exams. It also helps if a candidate has, at a minimum, a bachelor's degree. Reaching the level of warden usually requires a master's degree. Commissioners of DOCs are typically political appointees. In other words, they do not have civil service protection (that is, job security). They do not need to have any expertise in the field of criminal justice nor do they even need to have worked in the field of corrections. However, most have at least a minimal background in the area.

Retaining the good correctional managers and wardens

One of the biggest problems faced by prisons is the turnover of management. According to the Commission on Safety and Abuse, "the average tenure for a top corrections administrator in a state system is just three years" (Gibbons and de Katzenbach, 2006: 73). As determined by a survey of correctional managers, 29% of administrators hold their jobs, on average, for one year or less (Clem, 2003). There is a consensus that this is simply too short a time to improve or change things. It is difficult to keep not only good managers, but decent workers too.

Exhibit 16.1

Classics in corrections

John J. Dilulio's *Governing Prisons* (1987)

Governing Prisons is one of the first rigorous comparative studies of prison organization and management in the United States. This research conducted by John J. Dilulio, a conservative and controversial political scientist, examines the social science literature on corrections and finds it sadly lacking. He then identifies three different types of prison systems: Texas (a control model), Michigan (a responsibility model), and California (a consensual model). Dilulio traces the history of these models and the advantages and disadvantages of each. Dilulio favors prisons run by a mix of inmates that have limited power and prison administrators who are skilled in monitoring convicts, are compassionate, and have earned the respect of the inmates. These types of correctional facilities, he argues, are the most humane.

Solutions

The most important solutions for addressing the previously mentioned management difficulties often involve correctional workers staying out of the way of difficult bosses and attempts to give COs more power. These kinds of responses include properly managing your time, avoiding autocratic supervisors, properly training managers, empowering employees, facilitating unions and collective bargaining, and total quality management and unit management.

Properly managing your time

Numerous books, courses, and software programs help individuals make more effective use of their time. Some of the more well-known principles include determining how you currently spend your time, developing lists, prioritizing the lists, determining objectives, working toward those goals, writing down tasks, quickly getting to the gist of face-to-face meetings, selective use of the telephone, capitalizing on new technologies (for example, personal data assistants, PDAs), and reducing non-essential meetings and paperwork (Phillips and McConnell, 2005: 91–7).

Avoiding autocratic supervisors

Traditionally, wardens were political appointees. This meant that there was no necessity for them to have any practical experience in the field of corrections. They often ruled their organizations in an autocratic fashion. This philosophy and practice created a climate of fear and contributed to low worker morale and productivity. Over time, this situation has changed; although political connections never hurt, wardens typically have practical corrections experience and work their way up the chain of command. In order to cope with problem superiors, many COs try to get jobs in institutions where they will not be in constant contact with supervisors. They volunteer to spend the lion's share of their time up in watchtowers or devote a significant amount of their shifts to transporting prisoners. One alternative, which ultimately has negative consequences for any CO that chooses it, involves using up as many sick days as possible. The downside here is that often COs that frequently call in sick will come under the scrutiny of management, and they may be sanctioned for this kind of behavior.

Properly training managers

Starting in the 1980s, states began sending correctional managers to specialized training programs to improve many of their job-related skills, including communication, leadership, handling grievances, understanding new management practices, and the economy (Freeman, 2000: 322–9). Similar programs have been provided by the FBOP National Institute of Corrections, which "provide[s] training, technical assistance, information services, and policy/program development assistance to federal, state, and local corrections agencies" (www.nicic.org/AboutUs). These courses are available to senior-level correctional managers and leaders.

Employee empowerment

Allowing employees who previously had little or no ability for independent action to act with more autonomy is typically called employee empowerment (Freeman, 2000). An alternative definition is "letting employees solve their own problems and implement their own solutions; or letting the employees decide what needs to be done and go ahead and do it" (Phillips and McConnell, 2005: 66). Workers who are empowered are able to exert influence on organizational policy development and practices. In order to accomplish this, COs have formed unions, and some facilities have experimented with work groups, unit management, and the implementation of Total Quality Management (TQM) programs (Freeman, 2000: chapter 11).

Other techniques for employee delegation and empowerment entail being vigilant about "deadlines and follow-up" (Phillips and McConnell, 2005: 73). This includes being sensitive about the tasks that are delegated, determining how much of an actual task should be given to a subordinate, choosing the appropriate person to carry out a job, giving comprehensible instructions, offering appropriate incentives, and implementing some sort of control process (75–80).

Unions and collective bargaining

The process of unionization and collective bargaining has been slow to come to American prisons. In the 1940s, the only state that had a union was Connecticut. The movement took off in the 1960s with New York and Washington entering the fray. "By the 1970s, more than twenty states had formally authorized collective bargaining by public employees, and by the end of the twentieth century, more than half of the states had collective bargaining for at least some correctional employees" (Seiter, 2005: 334).

Essentially, collective bargaining refers to the contract entered into between management and the unions that represent the workers. It is understood that there is a mutually agreed–upon process for negotiating different aspects of the contact that are connected to wages, benefits, working conditions, and grievance procedures.

Total quality management and unit management

During the 1970s, recognizing that the old style of managing COs would not work anymore, many DOCs started experimenting with, and in some cases implementing, both corporate and participatory methods for running their correctional facilities (Bartollas, 2002: 261).

> [The corporate management model] emphasizes modern management techniques and participant management. Lines of authority and accountability are clear; feedback and quantitative evaluations are widely used. It did not take long for correctional administrators to discover that the new management theory did not solve the problems they faced in American prisons. By the

---

Exhibit 16.2

Film

Brubaker (1980)

Brubaker is a film (released in 1980) based on the real-life story of Tom Murton, the prison superintendent who between 1967 and 1968 confronted corruption and state-sanctioned murder and cover-ups in the Cummins Unit, one of Arkansas' most notorious prisons. Murton, played by actor Robert Redford, with the blessing of the state commissioner of corrections, enters Wakefield State prison, undercover as a prisoner, to observe and experience the problems firsthand. He quickly learns how convict bosses (trustees) practically run the place and strike terror into the lives of prisoners, while all the COs and warden appear thoroughly corrupt. Brubaker reveals his true identity to the prison authorities, is granted the position of warden, tries to improve prison conditions and practices, but confronts a variety of state prison administrators who are unwilling to reform the prisons under their control. When he finds unmarked graves on the prison farm, and evidence of corruption that extends up to the governor's office, the prison board fires him.

late 1980s, most of these correctional administrators saw that in spite of private-sector management theory, most prisons had more violence, worse conditions, and fewer programming opportunities than they had had under the autocrats of old. (261–2)

During the 1980s, many DOCs abandoned the shared-powers model and started moving toward a system where inmates wielded considerable power. The problem with this state of affairs was that prison gangs quickly filled up the power vacuum (Bartollas, 2002: 262). Started in 1966 by the FBOP, unit management is designed to break the correctional facility into small parts, push decision making downward, and try to increase contact between correctional workers and prisoners (Seiter, 2005: 317–18). In general, this approach is intended to improve staff–inmate communication. This is fostered by having the staff offices located right on the tiers.

Conclusion

Typically, programs that are designed to empower correctional employees in the management of correctional facilities are simply public relations exercises designed to temporarily pacify the COs until another fad or gimmick comes along. Most seasoned correctional workers are quick to realize this, which in turn creates bad morale, impedes sincere efforts to change, and forces institutions to carry on with maladaptive policies and practices and hostility by COs to their supervisors.

Key terms
Autocratic management: Supervisors, managers, and leaders of organizations give workers commands that the workforce think are unreasonable. These individuals are inflexible in their thinking and their actions.

Collective bargaining: A method where the union and the management decide to work out their differences though an established process that is typically supported by the legal system.

Total Quality Management (TQM): A method of operating a correctional facility that promotes decision-making from the rank and file. CO solutions are considered and implemented if they make sense to management.

Union: Organization that presses for increased pay and better job related benefits for its workers. Workers are responsible for paying dues.

Unit management: The corrections facility is broken down into small parts pushing decision-making down, and attempts to increase contact between COs and inmates.

SEVENTEEN

Privatization of corrections

Introduction

Over the history of corrections, the possibility that selected aspects of jails and prisons should be run by organizations other than the state has frequently been proposed and realized. This practice dates back at least to 1348 when prisoners would be used as galley slaves, and to 1598 when ship captains and merchants agreed to take inmates out of state facilities and transport them to America and other British colonies, where they would be forced into indentured servitude (Feeley, 2002).[1]

During the 1980s, renewed interest in having the private sector build and manage jail and prison facilities, and provide correctional services at the state and federal levels, occurred. Why did this happen?

> Since the early 1980s, when the race to incarcerate quickly outpaced available prison space, state and federal prison systems responded by constructing additional facilities ... Despite massive investment in prisons, corrections officials still had to turn to the private sector to house the overflow of the booming inmate population. Private prison companies, recognizing that corrections is indeed an industry, welcome the opportunity by building facilities in small towns where residents embrace the new business, even though wages would be meager. (Welch, 2011: 506)

What does this industry entail? Not only does it include the building and management of correctional facilities, but it also encompasses educational, food, medical, psychological, security, and transportation services (Austin and Irwin, 2001: 69–70). In 1984, the first private prison opened in Tennessee. In 1986, "there were just twenty-six hundred privately managed prison beds in the United States. By 1995, there were over sixty-three thousand. States like Tennessee considered privatizing their entire prison system" (Hallinan,

2003: 145). Approximately 264 of these kinds of facilities now exist in the United States.

According to the Bureau of Justice Statistics, "In 2014, 131,300 inmates were held in private prison facilities under the jurisdiction of 30 states and the BOP, a decrease of 2,100 prisoners from yearend 2013" (Carson, 2015: 13). The federal prison system "held 1,100 fewer prisoners in private prisons (down 3%), for a total of 40,000 or 19% of the BOP population. ... Seven states housed at least 20% of their inmate population in private facilities at year end 2014" (13). From 1999 to the present the number of inmates at private facilities "has grown 90%, from 69,000 prisoners at yearend 1999 to 131,300 in 2014. The use of private prisons was at a maximum in 2012, when 137,200 (almost 9%) of the total U.S. prison population were housed in private facilities" (13).

Regardless, the private correctional industry in the United States is expansive and an essential player in what has been labeled the Prison Industrial Complex (Christie, 1993/1994). The following section briefly reviews the origins and development of this concept.

Crime control industry

In 1956, American Sociologist C. Wright Mills, wrote *The Power Elite*, which argued that a vast network of individuals, organizations and American businesses work in concert to support an economy that is dominated by the military. He called this relationship the Military Industrial Complex (MIC). During the 1970s, criminologist Richard Quinney, in his book, *Class, State and Crime* (1977/1980), building upon Mills' concept, suggested that not only do we have a MIC, but we have a Social-Industrial Complex (SIC). The SIC, according to Quinney, was "an involvement of industry in the planning, production and operation of state programs. These state-financed programs like education, welfare, and criminal justice are social expenses necessary for maintaining social order and are furnished by monopolistic industries." Subsumed by the SIC is a Criminal Justice Industrial Complex. Quinney argued that large corporations benefit the most from this arrangement.

Christie (1993/1994), in his book *Crime Control as Industry*, outlined how recent trends indicate that we have an unfettered supply of individuals for the criminal justice system to monitor, and that a vast network of public and private enterprises financially benefits from this phenomenon. Though his argument was directed at all of the criminal justice systems in advanced industrialized countries, he mainly focused on the United States, particularly its correctional system. He looked at the rationale that led to an increase in the number of jails and prisons being built and operated, the rising numbers of inmates in the United States, and the political, economic, and cultural mechanisms that support it. In order to argue that the United States leads the world in incarcerated individuals, Christie reviewed how other countries have dealt with the problem of criminality and sanctioning offenders. He primarily blamed the American obsession with controlling lawbreakers at organizations such as the American Correctional Association and the process of privatization and its proponents.

Prison industrial complex

Others have built upon Christie's notion and fleshed it out to include the idea of a Prison Industrial Complex (PIC). According to journalist Schlosser (1998: 54), who first popularized the concept, a PIC is

> a set of bureaucratic, political, and economic interests that encourage increased spending on imprisonment, regardless of the actual need. The prison-industrial complex is not a conspiracy, guiding the nation's criminal-justice policy behind closed doors. It is a confluence of special interests that has given prison construction in the United States a seemly unstoppable momentum.

If Schlosser is correct, the whole panoply of nonprofit organizations and for-profit businesses is able to capitalize on this insatiable need to incarcerate individuals and build correctional facilities, ultimately to make money from the pain and suffering of others behind bars.

Since Schlosser's article, others have provided additional evidence of a number of businesses and corporations that have benefited from the PIC (for example, Sheldon and Brown, 2000; Sheldon, 2005), including confronting the PIC (for example, Platt, 2004; Mahmood, 2004). Some of these companies have their shares traded on the stock exchanges, including the Corrections Corporation of America (CCA), The Geo Group (formerly Wackenhut Corrections Corporation), Cornell Companies, and Community Educations Centers, which "account for over three fourths of the entire world wide market," and derive significant incomes from providing local, state, and federal prison services. Other companies such as Aramark and Canteen have done quite well supplying correctional services with food and meal services. These businesses are active and aggressive in their marketing through the World Wide Web, and practitioner-based organizations. For example, the American Correctional Association conference differs considerably from traditional scholarly conferences. At these venues there is a proliferation of private contractors trying to sell their wares to all sorts of prison systems in the United States. There is considerable discomfort among some segments of the public with the private prison system. For example, in 2013 The Geo Group wanted to name the stadium at Florida Atlantic University (Bishop,

2013). There was considerable backlash among selected students and faculty, which eventually led to the deal being cancelled.

Privatization is a highly contentious issue. Conservatives argue that the free market should not be constrained to selected industries, whereas "progressive liberals (and radicals) … complain that the pursuit of profit has no place in criminal justice" (Welch, 2011: 510). Those who support privatization suggest that the government has done a poor job of corrections, it is unnecessarily costly, inefficient, and the methods by which it is performed poor. "Critics, however, point out that claims of cost-effectiveness are incomplete and misleading; moreover, they stress that the state ought not sidestep its moral and ethical obligation to administer justice" (511).

The following outlines the arguments for and against privatization.

Advantages of privatization of correctional facilities

There are numerous arguments that have been presented for private prisons. In general:

> There are two levels of explanation for privatization: ideological and analytical. Proponents of an ideological explanation call for privatization because they favor a laissez-faire state. Proponents of the analytical explanation call for privatization as a means for controlling government expenditures…. Those in favor of private prisons say they save taxpayers money while maintaining facilities that operate more efficiently (20% less costs), and at a higher quality with lower recidivism rates than public ones. (Caplan, 2003: 15)

Alleged cost savings

Private prisons are amenable to conservatives and correctional planners. In general, they alleviate the unpredictability connected with construction costs, financing, and maintenance. Also prison populations fluctuate. A municipality or state does not want to make a major investment in infrastructure, only to find that in five years it is obsolete either because it does not achieve current correctional goals or because the number of inmates that the jurisdiction now has under its supervision has drastically decreased.

Private prison operators claim that they can build prisons at a fraction of the cost to build public ones. "Because private companies are not subject to the same construction rules as governments, they can build prisons for nearly 25 percent less and in half the time of comparable government funded construction projects" (Caplan, 2003: 15).

Another argument is the effect that private prisons may have on government pension systems and their reliance on public funding. It has been suggested that "it will reduce the public pension system's indebtedness because employees will be privately employed" (Caplan, 2003: 15–16).

The reality of these claims has been challenged by Camp and Gaes (2002) who report that compared to Bureau of Prisons facilities, private ones have demonstrated a higher staff turnover, escapes of prisoners, detection of contraband, and an overall compromised level of security to the public.

Disadvantages of privatization of correctional facilities

Private corporations that have operated correctional facilities have suffered from about five major problems. These include management issues, including labor practices, shady business practices, ethical concerns, poor or inadequate health care, and contributing to pressures for technology acquisition. (See K.C. Carceral's firsthand account of life inside a private prison (Exhibit 17.1).)

Exhibit 17.1

Classics in corrections

K.C. Carceral's *Prison, Inc.: A Convict Exposes Life Inside a Private Prison* (2005)

Although there are numerous memoirs and autobiographies of prisoners who have done time in state and federal prisons, this book is the only firsthand description of life behind bars in a private correctional facility. K.C. Carceral (not his real name), a well-educated convict, who spent close to two decades behind bars, describes, in appropriate detail, what it is like to be incarcerated in one of these facilities and how it differs from other publicly funded correctional institutions he was housed in. In brief, there are few staff and rehabilitative programs inside private facilities. Carceral spent four years in this prison and his book reviews the push in the United States for privatization and how prisoners conduct a sort of guerilla warfare against staff in these facilities.

Management issues

Over the past three decades there has been a litany of instances where the management has failed to properly supervise inmates, leading to complaints of violence, and escapes. When escapes do occur, it is typically the local jurisdiction that is responsible for apprehending the fleeing felon and bringing them into custody. "To help mitigate these concerns Arizona requires private facilities to have insurance policies that will reimburse state agencies should they have to intervene during an escape or a riot. However this only adds to the number of profiteers in the private prison enterprise – insurance companies" (Caplan, 2003: 16). Also often overlooked is that the contract must be supervised. So this needs to be factored into the purported cost savings (16).

Shady business practices

In the beginning, privatization creates competition, which can drive prices down as companies compete with each other; however, as fewer businesses enter the market, the corporations start increasing their costs to purchasers. Another problem concerns the fact that often after receiving a lucrative contract the provider will "sham" by providing fewer services or lower-quality items to further enhance their profit margin. On the other hand though, why is it assumed that private is worse than public – and more importantly, that it is a state's (country's) innate characteristic for public penalization versus private?

> Since privatization is driven by a profit motive, critics argue that managers tend to respond to the fiscal incentive to reduce costs at the expense of prisoners by downscaling programs and services. At the same time, privatization contributes to excessive use of incarceration since profits are generated through increased volume – that is, a steady expansion of the correctional population. (Welch, 2011: 511)

Ethical concerns

Privatization calls into question several ethical issues. Given that the government is responsible for arresting and adjudicating individuals charged with criminal offences, is it right for a corporation to profit from the misery of others? In private corrections, the staff often do not have the appropriate training to do their jobs properly. Privatization also makes it harder for the government to control what goes on in corporate-run prisons.

Poor or inadequate health care

Numerous convicts have suffered under private-run medical care providers. Some (for example, Prison Health Services) have continuously run afoul of state inspectors, regulators, and DOCs. Nevertheless, DOCs have continuously renewed their contracts, and often take the position that something is better than nothing. Moreover, although copious anecdotes exist, no empirical evidence exists to suggest that convicts suffer more under private prison regimes. In short, the reality of correctional facilities these days is that one cannot really talk about a system that is either public or private. We in fact have a hybrid system where selective aspects of correctional facilities are contracted out to the private sector. The private prison industry has fought back, sponsoring its own research and hiring correctional experts to do their bidding.

Contributes to technology consumption desires

One of the side-effects of the boom in new technologies produced by the private sector that are developed for the field of corrections is that "introducing new technologies such as electronic monitoring, thus creat[es] consumption desires among corrections officials. In turn, as company profits become increasingly contingent on corrections as a major growth industry in the United States for the foreseeable future, there is a strong economic interest in keeping corrections, especially imprisonment, large" (Lilly and Deflem, 1996: 12).

The shift to privatization of community corrections

Despite the rather large amount of scholarship and public debate about the privatization of corrections, little has been written on private entities running community corrections services and programs, despite the fact that "nationwide there are more clients served by private, locally operating, community correctional agencies than there are prisoners in private jails and prisons" (Alarid and Schloss, 2009: 279). There are approximately "300,000 misdemeanor probationers being supervised in 10 states by private agencies" (Schloss and Alarid, 2007). On the federal level, for example, the Bureau of Prisons "contracts with 250 community centers operated by the Salvation Army, Volunteers of America, and other private agencies" (Alarid and Schloss, 2009: 279).

In order for private entities to operate community corrections programs and services, states have passed Community Corrections Acts, "which transfer the authority for operating correctional programs from the state to local or private agencies. Local agencies and community boards are responsible for developing a range of community-based correctional options. As of 2008, 28 states have CCAs that have established community corrections partnerships between state, local, and private agencies" (Alarid et al., 2008). However, "state appropriations for full funding of these partnerships have been slow to develop compared to the overall probation growth rate. States that lack CCA legislation or funding mechanisms have contract options for the use of private agencies" (280).

In general, the private agencies providing community corrections "tend to be smaller and to range widely from facilities that manage the payment of fines and track community-service hours to privately owned and operated residential facilities such as work-release and halfway houses" (see Alarid et al., 2008). They also include "[state]-licensed drug treatment programs that partner with drug courts and probation agencies [offering] group counseling to offenders as part of the public health system" (280).

Some of the writing in this area has been done by representatives of state departments of probation and parole (for example, Bosco, 1998), the head of the American Parole and Probation Association (Paparozzi, 1998); a conservative think tank (for example, Reynolds, 2000), and a couple of pieces by scholars looking into the provision of probation services by private entities (for example, Schloss and Alarid, 2007; Alarid and Schloss, 2009). The reports by state representatives are generally descriptive in nature, and despite the use of the term "community corrections" in the title, most of the discussion refers to probation and/or bail. Some of this research looks at the arguments for and against the use of the private sector (profit and nonprofit) to provide community corrections services (Meyer and Grant, 1996). It would only seem natural that private entities wishing to expand profits would look to market segments where they could apply their expertise and turn a profit.

Conclusion

Some argue that private correctional facilities and community corrections are an imperfect but necessary solution to dealing with the problems of crowding and overcrowding and exert greater control over correctional populations. In short, the reality of correctional facilities these days is that one cannot really talk about a system that is either public or private. We in fact have a hybrid system where selective aspects of jails and prisons are contracted out to the private sector.

Key words

Community Corrections Act: "... transfer the authority for operating correctional programs from the state to local or private agencies" (Alarid et al., 2008).

Crime control industry: Realization that we have an unfettered supply of individuals for the criminal justice system to monitor, and that a vast network of public and private enterprises financially benefits from this phenomenon. Popularized by Nils Christie.

Criminal justice industrial complex: The set of linkages among both the public and private sector which perpetuate criminal justice institutions as the major solutions for dealing with crime and deviance in society.

Military industrial complex: The vast network of individuals, organizations, and American businesses work in concert to support an economy that is dominated by the military. Term popularized by C. Wright Mills.

Prison industrial complex: "… a set of bureaucratic, political, and economic interests that encourage increased spending on imprisonment, regardless of the actual need" (Schlosser, 1998: 54).

Privatization: When functions and services typically owned and/or managed by the state are turned over to the private sector to either own and/or manage.

Sham: When a business provides fewer services or lower quality items than promised in a contract to further enhance the profit margin.

Note

[1] It is tempting to include ship merchants and insurance companies that participated in the slave trade into this conversation, but this is more of a parallel practice, and not one embedded in the field of corrections. Likewise discussions about using inmates to support private enterprise, like the convict lease programs, are tangential to this discussion.

EIGHTEEN

Future of corrections

Introduction

What does the future hold for corrections in the United States? After careful reflection, internal debate, and considerable agonizing, I struggled about whether to end the book on an optimistic or a pessimistic note. Unfortunately, I could not come to a decision concerning which option was best. Some of the reforms I list are certainly things to celebrate, while scholars, practitioners, inmates, ex-cons, and activists will question others. Many of the suggestions may also work for a short period of time, while others may look good on paper but are not effective once put into practice.

Indeed, in order to improve the field of corrections, a comprehensive strategy must be taken. When I say this, I am not referring to the fact that we need better cooperation among the different branches of the criminal justice system, although this might be helpful. A more holistic approach, incorporating labor unions, foundations, social welfare organizations, social work agencies, and criminal justice actors, is preferable. This emphasis should involve people and organizations at the interlocking individual, community, legal, and political levels.

Regardless, this concluding chapter provides a glimpse of the future of corrections in the United States, and in doing so answers a number of questions. These include: What types of criminals might one expect to find in correctional institutions? What problems will jails and prisons encounter? And what are some emerging ideas that have been proposed? This chapter also outlines a number of scenarios we might expect in the future, and given the multiplicity of theories and types of crimes, this final section discusses how we can realistically reduce the number of people behind bars and orient the criminal justice and correctional systems more toward rehabilitation and less toward retribution.

Pessimism or optimism?

There are two basic and opposing ways of predicting the future: one is pessimistic and the other optimistic. In the pessimistic alternative, which can be as simple as maintaining the status quo, things will only get worse. Jail and prison populations will continue to grow, those behind bars will age, their health problems will increase, and there will be less money for suitable living conditions and programming. In a more drastic scenario, crime will increase, real and alleged perpetrators will continue to be incarcerated, and things will go from bad to worse (JFA Institute, 2007).

In an optimistic and somewhat utopian scenario, the frequency, intensity, and lethality of crime will subside until crime becomes a thing of the past. Those who were sentenced to long prison terms will be rehabilitated and eventually released into society. First-time drug offenders will also be released, receiving appropriate treatment in the community, and they will cease and desist committing crimes to support their drug habits. Let us, however, take a closer look at these contrasting perspectives.

The pessimistic scenario examined

The criminal justice system, and corrections in particular, is running out of options that would help improve the current state of affairs. The future does not look bright; most of the problems reviewed in this book are likely to affect jails and prisons, convicts, and correctional officers (COs) in the decades to come. At a minimum, these issues will confront a desensitized public, who alternatively may be obedient/deferent to authority, distrustful of the criminal justice system, apathetic, and poorly informed about contemporary correctional policies and practices. Resolving the problems and challenges reviewed in this book will keep researchers, practitioners, consultants, and activists busy for the foreseeable future.

Desensitized public

Americans are becoming more desensitized to the problems that do not immediately impact their lives. This is attributable to a number of factors. For instance, we are now barraged with numerous communications – including the proliferation of direct mail, cable television, email, the World Wide Web, satellite radio, and social media – that reach Americans on a daily basis. Given the amount of information that any one person receives, they may simply not have the time or interest to find out what is really going on in jails and prisons. In a similar fashion, many Americans feel they know everything about criminal justice and corrections because they regularly watch popular television shows like *CSI* or *Law and Order*. As outlined in Chapter 2, this militates against a proper understanding of realistic solutions for crime and those who commit crimes.

Obedience/deference to authority

Many individuals are all too willing to accept, believe in the infallibility of, and/or act obediently or deferentially to authority (Milgram, 1974). One of the reasons for this is that "[individuals] have little defense against the penalties that can be imposed for defiance" (Piven and Cloward, 1977: 6). Obedience to authority may also be a result of cost–benefit calculations that citizens have made, as they conclude that they have more to lose than to gain from criticizing (that is, protesting against) large powerful organizations like prisons, departments of corrections (DOCs), and governmental bodies. This attitude may also be a result of strong and hidden pressures to conform.

Distrust of the criminal justice system

It is popularly assumed that communities that are disproportionately affected by crime or in which a greater number of individuals are imprisoned (in the United States this would primarily include African Americans and Hispanics) will complain or protest against this pattern and, in some way, try to alter existing economic, political, or social conditions. Most members of the affected communities have a collective memory of repression, powerlessness, and isolation in the political sphere. Many segments of society are very distrustful of the criminal justice system (Gaventa, 1980; Lukes, 1974), and thus, they are reluctant to participate in the political process. Newly arrived immigrants, for example, particularly those from underdeveloped and developing countries and those who may have entered the country illegally, may fear that their status could be easily revoked. Immigrants may also face language barriers, may harbor a deep distrust of the criminal justice system, and may be less knowledgeable about their constitutional rights – all of which make them shy away from political participation.

Apathy

Many people are apathetic about participating in the political process (Ricci, 1984: 154). Political participation is not simply the act of voting. It can include working on behalf of a politician, signing a petition, or writing letters to the editor of a newspaper. The public may have a feeling that "if it does not affect me personally, why get involved?" or that their lone individual actions will not have much of an impact, causing them to question why they should get involved (for example, Lamb, 1975). Participating involves a series of cost–benefit calculations. Many people who are bothered by political or social conditions rationalize that they stand to lose more (that is, police harassment, absenteeism from work, and lost wages) than to gain in criticizing and/or protesting against the criminal justice system. In particular, these individuals cannot afford time off from their jobs or school to complain about social injustices that occur in their lives and/or community.

Policy ignorance and confusion

One of the perpetual problems of corrections is the "pendulum of politics," which is the tendency for policies and practices to come in and out of fashion. This phenomenon may frustrate corrections policies and practices because it constantly fluctuates between liberal and conservative initiatives. Also the definitions of social problems often shift, which leads to confusion among policy alternatives. This includes not only the political parties that are in power, but also the individuals who are tasked with implementing the new courses of action. In situations like this, neither the goals of rehabilitation nor of punitiveness are totally achieved. Perhaps this is not what is intended in the first place. Changing policies and practices can lead to anger, cynicism, and apathy on the part of inmates and correctional professionals alike (for example, Fleisher, 1996; Fabelo, 1997). Also because corrections is not a simple subject, many people are unwilling to appropriately educate themselves on this subject matter.

The graying prison population

One of the biggest problems is the graying of the prison population. One of the reasons for this pattern is the high number of individuals who were sentenced to life in prison in state and federal institutions. The graying of the prison population continues unabated, with more convicts serving life sentences and dying of old age or natural causes behind bars. Some prison systems allow elderly prisoners or younger convicts who are predicted to die in a few months to apply for "compassionate release." This may allow the convict to go home and die in the company of their loved ones. The problem is that few prisoners ever make it out the door before dying, as the application process may take many months to be officially approved. The graying prison population means that prison systems will need to spend even more money on special medical treatments to keep these individuals alive and to build specially designed facilities that allow for an expanded population of older inmates.

Women in jails and prisons

It is generally understood that the rate of crimes committed by females is increasing, which causes unique problems to the correctional facilities in which women convicts are housed. About 10% of all correctional populations consist of females. Unfortunately, the building rate for women's facilities has not increased as it has for men. Additionally, female convicts suffer qualitatively different problems than men, including a history of being victims of sexual abuse and the guilt surrounding their separation from their children. When a mother is incarcerated, there may not always be a spouse or relative who can care for her children. In a best-case scenario, the children may end up under the supervision of the inmate's mother, sister, or grandmother. Too often, however, the children fall under the care of a distant relative or the Department of Social Services (Ross and Richards, 2003: chapter 11).

Lack of funding

Without adequate funding, all other problems of the correctional enterprise are exacerbated, and this contributes to the revolving-door syndrome (that is, no sooner are prisoners released, then they commit a crime and/or violate the conditions of their probation or parole, and return to prison). Frequently, even the best-laid plans fail because the state either does not have enough money or squanders it with needless stopgap measures. It is unrealistic to expect that private organizations like charities and foundations will adequately pick up the slack in this respect.

The optimistic scenario examined

When we look to the field of corrections, few truly new solutions are being proposed. A handful of promising initiatives recently singled out include new technologies, a CompStat-like initiative for correctional personnel, selective release, DNA testing, and changes in drug policy and laws.

New technologies

Over time, advances in forensic/detection and communication technologies have made work-related equipment smaller, more portable, cheaper, and more widely available to criminal justice personnel. This may mean that the possibilities for monitoring those convicted of crimes are easier in the community than behind bars. To a limited extent, the introduction of new technologies may be of some aid to the corrections field (see Chapter 9).

Here, I am not referring to weaponry, such as pepper/OC spray, or restraints, like stun belts, but specifically to electronic monitoring (EM) or chemical castration. Although their connection to rehabilitation is questionable, these mechanisms and procedures can lead to cost savings only after correctional systems make an initial investment of money and properly train personnel to effectively use them. Also, these new mechanisms/procedures are not flawless. For example, individuals who are monitored by this technology may deactivate or modify an apparatus for their own benefit (Fabelo, 2000).

CompStat-like programs for corrections

In 1994, New York City Police Commissioner William Bratton introduced a new management philosophy and practice, which attempted to use timely statistics on crime rates and regular follow-up with senior command staff in order to better marshal the New York City Police Department's resources to combat crime. He called this CompStat (Bratton, 1998). Bratton and others claimed that reductions in NYC's crime rates can be attributed to CompStat. Although these claims have been contested, Mac Donald (2003) wrote that we should hold corrections professionals accountable, just as we are now making the police accountable through CompStat procedures. Mac Donald argues that there are plenty of rehabilitation programs, and – although her data is anecdotal – there may be some truth to her argument that not requiring probationers and parolees to finish such programs is not helping them to succeed after release.

Selective release

Some states, like Illinois and Kentucky, have realized that the last two decades of skyrocketing expenditures for corrections have had a minimal positive impact on the safety and well-being of their citizens. That is why they have implemented significant changes by releasing nonviolent inmates near the end of their sentences (Austin et al., 2003). Incarceration has also proved once again to have few rehabilitative results on those sentenced to jail or prison. Likewise state DOCs and the Federal Bureau of Prisons could improve screening and review procedures to speed up decision making in connection with compassionate release.

DNA testing

The revelations of wrongful convictions, as demonstrated in high-profile cases, have called into question the rush to judgment attitude of some criminal justice systems (Huff et al., 1996). These situations have led to an increased willingness of judges and juries to consider DNA evidence, and have convinced some governors in death penalty states to temporarily suspend the administration of the death penalty. DNA testing of individuals who are on death row (or in the general population) can lead, in some situations, to the release of convicts who would otherwise require constant monitoring and vigilance (Scheck et al., 2000). Such analysis can also reduce the expenditure involved in putting a person to death. When you factor in not only the costs of incarceration, but also any expenses related to appeals, this could mean millions of dollars saved. Why is the criminal justice system not pursuing this course in every case? DNA investigations are very resource intensive. There is a considerable amount of legal work in each of these situations, and currently people are exonerated mainly through the pro bono work of criminal lawyers.

Changes in drug policy and drug laws

Over the past five decades, several states (for example, Washington, Colorado, and the District of Columbia) have decriminalized and/or legalized both medicinal and recreational marijuana. This has led to different law enforcement procedures, a decrease in the size of jail and prison populations, and tax revenue benefits. Now selected elements in the criminal justice system can focus on more serious kinds of crimes and the people who commit them. Likewise, changes in federal drug policy, such as the Fair Sentencing Act of 2010, have addressed some of the sentencing disparities between the possession of powder cocaine and crack cocaine. Many individuals who are currently doing time in federal prisons, because of drug related convictions over the past few decades, have applied for clemency under the Obama administration.

Future challenges

How much do current events affect corrections in the United States? This is a difficult question to answer. The future is ultimately unknown, but there are developments on the horizon that can and may affect our country's jails and prisons, particularly the kinds of people who may be incarcerated in America's correctional facilities.

Consequences of the wars in Iraq and Afghanistan

The United States' military and political efforts in Iraq and Afghanistan could have several effects. When the troops finally pull out of conflict situations like this, there is the strong likelihood that violent crime in the United States may increase. As the history of other conflicts reflects, after major wars, domestic crimes in the United States typically increase. In particular, there have been significant periods in American history during which violent crime peaked, particularly after the Civil War, during Prohibition and the Great Depression, after World War II, and during the 1970s after the war in Vietnam (Monkkonen, 1981; Archer and Gartner, 1984; Gurr, 1989). Currently we have wings and tiers in prisons that are solely made up of veterans who have committed crimes during the immediate weeks and months following return. Much of this could have been prevented had they received adequate care from the United States Department of Veterans Administration.

Future causes of crime

Crime has numerous causes. Around the world, small civil wars, population growth, natural disasters, conflicting values, and limited or unequal access to food, employment, and natural resources (through destruction and depletion) are prime motivators for mass migrations, refugee problems, and unaddressed grievances. Over time, these factors will place a greater burden on governments, and, as we have learned, individuals and groups whose needs are not met may resort to crime as a means of both protest and survival. Indeed, the future will bring new challenges to the criminal justice system, with new classifications like cybercrime and environmental crime, and eventually, the legal system will need to better deal with individuals and organizations that have committed these offences.

The effects of 9/11

The terrorist attacks of 9/11 have had a dramatic effect on the practice of criminal justice in the United States. This reaction has been felt in the field of corrections, particularly through a lack of funding. More money has been spent on other branches of the criminal justice system and on homeland security (not to mention the wars in Iraq and Afghanistan), and corrections have come up short. The new set of domestic terrorism laws embedded in the PATRIOT Act has already resulted in an increase in Middle Eastern males and Muslims entering the criminal justice system. The corrections profession may also suffer from a tendency to profile members of certain ethnic groups (especially Arabic and Muslim males), many of whom will undoubtedly be sent to maximum security facilities. Some have been imprisoned in places like Guantanamo Bay, while others have been held in military brigs or Supermax prisons.

Solutions for dealing with current challenges

The future is ultimately unpredictable, and coming up with appropriate solutions is not easy. After reading this book, the student should understand that a number of current approaches are not actually effective. Poorly thought-out or designed policies or technological fixes will probably not help much in deterring or detecting possible criminals. There are still too many problems with these tools to make them as useful as their inventors currently claim they are. Similarly, target hardening will not deter the most dedicated individuals from committing crimes.

What is going to win the day in the fight against crime and the appropriate use and management of jails and prisons? Clearly, a multipronged approach is most beneficial. At the very least 12 specific policy recommendations for improving the general state of affairs in corrections can be advocated (Richards et al., 2011). These include: reducing the size of the correctional population, increasing the number of restorative justice programs, ending the war on drugs, demilitarizing the criminal justice system, ending punishment packages, restoring voting rights for felons, closing outdated and dangerous prisons, restoring federally funded post-secondary educational programs, properly preparing inmates for release, improving the provision of medical services, providing community resource centers, and providing residential treatment centers. Below, the more important ideas are reviewed in greater detail.

General solutions

International resolutions. A catalyst for speeding up the process of change might include resolutions (backed up by sanctions) passed by international governmental bodies such as the Council of Europe or the United Nations Human Rights Committee regarding criminal justice reform. Alternatively, federalization (for example, consent decrees) or the threat of this process may at least temporarily improve the level of safety and services in correctional facilities.

Demands for more accountability. Perhaps the revelations of the abuse that took place in Iraq's infamous Abu Ghraib prison (Hersh, 2004) will force Americans to demand more accountability, along with institutional and programmatic changes – not only in the foreign detention centers but also in those at home. Some analysts have argued that the National Commission on Safety and Abuse in Prisons (2005–6) was a direct outgrowth of this incident.

More transparency. More transparency has to occur. Increased and regular inspections of correctional institutions by outside parties, like the news media, scholars, and politicians, need to happen. Too often, inspections are simply public relations gestures, designed to pacify politicians and a less-than-informed public.

Increased resources. More money should be spent specifically on rehabilitative programs that have proven to reduce recidivism. Once the jail and prison populations are reduced to a manageable size, COs should be encouraged, through educational and salary incentives, to switch from their current roles – in which they basically function like parking lot and hotel attendants – to becoming true "Rehabilitation Officers," implementing and managing meaningful rehabilitation programs. This also means hiring more individuals whose sole purpose would be to rehabilitate convicts. Additional funding would also make the profession more attractive in terms of salary and benefits.

Sentencing reform. In an effort to minimize prisoner despair and reinforce the focus on rehabilitation, legislators should work hard to pass discretionary sentencing and indeterminate sentences for most, if not all, inmates convicted of felonies. Although this approach has its downsides, the merits override the drawbacks. Over the past decade, the number of people sentenced to life in prison has doubled. This kind of sanction has contributed to the overcrowded conditions in American jails and prisons.

In 2012, The Sentencing Project, a Washington, D.C.-based nonprofit criminal justice advocacy group, reported that in 2012 approximately 160,000 prisoners were serving life sentences in the U.S. state and federal prisons. Among this total, 49,000 are serving life without possibility of parole, an increase of 22.2% since 2008 (Nellis, 2013). All told this is about 6% of all people incarcerated in U.S. correctional facilities. Most "lifers" are behind bars because they have been convicted of crimes other than murder, burglary, and drug-related offences. This would be fine if there was some hope of eventual release, but only about 30% of lifers have the possibility of parole. What has caused this surge of sentencing individuals to life without parole? Part of the rationale can be traced to the reluctance of judges to hand down death penalties, because of both the recent exonerations based on DNA evidence and the growing strength of the anti–death penalty lobby.

From a humanitarian standpoint, it is important that criminal defense lawyers counsel their clients to plead to charges where life without parole is the better alternative to the death penalty. But why is it that so many lifers remain behind bars even if there is a possibility of parole? In short, parole boards are reluctant to grant these individuals parole, and governors have cut back on the number of individuals to whom they have granted clemency. Over the past decade, because of the horror stories connected to individuals who were granted parole and then committed heinous crimes (as in the case of, for example, Aimee's Law), governors seeking reelection or wanting to leave the office with an untarnished record have been hesitant to use this power to their advantage.

It must be understood that, for one reason or another, some people who are given a criminal sanction do change, while others – no matter how long the sentence or how severe the punishment – may never mend their ways. Moreover, as most individuals age and mature, they present a decreasing threat to society. Notwithstanding, over the past two decades, U.S. state and federal prison populations have grown at exponential rates. This makes it difficult to implement rehabilitative programs. It also makes the job of a CO more dangerous. A recent study by the Sentencing Project, based in Washington, D.C., concluded that the recidivism rate for lifers is considerably lower than that for the average person who is released from jail or prison. Thus, policies and practices in connection with life sentences should be reexamined. Parole boards and sentencing commissions must reexamine the purpose, intent, and effects of life sentences, and governors should begin reviewing more cases for executive clemency, particularly for cases that have merit.

Individual level[1]

In order to comprehensively combat crime, we must better deal with the social and emotional health of prisoners and their families, correctional personnel, and victims of crime. This means investing a greater amount of resources into improving children's lives, including expanding Head Start and after-school programs that emphasize prosocial activities like creative (for example, art and music) or physical (for example, sports) pursuits. Society should also heavily invest in parenting skills and mentorship programs.

Community level

The government must also provide more infrastructure in poorer neighborhoods, including safe parks, playgrounds, and schools. There should also be better training of criminal justice personnel to be more than law enforcers, enabling them to adopt more of a social work approach. Daycare workers and public school teachers should be better trained and paid, thus motivating them to not treat their job as simply a paycheck. Some people commit crimes as a cry for help or because they need more attention. Free counseling by competent therapists should be provided to all who need it, and our society should work to reduce or eliminate the stigma related to participating in counseling.

Organizational level

We can reduce prison populations by transferring many nonviolent inmates to community corrections programs. Traditionally, this has meant probation or parole. But, more recently, these programs have also come to rely on EM devices, house arrest, chemical castration, and intensive supervision, all of which have generally proved to keep inmates in check. In December 2003, for example, in order to deal with budget deficits, Kentucky started releasing numerous short-timers (those with less than a year on their sentence) who had been convicted of nonviolent crimes. This action had minimal effect on recidivism rates (Richards et al., 2004).

Once the jail and prison populations come down to a manageable size, COs should be encouraged through educational and monetary incentives, to become "rehabilitation officers," implementing and managing meaningful rehabilitation programs. Prison systems should be rewarded for their ability to rehabilitate inmates, not for simply preventing inmates from escaping. State DOCs should be given more money if their released inmates prove to commit fewer crimes. This also presupposes that an accurate measure of rehabilitation can be settled on.

Again, it must be understood that some individuals will never be appropriate for release into society. These people must be housed in secure facilities, but jails and prisons should really be reserved only for the most violent criminals.

Our correctional facilities should be smaller too. Large jails and prisons are costly to run, unnecessarily bureaucratic, and impersonal. Cost–benefit analyses must be conducted in order to determine what kinds of savings can truly be achieved by increasing scale. Smaller physical structures go a long way in minimizing the alienation of prisoners and COs alike. The older facilities can be torn down, or alternative uses found for them, such as homeless shelters or tourist attractions for the public to see "the way things used to be."

Within the remaining prisons and jails, we need to rethink the way prisoners are housed. Older, more experienced prisoners typically prey on younger prisoners. This leads to both physical and sexual violence. Over time, younger prisoners become socialized to prison life (that is, prisonization), making it more difficult for them to reenter society. Violent prisoners who have committed felonies should never be mixed with first-time offenders or people convicted of nonviolent crimes.

Over the past two centuries, American jails and prisons have adopted a fortress mentality. Wardens and correctional administrators should be more amenable to continuous inspection and should allow the public to take a regular look at what goes on behind bars. This may simultaneously serve as a deterrent against the abuse of inmates, and it might help "scare straight" juveniles at risk of a life of crime, providing them with a wake-up call to mend their ways.[2]

Legal system level

The legal system should be reformed. In particular, we should seriously consider legalizing many soft drugs or decriminalizing them, recognizing their use as a medical need rather than as a criminal activity. Hopefully this means that the prices will fall and be within the reach of those who use drugs; thus, their proclivity to commit crimes to support their habits will decrease. Additionally, we should tighten up restrictions on the sale and possession of handguns. Furthermore, we should fight the powerful lobbies that support the manufacture, sale, and use of handguns. Laws about handgun use should be revised so that only the police and the military can carry a gun, and no one else should be allowed to own or use one. Taking a page out of one of comedian Chris Rock's stand-up routines as an alternative, the government should find a way to make bullets very expensive.

Education and employment

The federal government should also implement a "No Prisoner Left Behind" program, which requires state correctional departments to ensure that all prisoners pass their GEDs (General Educational Development), and complete one or more practical technical training courses that will insure that the day that convicts walk out the door of a jail or prison they will be qualified for a well-paid job. Moreover, community college and university education should be facilitated for any prisoner upon request. We know that most inmates have few marketable skills to rely on when they get out of jail or prison. It is incumbent on the correctional system to ensure that these individuals have at least a high school education, a trade, and/or a university education.

Conclusion

I began this book with an ambitious goal of outlining the most important challenges, and potential and realistic solutions facing the field of corrections. I also pointed out, where appropriate, that many of our "solutions" have had unintended consequences, have exacerbated existing difficulties, or have created new ones. This is only natural because corrections is a system, and tinkering with one aspect can have an effect somewhere else in the process. We also need to be cognizant of doing more with less. There are some positive changes taking place in a piecemeal fashion, but nothing radical is happening in the field of corrections. Hopefully, many of the suggestions outlined in this book will pave the way to meaningful reform and help minimize problems in corrections for the next decade and beyond.

Although crime creates a considerable amount of pain, heartache, and controversy, and it costs individuals, families, communities, governments, and corporations substantial resources, perhaps there is a tolerable level of crime with which a society can live (Durkheim, 1895/1982). For example, during the 1960s and 1970s, citizens in advanced industrialized countries were constantly reminded through the media, educators, and personal experiences that street crime was increasing (Ross, 2014). This created a furor of public indignation and governmental responses that manifested in a "war on crime." While the rate of crime has increased and decreased in a cyclical fashion since that time, and the methods by which we respond to crime have been debated, and occasionally implemented, the crisis of *response* seems to have abated and been replaced by "the war on terrorism." Crime is disruptive to the normal functioning of the government's, businesses' and individuals' daily lives. However, policymakers, practitioners and politicians, as much as possible, need to avoid simplistic responses that can create a more dangerous environment or lead to the needless expenditure of resources.

Hopefully, the methodology, analysis, and suggestions outlined in this book will allow us to minimize the pain and suffering caused by incarceration, the danger, frustration, and boredom faced by correctional workers and convicts alike, and prevent researchers, policymakers, and practitioners from going down blind alleys. Needless to say, we must recognize that neither understanding the root causes of crime nor locking up everyone who breaks the law (that is, mass incarceration) will entirely eliminate illegal behavior. About the best we can do in this scenario is to use our power and knowledge to stay informed, to seek out reliable information, and to question that which seems confusing or based on faulty reasoning.

Although the aforementioned ideas are probably utopian in tone and objective, the amount and types of crime will not be impacted unless we engage in a radical rethinking of how we approach human relations. Unfortunately, this will probably not happen any time soon. Perhaps we can expect no more from research, policies, and practices sponsored by bureaucracies that are exceptionally rule-bound, by governments with limited vision, and by legislators who cannot see past the next election.

At best, the research will result in policy reviews that merely tinker with how prisoners are treated and managed. And so it goes, across the country, millions of Americans live in cages, academics conduct studies that do little more than rearrange the deck chairs on the proverbial *Titanic*, state DOCs talk of policy reforms, jail and prison conditions worsen, and taxpayers drown in consumer debt. Maybe it is time to close some correctional facilities and, instead of transferring the inmates, send them home to their families and communities. That way we can spend those saved public dollars on economic and community development (Clear and Cadora, 2003).

Researchers, policymakers, and prison activists clearly need to explore these wider contexts and implications, and to not be afraid of failure. Unfortunately prison change often takes place as a result of some sort of crisis, including underfunded budgets, failed privatization, failures of segregation, and class action lawsuits. Let us not wait until the next major crisis for thoughtful change to occur. Until American jails, prisons, and community corrections are reinvented in a proactive manner, and rationally thought-out policies and practices are implemented, especially those that have been controlled for unintended consequences, the number of people wasting away behind the razor wire and high walls will continue to grow. They represent the worst of a failed system that foreigners constantly point to as a lack of American ingenuity.

In the end, researching and writing this book has been a journey of sorts. I do not expect every reader to agree with the evidence I marshaled or my interpretations and conclusions; however, this effort should be the beginning (and not the end) of a serious and thoughtful dialogue on corrections in America, one that is necessary and ongoing.

Key terms

Alienation: Psychological and emotional distance that a person or group experiences. They feel disconnected to individuals, organizations, and work related environments.

Apathy: People do not work to change the things that bother them. They avoid participating in the political process.

Biometric screening: Using human characteristics (retina eye display and finger prints) to identify people.

CompStat: A relatively new management technique that includes weekly (or otherwise regular) meetings of senior police personnel (especially the chief/commissioner and district commanders) to review crime that has occurred in their sector/district/borough to monitor responses to reduce crime in those areas. This concept usually involves crime mapping and was pioneered in New York City during the early 1990s.

Cyber crime: Crime that is committed electronically through the World Wide Web.

Deference to authority: A tendency to believe and not oppose individuals who are in positions of authority.

DNA testing: Use of DNA (the carrier of genetic information) to determine guilt and innocence of an individual and to eliminate suspects.

Innocence project: Using DNA evidence, it works to overturn the convictions of individuals on death row.

Optimistic view: The frequency of incarcerating individuals will subside when crime becomes a thing of the past. The severity of conditions behind bars will improve.

Pendulum of politics: Government policies will switch between laws, policies, and practices that are supported by liberal regimes and over time the emphasis will shift to government policies that support the laws, policies, and practices of conservative regimes.

Pessimistic view: The frequency of people who are sentenced to correctional facilities will increase and the conditions inside jails and prison will worsen.

Prisonization: When a prisoner accommodates to the norms and routines of the correctional facility.

Target hardening: Added security measures to deter or protect potential and actual targets (includes metal detectors, concrete barriers, etc.).

Notes

[1] This section builds upon Ross (2006b).

[2] Needless to say, the Sacred Straight program had questionable findings (Finkenauer and Gavin, 1999). That is why I use the word *may* in this sentence.

References

Abbey, E. (1975). *The Monkey Wrench Gang*. New York: Harper.

Abbott, H.J. (1981). *In the Belly of the Beast*. New York: Random House.

Abu-Jamal, M. (1996). *Live from Death Row*. New York: Avon Books.

Aday, R. (1994). "Golden Years behind Bars: Special Programs and Facilities for Elderly Inmates," *Federal Probation*, Vol. 58, No. 2, pp. 47–54.

Adler, P. (2005). *Constructions of Deviance*. Belmont, CA: Wadsworth.

Alarid, L. and C.S. Schloss. (2009). "Attorney Views on the Use of Private Agencies for Probation Supervision and Treatment," *International Journal of Offender Therapy and Comparative Criminology*, Vol. 53, No. 3, pp. 278–91.

Alarid, L.F., P. Cromwell, and R. del Carmen. (2008). *Community-Based Corrections*. (7th Ed.). Belmont, CA: Wadsworth/Cengage.

Alleman, T. (2002). "Correctional Philosophies: Varying Ideologies of Punishment," in R. Gido and T. Alleman (eds.) *Turnstile Justice: Issues in American Corrections*. Upper Saddle, NJ: Prentice Hall, pp. 18–37.

Allen, H. and C.E. Simonsen. (2001). *Corrections in America: An Introduction*. (9th Ed.). Upper Saddle, NJ: Prentice Hall.

American Correctional Association. (1993). *Gangs in Correctional Facilities: A National Assessment*. Washington, D.C.: U.S. Department of Justice.

American Correctional Association. (2004). "Correctional Officers: Survey Summary," *Corrections Compendium*, Vol. 29, No. 5, pp. 10–17.

Amnesty International. (2001). *Abuse of Women in Custody: Sexual Misconduct and Shackling of Pregnant Women*. New York: Amnesty International. www.amnestyusa.org/women/custody/

Anderson, E. (1980). *Streetwise: Race, Class, and Change in an Urban Community*. Chicago, IL: University of Chicago Press.

Anderson, E. (1999). *Code of the Street*. New York: W.W. Norton & Company.

Andrews, D.A. and J. Bonta. (2006). *The Psychology of Criminal Conduct*. (4th Ed.). Cincinnati, OH: Anderson/LexisNexis.

Andrews, D., A. Zinger, R.D. Hoge, J.P. Bonta, P. Gendreau, and F.T. Cullen. (1990). "Does Correctional Treatment Work? A Clinically Relevant and Psychologically Informed Meta Analysis?" *Criminology*, Vol. 28, No. 3, pp. 369–404.

Anonymous. (1989). "Corrections and the Media," *Corrections Today*, Vol. 51, entire issue.

Anonymous. (1992). "Prison Envelope Art: Imagery in Motion," *Artpaper*, Vol. 12, pp. 16–17.

Anonymous. (1997). *America's Prisons: Opposing Viewpoints*. San Diego, CA: Greenhaven Press.

Anonymous. (1998a). "Access Prisons," *The Quill*, Vol. 86, No. 4, p. 4.

Anonymous. (1998b). "Freedom of Information," *The Quill*, Vol. 86, p. 29.

Anonymous. (1998c). "Pot Noodle Uses Hard Cell in Latest TV Work," *Meeting*, January 22, p. 3

Anonymous. (1999). "Common Myths and Misconceptions about Prisons and Prison Life," www.patrickcrusade.org/myths.htm

Archambeault, W. (2003). "Soar Like an Eagle and Dive Like a Loon," in J.I. Ross and S.C. Richards (eds.) *Convict Criminology*. Belmont, CA: Wadsworth, pp. 287–308.

Archambeault, W. (2006). "Imprisonment and American Indian Medicine Ways: A Comparative Analysis of Conflicting Cultural Beliefs, Values, and Practices," in J.I. Ross and L. Gould (eds.) *Native Americans and the Criminal Justice System: Theoretical and Policy Perspectives*. Boulder, CO: Paradigm Publishers, pp. 143–60.

Archambeault, W. (2014), "The Current State of Indian Country Corrections in the United States," in J.I. Ross (ed.) *American Indians at Risk*, Santa Barbara, CA: Greenwood ABC-CLIO, pp. 77–94.

Archer, D. and R. Gartner. (1984). *Violence and Crime in a Cross-National Perspective*. New Haven, CT: Yale University Press.

Armstrong, G.S., A.R. Gover, and D. Mackenzie. (2002). "The Development and Diversity of Correctional Boot Camps," in R. Gido and T. Alleman (eds.) *Turnstile Justice: Issues in American Corrections*. Upper Saddle, NJ: Prentice Hall, pp. 115–30.

Arrigo, B. (ed.). (1998). *Social Justice/Criminal Justice*. Belmont, CA: Wadsworth.

Arrigo, B. (2005). "Mental Health," in M. Bosworth (ed.) *Encyclopedia of Prisons & Correctional Facilities*. Thousand Oaks, CA: Sage Publications, pp. 593–6.

Austin, J. (1998). "The Limits of Prison Drug Treatment," *Corrections Management Quarterly*, Vol. 2, No. 4, pp. 66–74.

Austin, J. (2003). "The Use of Science to Justify the Imprisonment Binge," in J.I. Ross and S.C. Richards (eds.) *Convict Criminology*. Belmont, CA: Wadsworth, pp. 17–36.

Austin, J. and J. Irwin. (2001). *It's about Time*. Belmont, CA: Wadsworth.

Austin, J. and B. Krisberg. (1981). "Wider, Stronger and Different Nets: The Dialectics of Criminal Justice Reform," *Journal of Research on Crime and Delinquency*, Vol. 18, No. 1, pp. 165–96.

Austin, J., Marino A.B., L. Carroll, P.L. McCall, and S.C. Richards. (2001). "The Use of Incarceration in the United States," American Society of Criminology National Policy Committee. *Critical Criminology: An International Journal*, Vol. 10, No. 1, pp. 17–41.

Austin, J., S.C. Richards, and R.S. Jones. (2003). "Prison Release in Kentucky: A Convict Perspective on Policy Recommendations," *Offender Programs Report*, Vol. 7, No. 1, pp. 1, 13–16.

Baca, J. Santiago. (2001). *A Place to Stand.* New York: Grove Press.

Barak, G. (1995). "Media, Crime and Justice: A Case for Constitutive Criminology," in J. Ferrell and Clinton R. Sanders (eds.) *Cultural Criminology.* Boston, MA: Northeastern University Press, pp. 142–68.

Barak-Glantz, I. (1983). "Who's in the Hole?" *Criminal Justice Review*, Vol. 8, pp. 29–37.

Bartollas, C. (2002). *Invitation to Corrections.* Boston, MA: Allyn & Bacon.

Barker, T. and D.L. Carter. (1994). *Police Deviance* (3rd Ed.). Cincinnati, OH: Anderson.

Baskir, L.M. and W.A. Strauss (1987). *Chance and Circumstance: The Draft, the War, and the Vietnam Generation.* New York: Alfred A. Knopf.

Bayens, G., J.J. Williams, and J. Ortiz Smykla. (1997). "Jail Types Makes a Difference," *American Jails*, Vol. 11, No. 2, pp. 32–9.

Beck, A.J. and C. Johnson. (2012). Bureau of Justice Statistics, National Former Prisoner Survey: Sexual Victimization Reported by Former State Prisoners, 2008. Washington, DC: Bureau of Justice Statistics (May).

Beck, A.J. and L.M. Maruschak. (2001). "Mental Health Treatment in State Prisons, 2000)," *Bureau of Justice Statistics*, NCJ 188215.

Beck, A.J., P.M. Harrison, and D.B. Adams. (2007). *Sexual Violence Reported by Correctional Authorities, 2006* (NCJ 218914). Washington, DC: Bureau of Justice Statistics.

Beckett, K. and T. Sasson. (2003). *The Politics of Injustice.* (2nd Ed.). Thousand Oaks, CA: Sage Publications.

Bedau, H.A. (1982). *The Death Penalty in America.* New York: Oxford University Press.

Bell, W.R. (2002). *Practical Criminal Investigations in Correctional Facilities.* Boca Raton, FL: CRC Press.

Bell v. Wolfish 441 U.S. 520 (1979).

Bellin, E.Y., D.D. Fletcher, and S.M. Safer. (1993). "Association of Tuberculosis Infection with Increased time in or Admission to the New York City Jail System," *Journal of the American Medical Association*, Vol. 269, No. 17, pp. 2228–31.

Bender, D. (1997). *America's Prisons: Opposing Viewpoints.* San Diego, CA: Greenhaven Press.

Berger, P. and T. Luckmann. (1966). *The Social Construction of Reality.* New York: Anchor.

Bergin, T. (2013). *The Evidence Enigma: Correctional Boot Camps.* Surrey, England: Ashgate Publishing.

Berk, R.A., H. Ladd, H. Graziano, and J.H. Baek. (2003). "A Randomized Experiment Testing Inmate Classification Systems," *Criminology & Public Policy*, Vol. 2, No. 2, pp. 215–42.

Bishop, G. (2103). "A Company That Runs Prisons Will Have Its Name on a Stadium," *New York Times*, February 19, www.nytimes.com/2013/02/20/sports/ncaafootball/a-company-that-runs-prisons-will-have-its-name-on-a-stadium.html?_r=0.

Blakely, C.R. (2003). "Innovations in Prison and Inmate Classification: Gill Revisited," *The Prison Service Journal*, March, pp. 6–9.

Blakely, C.R. (2004a). "Prison Privatization and Neo-Liberalism: Ill-Effects for the Poor and Minority?" *The Prison Service Journal*, January, pp. 23–5.

Blakely, C.R. (2004b). "Private and State Run US Prisons Compared," *Probation Journal*, Vol. 51, No. 3, pp. 254–6.

Blakely, C.R. and V. Bumphus. (2005). "An Analysis of Civil Suits Filed against Private and Public Prisons: A Comparison of Title 42: Section (1983) Litigation Filed against Both Private and Public Prison Sectors since 1992," *Probation Journal*, Vol. 52, No. 1, pp. 6–75.

Blitz, C.L., N. Wolff, and J. Shi. (2008). "Physical Victimization in Prison: The Role of Mental Illness," *International Journal of Law and Psychiatry*, Vol. 31, No. 5, pp. 385–93.

Blumstein, A., J. Cohen, S. Morita, and D. Nagin. (1981). "On Testing the Stability of Punishment Hypothesis: A Reply," *Journal of Criminal Law and Criminology*, Vol. 72, pp. 1799–808.

Blumstein, A., J. Cohen, and D. Nagin. (1977). "The Dynamics of a Homeostatic Punishment Process," *Journal of Criminal Law and Criminology*, Vol. 67, No. 3, pp. 317–34.

Bogan, C.E. and M.J. English. (1994). *Benchmarking for Best Practices: Winning Through Innovative Adaptation*, New York, NY: McGraw-Hill.

Bohm, R.M. (2003). *Deathquest II: An Introduction to the Theory and Practice of Capital Punishment in the United States*. (2nd Ed.). Cincinnati, OH: Anderson.

Bonta, J., T. Rugge, T.L. Scott, G. Bourgon, and A.K. Yessine. (2008). "Exploring the Black Box of Community Supervision," *Journal of Offender Rehabilitation*, Vol. 47, No 3, pp. 248–70.

Bosco, R.J. (1998). "Connecticut Probation's Partnership with Private Sector." In National Institute of Corrections (ed.) *Topics in Community Corrections. Annual Issue: Privatizing Community Supervision*. Longmont, CO: National Institute of Corrections, pp. 8–12

Bottoms, A.E. (1999). "Interpersonal Violence and Social Order in Prisons," in M. Tonry and Joan Petersilia (eds.) *Prisons*. Chicago, IL: University of Chicago Press, Vol. 26, pp. 205–81.

Bourgois, P. (2002). *In Search of Respect: Selling Crack in El Barrio*. (2nd Ed.). New York: Cambridge University Press.

Bowers, W.J. and G.L. Pierce. (1980). "Deterrence or Brutalization? What is the Effect of Executions?" *Crime & Delinquency*, Vol. 26, Issue 4, pp 453–484.

Bowker, L.H. (1978). *Prison Subcultures*. Lexington, MA: Lexington Books.

Bowker, L.H. (1980). *Prison Victimization*. New York: Elsevier Science.

Boyd, S.E. (2009). "Implementing the Missing Peace: Reconsidering Prison Gang Management," *Quinnipiac Law Review*, Vol. 28, pp. 969–1018.

Braithwaite, J. (1989). *Crime, Shame and Reintegration*. Cambridge: Cambridge University Press.

Bratton, W. (1998). *The Turnaround: How America's Top Cop Reversed the Crime Epidemic*. New York: Random House.

Briggs, C.S., J.L. Sundt, and T.C. Castellano. (2003). "The Effect of Supermaximum Security Prisons on Aggregate Levels of Institutional Violence," *Criminology*, Vol. 41, No. 4, pp. 1341–76.

Britton, D. (1997). "Perceptions of the Work Environment among Correctional Officers: Do Race and Sex Matter?" *Criminology*, Vol. 35, No. 1, pp. 85–105.

Broder, J.M. (2003). "No Hard Time for Prison Budgets," *New York Times*, January 19, p. 5.

Brodsky, C.M. (1982). "Work Stress in Correctional Institutions," *Journal of Prison Jail Health*, Vol. 2, No. 2, pp. 74–102.

Bronner, E. (2012). "Poor Land in Jail as Companies Add Huge Fees for Probation," *New York Times*, July 12.

Brown, J.R. (2002). "Drug Diversion Courts: Are They Needed and Will They Succeed in Breaking the Cycle of Drug-Related Crime?" in L. Stolzenberg and S.J. D'Alessio (eds.) *Criminal Courts for the 21st Century*. (2nd Ed.). Upper Saddle, NJ: Prentice Hall, pp. 5–37.

Brown, P. (1986). "Probation Officer Burnout," *Federal Probation*, Vol. 50, No. 1, pp. 4–7.

Brownstein, H. (1995). "The Media and the Construction of Random Drug Violence," in J. Ferrell and C.R. Sanders (eds.) *Cultural Criminology*. Boston, MA: Northeastern University Press, pp. 45–65.

Bruton, J. (2004). *The Big House: Life inside a Supermax Security Prison*. Minneapolis, MN: Voyageur Press.

Buentello, S. and R.S. Fong. (1991). "The Detection of Prison Gang Development: An Empirical Assessment," *Federal Probation*, Vol. 55, pp. 66–9.

Burke, T.W., E. Rizzo, and C.E. O'Rear. (1992). "Do Officers Need College Degrees?" *Corrections Today*, Vol. 54, pp. 174–6.

Bynum, T. (1982). "Release on Recognizance: Substantive or Superficial Reform," *Criminology*, Vol. 20, pp. 67–82.

Byrne, J., F. Taxman, and D. Hummer. (2005). "Examining the Impact of Institutional Culture (and Cultural Change) on Prison Violence and Disorder: A Review of the Evidence on Both Causes and Solutions." Paper presented at the 14th World Congress of Criminology, Philadelphia, August 11.

Caplan, J. (2003). "Policy for Profit: The Private-Prison Industry's Influence Over Criminal Justice Legislation," *ACJS Today*, Vol. 26, No. 1, pp 15–20.

Camp, G. and C. Camp. (1985). *Prison Gangs: Their Extent, Nature, and Impact in Prisons*. Washington, D.C.: U.S. Department of Justice.

Camp, G. and G. Camp. (1999). *Corrections Yearbook (1999)*. Middletown, CT: Criminal Justice Institute.

Camp, C.G., G. Camp, and B. May. (2003). *The (2002) Corrections Yearbook*. Middletown, CT: Criminal Justice Institute.

Camp, S.D. and G. Gaes. (2002). "Growth and Quality of U.S. Private Prisons: Evidence from a National Survey," *Criminology & Public Policy*, Vol. 1, No. 3, pp. 427–49.

Camp, S.D., W.G. Saylor, and K.N. Wright. (2001). "Racial Diversity of Correctional Workers and Inmates: Organizational Commitment, Teamwork and Workers' Efficiency in Prisons," *Justice Quarterly*, Vol. 18, No. 2, pp. 411–27.

Campbell, C., C. McCoy, and C.A.B. Osigweh. (1990). "The Influence of Probation Recommendations on Sentencing Decisions and Their Predictive Accuracy," *Federal Probation*, Vol. 54, No. 4, pp. 13–20.

Canon, G. (2015). "Here's the Latest Evidence of How Private Prisons Are Exploiting Inmates for Profit," *Mother Jones*, June 17, www.motherjones.com/mojo/2015/06/private-prisons-profit.

Carceral, K.C. (2006). *Prison, Inc.: A convict exposes life inside a private prison*. New York, NY: New York University Press.

Carlson, J.R., R.H. Anson, and G. Thomas. (2003). "Correctional Officer Burnout and Stress: Does Gender Matter? *The Prison Journal*, Vol. 83, No. 3, pp. 277–88.

Carpenter, T. (2010). "KS prisons tested for asbestos," *The Topeka Capital Journal*, August 24, http://cjonline.com/news/state/2010-08-24/ks_prisons_tested_for_asbestos.

Carroll, L. (1988). *Hacks, Blacks, and Cons: Race Relations in a Maximum Security Prison*. Prospect Heights, IL: Waveland Press.

Carson, E.A. (2015). Prisoners in 2014, United States Department of Justice, Bureau of Justice Statistics (September 2015). NCJ 248955.

Cauchon, D. (1994). "The Alcatraz of the Rockies," *USA Today*, November 16, p. 6A.

Cecil, D.K. and J.L. Leitner. (2009). "Unlocking the Gates: An Examination of MSNBC Investigates–Lockup," *The Howard Journal*, Vol. 48, No. 2, pp. 184–99.

Champion, D.J. (1999). *Probation, Parole, and Community Corrections*. (3rd. Ed.). Upper Saddle River, NJ: Prentice Hall.

Champion, D.J. (2001). *Corrections in the United States: A Contemporary Perspective*. (3rd. Ed.). Upper Saddle, NJ: Prentice Hall.

Champion, D.J. (2002). *Probation, Parole, and Community Corrections*. (4th. Ed.). Upper Saddle River, NJ: Prentice Hall.

Champion, D.J. (2005). *Corrections in the United States: Contemporary Perspectives*. (4th. Ed.). Upper Saddle River, NJ: Prentice Hall.

Cheatwood, D. (1998). "Prison Movies: Films about Adult, Male, Civilian Prisons: 1929–1995," in F. Bayley and D. Hale (eds.) *Popular Culture, Crime & Justice*. Belmont, CA: Wadsworth, pp. 209–31.

Cheek, F.E. (1984). *Stress Management for Correctional Officers and Their Families*. College Park, MD: American Correctional Association.

Cheek, F.E. and M.D.S. Miller. (1983). "The Experience of Stress for Corrections Officers: A Double-Blind Theory of Correctional Stress," *Journal of Criminal Justice*, Vol. 11, No. 2, pp. 105–20.

Cherkis, J. (2007). "Hard Time: Federal Judge Slams the District for Overdetaining Inmates," *Washington City Paper*, April 6, pp. 6–7.

Chermack S. (1998). "Police, Courts, Corrections in the Media," in F. Bailey and D. Hale (eds.) *Popular Culture, Crime and Justice*. Belmont, CA: Wadsworth, pp. 87–99.

Chilton, B.S. (1991). *Prisons under the Gavel: The Federal Takeover of Georgia Prisons*. Columbus, OH: Ohio State University Press.

Christian, T.E. (1998). *Conflict Resolution and Conflict Management in Corrections*. Lanham, MD: American Correctional Association.

Christianson, S. (2004). *Innocent: Inside Wrongful Conviction Cases*. New York: New York University Press.

Christie, N. (1993/1994). *Crime Control as Industry*. London: Routledge.

Clark, P. (2010). "Preventing Future Crime with Cognitive Behavioral Therapy," *NIJ Journal*, No. 265, April NCJ.

Clear, T. (1994). *Harm in American Penology*. Albany, NY: State University of New York Press.

Clear, T. (2001). "Ten Unintended Consequences of the Growth in Imprisonment," in E.J. Latessa, A. Holsinger, J.W. Marquart, and J.R. Sorensen (eds.) *Correctional Contexts: Contemporary and Classical Readings*. Los Angeles, CA: Roxbury Publishing Company, pp. 497–505.

Clear, T. and E. Cadora. (2003). *Community Justice*. Belmont, CA: Wadsworth.

Clem, C. (2003). "Results of Data Analysis: NIC Needs Assessment on Correctional Management and Executive Leadership Development," *National Institute of Corrections*, www.nicic.org/library/018898.

Clements, C.B. (1996). "Offender Classification: Two Decades of Progress," *Criminal Justice and Behavior*, Vol. 23, No. 1, pp. 121–43.

Clemmer, D. (1958). *The Prison Community*. New York: Holt, Rinehart.

Cohen, A.K., G.F. Cole, and R.G. Bailey. (1976). *Prison Violence*. Lexington, MA: Lexington Books.

Cohen, J. (1983). "Incapacitating Criminals: Recent Research Findings," *Research in Brief*. Washington, D.C.: National Institute of Justice.

Cohen, L.P. (2006a). "A Law's Fallout: Women in Prison Fight for Custody," *Wall Street Journal*, February 27, p. 1.

Cohen, L.P. (2006b). "U.S. Custody Law Is the Exception," *Wall Street Journal*, February 27.

Cohen, S. (1985). *Visions of Social Control: Crime, Punishment and Classification.* Cambridge: Polity Press.

Cole, G. (1994). *The American Criminal Justice System.* Belmont, CA: Wasdworth.

Cole, G. (1995). *The American System of Criminal Justice.* (7th Ed.). Belmont, CA: Wadsworth.

Coleman, R.J. (1998). "A Cooperative Corrections Arrangement: A Blueprint for Criminal Justice in the 21st Century," *Corrections Now*, Vol. 3, No. 1, p. 1.

Colvin, M. (1992). *From Accommodation to Riot: The Penitentiary of New Mexico in Crisis.* Albany, NY: State University of New York Press.

Conover, T. (2001). *Newjack: Guarding Sing Sing.* New York: Vintage Books.

Converse, P. (1964). "The Nature of Belief Systems in Mass Publics," in D. Apter (ed.) *Ideology and Discontent.* New York: Free Press, pp. 206–61.

Corbet, R. and G.T. Marx. (1991). "Critique: No Soul in the New Machine: Technofallacies in the Electronic Monitoring Movement," *Justice Quarterly*, Vol. 8, No. 3, pp. 399–414.

Cornelius, H. (1988). "Conflict Resolution for Correctional Officer Training Programs," in J. Mugford (ed.) *Correctional Officer Training* (Proceeding from workshop, July 7–9, 1987) pp. 55–66, www.ncjrs.gov/pdffiles1/Digitization/111817-111818NCJRS.pdf.

CCA (Corrections Corporation of America). (2010). *Corrections Corporation of America on Pre-Release and Re-entry Services*, www.cca.com/inmate-services/inmate-families/reentry-programs-and-pre-release.

Coyle, A. (2003). *Humanity in Prison. Questions of Definition and Audit.* London: International Centre for Prison Studies.

Crawley, E. (2005). "Institutional Thoughtlessness in Prisons and Its Impacts on the Day-to-Day Lives of Elderly Men," *Journal of Contemporary Criminal Justice*, Vol. 21, No. 4, pp. 350–63.

Crisanti, A.S. and B. Freuh. (2011). "Risk of Trauma Exposure Among Persons with Mental Illness in Jails and Prisons: What Do We Really Know?" *Currant Opinion Psychiatry*, Vol. 24, No. 5, 431–35.

Cromwell, P.F., R.V. Del Carmen, and L.F. Alaird. (2002). *Community-Based Corrections.* Belmont, CA: Wadsworth.

Crouch, B. (1991). "Guard Word in Transition," in K.C. Haas and G.P. Alpert (eds.) *The Dilemmas of Corrections: Contemporary Readings.* (2nd Ed.). Prospect Heights, IL: Waveland.

Crouch, B.M. and J.W. Marquart. (1980). "On Becoming a Prison Guard," in B.M. Crouch (ed.) *The Keepers: Prison Guards and Contemporary Corrections.* Springfield, IL: W.I. Thomas, pp. 63–106.

Crowther, B. (1989). *Captured on Film: The Prison Movie.* London: B.T. Batsford.

Cullen, F.T. (2002). "Rehabilitation and Treatment Programs," in J.Q. Wilson and J. Petersilia (eds.) *Crime: Public Policies for Crime Control.* (2nd Ed.). Oakland, CA: ICS Press, pp. 253–89.

Cullen, F.T. (2006). "It's Time to Reaffirm Rehabilitation," *Criminology & Public Policy*, Vol. 5, No. 4, pp. 665–72.

Cullen, F.T., J. Cullen, and J. Wozniak. (1988). "Is Rehabilitation Dead? The Myth of the Punitive Public," *Journal of Criminal Justice*, Vol. 16, No. 4, pp. 303–17.

Cullen, F.T., B.S. Fisher, and B.K. Applegate. (2000). "Public Opinion about Punishment and Corrections," *Crime and Justice*, Vol. 27, No. 1, pp. 1–79.

Cullen, F.T. and P. Gendreau. (1989). "The Effectiveness of Correctional Rehabilitation: Reconsidering the 'Nothing Works' Debate," in L. Goodstein and D. MacKenzie (eds.) *American Prisons: Issues in Research and Policy*. New York: Plenum Publishing Company, pp. 23–44.

Cullen, F.T. and P. Gendreau. (2000). "Assessing Correctional Rehabilitation: Policy, Practice, and Prospects," in J. Horney (ed.) *Criminal Justice (2000): Volume 3 Policies, Processes, and Decisions of the Criminal Justice System*. Washington, D.C.: U.S. Department of Justice, National Institute of Justice, pp. 109–75.

Cullen, F. and K.E. Gilbert. (1982). *Reaffirming Rehabilitation*. Cincinnati, OH: Anderson Publishing.

Cullen, F., E.J. Latessa, V.S. Burton, and L.X. Lombardo. (1993a). "Correctional Orientation of Prison Wardens: Is the Rehabilitation Ideal Supported?" *Criminology*, Vol. 31, No. 1, pp. 69–92.

Cullen, F., E. Latessa, R. Kopache, L. Lombardo, and V. Burton. (1993b). "Prison Warden Job Satisfaction," *The Prison Journal*, Vol. 73, No. 2, pp. 141–61.

Cullen, F., B. Link, N. Wolfe, and J. Frank. (1985). "The Social Dimensions of Correctional Officer Stress," *Justice Quarterly*, Vol. 2, No. 4, pp. 505–33.

Czajkoski, E.H. (1973). "Exposing the Quasi-Judicial Role of the Probation Officer," *Federal Probation*, Vol. 37, pp. 9–13.

Davis, C.N. (1998). "Access to Prisons," *The Quill*, Vol. 86, pp. 19–29.

Davis, M.S. and D.J. Flannery. (2002). "The Institutional Treatment of Gang Members," *Correctional Management Quarterly*, Vol. 5, No. 1, pp. 37–46.

Davis, R. (2005). "At Jail, a 'Systems Overload,' " *Baltimore Sun*, April 21.

Dabney, D.A. and M.S. Vaughn (2000). "Incompetent Jail and Prison Doctors," *The Prison Journal*, Vol. 80, No. 2, pp. 151–83.

Deslich, S.A., Thistlethwaite, T., and Coustasse, A. (2013). "Telepsychiatry in Correctional Facilities: Using Technology to Improve Access and Decrease Costs of Mental Health Care in Underserved Populations," *The Permanente Journal*, Vol. 17, No. 3, pp. 80–6.

Dennis, N. (ed.). (1997). *Zero Tolerance: Policing in a Free Society*. London: IEA Health and Welfare Unit.

DiIulio, J.D. (1988). "What's Wrong with Private Prisons," *The Public Interest*, No. 92, Summer, pp. 66–83.

DiIulio, J.J. (1987). *Governing Prisons*. New York: Free Press.

DiIulio, J.J. (1991). *No Escape: The Future of American Corrections*. Cincinnati, OH: Basic Books.

Ditton, P.M. (1999). "Mental Health and Treatment of Inmates and Probationers," *Bureau of Justice Statistics*, NCJ 174463.

Domurand, F. (2000). "Who Is Killing Our Probation Officers: The Performance Crisis in Community Corrections," *Corrections Management Quarterly*, Vol. 4, No. 2, pp. 41–51.

Douglas, J.W., R. Raudla, and R.E. Hartley. (2015). "Shifting Constellations of Actors and Their Influence on Policy Diffusion: A Study of the Diffusion of Drug Courts," *Policy Studies Journal*, Vol. 43, No. 4, pp. 484–511.

Dow, M. (2004). *American Gulag*. Berkeley, CA: University of California Press.

Dowker, F. and G. Good. (1993). "The Proliferation of Control Unit Prisons in the United States," *Journal of Prisoners on Prisons*, Vol. 4, No. 1, pp. 95–110.

Ducksworth, J. (2010). "The Prisoner Reentry Industry," *Dialectical Anthropology*, Vol. 34, pp. 557–561.

Duncan, M.G. (1996). *Romantic Outlaws, Beloved Prisons*. New York: New York University Press.

Durham, A.M., III. (1993). "The Future of Correctional Privatization: Lessons from the Past," in G. Bowman, S. Hakim, and P. Seidenstat (eds.) *Privatizing Correctional Institutions*. New Brunswick, NJ: Transaction Publishers, pp. 33–50.

Durkheim, E. (1895/1982). *The Rules of the Sociological Method*. Translated by W.D. Halls. New York: Free Press.

Dyer, J. (1999). *The Perpetual Incarceration Machine: How America Profits from Crime*. Boulder, CO: Westview Press.

Edney, R.C. (2004). "To Keep Me Safe From Harm: Transgender Prisoners and the Experience of Imprisonment," *Deakin Law Review*, Vol. 9, No. 2, pp. 327–38.

Ellesworth, T. (ed.). (1996). *Contemporary Community Corrections*. (2nd Ed.). Prospect Heights, IL: Waveland Press.

Elrod, P. and M.T. Brooks. (2003). "I Mean You Ain't Really Learning Nothing [Productive]," in J.I. Ross and S.C. Richards (eds.) *Convict Criminology*. Belmont, CA: Wadsworth, pp. 325–46.

Estelle v. Gamble 429 U.S. 97 (1976).

Evans, M. and R. Morgan. (1998). *Preventing Torture: A Study of the European Convention for the Prevention of Torture and Inhumane or Degrading Treatment or Punishment*. London: Oxford University Press.

Fabelo, T. (1997). "The Critical Role of Policy Research in Developing Effective Correctional Policies," *Corrections Management Quarterly*, Vol. 1, No. 1, pp. 25–31.

Fabelo, T. (2000). "Technocorrections: The Promises, the Uncertain Threats," *Sentencing and Corrections: Issues for the 21st Century*. Washington, D.C.: U.S. Department of Justice.

Faith, K. (1997). "Media, Myths and Masculinization: Images of Women in Prison," in E. Adelberg and C. Currie (eds.) *Too Few to Count: Canadian Women in Conflict with the Law*. Vancouver, BC: Press Gang Publishers, pp. 181–219.

Farkas, M.A. (1990). "Professionalization: Is It the Cure-All for What 'Ails' the Corrections Officer," *Journal of Crime and Justice*, Vol. 13, No. 2, pp. 29–54.

Farkas, M.A. (1999). "Correctional Officer Attitudes toward Inmates and Working with Inmates in a 'Get Tough' Era," *Journal of Criminal Justice*, Vol. 27, No. 6, pp. 495–506.

Feeley M.M. (2002). "Entrepreneurs of Punishment: The Legacy of Privatization," *Punishment & Society*, Vol. 4, No. 3, pp. 321–44.

Feeley, M.M. and J. Simon. (1992). "The New Penology: Notes on the Emerging Strategy of Corrections and Its Implications," *Criminology*, Vol. 30, No. 4, pp. 449–74.

Feeley, M.M. and Van Swearingen, R. (2004). "The Prison Conditions Cases and the Bureaucratization of American Corrections: Influences, Impacts and Implications," *Pace Law Review*, Vol. 24, No. 2, pp. 433–76.

Ferrell, J. (1993). *Crimes of Style*. Boston, MA: Northeastern University Press.

Ferrell, J. and C.R. Sanders (eds.). (1995). *Cultural Criminology*. Boston, MA: Northeastern University Press.

Finckenauer, J.O. and P.W. Gavin. (1999). *Scared Straight: The Panacea Phenomenon Revisited*. Springfield, IL: Waveland Press.

Finn, M. and S. Muirhead-Steves. (2002). "Effectiveness of Electronic Monitoring with Violent Male Parolees," *Justice Quarterly*, Vol. 19, pp. 293–312.

Finn, P. (2000). *Addressing Correctional Officer Stress: Programs and Strategies*. Washington, D.C.: U.S. Department of Justice Programs.

Finn, P. and J. Esselman Tomz. (1996). *Developing a Law Enforcement Stress Program for Officers and Their Families*. U.S. Department of Justice. NCJ 163175.

Finn, P. and S. Kuck. (2005). "Stress among Probation and Parole Officers and What Can Be Done about It," *National Institute of Justice, Research in Practice*, June, NCJ 205620.

Fisher-Giorlando, M. (1987). "Prison Culture: Using Music as Data," Ph.D. Dissertation, Ohio State University.

Fisher-Giorlando, M. (2003). "Why I Study Prisons: My Twenty-Year Personal and Professional Odyssey and an Understanding of Southern Prisons," in J.I. Ross and S.C. Richards (eds.) *Convict Criminology*. Belmont, CA: Wadsworth, pp. 59–76.

Flanagan, T.J. and S.L. Caulfield. (1984). "Public Opinion and Prison Policy: A Review," *The Prison Journal*, Vol. 64, No. 2, 31–46.

Fleisher, M.S. (1989). *Warehousing Violence*. Newbury Park, CA: Sage Publications.

Fleisher, M.S. (1996). "Management Assessment and Policy Dissemination in Federal Prisons," *The Prison Journal*, Vol. 76, No. 1, pp. 81–92.

Fleisher, M.S. (1997). "Health Care in the Federal Bureau of Prisons," in J.M. Marquart and J.R. Stevenson (eds.) *Correctional Contexts: Contemporary and Classical Readings*. Los Angeles, CA: Roxbury Press, pp. 327–34.

Flynn, E.E. (1992). "The Graying of America's Prison Population," *The Prison Journal*, Vol. 72, Nos. 1 and 2, pp. 77–98.

Fong, R., R.E. Vogel and S. Buentello. (1992). "Prison Gang Dynamics: A Look Inside the Texas Department of Corrections," in P.J. Benekos and A.V. Merlo (eds.) *Corrections: Dilemmas and Directions*. Cincinnati, OH: Anderson Publishing, pp. 57–78.

Ford, M. Chandler and F.T. Moore. (1992). "Fiscal Challenges Facing Local Correctional Facilities," in P. Benekos and Alida V. Merlo (eds.) *Corrections: Dilemmas and Directions*. Cincinnati, OH: Anderson Publishing, pp. 1–22.

Foucault, M. (1977). *Discipline and Punish: The Birth of the Prison*. New York: Vintage Books.

Franklin, H.B. (1978). *The Victim as Criminal and Artist*. New York: Oxford University Press.

Franklin, H.B. (1982). *Prison Literature in America: The Victim as Criminal and Artist*. Westport, CT: Lawrence Hill and Company.

Franklin, R.H. (1998). "Assessing Supermax Operations," *Corrections Today*, Vol. 60, No. 1, pp. 126–28.

Freeman, R.M. (1998). "Public Perception and Corrections: Correctional Officers as Smug Hacks," in F. Bailey and D. Hale (eds.) *Popular Culture, Crime & Justice*. Belmont, CA: Wadsworth, pp. 196–208.

Freeman, R.M. (1999). *Correctional Organization and Management*. Boston, MA: Butterworth-Heinemann.

Freeman, R.M. (2000). *Popular Culture and Corrections*. Lanham, MD: American Correctional Association.

Friedman, A. (2014). "How Courts View ACA Accreditation," *Prison Legal News*, October, p. 18.

Fry, L. and W. Freeze. (1992). "Bringing the Convict Back In: An Ecological Approach to Inmate Adaptations," *Journal of Criminal Justice*, Vol. 20, No. 4, pp. 355–65.

Gaes, G.G. and S.D. Camp. (2004). *Measuring Prison Performance: Government Privatization and Accountability*. Walnut Creek, CA: Alta Mira Press.

Garland, G. (2005). "Contraband Floods Maryland Prisons: Officials Struggle to Stem Inflow of Drugs, Tobacco," *Baltimore Sun*, July 6.

Gaston, A. (1996). "Controlling Gangs through Teamwork and Technology," *Large Jail Network Bulletin*. Washington, D.C.: U.S. Department of Justice, National Institute of Corrections.

Gaventa, J. (1980) *Power and Powerlessness*. Urbana, IL: University of Illinois Press.

Gavora, J. (1996) "The prisoners' accomplice (Clinton Justice Department alleges violations of prisoners' rights in Supermax, Maryland's prison for the most dangerous prisoners)," *Policy Review*, Vol. 79, No. 6.

Gendreau, P. and J. Bonta. (1984). "Solitary Confinement Is Not Cruel and Unusual Punishment: People Sometimes Are!" *Canadian Journal of Criminology*, Vol. 26, pp. 467–78.

General Accounting Office. (2005). *Adult Drug Courts: Evidence Indicates Recidivism Reductions and Mixed Results for Other Outcomes*. Washington, D.C.: General Accounting Office.

Gerber, J. and E.J. Fritsch. (1994). "The Effects of Academic and Vocational Program Participation on Inmate Misconduct and Reincarceration," *Prison Education Research Report: Final Report*. Huntsville, TX: Sam Houston State University.

Gerber, J. and E.J. Fritsch. (2001). "Adult Academic and Vocational Correctional Programs: A Review of Recent Research," in E.J. Latessa, A. Holsinger, J.W. Marquart, and J.R. Sorensen (eds.) *Correctional Contexts: Contemporary and Classical Readings*. (2nd Ed.). Los Angeles, CA: Roxbury Publishing Company, pp. 268–90.

Gershon R.R., Mitchell C., Sherman M.F., Vlahov D., Lears M.K., Felknor S., and Lubelczyk, R.A. (2005). "Hepatitis B Vaccination in Correctional Health Care Workers," *American Journal of Infectious Control*, Vol. 33, No. 9, pp. 510–18.

Gibbons, J.J. and N. de B. Katzenbach (2006). *National Commission on Safety and Abuse in Prison*, www.prisoncommission.org.

Gibbs, J.J. 1993. "Problems and Priorities: Perceptions of Jail Custodians and Social Service Providers," *Journal of Criminal Justice*, Vol. 11, No. 1, pp. 327–49.

Gibbs, J.P. (1990). "Control as Sociology's Central Notion," *Social Science Journal*, Vol. 27 No. 1, pp. 1–27.

Gido, R.L. and T. Alleman (eds.). (2002). *Turnstile Justice: Issues in American Corrections*. (2nd Ed.). Upper Saddle, NJ: Prentice Hall.

Gilliard, D. (1999). *Prison and Jail Inmates at Midyear (1998) (BJS, USDOJ)*. Washington, D.C.: U.S. Department of Justice.

Glaze, L.E. and T.P. Bonczar. (2006). "Probation and Parole in the United States, 2005," *Bureau of Justice Statistics*, November, NCJ 215091.

Glaze, L.E. and D. Keable. (2014). "Correctional Populations in the United States, 2013," Washington, DC: Bureau of Justice Statistics, December, NCJ 248479.

Goffman, E. (1959). *The Presentation of Self in Everyday Life*. Garden City, NY: Doubleday.

Goffman, E. (1961). *Asylums: Essays on the Social Situation of Mental Patients and Other Inmates*. Garden City, NY: Doubleday.

Gondles, J.A. (1999). "Foreword," in R.M. Freeman (ed.) *Correctional Organization and Management*. Burlington, MA: Butterworth-Heinemann, p. v.

Grassian, S. (1983). "Psychopathological Effects of Solitary Confinement," *American Journal of Psychiatry*, Vol. 140, No. 11, pp. 1450–4.

Grassian, S. and N. Friedman. (1986). "Effects of Sensory Deprivation in Psychiatric Seclusion and Solitary Confinement," *International Journal of Law and Psychiatry*, Vol. 8, No. 1, pp. 49–65.

Greenberg, D. (1975). "The Incapacitative Effect of Imprisonment, Some Estimates," *Law and Society Review*, Vol. 9, No. 4, pp. 541–80.

Greene, D. (2005). "Abolition," in M. Bosworth (ed.) *Encyclopedia of Prisons & Correctional Facilities*. Thousand Oaks, CA: Sage Publications, pp. 2–5.

Grodzins, M. (1956). *The Loyal and the Disloyal: Social Boundaries of Patriotism and Treason*. Chicago, IL: University of Chicago Press.

Gurr, T.R. (ed.). (1989). *Violence in America, Vol. 1: The History of Crime*. Thousand Oaks, CA: Sage Publications.

Hagedorn, J. (1988). *People and Folks: Gangs, Crime and Underclass in a Rustbelt City*. Chicago, IL: Lakeview.

Hall, A. (1987). *System Wide Strategies to Alleviate Jail Crowding*. Washington, D.C.: National Institute of Justice.

Hall, A., D. Henry, J. Perlstein, and W.F. Smith. (1985). *Alleviating Jail Crowding: A Systems Perspective*. Washington, D.C.: National Institute of Justice.

Hallinan, J.T. (2003). *Going Up the River*. New York: Random House.

Hamm, M.S. (1995). *The Abandoned Ones: The Imprisonment and Uprising of the Mariel Boat People*. Boston, MA: Northeastern University Press.

Hamm, M.S. and J. Ferrell. (1994). "Rap, Cops, and Crime: Clarifying the Cop Killer Controversy," *ACJS Today*, Vol. 13, pp. 1, 3, 29.

Hammett, T.M., J. Epstein, J. Gross, M. Sifre, and T. Enor. (1995). *Update: HIV/AIDS and STDs in Correctional Facilities*. Washington, D.C.: Department of Justice, December.

Hammett, T., P. Harmon, and L. Maruschak. (1999). *1996–1997 Update: HIV/AIDS, STDs, and TB in Correctional Facilities*. Washington, D.C.: National Institute of Justice.

Hammond, A.F. (1989). "AIDS in Correctional Facilities: A New Form of the Death Penalty," *Washington University Journal of Urban and Contemporary Law*, Vol. 36, pp. 167–85.

Haney, C. (1993). "'Infamous' Punishment: The Psychological Consequences of Isolation," *National Prison Project Journal*, Vol. 8, No. 2, pp. 3–7, 21.

Haney, C. and M. Lynch. (1997). "Regulating Prisons of the Future: A Psychological Analysis of Supermax and Solitary Confinement," *New York University Review of Law and Social Change*, Vol. 23, pp. 477–570.

Harrison, P.M. and A.J. Beck. (2006). "Prisoners in 2005," *Bureau of Justice Statistics*, NCJ215092.

Hassine, V. (2002). "Prison Violence: From Where I Stand," in R. Gido and Ted Alleman (eds.) *Turnstile Justice: Issues in American Corrections*. Upper Saddle, NJ: Prentice Hall, pp. 38–56.

Hassine, V. (2004). *Life without Parole*. (3rd. Ed.). Los Angeles, CA: Roxbury.

Heater, M.L. (2000). "Age Sensitivity Training for Corrections Personnel," *Corrections Compendium*, Vol. 25, No. 6, June.

Heiner, R. (2001). *Social Problems: An Introduction to Critical Constructionism.* New York: Oxford University Press.

Hemmens, C. and E. Atherton. (2000). *Use of Force: Current Practice and Policy.* Lanham, MD: American Correctional Association.

Hemmens, C. and M.K. Stohr. (2001). "Correctional Staff Attitudes Regarding the Use of Force in Corrections," *Corrections Management Quarterly*, Vol. 5, pp. 26–39.

Hemmens, C., M.K. Stohr, M. Schoeler, and B. Miller. (2002). "One Step Up, Two Steps Back: The Progression of Perceptions of Women's Work in Prisons and Jails," *Journal of Criminal Justice*, Vol. 30, No. 6, pp. 473–89.

Henderson, M., F.T. Cullen, L. Carroll, and W. Feinberg. (2000). "Race, Rights, and Order in Prison: A National Survey of Wardens on the Racial Integration of Prison Cells," *The Prison Journal*, Vol. 18, No. 3, pp. 295–308.

Henrichson, C. and R. Delaney. 2012. "The Price of Prisons. What Incarceration Costs Taxpayers," *Federal Sentencing Reporter*, Vol. 25, No. 1, pp. 68–80.

Henriques, D.B. and A.W. Lehren. (2006). "Religion for Captive Audiences, with Taxpayers Footing the Bill," *New York Times*, December 10, pp. 1, 32.

Hensley, C., M. Koscheski, and R. Tewksbury. (2002). "Does the Participation in Conjugal Visitations Reduce Prison Violence in Mississippi? An Exploratory Study," *Criminal Justice Review*, Vol. 27, No. 1, pp. 52–65.

Hensley, P., S. Rutland, and P. Gray-Ray. (2002). "Conjugal Visitation Programs: The Logical Conclusion," in P. Hensley and Christopher Hensley (eds.) *Prison Sex: Practice and Policy*. Boulder, CO: Lynne Rienner, pp. 143–56.

Hepburn, J. (1985). "The Exercise of Power in Coercive Organizations: A Study of Prison Guards," *Criminology*, Vol. 23, No. 1, pp. 145–64.

Herman, E. and N. Chomsky. (1988). *Manufacturing Consent: The Political Economy of the Mass Media*. New York: Pantheon.

Hersh, S.M. (2004). *Chain of Command: The Road from 9/11 to Abu Ghraib.* New York: HarperCollins.

Hill, C. (2007). "Correctional Officers: Hiring Requirements and Wages," *Corrections Compendium*, Vol. 32, No. 3, pp. 12–27.

Hincle, P. (1996). "Prisons to Journalists: Drop Dead," *Extra! Newsletter of FAIR*, July 1, Vol. 9, No. 4, p. 13.

Hipp, J.R., Jesse J.R. Shah, and S. Turner. (2011). "Parolees' Physical Closeness to Social Services: A Study of California Parolees," *Crime & Delinquency*, Vol. 57, No. 1, pp. 102–29.

Honnold, J.A. and J.B. Stinchcomb. (1985). "Officer Stress," *Corrections Today*, December, pp. 46–51.

Hooks, G., C. Mosher, T. Rotolo, and L. Lobao. (2004). "The Prison Industry: Carceral Expansion and Employment in U.S. Counties, 1969–1994," *Social Science Quarterly*, Vol. 85, No. 1, pp. 37–57.

Hopper, C.B. (1970). *Sex in Prison: The Mississippi Experiment with Conjugal Visiting*. Baton Rouge, LA: Louisiana State University Press.

Hoshen, J., J. Sennott, and M. Winkler. (1995). "Keeping Tabs on Criminals," *IEEE Spectrum*, February, pp. 26–32.

Huff, R., A. Rattner, and E. Sagarin. (1996). *Convicted But Innocent: Wrongful Conviction and Public Policy*. Thousand Oaks, CA: Sage Publications.

Human Rights Watch. (1996). *All Too Familiar: Sexual Abuse of Women in U.S. Prisons*. New York: Human Rights Watch.

Human Rights Watch. (2001). *No Escape: Male Rape in U.S. Prisons*. New York: Human Rights Watch.

Human Rights Watch. (2012). *Old Behind Bars: The Aging Prison Population in the United States*. Human Rights Watch, January 27.

Hummel, R. (2002). "Boot Camp or Boot Hill? Troubled Teens Suffer From Too Much Tough Love," *Prison Legal News*, September, p. 1

Hylton, W.S. (2003). "Sick on the Inside," *Harpers*, August, pp. 43–54.

Innes, C.A. and V.D. Verdeyen. (1997). "Conceptualizing the Management of Violent Inmates," *Corrections Management Quarterly*, Vol. 1, No. 4, pp. 1–9.

Irwin, J. (1970). *The Felon*. Englewood Cliffs, NJ: Prentice Hall.

Irwin, J. (1985). *The Jail*. Berkeley, CA: University of California Press.

Irwin, J. (2005). *The Warehouse Prison: Disposal of the New Dangerous Class*. Los Angeles, CA: Roxbury Company.

Irwin, J. and J. Austin. (1997). *It's about Time. America's Imprisonment Binge*. Belmont, CA: Wadsworth.

Irwin, J. and D. Cressey. (1962). "Thieves, Convicts and Inmate Culture," *Social Problems*, Vol. 10, pp. 142–55.

Jackson, G. (1970). *Soledad Brother: The Prison Letters of George Jackson*. Chicago, IL: Lawrence Hill Books.

Jackson, S. and C. Maslach. (1982). "After-Effects of Job Related Stress: Families as Victims," *Journal of Occupational Behavior*, Vol. 3, No. 1, pp. 63–77.

Jacobs, J. (1977). *Stateville*. Chicago, IL: University of Chicago Press.

Jacobs, J.B. and H.A. Brooks. (1983). "The Mass Media and Prison News," in J.B. Jacobs (ed.) *New Perspectives on Prisons and Imprisonment*. Ithaca, NY: Cornell University Press, pp. 106–14.

Jacobson, C.A., J.T. Jacobson, and T.A. Crowe. (1989). "Hearing Loss in Inmates," *Ear and Hearing*, Vol. 10, No. 3, pp. 178–83.

Jacoby, J.E. (2002). "The Endurance of Failing Correctional Institutions: A Worst Case Scenario," *The Prison Journal*, Vol. 82, No. 2, pp. 168–88.

James, D.J. and L.E. Glaze. (2006). "Mental Health Problems of Prisons and Jail Inmates," *Bureau of Justice Statistics*, NCJ 213600.

JFA Institute. (2007). *Public Safety, Public Spending: Forecasting America's Prison Population, 2007–2011*. The Pew Charitable Trusts, www.pewtrusts.org/en/research-and-analysis/reports/2007/02/14/public-safety-public-spending-forecasting-americas-prison-population-20072011.

Johnson, B. (1994). "Exploring Direct Supervision: A Research Note," *American Jails*, March/April, pp. 63–4.

Johnson, R. (2002). *Hard Time: Understanding and Reforming the Prison*. (3rd Ed.). Belmont, CA: Wadsworth.

Jones, R. and T. Schmid. (2000). *Doing Time: Prison Experience and Identity among First Time Inmates*. Stamford, CT: JAI Press.

Kalinich, D.B. (1986). *Power, Stability, and Contraband: The Inmate Economy*. Prospect Heights, IL: Waveland Press.

Kappeler, V.E., M. Blumberg, and G.W. Potter. (1996). *The Mythology of Crime and Criminal Justice*. Prospect Heights, IL: Waveland Press.

Kappeler, V.E., R.D. Sluder, and G.P. Alpert. (1994). *Forces of Deviance: Understanding the Dark Side of Policing*. Prospect Heights, IL: Waveland Press.

Kauffman, K. (1988). *Prison Officers and Their World*. Cambridge, MA: Harvard University Press.

Kerness, B. and M. Ehehosi. (2001). *Torture in U.S. Prisons: Evidence of U.S. Human Rights Violations*. Philadelphia: American Friends Service Committee.

Kiekbusch, R., W. Price, and J. Theis. (2003). "Turnover Predictors: Causes of Employee Turnover in Sheriff-Operated Jails," *Criminal Justice Studies*, Vol. 16, No. 2, pp. 67–76.

Kifer, M., C. Hemmens, and M. Stohr. (2003). "The Goals of Corrections: Perspectives from the Line," *Criminal Justice Review*, Vol. 28, No. 1, pp. 47–69.

Kilgore, J. (2013). "Progress or More of the Same? Electronic Monitoring and Parole in the Age of Mass Incarceration," *Critical Criminology*, Vol. 21, No. 1, pp. 123–39.

King, David R. (1978). "The Brutalization Effect: Execution Publicity and the Incidence of Homicide in South Carolina," *Social Forces*, Vol. 57, No. 2, pp. 683–687.

Kindel, T. (1998). "Media Access: Where Should You Draw the Line," *Corrections Today*, Vol. 59, pp. 22–4.

Kleiman, M.A.R. (2003). "Faith-Based Fudging: How a Bush-Promoted Christian Prison Program Fakes Success by Massaging the Data."

Klein, M. (1997). *The American Street Gang*. New York: Oxford University Press.

Klein, N. (2000). *No Logo: Taking Aim at the Brand Bullies*. Toronto: Vintage Canada.

Kleining, J. and M. L. Smith. (2001). *Discretion, Community and Correctional Ethics*. Lanham, MD: Rowman & Littlefield.

Kleis, K.M. (2010). "Facilitating Failure: Parole, Reentry, and Obstacles to Success," *Dialectical Anthropology*, Vol. 34, No. 4, pp. 525–531.

Klofas, J.M. (1984). "Reconsidering Prison Personnel: New Views of the Correctional Officer Subculture," *International Journal of Offender Therapy and Comparative Criminology*, Vol. 28, No. 3, pp. 169–75.

Klofas, J. and H. Toch. (1982). "The Guard Subculture Myth," *Journal of Research in Crime and Delinquency*, Vol. 19, No. 2, pp. 238–54.

Korn, R. (1988). "The Effects of Confinement in the High Security Unit at Lexington," *Social Justice*, Vol. 15, No. 1, pp. 8–19.

Kratcoski, P. and G. Pownell. (1992). "Federal Bureau of Prisons Programming for Older Inmates," *Federal Probation*, Vol. 31, No. 1, pp. 28–35.

Krippendorf, K. (1981). *Content Analysis: An Introduction to Its Methodology*. Beverly Hills, CA: Sage Publications.

Kurki, L. and N. Morris. (2001). "The Purpose, Practices, and Problems of Supermax Prisons," in M. Tonry (ed.) *Crime and Justice, an Annual Edition*. Chicago, IL: University of Chicago Press, pp. 385–424.

Kutscher, B. (2013). "Rumble over Jailhouse Healthcare: As States Broaden Outsourcing to Private Vendors, Critics Question Quality of Care and Cost Savings," Modern Healthcare, August 31, www.modernhealthcare.com/article/20130831/MAGAZINE/308319891.

Lamb, C. (1975). *Political Power in Poor Neighborhoods*. New York: J. Wiley & Sons.

Lambert, E. (2004). "The Impact of Job Characteristics on Correctional Officer Staff Members," *The Prison Journal*, Vol. 84, No. 2, pp. 208–27.

Landenberger, N.A., and M. Lipsey. (2005). "The Positive Effects of Cognitive-behavioral Programs for Offenders: A Meta-analysis of Factors Associated With Effective Treatment," *Journal of Experimental Criminology*, Vol. 1, No. 4, pp. 451–76.

Lankenau, S.E. (2001). "Smoke 'Em If You Got 'Em: Cigarette Black Markets in U.S. Prisons and Jails," *Prison Journal*, Vol 81, pp. 142–161.

Lasky, G.L. and D.J. Strebalus. (1986). "Occupational Stressors among Federal Correctional Officers Working in Different Security Levels," *Criminal Justice Behavior*, Vol. 13, No. 3, pp. 317–27.

Latessa, E.J. and H.E. Allen. (1999). *Corrections in the Community*. (2nd. Ed.). Cincinnati, OH: Anderson Publishing.

Latessa, E.J., F.T. Cullen, and P. Gendreau. (2002). "Beyond Correctional Quackery: Professionalism and the Possibility of Effective Treatment," *Federal Probation*, Vol. 66, No. 1, pp. 43–9.

Latham, G.P. and K.N. Wexley. (1981). *Increasing Productivity through Performance Appraisal*. Menlo Park, CA: Addison-Wesley Publishing Company.

Lavigne, Y. (1989). *Hell's Angels: Three Can Keep a Secret If Two Are Dead*. Toronto: Lyle Stuart.

Lawrence, R. and S. Mahan. (1998). "Women Corrections Officers in Men's Prisons: Acceptance and Perceived Job Performance," *Women and Criminal Justice*, Vol. 9, No. 3, pp. 63–86.

Lee, S. (2012) "By the Numbers: The U.S.'s Growing For-Profit Detention Industry," June 20, www.propublica.org/article/by-the-numbers-the-u.s.s-growing-for-profit-detention-industry.

Lerner, J.A. (2002). *You Got Nothing Coming: Notes of a Prison Fish*. New York: Broadway.

Lerner, M. (1991). *Surplus Powerlessness: The Psychodynamics of Everyday Life and the Psychology of Individual and Social Transformation*. Amherst, NY: Humanity Books.

Lemert, M. (1993). "Visions of Social Control: Probation Considered," *Crime & Delinquency*, Vol. 39, No. 4, pp. 447–61.

Levinson, R.B., J.B. Stinchcomb, and J.J. Greene III. (2001). "Correctional Certification: First Step toward Professionalization," *Corrections Today*, Vol. 63, No. 5, pp. 125–38.

Lichter, R.S., S. Rothman, and L.S. Lichter. (1986). *The Media Elite*. Bethesda, MD: Adler and Adler.

Liebling, A. (1999). "Doing Research in Prison: Breaking the Silence?" *Theoretical Criminology*, Vol. 3, No. 2, pp. 147–73.

Liebman, J.S., J. Fagan, V. West, and J. Lloyd. (1999). "Capital Attrition: Error Rates in Capital Cases, 1973–1995," *Texas Law Review*, Vol. 78, pp. 1839–1865.

Lilly, R.J. and Deflem, M. (1996). Profit and Penalty: An Analysis of the Corrections-Commercial Complex, *Crime & Delinquency*, Vol. 42, No. 1, pp. 3–20.

Lindquist, C.A. and J.T. Whitehead. (1986). "Burnout, Job Stress, and Job Satisfaction among Southern Correctional Officers: Perceptions and Causal Factors," *Journal of Criminal Justice*, Vol. 10, No. 4, pp. 5–26.

Liptak, A. (2005). "To More Inmates, Life Term Means Dying Behind Bars," *New York Times*, October 2, pp. 1, A18–A19.

Lockwood, D. (1980). "Reducing Prison Sexual Violence," in R. Johnson and H. Toch (eds.) *The Pains of Imprisonment*. Beverley Hills, CA: Sage Publications, pp. 257–65.

Logan, C.H. (1993). "Criminal Justice Performance Measures for Prisons," in J.J. DiIulio Jr. (ed.) *Performance Measures for the Criminal Justice System*. Washington, D.C.: Office of Justice Programs, pp. 19–41. USDOJ OJP NCJ-143505.

Logan, C.H. and B.W. McGriff. (1989). *Comparing Costs of Public and Private Prisons: A Case Study*. Washington, D.C.: National Institute of Justice Research in Action.

Lombardo, L.X. (1989). *Guards Imprisoned*. (2nd Ed.). Cincinnati, OH: Anderson Publishing.

Lopiano-Misdom, J. and J. De Luca. (1997). *Street Trends: Today's Alternative Youth Cultures Are Creating Tomorrow's Mainstream Markets*. New York: HarperCollins Business.

Lovell, D., K. Cloyes, D. Allen, and L. Rhodes. (2000). "Who Lives in Super-Maximum Custody?" *Federal Probation*, Vol. 64, No. 1, pp. 33–8.

Lucken, K. (1998). "Contemporary Penal Trends: Modern or Post Modern?" *British Journal of Criminology*, Vol. 38, No. 1, pp. 106–23.

Lukes, S. (1974). *Power: A Radical View*. London: Macmillan.

Lynch, M. (1998). "Waste Managers? New Penology, Crime Fighting and Parole Agent Identity," *Law and Society Review*, Vol. 32, No. 4, pp. 839–69.

Lynch, M. (2007). *Big Prisons, Big Dreams: Crime and the Failure of America's Penal System*. New Brunswick, NJ: Rutgers University Press.

Lynch, M. and W.B. Groves. (1986/1989). *A Primer in Radical Criminology*. Albany, NJ: Harrow and Heston.

Lynd, S. (2004). *Lucasville: The Untold Story of a Prison Uprising*. Philadelphia, PA: Temple University Press.

Mac Donald, H. (2003). "How to Straighten Out Ex-Cons," *City Journal*, Spring, Vol. 13, No. 2, pp. 24–37.

Mackenzie, D. (2000). "Evidence-Based Corrections: Identifying What Works," *Crime and Delinquency*, Vol. 46, No. 4, pp. 457–72.

MacKenzie, D.L. (2006). *What Works in Corrections: Reducing the Criminal Activities of Offenders and Delinquents*. New York: Cambridge University Press.

Mackenzie, D.L. and C. Souryal. (1991). "Boot Camp Survey: Rehabilitation, Recidivism Reduction Outrank Punishment as Main Goals," *Corrections Today*, Vol. 53, No. 1, pp. 90–6.

Magaletta, P.R., Fagan, T.J., and Peyrot, M.F. (2000). "Telehealth in the Federal Bureau of Prisons: Inmates' Perceptions," *Professional Psychology: Research and Practice*, Vol. 31, No. 5, pp. 497–502.

Mahan, S. and R. Lawrence. (1996). "Media and Mayhem in Corrections: The Role of the Media in Prison Riots," *The Prison Journal*, Vol. 76, No. 4, pp. 1–18.

Mahmood, M. (2004). "Collateral Consequences of the Prison-Industrial Complex," *Social Justice*, Vol. 31, Nos. 1–2, pp. 31–5.

Mallicoat, S. (2005). "Correctional Officer Pay," in M. Bosworth (ed.) *Encyclopedia of Prisons & Correctional Facilities*. Thousand Oaks, CA: Sage Publications, pp. 185–7.

Mancini, C. and D.P. Mears (2013). "The Effects of Agency Scandal on Public Views Toward the Correctional System," *Criminal Justice Review*, Vol. 38, No. 1, pp. 5–28.

Marquart, J.W. (1986). "The Use of Physical Force by Prison Guards: Individuals, Situations, and Organizations," *Criminology*, Vol. 24, No. 2, pp. 347–66.

Marquart, J.W., M.B. Barnhill, and K. Balshaw-Biddle. (2001). "Fatal Attraction: An Analysis of Employee Boundary Violations in a Southern Prison System, 1995–1998," *Justice Quarterly*, Vol. 18, No. 4, pp. 877–910.

Marquart, J.W., D.E. Merianos, J.L. Hebert, and L. Carroll. (1997). "Health Condition and Prisoners: A Review of Research and Emerging Areas of Inquiry," *The Prison Journal*, Vol. 77, No. 1, pp. 184–208.

Marquez, J. and D. Thompson. (2006). "Prison 'Peacekeeper' Wielded Influence," *Associated Press*, January 22, www.nctimes.com/articles/(2006)/01/23/news/state/12206(193342.txt.

Martinson, R. (1974). "What Works – Questions and Answers about Prison Reform," *Public Interest*, Vol. 35, No. 1, pp. 22–54.

Martinson, R. (1979). "New Findings, New Views, a Note of Caution Regarding Sentencing Reform," *Hofstra Law Review*, Vol. 7, No. 2 pp. 243–58.

Maruschak, L.M. (2005). "HIV in Prisons, 2003," *Bureau of Justice Statistics*, September.

Massey, D. (1989). *Doing Time in American Prisons: A Study of Modern Novels*. New York: Greenwood Press.

Mathiesen, T. (1974). *The Politics of Abolition*. New York: J. Wiley.

Mauer, M. (1996). "Tales of a Criminal Justice Reformer," *Criminal Justice Ethics*, Vol. 15, No. 1, pp. 2–6.

Mauer, M. and M. Chesney-Lin. (2003). *Invisible Punishment*. New York: New Press.

Maur, M. (2006). *The Race to Incarcerate*. (Revised Ed.). New York: New Press.

May, J.P. and K.R. Pitts (eds.). (2000). *Building Violence: How America's Rush to Incarcerate Creates More Violence*. Thousand Oaks, CA: Sage Publications.

Mays, G.L. and R. Ruddell. (2007). *Making Sense of Criminal Justice: Policies and Practices*. New York: Oxford University Press.

Mays, G.L. and R. Ruddell (2015). *Making Sense of Criminal Justice: Policies and Practices* (2nd Ed.). New York: Oxford University Press.

McAuley, L. (1994). "Exploding Myths about Correctional Industries," *Corrections Today*, Vol. 56, p. 8.

McCarthy, B. and B.J. McCarthy, Jr. (1997). *Community-Based Corrections*. (3rd Ed.). Belmont, CA: Wadsworth.

McCarthy, B., B.J. McCarthy, Jr., and M.C. Leone. (2001). *Community-Based Corrections*. (4th Ed.). Belmont, CA: Wadsworth.

McCarthy, B.J. (1996). "Keeping an Eye on the Keeper: Prison Corruption and Its Control," in M.C. Braswell, B.R. McCarthy, and B.J. McCarthy (eds.) *Justice, Crime, and Ethics*. (2nd. Ed.) Cincinnati, OH: Anderson, pp. 229–41.

McCleary, R. (1978/1992). *Dangerous Men: The Sociology of Parole*. New York: Harrow and Heston.

McClosky, H. (1964). "Consensus and Ideology in American Politics," *American Political Science Review*, Vol. 58, No. 2, June, pp. 361–82.

McDonald, D.C. (1999). "Medical Care in Prisons," in M. Tonry and J. Petersilia (eds.) *Prisons*. Chicago, IL: University of Chicago Press, pp. 427–78.

McKinnon, K.M. (2004). "Overcrowding," in M. Bosworth (ed.) *Encyclopaedia of Prisons & Correctional Facilities*. Thousand Oaks, CA: Sage Publications, pp. 656–8.

McLaughlin, E. and J. Muncie. (2002). *Controlling Crime*. (2nd. Ed.). Thousand Oaks, CA: Sage Publications.

McLemore, M. (2008). "Access to Condoms in U.S. Prisons," *HIV/AIDs Law Review*, Vol. 13, No. 1, pp. 20–4.

McNamara, M. (2014). "Better To Be Out in Prison Than Out in Public: LGBTQ Prisoners Receive More Constitutional Protection If They Are Open About Their Sexuality While in Prison," *Law & Sexuality: A Review Of Lesbian, Gay, Bisexual & Transgender Legal Issues*, Vol. 23, No. 1, pp. 135–54.

McShane, M. and W. Krause. (1993). *Community Corrections*. New York: Macmillan.

McVay, D., V. Shiraldi, and J. Ziedenberg. (2004). "Treatment or Incarceration: National and State Findings in the Efficacy and Cost Savings of Drug Treatment versus Imprisonment," *Justice Policy*, Vol. 1, pp. 1–13.

Mears, D.P. (2006). *Evaluating the Effectiveness of Supermax*. Washington, D.C.: Urban Institute, www.urban.org/url.cfm?ID=411326.

Mekhjian, H., J.W. Turner, M. Gailiun, and T.A. Mccain. (1999). "Patient Satisfaction with Telemedicine in a Prison Environment," *Journal of Telemedicine and Telecare*, Vol. 5, No. 1, pp. 55–61.

Merlo, A. (1992). "Ethical Issues and the Private Sector," in P.J. Benekos and A.V. Merlo (eds.) *Corrections: Dilemmas and Directions*. Cincinnati, OH: Anderson/ACJS Monograph Series, pp. 23–36.

Merton, R.K. (1936). "The Unanticipated Consequences of Purposive Social Action," *American Sociological Review*, Vol. 1, No. 6, pp. 894–904.

Meskell, M.W. (1999). "An American Resolution: The History of Prisons in the United States from 1777 to 1877," *Stanford Law Review*, Vol. 51, No. 4, pp. 839–65.

Meyer, J. and A. Grant (1996). "The Privatization of Community Corrections. Queensland, Australia: Center for Applied Psychology and Criminology. Bond University, http://epublications.bond.edu.au/hss_pubs/48.

Mieszkowski, K. (1998). "She Helps Them Help Themselves," *Fast Company*, May 31, www.fastcompany.com/34620/she-helps-them-help-themselves.

Milgram, S. (1974). *Obedience to Authority*. London: Harper and Row.

Miller, J. (1995). "Struggles over the Symbolic: Gang Style and Meanings of Social Control," in J. Ferrell and C.R. Sanders (eds.) *Cultural Criminology*. Boston, MA: Northeastern University Press, pp. 213–34.

Miller, J.G. (1996). *Search and Destroy: African American Males and the Criminal Justice System*. New York: Cambridge University Press.

Miller, J.M. and L.H. Selva. (1994). "Drug Enforcement's Double-Edged Sword: An Assessment of Asset Forfeiture Programs," *Justice Quarterly*, Vol. 11, No. 2, pp. 313–35.

Mills, C.W. (1956). *Power Elite*. New York: Oxford University Press.

Monkkonen, E.H. (1981). *Police in Urban America, 1860–1920*. Cambridge: Cambridge University Press.

Moore, J.W. (1978). *Homeboys: Gangs, Drugs and Prison in the Barrios of Los Angeles*. Philadelphia, PA: Temple University Press.

Morey, Anne. (1995). "The Judge Called Me an Accessory: Women's Prison Films, 1950–1962," *Journal of Popular Film and Television*, Vol. 23, No. 2, pp. 80–7.

Morgan, R.D., A.R. Patrick, and P.R. Magaletta. (2008). "Does the Use of Telemental Health Alter the Treatment Experience? Inmates' Perceptions of Telemental Health Versus Face-to-face Treatment Modalities," *Journal of Consulting and Clinical Psychology*, Vol. 76, No. 1, pp. 158–62.

Moriary, L. and C. Fields. (1999). "Debating Correctional Controversies: Is the Segregation on HIV-Positive Inmates Ethical?" *The Prison Journal*, Vol. 78, No. 1, pp. 100–18.

Morris, N. (1974). *The Future of Imprisonment*. Chicago, IL: University of Chicago Press.

Morris, N. and M. Tonry. (1990). *Between Prison and Probation*. New York: Oxford University Press.

Morrow, C.K. (1982). "Sick Doctors: The Social Construction of Professional Deviance," *Social Problems*, Vol. 30, pp. 92–108.

Moss, A. (2008). "Sexual Misconduct." In P.M. Carlson and J.S. Garrett (eds.). *Prison and Jail Administration* (2nd Ed.). Sudbury, MA: Jones & Bartlett, pp. 275–289.

Munro-Bjorklund, V. (1991). "Popular Cultural Images of Criminals and Convicts since Attica," *Social Justice*, Vol. 18, No. 3, pp. 48–70.

Murphy, D.S. (2003). "Aspirin Ain't Gonna Help the Kind of Pain I'm in: Health Care in the Federal Bureau of Prisons," in J.I. Ross and S.C. Richards (eds.) *Convict Criminology*. Belmont, CA: Wadsworth, pp. 247–66.

Murton, T.O. (1976). *The Dilemma of Prison Reform*. New York: Praeger.

Nagel, R. (2009). "The Myth of the General Right to Bail," *Public Interest*, Vol. 98, No. 1, pp. 84–97.

Nagin, D.S. and J.V. Pepper (eds.). (2012). *Deterrence and the Death Penalty*, Washington, DC: National Research Council.

National Advisory Commission on Criminal Justice Standards and Goals. (1973). *Task Force Report: Corrections*. Washington, D.C.: US Government Printing Office.

National Center for State Courts. (1975). *An Evaluation of Policy-Related Research on the Effectiveness of Pretrial Release Programs*. Denver, CO: National Center for State Courts.

National Institute of Corrections. (1997). *Supermax Housing: A Survey of Current Practice: Special Issues in Corrections*. Longmont, CO: U.S. Department of Justice, National Institute of Corrections.

National Institute of Justice (1998). *Law Enforcement and Corrections Family Support: Solicitation for Research, Evaluation, Development, and Demonstration Projects*, March.

Neal, D. (ed.). (2002). *Supermax Prisons: Beyond the Rock*. Lanham, MD: American Correctional Association.

Nellis, A. (2013). "Life Goes On: The Historic Rise in Life Sentences in America," The Sentencing Project, September 2013, http://sentencingproject. org/doc/publications/inc_Life Goes On 2013.pdf.

Nelson, W.R. and R.M. Davis. (1995). "Podular Direct Supervision: The First Twenty Years," *American Jails*, Vol. 9, No. 3, pp. 11–22.

Newbold, G. and J.I. Ross. (2013). "Convict Criminology at the Crossroads," *The Prison Journal*, Vol. 93, No.1, pp. 3–10.

Newbold, G., J.I. Ross, R.S. Jones, S.C. Richards, and M. Lenza. (2014). "Prison Research from the Inside: The Role of Convict Auto-Ethnography," *Qualitative Inquiry*, Vol. 20, No. 4. pp. 439–48,

Nink, C., C.B. Johnson, T. Oldbury, G. Cheeseman, and R. Rodriguez, (2005). "Job Corps: A Training Program Pipeline to the Corrections Profession," *Corrections Today*, Vol. 67, pp. 84–6.

Odo, J., E.C. Onyeozili, and I.D. Onwudiwe. (2005). "Boot Camps," in M. Bosworth (ed.) *Encyclopaedia of Prisons & Correctional Facilities*. Thousand Oaks, CA: Sage Publications, pp. 79–81.

Ogden, A. (2001). "Do Prison Inmates Have a Right to Vegetarian Meals," *Vegetarian Journal*, March, www.vrg.org/journal/vj(2001).mar/(2001). marprison.htm (Downloaded August 15, 2007).

Ogden, T.G. and C. Horrocks. (2001) "Pagers, Digital, Audio, and Kiosk-Officer assistants," *Federal Probation*, Vol. 65, No. 2, pp. 35–7.

Ogle, R. (1999). "Prison Privatization: An Environmental Catch 22," *Justice Quarterly*, Vol. 16, No. 3, pp. 579–600.

Ojmarrh M., D. Layton Mackenzie, G.J. Styve, and A.R. Gover. (2000). "The Impact of Individual, Organizational and Environmental Attributes on Voluntary Turnover among Juvenile Correctional Staff," *Criminology*, Vol. 17, No. 2, pp. 333–53.

Owen, B. (1988). *The Reproduction of Social Control: A Study of Prison Workers at San Quentin*. Greenwood, CT: Praeger.

Owen, B. (1998). *In the Mix: Struggle and Survival in a Women's Prison*. Albany, NY: State University of New York Press.

Owen, B. (2005). "Women's Prisons," in M. Bosworth (ed.) *Encyclopedia of Prisons & Correctional Facilities*. Thousand Oaks, CA: Sage Publications, Vol. 2, pp. 1051–5.

Page, J. (2011a). *The Toughest Beat: Politics, Punishment, and the Prison Officers Union in California*. New York: Oxford University Press.

Page, J. (2011b). "Prison Officer Unions and the Perpetuation of the Penal Status Quo," *Criminology & Public Policy*, Vol. 10, No. 3, pp. 735–70.

Palmer, T. (1975). "Martinson Revisited," *Journal of Research in Crime and Delinquency*, Vol. 12, No. 2, pp. 133–52.

Paparozzi, M.A. (1998). "Whether Public or Private, It's the Results that Matter." In National Institute of Corrections (Ed.) *Topics in Community Corrections: Annual Issue: Privatizing Community Supervision*. Longmont, CO: National Institute of Corrections, pp. 3–7.

Parent, D.G. (2003). Correctional Boot Camps: Lessons From a Decade of Research. Washington, DC, United States Department of Justice, NIJ NCJ 197018.

Parenti, M. (1995). *Democracy for the Few*. New York: St. Martin's Press.

Parish, J.R. (1990). *Prison Pictures from Hollywood*. Jefferson, NC: McFarland.

Parsonage, W.H. (1990). "Worker Safety in Probation and Parole," Report supported by TA number 89C7002 from the National Institute of Corrections.

Parsonage, W.H. and W. Conway Bushey. (1989). "The Victimization of Probation and Parole Officers in the Line of Duty: An Exploratory Study," *Criminal Justice Policy Review*, Vol. 2, No. 4, pp. 372–91.

Parsons, T. (1951). *The Social System*. Glencoe, IL: The Free Press.

Patrick, S. and R. Marsh. (2001). "Current Tobacco Policies in U.S. Adult Male Prisons," *The Social Science Journal*, Vol. 38, No. 1, pp. 27–37.

Pattillo, M., D. Weiman, and B. Western (eds.). (2004). *Imprisoning America: The Social Effects of Mass Incarceration*. New York: Russell Sage Foundation.

Pell v. Procunier 4147 U.S. 817 (1974).

Pepinsky, H.E. and P. Jesilow. (1985). *Myths that Cause Crime*. Cabin John, MD: Seven Locks Press.

Pepinsky, H.E. and R. Quinney (eds.). (1991). *Criminology as Peacemaking*. Bloomington, IN: Indiana University Press.

Petersilia, J. (2003). *When Prisoners Come: Parole and Prisoner Re-entry*. New York: Oxford University Press.

Peterson, R.D. and D.J. Palumbo. (1997). "The Social Construction of Intermediate Punishment," *The Prison Journal*, Vol. 77, No. 1, pp. 77–91.

Pfaff, J.F. (2012). "The Micro and Macro Causes of Prison Growth," *Georgia State University Law Review*, Vol. 28, No. 4, pp. 1239–74.

Piven, F. Fox and R. Cloward. (1977). *Poor People's Movements*. New York: Pantheon.

Phillips, R.L. and C.M. McConnell. (2005). *The Effective Corrections Manager: Correctional Supervision for the Future* (2nd Ed.). Sudbury, MA: Jones and Bartlett.

Platt, T. (2004). "Challenging the Prison-Industrial Complex: A Symposium," *Social Justice*, Vol. 31, Nos. 1–2, pp. 7–8

Pogrebin, M.R. and E.D. Poole. (1997). "The Sexualized Work Environment: A Look at Women Jail Officers," *The Prison Journal*, Vol. 77, No. 1, pp. 41–57.

Pollock, J.M. (2004). *Prisons and Prison Life: Costs and Consequences*. Los Angeles, CA: Roxbury Press.

Pollock, J.M., N. Hogan, E. Lambert, J.I. Ross, and J. Sundt. (2012). "A Utopian Prison: Contradiction in Terms?" *Journal of Contemporary Criminal Justice*, Vol. 28, No. 1, pp. 60–76.

Pollock-Byrne, J. (1986). *Sex and Supervision: Guarding Male and Female Inmates*. Greenwood, CT: Greenwood Press.

Pollock-Byrne, J. (1990). *Women, Prison and Crime*. Pacific Grove, CA: Brooks/Cole.

Pratt, T.C., J. Maahs, and C. Hemmens. (1999). "The History of the Use of Force in Corrections," in C. Hemmens and E. Atherton (eds.) *Use of Force: Current Practice and Policy*. Lanham, MD: American Correctional Association, pp. 13–22.

Pratt, T.C., J. Maahs, and S.D. Stehr. (1998). "The Symbolic Ownership of the Corrections 'Problem': A Framework for Understanding the Development of Corrections Policy in the United States," *The Prison Journal*, Vol. 4, No. 4, pp. 451–64.

Preston, F.W. and R. Roots. (2004). "Law and Its Unintended Consequences," *American Behavioral Scientist*, Vol. 47, No. 11, pp. 371–5.

Price, M. (2005). "Compassionate Release," in M. Bosworth (ed.) *Encyclopedia of Prisons and Correctional Facilities*. Thousand Oaks, CA: Sage Publications, Vol. 1, pp. 150–1.

Quinney, R. (1980). *Class, State, and Crime* (2nd Ed.). New York: David McKay.

Quinney, R. (1985). "Myth and the Art of Criminology," *Legal Studies Forum*, Vol. 9, No. 3, pp. 291–9.

Rafter, N.H. (2000). *Shots in the Mirror: Crime Films and Society*. New York: Oxford University Press.

Ralph, P., R.J. Hunter, J.W. Marquart, S.J. Cuvelier, and D. Merlo. (1996). "Exploring the Differences between Gang and Nongang Prisoners," in C.R. Huff (ed.) *Gangs in America*. Thousand Oaks, CA: Sage Publications, pp. 123–38.

Reiman, J. (1979/2003). *The Rich Get Richer and the Poor Get Prison*. (7th Ed.). Boston, MA: Allyn & Bacon.

Reisig, M. and N. Lovrich. (1998). "Job Attitudes among Higher-Custody State Prison Management Personnel: A Cross-Sectional Comparative Assessment," *Journal of Criminal Justice*, Vol. 26, No. 3, pp. 213–26.

Reisig, M.D. and T.C. Pratt. (2000). "The Ethics of Correctional Privatization: A Critical Examination of the Delegation of Coercive Authority," *The Prison Journal*, Vol. 80, No. 2, pp. 210–22.

Reutter, D. (2016) "Florida's Department of Corrections: A Culture of Corruption, Abuse and Deaths," *Prison Legal News*, February 2, www.prisonlegalnews.org/news/issue/27/2/#article-18958.

Reynolds, M.O. (2000). *Privatizing Probation and Parole*, NCPA Policy Report No. 233. Dallas, TX: National Center for Policy Analysis, www.ncpa.org/pdfs/st233.pdf.

Rhine, E.E., W.R. Smith, R.W. Jackson, with P.B. Burke and R. Labelle. (1991). *Paroling Authorities: Recent History and Current Practice*. Laurel, MD: American Correctional Association.

Ricci, D.M. (1984). *The Tragedy of Political Science*. New Haven, CT: Yale University Press.

Richards, S.C. (1998). "Critical and Radical Perspectives on Community Punishment: Lesson from the Darkness," in J.I. Ross (ed.) *Cutting the Edge: Current Perspectives in Radical/Critical Criminology and Criminal Justice*. New York: Praeger, pp. 122–44.

Richards, S.C. (2003). "Beating the Perpetual Incarceration Machine," in S. Maruna and R. Immarigeon (eds.) *Ex-Convict Reentry and Desistance from Crime*. Albany, NY: SUNY Press, pp. 201–32.

Richards, S.C. (2004). "Penitentiary Dreams: Books Will Take You Anywhere You Want to Go," *The Journal of Prisoners on Prisons*, Vol. 13, pp. 60–73.

Richards, S.C. and M.J. Avey. (2000). "Controlling State Crime in the United States of America: What Can We Do About the Thug State?" In J.I. Rosso (ed.) *Varieties of State Crime and its Control*. Monsey, NY: Criminal Justice Press, pp. 31–57.

Richards, S.C., J. Austin, and R.S. Jones. (2004). "Thinking about Prison Release and Budget Crisis in the Blue Grass State," *Critical Criminology: An International Journal*, Vol. 12, No. 3, pp. 243–63.

Richards, S.C. and R.S. Jones. (1997). "Perpetual Incarceration Machine: Structural Impediments to Post-Prison Success," *The Journal of Contemporary Criminal Justice*, Vol. 13, No. 1, pp. 4–22.

Richards, S.C., C.D. Rose, and S.O. Reed. (2006). "Inviting Convicts to College: Prison and University Partnership," in *The State of Corrections: (2005) Proceedings ACA Annual Conferences*. Lanham, MD: American Correctional Association, pp. 171–80.

Richards, S.C. and J.I. Ross. (2003). "A Convict Perspective on the Classification of Prisoners," *Criminology & Public Policy*, Vol. 2, No. 2, pp. 242–51.

Richards, S.C. and J.I. Ross. (2007). "The New School of Convict Criminology: How Might Prison College Programs Rehabilitate Prisoners?" in L.F. Alarid and P. Reichel (eds.) *Introduction to Corrections: Supervising Men and Women*. Boston, MA: Allyn & Bacon.

Richards, S.C., J.I. Ross, R.S. Jones, G. Newbold, D.S. Murphy, and R.S. Grigsby. (2011). "Convict Criminology: Prisoner Re-Entry Policy Recommendations," in I.O. Ekunwe and R.S. Jones (eds.) *Global Perspectives on Re-entry*. Tampere, Finland: Tampere University Press, pp. 198–222.

Richards, S.C., J.I. Ross, G. Newbold, M. Lenza, R.S. Jones, D.S. Murphy, and R.S. Grigsby. (2012). "Convict Criminology, Prisoner Reentry, and Public Policy Recommendations," *Journal of Prisoners on Prisons*, Vol. 21, No. 1, pp. 16–35.

Rideau, W. (1992). "The Sexual Jungle," in W. Rideau and R. Wikberg (eds.) *Life Sentences: Rage and Survival behind Bars*. New York: Times Books, pp. 73–107.

Rideau, W. and R. Wikberg. (1992). *Life Sentences: Rage and Survival behind the Bars*. New York: Times Books.

Riveland, C. (1997). "The Correctional Leader and Public Policy Skills," *Corrections Management Quarterly*, Vol. 1, No. 3, pp. 22–5.

Riveland, C. (1998). *Supermax Prison: Overview and General Considerations*. Longmont, CO: National Institute of Corrections.

Riveland, C. (1999). "Prison Management Trends: 1975–2025," in M. Tonry and J. Petersilia (eds.) *Prisons*. Chicago, IL: University of Chicago Press, pp. 163–203.

Robbins, I.P. (1986). "Privatization of Corrections: Defining the Issues," *Federal Probation*, Vol. 50, pp. 24–30.

Roberts, J. (ed.). (1994). *Escaping Prison Myths*. Washington, D.C.: The American University Press.

Rogers, R. (1993). "Solitary Confinement," *International Journal of Offender Therapy and Comparative Criminology*, Vol. 37, No. 4, pp. 339–49.

Rolland, M. (1997). *Descent into Madness: An Inmate's Experience of the New Mexico State Prison Riot*. Cincinnati, OH: Anderson Publishing.

Roman, J., W. Townsend, and A. Bhati. (2003). *National Estimates of Drug Court Recidivism Rates*. Washington, D.C.: National Institute of Justice, U.S. Department of Justice, July.

Roots, R. (2005). "New Generation Prisons," in M. Bosworth (ed.) *Encyclopaedia of Prisons & Correctional Facilities*. Thousand Oaks, CA: Sage Publications.

Rose, C.D., S.O. Reed, and S.C. Richards. (2005). "Inviting Convicts to College: A Free College Preparatory Program for Prisoners," *Offender Programs Report*, Vol. 8, No. 6, pp. 81, 91–3.

Ross, J.I. (1983). "Jail Dehumanizing Say Abolitionists," *Now*, June 2–8, p. 5.

Ross, J.I. (1998). "The Role of the Media in the Creation of Public Police Violence," in F. Bayley and D. Hale (eds.) *Popular Culture, Crime & Justice*. Belmont, CA: Wadsworth, pp. 100–10.

Ross, J.I. (ed.). (1998/2009). *Cutting the Edge: Current Perspectives in Radical/ Critical Criminology and Criminal Justice*. (2nd Ed.). New Brunswick, NJ: Transaction Publishers.

Ross, J.I. (1999). "Content Analysis of the *Baltimore Sun*'s Coverage of Prison Issues," Unpublished.

Ross, J.I. (2000). "Grants-R-Us: Inside A Federal Grant Making Research Agency," *American Behavioral Scientist*, Vol. 43, No. 10, August, pp. 1704–23.

Ross, J.I. (ed.). (1995/2000a). *Controlling State Crime*. (2nd. Ed.). New Brunswick, NJ: Transaction Publishing.

Ross, J.I. (ed.). (2000b). *Varieties of State Crime and Its Control*. Monsey, NJ: Criminal Justice Press.

Ross, J.I. (2000c). *Making News of Police Violence*. Westport, CT: Praeger.

Ross, J.I. (2003). "(Mis)representing Prisons: The Role of Our Cultural Industries," in J.I. Ross and S.C. Richards (eds.) *Convict Criminology*. Belmont, CA: Wadsworth, pp. 37–56.

Ross, J.I. (2006a). "Is the End in Sight for Supermax," *Forbes* On-line, April 18, www.forbes.com/2006/04/15/prison-supermax-ross_cx_jr_06slate_0418super.html

Ross, J.I. (2006b). "Jailhouse Blues," *Forbes* On-line, April 18, www.forbes.com/(2006)/04/15/prison-Jeffrey-ross_cx_jr_06slate_0418ross.html

Ross, J.I. (2006c). "Close Juvenile Boot Camps," *Tampa Tribune*, February, p. 19.

Ross, J.I. (2007). "Supermax Prisons," *Society*, March/April, Vol. 44, No. 3, pp. 60–4.

Ross, J.I. (2008a). "Gangs in Prison," in D. Brotherton and L. Kontos (eds.) *Encyclopedia of Gangs*. Westport, CT: Greenwood Press, pp. 98–101.

Ross, J.I. (2008b). "Analyzing Contemporary Introductory Textbooks on Correctional Administration/Management/Organization," *Journal of Criminal Justice Education*, Vol. 19, No. 3, pp. 446–60.

Ross, J.I. (2008c). *Special Problems in Corrections*. Upper Saddle, NJ: Prentice Hall.

Ross, J.I. (2010). "Resisting the Carceral State: Prisoner Resistance From the Bottom Up," *Social Justice*, Vol. 36, No. 3, pp. 28–45.

Ross, J.I. (2011a). "Deconstructing the Prisoner Re-Entry Industry/Complex: Origins of the Term and a Critique of Current Literature/Analysis," in I.O. Ekunwe and R.S. Jones (eds.) *Global Perspectives on Re-entry*. Tampere, Finland: Tampere University Press, pp. 173–97.

Ross, J.I. (2011b). "Challenges of Reporting on Corrections: An Exploratory Study Derived from Interviews with American Reporters Who Cover Jails and Prisons," *Corrections Compendium*. Spring, pp. 7–13.

Ross, J.I. (2011c). "Moving Beyond Soering: US Prison Conditions as an Argument against Extradition to the United States," *International Criminal Justice Review*, Vol. 21, No. 2, pp. 156–68.

Ross, J.I. (2011d). "Patient Evaluations R Us: The Dynamics of Power Relations inside a Forensic Psychiatric Facility from the Bottom Up," in L.M. Johnson (ed.) *Experiencing Corrections*, Thousand Oaks, CA: Sage Publications, pp. 55–72.

Ross, J.I. (2012a). "Debunking the Myths of American Corrections," *Critical Criminology*, Vol. 20, No. 4, pp. 409–21

Ross, J.I. (2012b). "Why a Jail or Prison Sentence is increasingly like a Death Sentence," *Contemporary Justice Review*, Vol. 15, No. 3, pp. 309–22.

Ross, J.I. (ed.) (2013a). *The Globalization of Supermax Prisons*, New Brunswick, NJ: Rutgers University Press.

Ross, J.I. (2013b). "The Invention of the American Supermax Prison," in J.I. Ross (ed.). *The Globalization of Supermax Prisons*, New Brunswick, NJ: Rutgers University Press, pp. 10–24.

Ross, J.I. (2013c). "Deconstructing Correctional Officer Deviance: Towards Typologies of Actions and Controls," *Criminal Justice Review*, Vol. 38, No. 1, pp. 110–26.

Ross, J.I. (2014). "Misidentified and Misunderstood: Extremists and Extremist Groups Incarcerated in U.S. Correctional Facilities," in G. Michaels (ed.). *Extremism in America*. Gainesville, FL: The University Press of Florida, pp. 274–93.

Ross, J.I. (2015). "Varieties of Prison Voyeurism: An Analytic/Interpretive Framework," *The Prison Journal*, September, Vol. 95, No. 3, pp. 397–417.

Ross, J.I., S. Darke, A. Aresti, G. Newbold, and R. Earle. (2014). "The Development of Convict Criminology Beyond North America," *International Journal of Criminal Justice*, Vol. 24, No. 2, pp. 121–33.

Ross, J.I. and S.C. Richards. (2002). *Behind Bars: Surviving Prison.* Indianapolis, IN: Alpha Books.

Ross, J.I. and S.C. Richards (eds.). (2003). *Convict Criminology.* Belmont, CA: Wadsworth.

Ross, J.I. and S.C. Richards. (2009). *Beyond Bars: Rejoining Society after Prison.* Indianapolis, IN: Alpha Books.

Ross, J.I., S.C. Richards, G. Newbold, R.S. Jones, M. Lenza, D.S. Murphy, R. Hogan, and G.D. Curry. (2011). "Knocking on the Ivory Tower's Door: The Experience of Ex-Convicts Applying For Tenure-Track University Positions," *Journal of Criminal Justice Education*, Vol. 22, No. 2, pp. 267–85.

Ross, J.I. and D.L. Rothe (2013). "Guantánamo: America's Foreign Supermax Prison," in J.I. Ross (ed.). *The Globalization of Supermax Prisons.* New Brunswick, NJ: Rutgers University Press, pp. 160–76.

Ross, J.I., R. Tewksbury, and M. Zaldivar. (2015). "Analyzing For-profit Colleges and Universities that Offer Bachelors, Masters and Doctorates to Inmates Incarcerated in American Correctional Facilities," *Journal of Offender Rehabilitation*, Vol. 54, No. 8, pp. 585–98.

Ross, J.I., M. Zaldivar, and R. Tewksbury. (2015). "Breaking Out of Prison and into Print? Rationales and Strategies to Assist Educated Convicts Conduct Scholarly Research and Writing Behind Bars, *Critical Criminology: An International Journal*, Vol. 23, No. 1, pp. 73–83.

Rothman, D.J. (1971/(2002). *The Discovery of the Asylum: Social Order and Disorder in the New Republic.* (Revised Ed.). New York: Aldine.

Rothman, D.J. (1980). *Conscience and Convenience: The Asylum and Its Alternatives in Progressive America.* Boston, MA: Little, Brown and Company.

Ruddell, R., Decker, S.H., and Egley Jr., A. (2006). "Gang Intervention in Jails: A National Analysis," *Criminal Justice Review*, Vol. 31, No. 1, pp. 33–46.

Ruggerio, M., E. Greenberger, and L.D. Steinberg. (1982). "Occupational Deviance Among Youth Workers," *Youth and Society*, Vol. 13, pp. 423–448.

Ruiz, J.D., F. Molitor, R.K. Sun, J. Mikanda, and M. Facer. (1999). "Prevalence and Correlates of Hepatitis C Virus Infections among Inmates Entering the California Correctional System," *Western Journal of Medicine*, Vol. 170, No. 3, pp. 156–60.

Sanders, C.R. (2009). *Marginal Conventions: Popular Culture, Mass Media, and Social Deviance.* Bowling Green, OH: The Popular Press.

Sanders, C.R. and E. Lyon. (1995). "Repetitive Retribution: Media Images and the Cultural Construction of Criminal Justice," in J. Ferrell and C. Sanders (eds.) *Cultural Criminology.* Boston, MA: Northeastern University Press, pp. 25–44.

Saum, C., H. Surratt, J. Inciardi, and R. Bennett. (1995). "Sex in Prison: Exploring the Myths and Realities," *The Prison Journal*, Vol. 75, No. 4, pp. 413–31.

Savicki, V., E. Cooley, and J. Gjesvold. (2003). "Harassment as a Predictor of Job Burnout in Correctional Officers," *Criminal Justice and Behavior*, Vol. 30, No. 5, pp. 602–19.

Saxbe v. Washington Post 417 U.S. 843 (1974).

Scheck, B., P. Neufeld, and J. Dwyer. (2000). *Actual Innocence: Five Days to Execution, and Other Dispatches from the Wrongly Convicted*. New York: Doubleday.

Schicher, D. (1992). "Myths and Realities in Prison Siting," *Crime and Delinquency*, Vol. 38, No. 1, pp. 70–88.

Schichor, D. (1999). "Privatizing Correctional Institutions. An Organizational Perspective," *The Prison Journal*, Vol. 79, No. 2, pp. 226–49.

Schiller, H.I. (1989). *Culture Inc. The Corporate Takeover of Public Expression*. New York: Oxford University Press.

Schloss, C.S., and L.F. Alarid. (2007). "Standards in the Privatization of Probation Services: A Statutory Analysis," *Criminal Justice Review*, Vol. 32, No. 3, pp. 233–45.

Schlosser, E. (1998). "The Prison Industrial Complex," *The Atlantic Monthly*, December, pp. 51–77.

Schmalleger, F. (1999). *Criminal Justice Today: An Introductory Text for the 21st Century*. (5th Ed.). Upper Saddle, NJ: Prentice Hall.

Schmalleger, F. (2006). *Criminology Today*. Upper Saddle, NJ: Prentice Hall.

Scott, S. (2012). "One is Not Born, But Becomes a Woman: A Fourteenth Amendment Argument in Support of Housing Male-to-Female Transgender Inmates in Female Facilities," *University of Pennsylvania Journals of Constitutional Law*, Vol. 15, pp. 1259–97.

Sechrest, D.K. and D.A. Josi. (1999). "A Pragmatic Approach to Parole Aftercare: Evaluation of a Community Reintegration Program for High-Risk Youthful Offenders," *Justice Quarterly*, Vol. 16, No. 1, pp. 51–80.

Seiter, R. (2005). *Corrections: An Introduction*. Upper Saddle, NJ: Prentice Hall.

Seith, E.W. (1989). "Less Eligibility: The Upper Limits of Penal Policy," *Criminal Justice Policy Review*, Vol. 3, No. 2, pp. 159–83.

Sentementes, G.G. (2005). "City in Central Booking Lawsuit," *Baltimore Sun*, September 30.

Shadoian, J. (1979). *Dreams and Dead Ends: The American Gangster/Crime Film*. Cambridge, MA: MIT Press.

Sheldon, R.G. (2005). "Prison Industrial Complex," in M. Bosworth (ed.). *Encyclopaedia of Prison & Correctional Facilities*. Thousand Oaks, CA: Sage Publications, pp. 725–9.

Sheldon, R.G. and W.B. Brown. (2000). "The Crime Control Industry and the Management of the Surplus Population," *Critical Criminology: An International Journal*, Vol. 9, No. 1, pp. 39–62.

Siever, R. (2005). "HMOs Behind Bars: Constitutional Implications of Managed Health Care in the Prison System," *Vanderbuilt Law Review*, Vol. 54, No. 4, pp. 407–26.

Sigler, R. and C.L. Shook. (1995). "The Federal Judiciary and Corrections: Breaking the 'Hands-Off' Doctrine," *Criminal Justice Policy Review*, Vol. 7, Nos. 3–4, pp. 245–54.

Slate, R. and R.E. Vogel. (1997). "Participative Management and Correctional Personnel: A Study of the Perceived Atmosphere for Participation in Correctional Decision Making and Its Impact on Employee Stress and Thoughts about Quitting," *Journal of Criminal Justice*, Vol. 25, No. 5, pp. 397–408.

Slate, R.N., R.E. Vogel, and W.W. Johnson. (2001). "To Quit or Not to Quit: Perceptions of Participation in Correctional Decision Making and the Impact of Organizational Stress," *Corrections Management Quarterly*, Vol. 5, No. 2, pp. 68–78.

Slater, D. (2003). "Lights, Camera, Lockdown," *Legal Affairs*, May/June, www. legalaffairs.org/issues/May-June-(2003)/review_slater_mayjun03.msp (Downloaded August 15, 2007).

Smith, B.V. (2008). "The Prison Rape Elimination Act: Implementation and Unresolved Issues," *American University Criminal Law Briefing*, Vol. 3, No. 2, pp. 19–28.

Smith, H.P. and R.M. Kaminski. (2010). "Inmate Self-injurious Behaviors: Distinguishing Characteristics Within a Retrospective Study," *Criminal Justice and Behavior*, Vol. 37, pp. 81–96.

Smith, H.P. and R.M. Kaminski. (2011). "Self-injurious Behaviors in State Prisons: Findings From a National Survey," *Criminal Justice and Behavior*, Vol. 38, pp. 26–41.

Soderstrom, I.R. and W.M. Wheeler. (1999). "Is It Still Practical to Incarcerate the Elderly Offender?" in C.B. Fields (ed.) *Controversial Issues in Corrections*. Boston, MA: Allyn and Bacon, pp. 72–89.

Souryal, S. (2009). "Deterring Corruption by Prison Personnel: A Principle-based Perspective," *Prison Journal*, Vol. 89, pp. 21–45.

Speck, E. (2010). "Human Services and the Prisoner Reentry Industry," *Dialectical Anthropology*, Vol. 34, No. 4, pp. 483–449.

Speed Weed, W. (2001). "Incubating Disease. Prisons Are Rife with Infectious Illnesses – and Threaten to Spread Them to the Public," *Mother Jones*, July 10, www.motherjones.com/news/special_reports/prisons/print_disease.html.

Stastny, C. and G. Tyrnauer. (1982). *Who Rules the Joint? The Changing Political Culture of Maximum-Security Prisons in America*. Lexington, MA: Lexington Books.

State of New York. (1972). *Attica: The Official Report of the New York State Special Commission on Attica*. New York: Praeger.

Steadman, H.J. and J. Cocozza (eds.). (1993). *Mental Illness in America's Prisons*. Seattle, WA: National Coalition for the Mentally Ill in the Criminal Justice System.

Stephan, J.J. (2004). *State Prison Expenditures, 2001*. U.S. Department of Justice. Office of Justice Programs. Bureau of Justice Statistics. Special Report. June, NCJ 202949, www.bjs.gov/content/pub/pdf/spe01.pdf

Stephan, J.J. (2008). *Census of State and Federal Correctional Facilities, 2005*. U.S. Department of Justice. Office of Justice Programs. Bureau of Justice Statistics, October, NCJ 222182.

Stewart, C.H. (1998). "Management Response to Sexual Misconduct between Staff and Inmates," *Correctional Management Quarterly*, Vol. 2, pp. 81–88.

Stichman, A.J. (2002). "The Sources and Impact of Inmate Perceptions of Correctional Officers' Bases of Power" (Ph.D. dissertation). Cincinnati, OH: University of Cincinnati.

Stinchcomb, J.B. (1985). "Why Not the Best? Using Assessment Centers for Officer Selection," *Corrections Today*, Vol. 47, p. 9.

Stinchcomb, J.B. (1998). "Quality Management in Corrections Implementation Issues and Potential Policy Implications," *Criminal Justice Policy Review*, Vol. 9, No. 1, pp. 123–36.

Stinchcomb, J.B. (1999). "Recovering from the Shocking Reality of Shock Incarceration – What Correctional Administration Can Learn from Boot Camp Failures," *Corrections Management Quarterly*, Vol. 2, No. 4, pp. 43–52.

Stinchcomb, J.B. (2000). "Developing Correctional Officer Professionalism: A Work in Progress," *Corrections Compendium*, Vol. 25, pp. 1–4, 18–19.

Stohr, M.K., G.L. Mays, A. Beck, and T. Kelley. (1998). "Sexual Harassment in Women's Jails," *Journal of Contemporary Criminal Justice*, Vol. 14, No. 2, pp. 135–55.

Stohr, M.K., C. Hemmens, M. Kifer and M. Schoeler. (2000). "We Know It, We Just Have to Do It: Perceptions of Work in Prisons and Jails," *Prison Journal*, Vol. 80, pp. 126–50.

Stojkovic, S. (1984). "Social Bases of Power and Control Mechanisms Among Prisoners in a Prison Organization," *Justice Quarterly*, Vol. 1, pp. 511–28.

Stojkovic, S. and M.A. Farkas. (2003). *Correctional Leadership: A Cultural Perspective*. Belmont, CA: Wadsworth.

Stolz, B.A. (1997). "Privatizing Corrections: Changing the Corrections Policy-Making Subgovernment," *The Prison Journal*, Vol. 77, No. 1, pp. 92–111.

Stone, J. (2005). "Elmira Reformatory," in M. Bosworth (ed.) *Encyclopedia of Prisons and Correctional Facilities*. Thousand Oaks, CA: Sage Publications, pp. 286–8.

Stuever, H. (2000). "Radical Chic: Benetton Takes on the Death Penalty," *Washington Post*, January 25, p. C1.

Suedfeld, P. (1974). "Solitary Confinement in the Correctional Setting: Goals, Problems, and Suggestions," *Corrective and Social Psychiatry*, Vol. 141, pp. 10–20.

Suedfeld, P., C. Ramirez, J. Deaton, and G. Baker-Brown. (1982). "Reactions and Attributes of Prisoners in Solitary Confinement," *Criminal Justice and Behavior*, Vol. 9, pp. 303–40.

Sullivan, L.E. (1990). *The Prison Reform Movement: Forlorn Hope*. Boston, MA: Twayne Publishers.

Surette, R. (1998). "Prologue: Some Unpopular Thoughts about Popular Culture," in F. Bayley and D. Hale (eds.) *Popular Culture, Crime & Justice*. Belmont, CA: Wadsworth, pp. viv–xxiv.

Surette, R. (1999). "Media Echoes: Systematic Effects of News Coverage," *Justice Quarterly*, Vol. 16, pp. 601–20.

Swanson, C.G., G. Rohrer, and M.S. Crow. (2010). "Is Criminal Justice Education Ready for Reentry?" *Journal of Criminal Education*, Vol. 21, No. 1, pp. 60–76

Sykes, G. (1958). *The Society of Captives*. Princeton, NJ: Princeton University Press.

Sykes, G. and S.L. Messinger. (1960). "The Inmate Social System," in R.A. Cloward et al. (eds.) *Theoretical Studies in the Social Organization of the Prison*. New York: Social Science Research Council, pp. 6–8.

Tafoya, W. (1986). "A Delphi Forecast of the Future of Law Enforcement," Ph.D. Dissertation, University of Maryland.

Taggert, W.A. (1997). "The Nationalization of Corrections Policy in the American States," *Justice Quarterly*, Vol. 14, No. 3, pp. 429–42.

Talbott, F. (1988). "Reporting from behind the Walls," *The Quill*, Vol. 76, pp. 16–20.

Talbott, F. (1989). "Covering Prisons," *Editor & Publisher*, April 22, pp. 74–78.

Taylor, I., P. Walton, and J. Young. (1973). *The New Criminology*. London: Routledge and Kegan Paul.

Taylor, J.M. and R. Tewksbury. (2002). "Postsecondary Correctional Education: The Imprisoned University," in R. Gido and T. Alleman (eds.) *Turnstile Justice*. Upper Saddle, NJ: Prentice Hall, pp. 145–75.

Terry, C. (2003). "From C-Block to Academia: You Can't Get There from Here," in J.I. Ross and S.C. Richards (eds.) *Convict Criminology*. Belmont, CA: Wadsworth, pp. 95–119.

Testa, M. (2015). "Imprisonment of the Mentally Ill: A Call for Diversion to the Community Mental Health System," *Albany Government Law Review*, Vol. 8, pp. 405–38.

Thomas, J. (1988). *Prisoner Litigation: The Paradox of the Jailhouse Lawyer*. Totowa, NJ: Rowman and Littlefield.

Thomas, J. (2005). "Types of Clemency," in M. Bosworth (ed.) *Encyclopedia of Prisons & Correctional Facilities*. Thousand Oaks, CA: Sage Publications, pp. 134–7.

Thompkins, D.E., Curtis, R., and Wendel, T. (2010). "Forum: The Prison Reentry Industry," *Dialectical Anthropology*, Vol. 34, No. 4, pp. 427–9.

Thompson, A., Nored, L.S., and Cheeseman Dial, K. (2008). "The Prison Rape Elimination Act (PREA): An Evaluation of Policy Compliance with Illustrative Excerpts," *Criminal Justice Policy Review*, Vol. 19, No. 4, pp. 414–37.

Thompson, C.W. (1998). "Prison Company Assailed: Report Slams Firm Hoping to Build D.C. Facility," *Washington Post*, October 8, pp. B1, B9.

Thompson, J.A. and G.L. Mays (eds.). (1991). *American Jails: Public Policy Issues*. Chicago, IL: Nelson-Hall.

Toberg, M. (1983). "Bail Bondsmen and Criminal Courts," *Justice System Journal*, Vol. 8, pp. 141–56.

Toch, H. (2001). "The Future of Supermax Confinement," *The Prison Journal*, Vol. 81, pp. 376–88.

Toch, H. and J. Klofas. (1982). "Alienation and Desire for Job Enrichment among Correctional Officers," *Federal Probation*, Vol. 46, No. 1, pp. 35–44.

Toller, W. and B. Tsagaris. (1996a). "A Comparison of Gang Members and Non-Gang Members in a Prison Setting. *The Prison Journal*, Vol. 81, No. 2, pp. 50–60.

Toller, W. and B. Tsagaris. (1996b). "Managing Institutional Gangs: A Practical Approach, Combining Security and Human Services," *Corrections Today*, Vol. 58, No. 6, pp. 110–11, 115.

Toobin, J. (2014). "This Is My Jail," *New Yorker*, April 14, www.newyorker.com/magazine/2014/04/14/this-is-my-jail.

Tonry, M. (2004). *Thinking about Crime: Sense and Sensibility in Penal Culture*. New York: Oxford University Press.

Torr, J.D. (1999). *Drug Abuse: Opposing Viewpoints*. San Diego, CA: Greenhaven Press.

Travis, J. (2005). *But They All Come Back: Facing the Challenges of Prisoner Reentry*. Washington, DC: Urban Institute.

Travisino, A.P. (1980). "Brubaker: The Crusader Strikes Out," *On the Line*, Vol. 3, No. 6, p. 1.

Tregea, W.S. (2003). "Twenty Years Teaching College in Prison," in J.I. Ross and S.C. Richards (eds.) *Convict Criminology*. Belmont, CA: Wadsworth, pp. 59–76.

Tregea, W.S. (2014). *Prisoners on Criminology: Convict Life Stories, and Crime Prevention*. Lanham, MD: Lexington Books.

Triple, H.R., J. Mullings, and K. Scarborough. (1996). "Work Related Stress and Coping among Correctional Officers: Implications from Organizational Literature," *Journal of Criminal Justice*, Vol. 24, No. 4, pp. 291–308.

Tucker, L. (no date). "Rasha Drachkovitch and The Lockup Interview," *Film Monthly*, www.filmmonthly.com/interviews/rasha_drachkovitch_and_the_lockup.html.

Tunnell, K.D. (1992). "99 Years Is Almost for Life: Punishment for Violent Crime in Bluegrass Music," *Journal of Popular Culture*, Vol. 26, No. 1, pp. 165–81.

Tunnell, K.D. (1995). "A Cultural Approach to Crime and Punishment, Bluegrass Style," in J. Ferrell and C.R. Sanders (eds.) *Cultural Criminology*. Boston, MA: Northeastern University Press, pp. 80–115.

Tunnell, K.D. (2000). *Living Off Crime*. Chicago, IL: Burnham Publishing.

United States. (2006). *Occupational Outlook Handbook, 2006–2007*. U.S. Bureau of Labor Statistics, US Government Printing Office.

Useem, B. (1985). "Disorganization and the New Mexico Prison Riot of 1980," *American Sociological Review*, Vol. 50, pp. 677–88.

Useem, B. and P. Kimball. (1989). *States of Siege: U.S. Prison Riots, 1971–1986*. New York: Oxford University Press.

Useem, B., C. Graham Camp, G.M. Camp, and R. Dugan. (1995). *Resolution of Prison Riots. National Institute of Justice Research in Brief*, October, NCJ155283.

Valentine, B. and R. Schober. (2000). *Gangs and Their Tattoos: Identifying Gangbangers on the Street and in Prison*. Boulder, CO: Paladin.

Valentine, G. and B. Longstaff. (1998). "Doing Porridge: Food and Social Relations in a Male Prison," *Journal of Material Culture*, Vol. 3, No. 2, pp. 131–52.

Vaughn, M.S. (1997). "Civil Liability against Prison Officials for Prescribing and Dispensing Medication and Drugs to Prison Inmates," *The Journal of Legal Medicine*, Vol. 18, No. 3, pp. 315–44.

Vaughn, M.S. and L. Carroll. (1998). "Separate and Unequal: Prison versus Free World Medical Care," *Justice Quarterly*, Vol. 15, pp. 3–40.

Vetter, H.J. and R. Adams. (1970). "Effectiveness of Probation Caseload Sizes: A Review of the Empirical Literature," *Criminology*, Vol. 8, No. 4, pp. 333–43.

Villaume, A.C. (2005). "'Life without Parole' and 'Virtual Life Sentences': Death Sentences by Any Other Name," *Contemporary Justice Review*, Vol. 8, pp. 265–77.

Vohryzek-Bolden, M. and T. Croisdale. (1999). *Overview of Selected States' Academy and In-Service Training for Adult and Juvenile Correctional Employees*. Longmont, CO: National Institute of Corrections.

Vollmer, H.M. and D.L. Mills. (1966). *Professionalization*. Englewood Cliffs, NJ: Prentice Hall.

Von Zielbauer, P. (2005a). "As Health Care in Jails Goes Private, 10 Days Can Be a Death Sentence," *The New York Times*, February 27, pp. A1, A26–A29.

Von Zielbauer, P. (2005b). "Inside City's Jails, Missed Signals Open Way to Season of Suicides," *The New York Times*, February 28, pp. A1, A18–A19.

Wacquant, L. (2002). "The Curious Eclipse of Prison Ethnography in the Age of Mass Incarceration," *Ethnography*, Vol. 3, No. 4, pp. 371–391.

Ward, D. (1994). "Alcatraz and Marion: Confinement in Super Maximum Custody," in J. Roberts (ed.) *Escaping Prison Myths*. Washington, D.C.: The American University Press, pp. 81–93.

Warr, M., R.F. Meier, and M.L. Erickson. (1983). "Norms, Theories of Punishment, and Publicly Preferred Penalties for Crimes," *Sociological Quarterly*, Vol. 24, No. 1, pp. 75–91.

Webb, G.L. and D.G. Morris. (2002). "Working as a Prison Guard," in T. Gray (ed.) *Exploring Corrections: A Book of Readings*. Boston, MA: Allyn & Bacon, pp. 69–83.

Weinberg, R.B., J.H. Evans, C.A. Otten, and H.A. Marlowe. (1985). "Managerial Stress in Corrections Personnel," *Corrective and Social Psychiatry and Journal of Behavior Technology Methods and Therapy*, Vol. 31, No. 2, pp. 9–95.

Weinstein, C. (2000). "Even Dogs Confined to Cages for Long Periods of Time Go Berserk," in J.P. May and K.R. Pitts (eds.) *Building Violence: How America's Rush to Incarcerate Creates More Violence*. Thousand Oaks, CA: Sage Publications, pp. 118–24.

Welch, M. (1994). "Jail Overcrowding: Social Sanitation and the Warehousing of the Urban Underclass," in A.R. Roberts (ed.) *Critical Issues in Crime and Justice*. Thousand Oaks, CA: Sage Publications, pp. 251–76.

Welch, M. (1996). *Corrections: A Critical Approach*. New York: McGraw-Hill.

Welch, M. (1998). "Critical Criminology, Social Control, and an Alternative View of Corrections," in J.I. Ross (ed.) *Cutting the Edge: Current Perspectives in Radical/Critical Criminology and Criminal Justice*. New York: Praeger, pp. 107–21.

Welch, M. (2002). *Detained: Immigration Laws and the Expanding I.N.S. Jail Complex*. Philadelphia, PA: Temple University Press.

Welch, M. (2004). *Corrections: A Critical Approach*. (2nd Ed.). New York: McGraw-Hill.

Welch, M. (2011). *Corrections: A Critical Approach*. (3rd Ed.). New York: Routledge.

Welsh, W.N. (1992). "The Dynamics of Jail Reform Litigation: A Comparative Analysis of Litigation in California Counties," *Law & Society Review*, Vol. 26, No. 3, pp. 591–626.

Welsh, W.N. (1995). *Counties in Court: Jail Overcrowding and Court Ordered Reform*. Philadelphia, PA: Temple University Press.

Welsh, W.N. and P.W. Harris. (2004). *Criminal Justice: Policy and Planning*. (2nd Ed.). Cincinnati, OH: Anderson/LexisNexis.

West, A.D. and Seiter, R.P. (2004). "Social Worker or Cop? Measuring the Supervision Styles of Probation & Parole Officers in Kentucky and Missouri," *Journal of Crime & Justice*, Vol. 27, No. 2, pp. 27–57.

Whitehead, J. (1985). "Job Burnout in Probation and Parole: Its Extent and Intervention Implications," *Criminal Justice & Behavior*, Vol. 12, No. 1, pp. 91–110.

Whitehead, J. (1987). "Probation Officer Burnout: A Test of Two Theories," *Journal of Criminal Justice*, Vol. 15, No. 1, pp. 25–35.

Whitehead, J. and C. Lindquist. (1986). "Correctional Officer Job Burnout: A Path Model," *Journal of Crime & Delinquency*, Vol. 23, No. 1, pp. 23–42.

Wicker, T. (1980/1994). *A Time to Die: The Attica Riot*. Lincoln, NE: University of Nebraska Press.

Wilkinson, W.R. (2005). *Prison Work: A Tale of Thirty Years in the California Department of Corrections*, Columbus, OH: Ohio State University Press.

Williams, V.L. and M. Fish. (1974). *Convicts, Codes, and Contraband: The Prison Life of Men and Women*. Cambridge, MA: Ballinger.

Willett, J. (2004). *Warden: Prison Life and Death from the Inside Out*. Houston, TX: Bright Sky Press.

Wilper, A.P., S. Woolhandler, J.W. Boyd, K.E. Lasser, D. McCormick, D.H. Bor, and D.U. Himmelstein. (2009a). "Health Status and Access to Care for Inmates Is Substandard across the Country," *Journal of Clinical Outcomes Management*, Vol. 16, No. 3, pp. 106–7.

Wilper, A.P., S. Woolhandler, J.W. Boyd, K.E. Lasser, D. McCormick, D.H. Bor, and D.U. Himmelstein. (2009b). "The Health and Health Care of US Prisoners: Results of a Nation-wide Survey," *American Journal of Public Health*, Vol. 99, No. 4, pp. 666–72.

Winterdyk, J. and R. Ruddell. (2010). "Managing Prison Gangs: Results from a Survey of U.S. Prison Systems," *Journal of Criminal Justice*, Vol. 38, No. 4, pp. 730–6.

World Health Organization. (2007). "Effectiveness of Interventions to Address HIV in Prisons." Geneva, Switzerland: World Health Organization.

Worley, R. and K.A. Cheeseman. (2006). "Guards as Embezzlers: The Consequences of 'Nonshareable Problems' in Prison Settings," *Deviant Behavior*, Vol. 27, No. 2, pp. 203–22.

Worley, R.M. and V.B. Worley. (2011). "Guards Gone Wild: A Self Report Study of Correctional Officer Misconduct and the Effect on Institutional Deviance On 'Care' Within the Texas Prison System," *Deviant Behavior*, Vol. 32, pp. 293–319.

Worley, R.M. and V.B. Worley. (2013). "Games Guards Play: A Self-report Study of Institutional Deviance within the Texas Department of Criminal Justice," *Criminal Justice Studies*, Vol. 26, No. 1, pp. 115–132.

Worley, R.M., R. Tewksbury, and D. Frantzen. (2010). "Preventing Fatal Attractions: Lessons Learned from Inmate Boundary Violations in a Southern Penitentiary System," *Criminal Justice Studies*, Vol. 23, pp. 347–360.

Wright, E.O. (1973). *The Politics of Punishment*. New York: HarperCollins.

Wright, J.H. (1991). "Life without Parole: The View from Death Row," *Criminal Law Bulletin*, Vol. 27, pp. 334–57.

Wright, K.N., W.G. Saylor, E. Gilman, and S. Camp. (1997). "Job Control and Occupational Outcomes among Prison Workers," *Justice Quarterly*, Vol. 26, No. 3, pp. 213–26.

Wright, L. (2008). "Health Care in Prison Thirty Years After Estelle v. Gamble," *Journal of Correctional Health Care*, Vol. 14, No. 1, pp. 31–5.

Wright, T. (1993). "Correctional Employee Turnover: A Longitudinal Study," *Journal of Criminal Justice*, Vol. 21, No. 2. pp. 131–42.

Yates, M.T. (2009). "Congressional Debates Over Prison Education: A Critical Discourse Analysis" (Ph.D. dissertation). Georgia Sate University.

Young, J. (2006). "Waters Seeks to Sway AIDS Group on Prisoner Testing," *The Hill*, September 12, p. 5

Zaner, L. (1989). "The Screen Test: Has Hollywood Hurt the Corrections Image?" *Corrections Today*, Part 51, pp. 64–98.

Zinger, I., C. Wichmann, and D.A. Andrews. (2001). "The Psychological Effects of 60 Days in Administrative Segregation," *Canadian Journal of Criminology*, Vol. 43, pp. 47–83.

Zumbrun, J. (2007). "Celebs Put Their Best Foot Forward," *Washington Post*, July 18, pp. C1–C2.

Zupan, L.L. (1986). "Gender-Related Differences in Correctional Officers' Perceptions and Attitudes," *Journal of Criminal Justice*, Vol. 20, pp. 297–309.

Zupan, L.L. (1992). "The Progress of Women Correctional Officers in All-Male Prisons," in I.L. Moyers (ed.) *The Changing Roles of Women in the Criminal Justice System*. Prospect Heights, IL: Waveland Press, pp. 232–44.

Zupan, L.L. (2002). "The Persistent Problems Plaguing Modern Jails," in T. Gray (ed.) *Exploring Corrections: A Book of Readings*. Boston, MA: Allyn & Bacon, pp. 37–63.

Zupan, L.L. and B.A. Menke. (1988). "Implementing Organizational Change: From Traditional to New Generation Jail Operations," *Policy Studies Review*, Vol. 7, pp. 615–25.

Zupan, L.L. and B.A. Menke. (1991). "The New Generation Jail: An Overview," in Joel A. Thompson and G.L. Mays (eds.) *American Jails: Public Policy Issues*. Chicago, IL: Nelson-Hall, pp. 181–94.

Zweig, J.M., R.L. Naser, J. Blackmore, and M. Schaffer. (2006). "Addressing Sexual Violence in Prisons: A National Snapshot of Approaches and Highlights of Innovative Strategies, Final Report." Washington, D.C.: National Institute of Justice, www.ncjrs.gov/pdffiles1/nij/grants/216856.pdf.

Index

Note: Page numbers in **bold** indicate definitions of key terms. Page numbers in *italics* refer to exhibit boxes and page numbers followed by the letter "n" indicate footnotes.

CPSIA information can be obtained
at www.ICGtesting.com
Printed in the USA
LVHW100330261120
672679LV00008B/624